PELICAN BOOKS

A314

THE PELICAN HISTORY OF THE WORLD

A HISTORY OF THE UNITED STATES

VOLUME TWO

A HISTORY OF
THE UNITED STATES

BY

R. B. NYE AND J. E. MORPURGO

VOLUME TWO

THE GROWTH OF
THE UNITED STATES

*

PENGUIN BOOKS

Penguin Books Ltd, Harmondsworth, Middlesex

U.S.A.: Penguin Books Inc., 3300 Clipper Mill Road, Baltimore 11, Md

CANADA: Penguin Books (Canada) Ltd, 47 Green Street,
Saint Lambert, Montreal, P.Q.

AUSTRALIA: Penguin Books Pty Ltd, 762 Whitehorse Road,
Mitcham, Victoria

SOUTH AFRICA: Penguin Books (S.A.) Pty Ltd, Gibraltar House,
Regent Road, Sea Point, Cape Town

—

First published 1955

Made and printed in Great Britain
by The Whitefriars Press Ltd
Tonbridge

CONTENTS OF VOLUME II

LIST OF MAPS

7928

CHAPTER 22

THE AGE OF GOOD FEELINGS
1814–28

THE reaction of war-weary Americans to news of the Treaty of Ghent was swift and spontaneous; bells rang, parades formed, schools dismissed, newspapers broke out headlines to proclaim the passage 'from gloom to glory'. Yet 'Mr Madison's War' accomplished nothing in a military or a political sense. The Treaty realized none of the United States' war aims, neither the officially-pronounced policies of Madison nor the privately-expressed hopes of the 'War Hawks', whose clamours for blood and soil had been loudest. The slogan of victory, 'Not one inch of territory lost or ceded!' had a different ring from the Westerner's triumphant 'On to Canada!' of 1812. The conflict cost a huge sum of money, dislocated business and foreign trade, raised the national debt to astronomical figures, deranged currency values, and exposed glaring cracks in the national political façade. Its record of fumbling, bickering, and unpreparedness remains unmatched by any subsequent American military experience.

But still the war seemed to be a victory, and marked a turning point in American history. It gave a tremendous lift to national morale; after all, American forces had met and presumably defeated for the second time (or at least had not been defeated by) the world's greatest military and naval power, albeit that that power's right hand was elsewhere engaged at the time. True, the war might have been avoided if American statesmanship had been of sufficient skill and calibre to avoid it. True, it might have been fought with France, on possibly better grounds. But from an American viewpoint, the war gave notice to the rest of the world that the United States had arrived as a nation, with aims of its own to be fought for. In it Americans proved something to themselves — that they could fight in defence of their interests, that they could blunder and vacillate, and still not lose the war. The bumbling campaigns, the incompetent commanders, the charred remnants of White House and Capitol, the solid ring of the British blockade, the captured merchantmen and impressed seamen – these could be forgotten if one chose to remember the *Constitution* and the *Guerriere*, Perry's gallant 'We have met the enemy and they are ours', or Pakenham's veterans littering the field at New Orleans, cut down by the long rifles of the Kentuckians. 'Who would not be an American?' trumpeted *Niles' Register*. 'Long live the republic! All hail! Last asylum of oppressed humanity!' If the eagle screamed, the indecisiveness of the conflict left little real ill-feeling between American and Briton. When the newspaper talk died down and the orators stilled, old imprecations and recent insults were more or less forgotten, and British-American relations remained fairly friendly until disturbed by the Civil War.

The conclusion of the war marked the end of a lingering American colonial complex. It was hardly 'a second war of independence', but in a subtle, metaphysical sense there is some reason for so calling it. The 'submission' policies of Jefferson, which had clearly engendered a national feeling of uncertainty and inferiority in foreign affairs, promptly disappeared in the waving folds of Francis Scott Key's 'Star Spangled Banner'. Out of the old clash between a growing national self-consciousness and the old persistent feeling of dependence on Europe, came a newer spirit of self-reliance. Troops from different states and sections fought side by side under the command of Scott, a Virginian, and Jackson, a Tennessean, and the raw troops from the new Western settlements won some memorable victories they were not likely to forget. The sectional grievances and selfish demands of certain states and groups had been dragged into the open, the malcontents exposed to public view in wartime; 'Hartford Convention' and 'Bluelight Federalist' were political terms of contempt for twenty years. The war knit the nation together and matured it. 'It has renewed', said Swiss Albert Gallatin, who had served in Jefferson's cabinet, 'and reinstated the national feeling and character which the Revolution had given, and which were daily lessening. The people now have more general objects of attachment. . . . They are more Americans, they feel and act more as a nation.'

Hitherto America had faced east, despite its political independence. Until 1815 its trade was foreign trade, its problem in foreign affairs that of maintaining neutrality in European muddles, its problems of statesmanship those of foreign diplomacy, even its political theory conditioned by a preference for England or France. After the treaty of Ghent America turned to the great hazy untouched West, where half a continent lay empty and exposed, ready for exploitation. America could concentrate on its domestic problem of perfecting political and social organization, and of westward expansion, with less concern for European standards, ideals, and entanglements. American indifference to European affairs after 1815 was such that even Napoleon's return from Elba excited little attention in the press. Isolationism had begun.

Nineteenth-century America believed in two contrasted worlds, the Old and the New. The Old World of England and Europe was corrupt, tyrannical, regressive, plagued by wars and ancient hatreds. The New World was democratic, free, progressive, hopeful. The objective of American diplomacy, it was assumed, must be to keep these worlds apart, lest the taint of the Old besmirch the fresh *tabula rasa* of the New.

The first generation of American statesmen – Washington, Adams, Jefferson, Hamilton, Richard Henry Lee, and others – insisted that the United States should avoid whenever possible entanglements in Old World politics. Washington's Farewell Address (written with Hamilton's aid) was the classic statement of the view which set the prevailing pattern of American foreign policy.

At the same time it was apparent that the United States had close commercial, political, and cultural ties with the Old World, and that to follow a private path would be difficult if not impossible. In winning their independence, Americans found it necessary to seek an ally in France, and powerful European nations – England, Spain, and France – had large territorial possessions on America's doorstep. There were certain accepted positions on foreign affairs that the United States believed it must maintain – freedom of the seas, freedom of foreign trade, neutrality in European disputes, national integrity, and above all others, the promotion of the cause of liberty throughout the world. In practice, American diplomats often found these difficult. Did maintenance of freedom of the seas, for example, justify involvement in a European war? Did assistance to South American or European revolutions justify entanglement in European affairs? If so, how far should the United States go in aiding Greeks and Hungarians in throwing off oppression? Should American policy, when it agreed with that of a European power, be pursued jointly or alone? Ought the United States to assume responsibility for a hemispheric pan-American bloc?

In answering these and similar questions, the makers of American foreign policy during the first half of the nineteenth century followed closely the principles laid down by Washington and the first generation. Nearly every statement of foreign policy after 1815 was predicated on the assumption that the United States was detached from Europe, should remain so, and must always be free to pursue its own special diplomatic ends. American diplomats during the period had to find solutions to increasingly complex issues of foreign policy within this framework.

After the War of 1812, however, the American public was much less interested in external foreign relations than it was in the business of augmenting and expanding the nation it had constructed out of two wars and a generation of experiment; in other words, developing modern America. Certain factors operated in that development, producing in pre-Civil War America a particular intellectual and cultural pattern, shaped in time and place by the facts of the present and of the immediate past. Two of these factors, nationalism and romanticism, impressed themselves deeply on the personality of the period.

The feeling of 'Americanism' was of course not recent nor its roots shallow. The Revolution, Americans believed, created a new nation fullborn, and the War of 1812 simply completed its independence. Politically there was no doubt of America's separate national existence. Economically, the most pressing problem since 1776 had been to develop that nation into an economic unit, the more effectively to compete in foreign trade with the established mercantile nations – another reason for a nationalistic trend. At the same time, it was apparent that those British institutions, manners, and mores transplanted to American soil in the seventeenth century were subtly and surely flowering into something indigenous and American. Geographically far removed from the parent nation for more than a hundred and fifty years, America had already modified and changed English ideas, law, theology, manners, language, literature, society, and custom into a recognizably native culture long before the revolutionary break, which merely speeded up the process. And there had been, since 1790, growing migration to the United States of non-British peoples, further intensifying the cultural cleavage with the mother country. Furthermore, within this cultural framework sectional differences were beginning to appear, growing sharper as time passed, in dialect, manners, economics, society, tastes, needs – the citified commercial Middle States of New York, Pennsylvania, and New Jersey; rural, Calvinist New England; the semi-feudal agrarian South; the bumptious, sprawling West – not one America, but many in one, the 'e pluribus unum' of the coinage made real. Amidst all this was the plain hard fact of the frontier, which as it moved westward became the hither edge of a civilization more and more removed from Europe and increasingly American. Early eighteenth-century Boston, though by no means culturally or temperamentally British, was only a ship's voyage from London; nineteenth-century Pittsburgh and Wheeling, behind the mountain wall, grew in a new and alien world. And beneath the rising tide of nationalism lay the shreds of the old colonial sense of mission and destiny, the idealism of those who came to the shores of Massachusetts to make a new Jerusalem in this green and pleasant land. Small wonder that by 1815 America resounded with cries for a native culture, a native tradition, a realization of its native self.

Early nineteenth-century America, of course, grew up in an age of romanticism, with a tendency to exalt the common man, to stress the potentialities of the individual, to break the rigid bonds of tradition and form. The romantic movement of the late eighteenth century, as it reached America in the early nineteenth century, wrought profound and significant changes in the temper of American life. The legacy of belief in inevitable progress, left behind by the preceding generation, buttressed the nation's romantic faith in its own powers and blew on it the breath of hope. America faced the future with dynamic eagerness, confident of solving its problems. 'We are the pioneers of the world,' reflected Herman Melville. 'God has predestined, mankind expects, great things from our race, and great things we feel in our soul. The most of the nations must soon be in the rear. We are . . . the advance guard, sent on through the wilderness of untried things.'

The optimistic nationalism that characterized the period was not a wholly narrow and insular one. The literate population of the United States was still for the most part British in origin, and old ties with England and Europe not easily broken. After concluding two wars against Britain, separated by a brief period of internal adjustment, the United States felt sufficiently secure to take another look at England and Europe – but with a self-consciously American attitude, neither imitative nor colonial. After 1814 American scholars, writers, and travellers eagerly sought out and brought back with them from abroad the ideas, treasures, and attitudes of the Old World, yet always with the accepted underlying assumption that they were not copying Europe, but absorbing it. Young men like Motley, Bancroft, Ticknor, and Everett studied at German universities; Emerson visited Wordsworth and Coleridge; Longfellow travelled in Germany, Italy, and Spain; Irving went to England, Spain, and

Germany. These and others like them re-established enthusiastic communication with older civilizations. American culture of the period therefore displayed all the hallmarks of contemporary European thought, with the addition of such characteristic American traits as a belief in the superiority of democracy, an optimistic and expansive attitude, and a greater sense of an older Puritan moralism and rigidity. America must 'prove to the world', wrote Charles Ingersoll in 1823, 'that the best patronage of religion, science, literature, and the arts, of whatever the mind can achieve, is SELF-GOVERNMENT.'

This blending of nationalism and cosmopolitanism is aptly illustrated by the literary trends of the period. American authors and critics, groping for some concept of a national culture, could not quite decide whether to be Americans or geniuses; in them the hope lingered that they might be both. With their military and political affairs apparently for the moment stabilized, they turned energetically to the problem of establishing a national culture, though not at all certain what it should be. The journals of the time were filled with laments for the lack of a native cultural tradition, coupled with loud demands for its creation. Under pressure from the nationalistic urge from at home, and the drive of European romanticism from abroad, American critics hopefully awaited the appearance of an American Scott or an American Wordsworth. In their haste to acclaim him, they were often premature, hailing every dull poem as a 'new American epic' or every tedious novelist as an 'American Austen' or a 'native Scott'.

In attempting to create a native culture, the American of the first three decades of the century felt it his patriotic duty to answer the attacks of European (especially British) writers on America. Badgered by foreign critics, uncertain of their own status in the world, and subjected to the abuse of magazines such as the Tory *Quarterly* and *Blackwood's*, they displayed an exaggerated but understandable pugnacity and sensitivity – *le patriotisme irritable* that de Tocqueville noted. Replies to foreign attacks were not easily fashioned, for

American literary and artistic production was hardly distinguished. If Britain could display Burns, Byron, Scott, Wordsworth, Coleridge, Jane Austen, and a myriad of others, to whom could America point with pride? Dwight, Barlow, Dennie, Paulding, Drake, Freneau, Halleck, and company. The shadow of Byron and Wordsworth lay over American verse; Scott, whose books sold a half-million copies in the United States by 1823, dominated American fiction. Sydney Smith's sneering query, 'Who reads an American book?' was hard to answer.

Yet there was something developing. Americans discovered that the frontier blockhouse was as satisfactory a background for romantic fiction as a castle on the Rhine or in the Scottish lowlands; Deerslayer in his buckskin was as exciting a figure as a knight in armour; Indians were adversaries as worthy as Moors or clansmen. Cooper, Bryant, young Longfellow, Poe, and a few others provided a partial answer to Smith, and Washington Irving a much more convincing one. Irving, who showed that art could be both good and national, pointed the way toward the development of a native cultural tradition. William Ellery Channing expressed the hope that Irving and a few others seemed to justify, that America, with its concept of liberty and with its freedom from much of the Old World's corruption and error, might yet evolve a cultural tradition that would 'give new impulses to the human mind'.

The place of religion in American life in the early nineteenth century was still secure, though not so central as it had once been. The Revolutionary War disrupted churches and weakened their position by shifting interest from religious to political affairs. The separation of church and state, begun by the Bill of Rights and completed by the states, became a fact, while the dominance of Calvinism in American life, already threatened during the later eighteenth century, was further endangered by a growing trend towards secularism.

Seventeenth-century Puritanism, exemplified in the New England colonies of Plymouth and Massachusetts Bay, was a unified, internally balanced system of beliefs and practices, embracing ethics, politics, science, economics, and social thought. It controlled the thought of the American seventeenth century. After 1750 Calvinistic Christianity was gradually buried beneath a heavy coating of political and economic facts to which its theology had little relevance. But for fifty-odd years it was neither effectively disputed nor openly discarded, despite the inroads made into its domain by the Methodism of the 1740s and the deism of the 1790s. It was simply ignored as something of little consequence in practical living, although occasional flares of revitalization might occur within it. By the time of the War of 1812 Puritanism had lost its hold on American life, though its impression remained on generations to come.

The decline and fall of American Puritanism came as the result of a variety of internal and external causes. It was always a difficult creed to hold, containing seemingly irreconcilable principles which had to be kept in alignment by constant argument and adjustment. Its concepts of God, freewill, knowledge and revelation, sin, and moral duty were maintained throughout the seventeenth century in delicate intellectual and imaginative balance; to later generations of ministers and laity they seemed less capable of proof or reconciliation. As the concepts themselves came under the scrutiny of a rationalistic, hard-headed age, the system they supported disintegrated – like Holmes' 'one-hoss shay', which pure logic could no longer hold together.

Puritanism was, of course, under constant pressure from without. As the nation turned to a mercantile and industrial economy, the emphasis of living shifted from other-worldliness to this-worldliness. Cities grew, a new wealthy, sophisticated urban class rose and prospered, while piety suffered. The single-minded purpose of the original Puritans disappeared in the mercantile economics of a maturing eighteenth-century society, where neither Jonathan Edwards nor Cotton Mather could recall it. It became difficult, as one observer noted, for reasonable folk to regard their decent, orderly, and wealthy neighbours as inherently sinful and lost, even though they did not belong to the proper orthodox church. 'Protestantism', remarked Lowell later, 'had made its fortune and no longer protested.' The rationalism of Newton and Franklin had no place for Puritan logic, nor for its concepts of the universe and human nature. Deism, Methodism, Baptism, and Unitarianism were better equipped to meet the needs of the times, and more adaptable to the rational, individualistic, secular spirit of the late eighteenth and early nineteenth century. By substituting an optimistic, expansive religious philosophy for one of gloomy determinism, the newer sects freed the active spirit of the age from the inhibitions imposed on it by traditional Calvinism.

For that matter, the whole drift of contemporary political thought moved directly away from the Puritan idea of the state and its function. The concept of natural rights, the social compact theory, the new feeling of equality, liberty, and fraternity – all these were incompatible with the Puritan tradition of oligarchy. The early Puritans' conviction that they were God's chosen people faded with the rise of nationalism; the wedge driven between church and state by eighteenth-century constitutional thinkers weakened the older system still more. By 1814, after a half-century's defence, Puritanism found itself in contradiction to the main trends of American political thought. Its theology was opposed to contemporary science; its theocracy in conflict with contemporary ideas of democracy; its basic ethic at variance with nineteenth-century social, political, and economic facts.

At the close of the eighteenth century the established orthodox churches were at a low ebb. The Great Awakening of mid-century split the Congregationalists into warring wings of 'New Lights' and 'Old Lights', while Methodism and deism sapped their strength. Presbyterians noted the decline of their churches with alarm; in 1782 only two students at Princeton, long a Presbyterian stronghold, professed the true faith. President Timothy Dwight at Yale inveighed against 'infidelity', while the Congregationalist-

Unitarian controversy split Harvard's theological faculty and led later to the founding of Andover by the defeated conservatives. The Episcopal Church in the South, thought Chief Justice Marshall, was 'too far gone to be revived'. Timothy Flint, a frontier missionary, reported from the West that 'in these new regions, too, of the most absolute independence, you see all the wanderings of human thought, every shade of faith . . .' There were a good many frontiersmen who swore by Tom Paine and proudly called themselves 'nullifidians', and a preacher could never be sure how he would be received in the hinterlands. Even in Catholic Louisiana Voltaire and Diderot were popular, while a visitor to St Louis left it with the firm impression that every Frenchman was an infidel.

In the chaos following the breakdown of the old faiths, several new ones or variations of older ones appeared on the theological scene. Unitarianism, whose appeal was largely limited to the cultivated upper classes, became an influential force in New England and the East. The visit of the great Hazlitt's father to New England in 1783–5, and the work of liberal Congregationalists such as Thomas Barnard and John Prince before him, had direct consequences. The Episcopal King's Chapel in Boston took a Unitarian stand in 1784; in the next sixteen years all but a few of the city's churches followed suit. The appointment of a Unitarian, Henry Ware, as Hollis Professor of Divinity at Harvard in 1805, marked the end of Puritan dominance in the cradle of New England Calvinism. Universalism, called derisively for its simple creed 'the poor man's Unitarianism', established itself in Massachusetts as early as 1779. Both of these sects, with their stress on the worth of human nature, their emphasis on the social and humanitarian rather than the credal aspects of religion, and their belief in the efficacy of the individual, were in closer agreement with the mood of the period than was orthodox Calvinism. They gave respectability and organized status to liberal religious thought as deism had failed to do. Not long after 1800 the majority of established churches from Maine to Maryland made the transition to Unitarian-Universalist principles without a serious break in the church organization.

Neither the older Puritanism nor the newer Unitarianism carried religion to the West. The opening of the transmountain areas and the swift rush of settlement westward meant great new opportunities for churchly expansion. The Presbyterians, of the older sects, were best situated to take advantage of it, since the last wave of pre-Revolutionary migration scattered Scotch-Irish Presbyterians north and south along the mountain frontier. In 1801 the Congregationalists and Presbyterians joined in a 'Plan of Union' to Christianize the West, and pushed their brands of orthodoxy into Ohio, Michigan, western New York, and Illinois, where migration from New England and the Middle States was largest.

The greatest successes in the West, however, were those of the Baptists and Methodists, whose organization, doctrines, and temperament were admirably fitted to frontier conditions. Both were loosely organized, flexible in creed, simple in theology. They both stressed religious elements particularly appropriate to the frontier – emotionalism, personal conversion, directness – emphasizing the importance of the individual in religion rather than church or creed. The shouting, hymn-singing, camp-meeting of the itinerant evangelist made theology a personal and communal matter; the week-long revivals were social as well as religious events. Bishop Francis Asbury, the superb administrator and organizer who introduced into the West the 'circuit rider' system used by the Wesleys in England, found it perfectly adapted to the scattered settlements, just as the Baptists found their 'lay preacher' system equally well suited. Asbury, who travelled over 300,000 miles in the saddle himself, sent hundreds of circuit-riding ministers like the redoubtable Peter Cartwright into remote backwoods areas, creating a string of Methodist outposts. The Baptists and Methodists captured the lower Northwest and the Southwest, and pushed churches far into the New England-settled Great Lakes areas.

Probably the greatest factor in the death of Puritanism was the wave of evangelism that swept like a prairie fire across America after 1800. In the Northeast, where Unitarianism and even Universalism never really appealed to the ordinary man, the Methodists sparked a rebirth of religious fervour that eventually evangelized half of the area – by 1802 one-third of the students at godless Yale affirmed conversion. Revivalist techniques, worked out in the Great Awakening a half-century before, fired Congregational and Presbyterian churches all over New England with what Timothy Dwight called 'that strange new-birth, that Methodistic grace'. The wave rolled swiftly west, where the Baptists and Methodists held sway. The great evangelist James McGready carried the flame of 'old time religion' through the Carolinas into Kentucky and Tennessee, followed by torchlit camp-meetings, shouting, singing, hysteria, and other stigmata of sudden public conversion. From the mountainous Southwest it spread west and north into the lower fringes of Ohio, Indiana, Michigan, and Illinois, cutting across sectarian lines and striking impartially into all the churches. The Methodists and Baptists, accustomed as they were to emotionalism, welcomed the evangelistic torch-bearers eagerly. The Presbyterians hung back, and the Congregationalists opposed them for a quarter of a century, but revivalism flourished nonetheless. The largest meeting was probably that at Cain Ridge, Kentucky, in 1801, where roughly 20,000 people gathered for a week in fervent hysterical worship, egged on by Baptist, Methodist, and Presbyterian exhorters. The Second Awakening shook orthodoxy on its already unsteady foundations, broke up into an astonishing variety of new schismatic sects, and left the Baptists and Methodists the undisputed masters of the West. From it came the Christian Church, the Campbellites, the United Brethren, the Rappites, and many more.

The evangelical Second Awakening of the early nineteenth century was in effect a theological manifestation of the democratizing temper of the era. With the old faiths apparently out of touch with the people and the times, the newer and less orthodox churches – by appealing to the common man and emphasizing ideas of individual worth, progress and equality of believers – met the religious demands of the day as surely and squarely as Jacksonian democracy met contemporary political desires. Splitting the old sects and creating new ones, the wave of revivalism encouraged the dissenting factions to challenge directly the domination of the orthodox churches of the East as well as of the West, and of the conservative, federalist classes who supported them. The break with Puritanism was clean and complete, as clear and certain as Jacksonian democracy's break with the older political tradition.

After 1800 Calvinism no longer dominated American life and thought. Yet its stamp remained strong on the American character – its moral fervour or 'Yankee conscience', its crusading spirit, its dreams of social reconstruction, its tremendous driving energy. The United States was still under the control of an aggressive Protestantism. Congregationalists, Baptists, Presbyterians, Methodists and the others might argue matters of creed interminably, but they all frowned on deviations from the moral, the accepted, the pious – a check on the rebelliousness and individualism of romanticism. There was no American Byron to scandalize New England, no atheist Shelley at Harvard, no illicit romance in Emerson's past. The disputatious diversity of American sects carried to the ultimate the implications of the Reformation, but never denied them; no American could escape the effects of nearly two hundred years of Puritanism.

America was optimistic, nationalistic, romantically hopeful, self-consciously young, trying hard to find the stability, confidence, and maturity of the older nations, hoping to establish itself as a nation in the shortest possible time. Perhaps it flexed its muscles in public too much, chased 'refinement' and sensibility too eagerly, played the pugnacious youngster too hard. But it was, or at least believed itself to be, an *achieved* democracy possessed of something that England, France, and the rest of the world did not have.

At the close of 'Mr Madison's War' the United States turned with a sigh of relief to the matter at hand, that of realizing its self-made promises. Mr Madison's party, having concluded its inept prosecution of an unpopular and inconclusive war, surprisingly enough emerged from it covered with popular glory, its Federalist opposition melted away. The Republican party, taking a stronger nationalistic position than even Hamilton's party maintained in its palmiest days, attracted to it all but the most irreconcilable Federalists, whose popularity had rapidly declined since the Hartford Convention. The Presidential election of 1816, a colourless affair, showed that party politics had reached very nearly a dead level. To decry partisanship became the fashion of the day, and even that king of partisans, Andrew Jackson, advised that 'Now is the time to exterminate the monster called party spirit . . . and perhaps have the pleasure of uniting a people heretofore politically divided'. Madison chose Secretary of State Monroe as his successor, while the Federalists did not bother to name an official candidate. Monroe carried all but three states, whose electors supported Rufus King of New York.

James Monroe of Virginia was neither a distinguished statesman nor an acute politician, though he had, as John Quincy Adams phrased it, 'a mind sound in its ultimate judgements and firm in its final conclusions'. He did have wide experience in politics – Senator from Virginia, Governor of Virginia, minister to France and England, Secretary of State – a solid but not brilliant record. A congenital middle-of-the-roader, he was so eminently fitted to govern the United States during a period of indecision that his two terms as President became known as 'the era of good feelings'. There was, of course, an internal balance of powers from 1816 to 1824 that lent some logic to the name, but the period was more accurately one of transition rather than of 'good feelings', peaceful only because political forces were busy regrouping for new conflict. For the placid soil of Monroe's era contained the seeds of sectional interests, soon to germinate. The rise of manufacturing in New England,

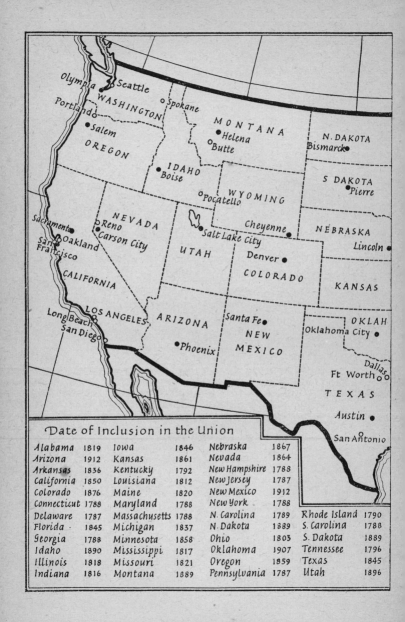

Olympia · Seattle
WASHINGTON   ○ Spokane
Portland
● Salem
OREGON   ● IDAHO
              Boise   MONTANA
                           ● Helena
                           ● Butte   N. DAKOTA
                                        Bismarck ●

                           WYOMING   S. DAKOTA
              ○ Pocatello   Pierre ●

Sacramento   NEVADA   ○ Salt Lake City   Cheyenne   NEBRASKA
● Reno   Carson City   ●
San   ● Oakland   Lincoln ●
Francisco   UTAH   Denver ●
CALIFORNIA   COLORADO
                                         KANSAS
Long Beach ● LOS ANGELES   ARIZONA
San Diego   Santa Fe ●   OKLAH
                           NEW   Oklahoma City ●
              ● Phoenix   MEXICO
                                         Dallas ○
                                         Ft Worth ○
                                         TEXAS
                                         Austin ●
                                         San Antonio ○

Date of Inclusion in the Union

State	Year	State	Year	State	Year	State	Year
Alabama	1819	Iowa	1846	Nebraska	1867		
Arizona	1912	Kansas	1861	Nevada	1864		
Arkansas	1836	Kentucky	1792	New Hampshire	1788		
California	1850	Louisiana	1812	New Jersey	1787		
Colorado	1876	Maine	1820	New Mexico	1912		
Connecticut	1788	Maryland	1788	New York	1788		
Delaware	1787	Massachusetts	1788	N. Carolina	1789	Rhode Island	1790
Florida	1845	Michigan	1837	N. Dakota	1889	S. Carolina	1788
Georgia	1788	Minnesota	1858	Ohio	1803	S. Dakota	1889
Idaho	1890	Mississippi	1817	Oklahoma	1907	Tennessee	1796
Illinois	1818	Missouri	1821	Oregon	1859	Texas	1845
Indiana	1816	Montana	1889	Pennsylvania	1787	Utah	1896

STATES AND PRINCIPAL CITIES

○ NEW YORK — over 1 million inhabitants
○ Toledo — over 200.000 inhabitants
● State Capital

Vermont	1791
Virginia	1788
Washington	1889
W Virginia	1863
Wisconsin	1848
Wyoming	1890

Abbreviations used on the Map

CONN. = Connecticut
DEL. = Delaware
MD = Maryland
MASS. = Massachusetts
MINN. = Minnesota
MISS = Mississippi
N.H. = New Hampshire
N.J. = New Jersey
R.I = Rhode Island
VT = Vermont

stimulated by embargo and war, the spread of cotton in the South, and the opening of the agricultural West meant a readjustment of sectional economic interests with unforeseen political consequences. The 'Virginia Dynasty', stretching from Washington to Monroe and broken only by John Adams, was nearly finished. The war and the West ended it, bringing into the political spotlight a new cast of leaders – Henry Clay of Kentucky, John C. Calhoun of South Carolina, New England's Daniel Webster, and John Quincy Adams, and of course Andrew Jackson.

Except for the delivery of the Monroe Doctrine, the record of American foreign affairs from 1816 to 1840 showed few important developments. The whole of Spanish Florida became American property in 1819, and the problem of whether or not to recognize the new revolutionary South American republics was deferred by observing a policy of favourable neutrality until their recognition seemed expedient. Although relatively uninterested in the tangled diplomatic manœuvrings of Europe, the United States still saw a threat to its power in the Western hemisphere in the formation of the Holy Alliance, and in the apparent design of the major European powers to crush revolution in Spain, Italy, Portugal, Greece, or wherever it raised its head. There was also a strong suspicion that Europe, particularly Britain, might move into the South American republics recently liberated by Bolivar. Therefore, in his annual message to Congress in 1823, Monroe laid down the broad outline of foreign policy eventually known as the Monroe Doctrine.

The basis of Monroe's doctrine rested on two main principles – the principle of non-colonization, that Europe should not be allowed to found new dependencies in the western hemisphere; and the principle of non-intervention, that Europe should never so interfere with the nations of that hemisphere as to endanger their independence or form of government. 'The political system of the allied powers is essentially different . . . from that of America', Monroe wrote. ' . . . We should consider any attempt on their part to extend their system to any portion of this hemisphere as dangerous to our peace and safety', thus drawing a sharp line of political demarcation between Europe and both Americas. The fundamental ideas of the Doctrine were implicit in the foreign policies of Washington, John Adams, and Jefferson. Monroe's message, however, clarified matters by stating in precise and explicit terms the principles of hemispheric separation, non-intervention, and avoidance of foreign entanglement. His forthright enunciation of American dominance over the whole Western half of the world irritated and annoyed Europe (particularly Canning and Metternich, and Canada). It was received at best with mixed feelings by these South American republics whose future it was designed to safeguard. Nevertheless the Monroe Doctrine remained a basic principle of American foreign policy, brought to issue in the Mexican troubles some thirty years later.

The ultra-nationalistic trend of the 'era of good feelings' was evident in the programme of legislation laid out by Congress during Monroe's administration. His inaugural address of 1815 asked for a stronger military, a solid uniform national currency, a protective tariff for war-born American industry, and a system of roads and canals to improve communications between the seaboard ports and the West. All these requests were speedily granted, the moribund Federalist party acceding with alacrity to what was essentially its own historic programme. New England's commercial interests objected, fearing that a tariff would damage foreign trade and that the road-canal system might favour the agricultural West, but they received short shrift. Meanwhile, while the Republicans strengthened the position of the federal government in political and commercial affairs, the Supreme Court, under able and obstinate Chief Justice John Marshall of Virginia, gave them legal assistance.

Marshall, one of John Adams' appointees, dominated the Court for thirty-four years (1801–35). An avowed Federalist, he lost no opportunity, in both important and obscure cases, to emphasize the supremacy of federal power and interest over that of the states, and the supremacy of the judiciary over the executive and legislative branches of the government. Hardly learned in law, Marshall was less the technical jurist than the juridical statesman, willing to look beyond the case at hand to the needs of a new people and of an expanding nation. During his term of office he handled more than fifty cases involving important constitutional issues, and decided each from the point of view of Federalistic political philosophy. As a result Marshall became the greatest single influence on the shape of American constitutional law.

Marbury versus Madison (1803) established the principle of judicial review, that is, the right of the Supreme Court to declare void and unconstitutional an act or portion of an act of Congress or state legislature. Fletcher versus Peck (1810) established the inviolability of contracts, placing them beyond the reach of state courts and governments, while in Dartmouth College versus Woodward (1819) he maintained that corporation charters were also contracts, a decision that later proved important to an expanding industrial economy. McCulloch versus Maryland (1819) and Osburn versus Bank of the United States (1824) affirmed the superiority of federal over state law and the Hamiltonian principle of implied constitutional power – that the federal government may do things not specifically stated in the Constitution that it may do, if its purpose agrees with the spirit of the Constitution and with the national interest. Hammering at these principles in decision after decision, with the majority of the Court behind him, Marshall's idea of federal supremacy fitted the prevailing nationalistic trend. Whatever the fate of the Federalist party, he wrote its ideas into constitutional law and won its old fight with the Jeffersonians.

From the Louisiana purchase to the entry of Wisconsin (the last state east of the Mississippi to enter the union) in 1848, the area added to the nation was larger than all Europe west of Russia. 'The rise of the new West', remarked a later historian, Frederick Jackson Turner, 'was the most significant fact in American history in the years immediately following the War of 1812.'

The West grew with phenomenal speed. In the first thirty-six years of the Republic, five new states joined the Union – Vermont, Tennessee, Kentucky, Ohio, and Louisiana. But six new states entered in only seven years after the close of the War of 1812, five of them carved from frontier territory – Indiana (1816), Mississippi (1817), Illinois (1818), Alabama (1819), Maine (1820), and Missouri (1821). The centre of population swiftly shifted westward. At the time of Washington's inauguration, less than six per cent of the country's population lived west of the Alleghany–Appalachian mountain ranges. By 1820 the figure stood at twenty-seven per cent and still growing; Ohio's population exceeded that of Massachusetts, while Louisiana and Missouri, the most western of the new states, had more than fifty thousand inhabitants. As early as 1796 a British traveller in Pennsylvania reported seeing 'ten and twenty waggons at a time . . . on their way to Pittsburgh and other parts of Ohio, from thence to descend down the river to Kentucky'. Another observer, watching the flatboats loaded with wagons dotting the Ohio river, remarked that 'there is scarcely a day . . . but that there is a greater or less number of boats floating down its gentle current', to the tune of 'Hi-O, away we go Floating down the river on the O-Hi-O'.

The great migration flowed down established waterways, through convenient mountain passes, and over the new national turnpikes that were built after 1818. New Eng landers followed the Connecticut and Housatonic rivers into Maine and over into upper New York State, where the Great Genesee Road began. The Hudson and Mohawk valleys opened up on western New York, joining lake and river routes that continued on to Ohio and Michigan. From Philadelphia and the Middle States Braddock's Road led to Pittsburgh, where the Allegheny and Monongahela rivers met to form the Ohio, the gateway to Ohio, Kentucky, Tennessee, southern Indiana and Illinois, and the Southwest. Migrants from Virginia and the southern seaboard could follow Boone's Wilderness Road through Cumberland Gap into Kentucky, or the new National Pike from Maryland to Wheeling and on into Ohio, Indiana, and Illinois. The Jonesboro Road carried migrants from North Carolina into Tennessee, while another route ran from South Carolina through Georgia into Alabama, Mississippi, and Louisiana. These roads seemed to be always full. At Zanesville, Ohio, fifty wagons a day crossed the Muskingum river; during one nine-day period in 1817, two hundred and sixty wagons passed a given point on the turnpike in upper New York State. On the southern route a traveller coming eastward counted 3,800 persons headed west towards Alabama and Mississippi. In its first year of operation, the Erie Canal carried 13,111 boats and 40,000 persons west. 'Old America', commented an observer in 1817, 'seems to be breaking up and moving westward.'

Some families travelled alone, with a single horse and wagon piled high with furniture and children, a barefooted wife walking behind. Others banded together for mutual assistance, and occasionally groups as large as 200 from a single area planned and made the trip, electing a leader and appointing trail committees. Cattle, horses, sheep, and hogs were driven before the caravan, tended by slaves in the case of the few wealthy Southerners who made the trip. For those able to afford it, flatboat or steamboat transportation made travel swifter; the poor simply walked, going West 'because everybody says it's good land'. From Virginia and the Carolinas, Southerners moved into Tennessee, Kentucky, Alabama, Mississippi, and Louisiana (and later into Arkansas and Texas), taking with them cotton economics and slavery. A few, like Lincoln's father, filtered north into southern Ohio, Illinois, and Indiana, giving that region a slightly Southern cast it still retains. The rich flat loam of the Northwest drew New England farmers, tired of the hard-scrabble acreage of Maine and Massachusetts, and attracted frustrated labourers and artisans from the densely-populated Eastern cities – giving a Puritan, Yankee stamp to the towns of Ohio, Michigan, northern Indiana and Illinois, and later

Wisconsin. Though most of them stopped at the Mississippi, the nation sent probing fingers in the huge, vaguely-known, rolling plains of the trans-river area, hitherto the domain of trappers, hunters, fur companies, and Indians. Jefferson sent Meriwether Lewis and William Clark up the Missouri to the Pacific Northwest in 1804, while John Jacob Astor sent two expeditions to the Oregon country and planted a post of his Pacific Fur Company at Astoria in 1811–12. The Wisconsin–Minnesota–Dakota territory was already the base of a highly organized fur trade, and missionaries, both Catholic and Protestant, followed the trappers into the westernmost reaches of the wilderness.

Behind the westward push was the desire for good, cheap land. The long argument over the disposal of the public domain, dating back to the Articles of Confederation, was settled by a series of decisions that favoured the settler rather than the private company or speculator. The Ordinance of 1785, coupled with the Northwest Ordinance of 1787, provided a pattern for surveying, selling, and settling the western lands. Successive changes in land laws led finally to the act of 1820 which established the minimum size of grants at 80 acres, the minimum price at $1.25 an acre, and certain favourable credit terms. While the new laws did not entirely eliminate the speculator, it at least made his job more difficult and the emigrant's acquisition of a good-sized farm somewhat easier.

Cheap land was lure enough, but there was also the pressure of economic conditions in the crowded, war-dislocated cities of the East to drive men West. American manufacturing, hurt by embargo and blockade, faltered uncertainly for nearly a decade after the War of 1812. Periodic business recessions, as the national economy adjusted to peace, were immediately reflected by increases in the westward flow, at its highest during the depression years of 1819 to 1821. The shipping interests of New England ran into stiff competition from European merchantmen, while the growth of New York, New Orleans, and Baltimore, plus the opening of canals and turnpikes, almost killed off the lesser

New England ports. Western wheat, sheep, cattle, and even vegetables – especially as transportation routes opened Eastern markets to them – pushed the New England farmer hard; freight rates between Buffalo and New York dropped from $100 to $8 a ton when the Erie Canal opened. From the seaboard South, where tobacco quickly wore out soil, the lush bottom lands of the West attracted farmers who raised cotton, tobacco, and wheat. The Southern yeoman farmer, artisan, and non-slaveholder often found the West a convenient and attractive escape from the economic and political domination of the great planters and merchants of the seaboard cities; the old conflict between back-country and coastal areas in Pennsylvania, Virginia, and the Carolinas helped to drive back-country men farther west in search of political and economic independence.

The removal of the Indian threat in the Northwest and Southwest after 1800 provided an additional impetus to the westward movement. 'Mad Anthony' Wayne's victory over Little Turtle's Miamis at Fallen Timbers in northwestern Ohio in 1794 broke the back of Indian resistance in the Ohio–Michigan–Indiana area, impressing the British so much that they speeded up evacuation of their Great Lakes military outposts, and with the failure of Tecumseh's confederacy, after Harrison's inconclusive clash with him at Tippecanoe in 1811, the Indian menace virtually came to an end. The Indians gave ground grudgingly in a series of bloody minor actions; it was not until after the Black Hawk War in 1832 that the westernmost settlers could forget the torch and scalping knife.

American institutions and American character received their shape and pattern from diverse influences – from Europe, from Puritan protestantism, from the environment of the land itself – but certainly one of the most powerful of these influences was the frontier. The growth and development of modern European nations has been conditioned by the fact that their expansion was confined within fairly definite limits, marked by national boundaries; in order to continue expansion one nation was forced to absorb or conquer others. This was not true of the United States. The early seventeenth-century colonies fringing the sea-coast found only a negligible Indian civilization between them and seemingly illimitable space. The early settlers came, subdued the wilderness and the Indian, evolved a government, and progressed from primitive agricultural society to complex industrial or agricultural civilization within a few years. Inland, perhaps only a few miles, the process was being repeated again and again, over a period of nearly 250 years, until the Pacific Ocean stopped it. Conflict with neighbouring nations was indirect rather than direct. There were no equal states to meet and subdue, no established or well-developed cultures to absorb or dominate – and the frontier could always move West. The settlement itself was fortunately accomplished by a homogeneous people, of the same race, language, stock, religion, and political and social ideals, whose minor cultural differences were easily assimilated.

The frontier meant a constant return to primitive conditions at the edge of the settlement line, a constant repetition of an evolutionary development from simple to complex civilization as that line moved westward. This perennial rebirth of civilization, perennial contact with primitive conditions, perennial social fluidity, had much to do with the distinctive temper of America and Americans. For as the frontier moved westward it became more and more native, geographically and culturally more removed from Europe, less subject to Old World intellectual, religious, and economic influences. In Hawthorne's extravagant phrase, beyond the mountains lay land 'on which the damned shadow of Europe had not fallen'. This is the difference between William Bradford and Abraham Lincoln, John Smith and Daniel Boone, Thomas Jefferson and Andrew Jackson, George Washington and William Jennings Bryan – all Americans, yet as unlike as the ages that produced them, the country they lived in, and most of all as diverse as the frontiers that shaped them.

349

The Atlantic Coast, the frontier of Smith and Bradford, was an English frontier, retaining much of British culture, habit, manner, and mode of thought. In the late seventeenth century, the line of settlement moved inland up the waterways to the mountain fall line and beyond, to the Wyoming Valley of Pennsylvania, Pittsburgh, eastern Tennessee, the Georgia uplands, Boone's Kentucky. By the late eighteenth century it had moved on – despite efforts to stop it with the Proclamation of 1763 – into the Ohio country, western Tennessee and Kentucky, to the threshold of the Northwest. A quarter of a century later the frontier lay at the Mississippi; then swiftly leaping to the Pacific, it worked slowly across the plains behind the Rocky Mountains, filling in the Missouri basin and the desert Southwest. The census of 1890 noted that there existed no more arable free land with a population density of less than two per square mile. Thus the frontier was declared officially dead, but its imprint on America is eternally present.

The men who went West with this frontier were a varied group, but contemporary observers and later historians identified five main types. A spectator standing at Cumberland Gap in 1790, or at Zanesville in 1810, or at South Pass in the Rockies in 1870, might have seen them pass by in almost the same order. First came the explorer, half-Indian, half-adventurer, driven west by his desire to see what lay beyond the next mountain range or across the hazy plain. He brought back tales of great virgin pine and hardwood trees a hundred feet high, stretching in a tremendous forest belt four hundred miles long and three hundred miles wide; of fertile tall-grass prairies and black bottom lands; of clear streams and thousands of blue lakes; of deer and turkeys and squirrels and rabbits. After him came the hunter and trapper, living by his rifle and bringing his skins back to some trading outpost, there to stand mute and uncomfortable until he had received his salt, powder, and bullets and could disappear into the wilderness again. He marked trails, found passes and fords, and knew which Indians were friendly and which savage. The pioneer farmer followed him, to build a rude cabin on squatter's land, clear a plot for a few vegetables, hunt, trap, and raise a family. When he heard the sound of a neighbour's axe, he moved on, or his sons did.

On his heels came the settler, who bought his land and built a better house with a chimney, rooms, and perhaps glass windows. He cleared more acres, drove a well, built bridges, mills, stores, schools, and churches, organized an elementary government, raised grain, fruit, and cash crops. When others came he might sell his land at a higher price and move on, or he might stay to merge with the growing community. In 1840 there were men in Michigan and Wisconsin who had moved five times, each time farther west; Lincoln's father liked to tell (with typical Western hyperbole) about a family that moved so often that the chickens were trained to walk to the wagon, lie down, and put their feet up to be tied for the trip. Last to arrive were the men of capital and professional skill – lawyers, bankers, editors, ministers, artisans, speculators, and politicians, the men who rounded out the social, political, and economic society, the men who stayed. They built handsome houses of frame or brick, better churches and schools, distilleries, factories, warehouses, put up fences and laid out streets and roads, introduced better strains of livestock and seed. Thus the cycle was complete, but beginning all over again somewhere to the west, a cycle accomplished with incredible speed. Some of Chicago's first settlers were still alive when it had become one of the nation's five largest cities.

What sort of man did this process produce? He was, first of all, nationally minded. The Atlantic coast was strongly influenced by Europe, but the area west of the mountains was much less so – it was simply American, a blend of Yankee, Southerner, Scotch-Irish, Pennsylvania Dutch, city man, farmer, and whatever else came west. None of the new Western states had any colonial history. They were children of the Federal government, which surveyed their land and sold it to them, helped them finance it, protected them against Indians and British (sometimes none too well), governed them as territories, and admitted them as states. Both Southwest and Northwest were nationalistic in thought until split by slavery and states-rights.

The frontier American was, by past and present circumstance, a strong believer in equality. European travellers noted that even in the cities workmen did not tip their hats or say 'Sir', that servants ate at the family table, that titles such as 'Judge' and 'Colonel' were so liberally bestowed as to be meaningless. The runaway servant and the earl's son faced starvation, Indians, the forest, and opportunity on an equal footing, for the frontier gave every man his chance. Each man counted as one, and how much he counted depended on his own brain and hands. And by *equality* the frontier meant not only social and political equality, but equality of economic opportunity – each to his own, and devil take the hindmost.

Frontier man was a self-reliant individualist. He was his own master, and had only himself to blame for failure. There was no store to sell salt to the pioneer, who travelled to the nearest salt-lick or trading post to get it. If his axe-handle broke, he whittled a new one. Illness he simply waited out or cured with what herb remedies he could devise. He built his own house, made many of his own tools, raised most of his food and made much of his clothing. As the Philadelphia *Inquirer and Daily Courier* pointed out in an editorial on prospects in Illinois:

The tendency of a new country being to develop and bring forward youthful talent, exerts a highly favorable influence upon boldness, force, and originality of intellect.

This feeling of self-reliance carried over into his political, social, and economic life. It was no accident that the West soon became known as an area of political intransigeance, as Lord Bryce later observed. From the farmers of Daniel Shays to Jefferson's back-country supporters to Jackson's muddy-booted followers to Bryan's embattled farmers the line of Western political revolt is clear and marked.

Yet with all his individualism, the pioneer developed a

fairly strong feeling of social solidarity and recognized the value of co-operative effort in dealing with the ever-present problems of frontier life – the wilderness, the Indian, loneliness, isolation. He organized militia, fire companies, barn- and house-raisings, cornhusking bees, and so on, as testimony to his feeling of group responsibility. The dances held on the green with bran or sawdust scattered on the ground (the 'brandance' and later 'barndance') with the fiddler scraping away at 'Old Dan Tucker' or 'Zip Coon', the rooster and gander pulls, the horseraces and camp-meetings, all helped to temper frontier individualism with a sense of social unity.

Frontier man was also a convinced optimist. If things went badly, there was always the chance that somewhere to the West they might go better. Thus the New Englanders sang on their way west:

> Come all ye Yankee Farmers who wish to change your lot,
> Who've spunk enough to travel beyond your native spot,
> And leave behind the village where Ma and Pa do stay,
> Come follow me and settle in Michigania –
> Yea, Yea, in Michigania.

Or the pioneers of Wisconsin:

> When we've wood and prairie land,
> Won by our toil,
> We'll reign like kings in fairy land,
> Lords of the soil!

He was also a materialist, accustomed to dealing in the concrete and the present, for the frontier afforded little time for reflection and placed little value on abstractions. 'Men must learn the languages of the rifle, the axe, and the plough', remarked a frontier minister, 'before they learn the lessons of Grecian and Roman philosophy and history.' There was much to be done simply to survive; the tomahawk, wet powder, starvation, and sickness were excessively real.

He had his vices as well as his virtues. Individualism and self-reliance could turn into plain disregard for law and order. Justice on the frontier could be primitive and self-administered, a matter of knife, fist, or gun. Theft was common, murder or rape not unusual, eye-gouging and ear-biting fights normal. Frontier life in its early stage could be unruly, brutal, and irreligious, though this phase usually did not last long when the church and women moved in. The Baptist, Methodist, Presbyterian, Congregational, and Campbellite circuit-riding preachers, their faiths founded on the rigid moral standards of old-fashioned Calvinism, carried law and order into backwoods settlements and exerted a powerful force against gambling, vice, drunkenness, and violence. The influence of the frontier wife was even greater. Foreign observers noted, as early as the mid eighteenth century, the growing importance of women in American life, especially in the West. As soon as the settler arrived with his wife and family, she subtly but emphatically began to impose standards of discipline, refinement, morality, and order on frontier chaos – as Tom Sawyer's Aunt Sally civilized Tom and Huckleberry Finn.

This lack of self-discipline, typical of the frontier, never quite disappeared from its character. The frontiersman liked to do things in a hurry and often regarded careful, finished work as a waste of time; he slashed the forests, gutted the soil, threw up jerry-built buildings, polluted the streams, and exterminated the game. In one large midwestern city two of the largest buildings actually fell down because of poor construction; firebells clanged nightly as matchbox houses flamed; bridges fell in; roads were lost in mire; trains collided and steamboats blew up. At least some of the defeats in the War of 1812 and in the Revolution can be laid to the Westerner's dislike of training and discipline, while the tone of legislative debates, punctuated by fist-fights and knife-brandishings, was sometimes hardly statesmanlike.

Frontier man tended to be impatient of culture and learning, for he placed great store by the ability to do many things passably well. As Emerson noted in *Self-Reliance*, the American admired the jack-of-all trades, the man who could farm, keep store, argue in court, serve in Congress, speculate in land, and run a bank. The specialist he viewed with dim suspicion; the learned man, the artist, the thinker he dismissed as an impractical theorist. Frontier society was produced by and organized for the average man, and those with unusual talents or highly developed sensitivities sometimes found it an uncomfortable and frustrating environment.

All in all, the frontiersmen were exuberant, vital, proud, ambitious men. Those who crossed the mountains were engaged in one of the greatest enterprises in history. Within two generations they transformed millions of acres of forest into farms, villages, and cities, and tamed a vast tract larger than Western Europe into civilization. The pioneer sensed the magnificence of the undertaking, and took pride in his part in it. It is not to be wondered, therefore, that he became fiercely proud of himself and his homeland and convinced of the superiority of both. It was this feeling that led the Kentucky preacher to define Heaven as 'a real Kentuck of a place', or the frontiersman to create legends around Davy Crockett, who could swallow thunderbolts and ride lightning bareback. 'The coarseness and strength combined with acuteness and inquisitiveness; that practical, inventive turn of mind, quick to find expedients; that masterful grasp of material things, lacking in the artistic but powerful to effect great ends; that restless, nervous energy, that dominant individualism, working for good and evil; and withal that buoyancy and exuberance which comes with freedom – these', wrote Frederick Jackson Turner, 'are the traits of the frontier, or traits called out elsewhere because of the existence of the frontier.'

The impact of the new West on the national economy was great. The War of 1812 revealed serious weaknesses in the national financial structure, and the settlement of the West intensified them. After the Bank of the United States was refused a renewal of its charter in 1811, national banking business fell to the state banks, many of them small and shaky. The demand for credit from speculators and landbuyers pushed them to the limit, with the result that Western banks over-extended themselves in making loans to settlers who needed money not only to purchase land but to buy tools, seeds, and finished goods. Cheap, fast, easy credit – and hang the consequences – was exactly to the Westerner's liking. Careless banking practices produced so-called 'wild-cat' banks, until in 1814 all state banks except those in thrifty New England stopped specie payments. With credit and currency gyrating wildly, the Federal government in 1817 created the Second Bank of the United States to stabilize credit and to inaugurate more conservative lending policies. The course pursued by the Second Bank placed the national credit on a more even keel, but in the process it wrecked many of the smaller banks in the West and South, collapsing land values, forcing mortgage foreclosures, and precipitating the depression of 1819–21. A large part of the city of Cincinnati, for example, including hotels, iron-works, buildings, and lots, fell into the hands of the Bank when the bubble burst. Since the panic that followed hit the West particularly hard, and removed the easy credit the West wanted, the Bank became a bitterly hated thing west of Pittsburgh. Western states fought back with debtor-relief and loose banking laws, but the Supreme Court usually overruled them. The roots of the conflict between debtor West and creditor East, between farmer and 'Wall Street', a conflict that flared up again and again until Bryan's time, lay in this post-war push to the West.

A second economic problem, partially though not wholly of the West's creating, was the tariff. Manufacturers, working at forced draft behind the walls of embargo and blockade, demanded tariff protection against European competition. British ships in American ports sometimes auctioned off whole cargoes to the highest bidder, undercutting American prices and robbing the middleman. In addition, the West was rapidly becoming a producing and consuming area of great importance. Demands for a protective tariff grew louder through the post-war years, until Henry Clay of Kentucky believed the time ripe for a planned national economy centred on such a tariff. Clay's 'American system' was intended to make the United States as nearly as possible into a closed, self-supporting economic unit. A tariff that encouraged and developed industry would, it was presumed, provide employment for displaced non-agricultural workers. The agricultural West would feed the industrial East and the cotton-tobacco South, while the textile mills of the South clothed the West and East, both West and South serving as consumer markets for the manufacturing East. The revenue from the tariff, on the other hand, could be used to provide the roads and canals that the West and South needed. Clay's system, which some New Englanders and Southerners considered anything but American, was in effect a cloudy recognition of growing economic sectionalism, a way of balancing sectional interests against each other for a common good.

Sectional interests were far too strong, however, for any such careful compromise, though elements of Clay's system appeared in the tariffs of 1816, 1824, and 1828. The strongest demands for a protective tariff came from the Middle and Western States, which were anxious to develop home markets. The South, which bought manufactured articles from Europe and sent much of its cotton abroad, wanted no part of it. New England's manufacturing interests deemed protection a necessity; its merchants and shippers feared a looser tariff policy would ruin their trade entirely.

Economic development of the West also created a demand for cheap and easy trade routes to the East and to the sea. The West therefore demanded aid from the Federal and state governments, since these were the only agencies with sufficient capital to underwrite huge road and canal projects. There was some doubt in the East whether Federal monies could be used for purposes benefiting but one or a few States, but Western clamour was too loud to disregard. As a result, construction of Cumberland National Road started in 1811, partially financed by Federal funds, and was completed in 1818. Six hundred miles long, sixty feet wide with a twenty foot macadamized strip down the middle, the 'National Pike' stretched from Cumberland, Maryland, over the mountains to Wheeling, Virginia, where it met the Ohio river. It continued on to Zanesville, Ohio, Terre Haute in Indiana, and eventually to the Mississippi at Vandalia, Illinois – a huge artery pulsing with commercial traffic moving at eight miles an hour. Meanwhile, the State of New York began construction of the Erie Canal in 1817, completing it in 1825 and linking the Atlantic and the Hudson river with the Great Lakes. The 'Big Ditch' 363 miles long (only four feet deep) connected New York and Europe with the thriving Western cities of Buffalo, Chicago, Cleveland, and Detroit; Governor Clinton's ceremonial pouring of two kegs of Lake Ontario water into New York Harbour was not a meaningless gesture.

Pennsylvania organized an intricate system of rivers, canals, and roads (even a steam-powered winch to haul boats up an inclined plane and over the mountains) connecting Pittsburgh with Philadelphia. Within twenty years a network of canals covered Ohio and portions of Indiana, linking the Ohio directly to the Great Lakes. Then, as the states built better toll roads, a stage-coach system sprang up, linking cities where canals and rivers could not. Steamboats appeared on the Western lakes and rivers; a scheduled steamboat run between Pittsburgh and New Orleans started in 1811. Later, when railroads pushed into the plains states across the Mississippi, the process was repeated with minor variations.

The effect of the new West in politics was particularly strong. The 'era of good feelings' drew to an end. The five new states added to the Union after the war of 1812 had definite political desires of their own, and their entrance upset the delicate balance of sectional politics. It was no longer Northeast against South, but a three-cornered conflict among North, South, and West, with the West throwing its weight to whatever side it felt most advantageous. Western ways and interests were not those of the older states; the Federalist aristocracy of the Northeast and the planter-politicians of the Southern seaboard feared the bumptious and aggressive frontiersmen. These Westerners were arrogantly democratic, jealous of their individual prerogatives, insistent on their own interests, and suspicious of centralized government unless they wanted something from it. They wanted a good many things – new laws of voting franchise and governmental representation; easy credit and elastic currency; internal improvements; tariffs; political power – and they raised a good many questions about such matters as slavery, the political rights of minorities, equalizing processes, economic opportunities. The farmers in the western counties of New York and Virginia, for example, forced a redrafting of their state constitutions, while the constitutions of the new Western states, with provisions for manhood suffrage, weak executives, short-term offices, and open election laws, reflected a determination to keep government close to the settler. The day of Andrew Jackson was not far off.

The imbalance caused by the emergence of the West in political affairs was evidenced by the first serious appearance of the slavery question in national politics. Before the close of the War of 1812, slavery was considered, North and South alike, as a temporary and regrettable rather than a permanent and desirable institution; both non-slaveholders and slaveholders were quite willing to subject the system to critical examination. Washington and Jefferson, among other Virginians, had freed their slaves. The elimination of the slave trade, beginning in 1808 under Constitutional guarantee, aroused little opposition from the South at the time; for that matter, neither did the anti-slavery provisions of the Northwest Ordinance of 1787. By 1804 most Northern states had abolished slavery, while in various Southern states, especially in back-country and border areas, active anti-slavery societies campaigned openly against it. Yet after 1816 there was a noticeable asperity in discussions of the slavery question – a warning, said Jefferson, 'like a firebell in the night'.

There were several reasons for this. The great Virginia tradition of liberalism lost ground slowly but surely after

1800 to the aristocratic tradition of South Carolina; the South, during the 'era of good feelings', was in the process of transferring its allegiance from the tradition of Jefferson to the tradition of Calhoun. In another fashion, the cleavage between North and South on other matters – on the tariff, on the war, on trade – indicated an approaching clash of sectional economic and political interests. Most important of all, however, were the problems tied up with the spread of cotton culture. Eli Whitney's cotton 'gin', the development of new strains of cotton, a growing post-war market, and the opening of the rich 'Black Belt' lands of the South-west made cotton an extremely lucrative cash crop. England's textile industry, revolutionized by the introduction of new machinery, demanded raw cotton in increasing quantities, and by 1815 New England had also developed textile mills of its own. How Cotton became King in the South is graphically shown by the production figures. In 1791–5 the South raised five million pounds of cotton. In the period 1800–5 production jumped to sixty million pounds; by 1845 it rose to four hundred million pounds; by 1850, 1000 million pounds. Cotton required a large, steady supply of cheap unskilled labour, and the Negro slave fitted the need perfectly. At the same time, it was found that the hot lands of Louisiana and Mississippi delta country were ideal for sugar-cane, while tobacco culture moved into Kentucky and Tennessee. All needed cheap labour. In 1800 there were about one million Negroes in the U.S., almost wholly concentrated in the Southern states. In 1808, when the importation of slaves ceased, the figure stood at one and three-quarter millions. By 1840 there were two and three-quarter millions, and by 1860 four and a half millions. In the state of Alabama, at one point in the 1850s, Negroes made up 87 per cent of the total population. The property value of all slaves in the South was estimated at one thousand three hundred and fifty million in the 1840s, and at 4000 million dollars by 1860.

By 1820 it was perfectly clear to the South that abolishing slavery meant abolishing the economic foundation of Southern society. Anti-slavery sentiment could be muzzled or diverted in the South, but not in the North, nor could action by the Federal government against slavery in the South and Southwest be avoided if the free states unanimously supported it. Preservation of their political power in Congress therefore became a matter of utmost importance to the slave-holding states. The tendency had been, as the nation moved West, to maintain a rough balance of power between slave and free state blocs in Washington. The Northeast and Northwest, however, had gained a million more than the South and the Southwest in population since the 1790 census, thereby gaining proportionately more seats in the House; in addition, a slave counted only three-fifths of a free labourer in determining that representation. Only in the Senate were all sections equally represented.

Of the original thirteen colonies, seven became free states and six slave. From 1791 to 1819 four more free states were admitted and five slave. When Missouri applied for entrance to the Union in 1819, both Northerners and Southerners in Congress carefully scrutinized the terms of its admission. Tallmadge of New York introduced a House bill requiring Missouri to enter the Union with a plan for emancipating its slaves; the bill immediately started an argument that some feared might flare into actual war. The question was actually much larger than Missouri. Slavery was already barred from the Northwest Territory, but not from those lands acquired by the Louisiana Purchase. Should Missouri and all other states subsequently carved from the Purchase be admitted as slave states, the balance of Federal political power tipped toward the South and slavery. If they were to be free states, their entry favoured the North and emancipation. At stake lay the political control, present and future, of the Union.

In 1820 it was still possible to find a compromise. Henry Clay of Kentucky arranged a plan whereby Missouri entered as a slave state, but Maine, the next addition, would be free, thus preserving the existing balance. At the same time Congress agreed to exclude slavery for ever from all Louisiana Purchase territory north of the parallel 36° 30′, a continuation of the Mason and Dixon line (the boundary between Pennsylvania and Maryland) and the Ohio river. But the Missouri Compromise delayed rather than settled the solution to the problem of slavery and its extension westward, and everyone knew it. 'It is hushed, indeed, for the moment', wrote Jefferson from Monticello. 'But this is a reprieve only, not a final sentence.' The tocsin of disunion had already sounded.

The election of 1824 brought the 'era of good feelings' to an abrupt end. Outwardly, as the campaign year approached, the virtual one-party government of the preceding eight years seemed to be unopposed. The old Federalist party was practically dead, but within the Republican party there was a three-way struggle for control among representatives of Northeastern manufacturers, Southern cotton-planters, and Western farmers. Their clashing sectional interests were thrown into bold relief by the variety of candidates they put forward and by the campaign they waged. Among the numerous aspirants to the Presidency who jockeyed for position after 1822, the choice narrowed down to four – one New Englander, one Southerner, and two Westerners. John Quincy Adams of Massachusetts, son of the second President, had probably the best qualifications of anyone in America for the office, though he was a poor practical politician. William Crawford of Georgia, who had the support of the seaboard South, was a Southern aristocrat of the states-rights school; his ill-health made him a doubtful candidate. John C. Calhoun of South Carolina, the most brilliant Southerner in Congress, declared himself out of the running in exchange for the vice-presidential nomination.

The two men from the West, Henry Clay and Andrew Jackson, presented an interesting study in contrasts and similarities. Clay, whose father was a back-country Baptist preacher, was as much a typical product of the Kentucky frontier as Jackson was of neighbouring Tennessee. As a young man Clay had been one of the leading 'War Hawks' and an ardent supporter of Western regional interests. In middle age, as he came into greater contact with the East and Europe, he shifted toward a nationalist position. Clay had all the charm and personal magnetism that Adams lacked; the true politician's ability to adjust, placate, and compromise; and a clear and able mind. Of all the candidates for the office he was the single one with what would to-day be called a platform – that is, his 'American System'.

Andrew Jackson of Tennessee was the most colourful and controversial figure of the four. Born in poverty in South Carolina to a Scotch-Irish linen-draper, Jackson fought as a boy in the Revolution and carried to his grave the scar of a British officer's sword-cut. After the war he wandered to Tennessee, picked up a smattering of law, traded in horses, farmed, served on the bench and in Congress, and ran into debt keeping a store. His services in the war of 1812 and later against the Indians made him a national military hero. A proud, hard-driving man, Jackson had a violent temper, strong principles, and a keen political sense. He was very nearly the perfect exemplification of Western man, with all his faults and virtues – suspicion of the rich and well-born, faith in the crowd, belief in equality, hatred of special privilege, nationalistic pride – traits present in different mixtures in other Westerners such as Clay, Benton, and Lincoln, but most throughly mixed in Jackson.

The election of 1824 revealed how sharply the nation was split on sectional lines. Adams carried New England and New York. Crawford, who suffered a stroke shortly before the election, took only Virginia and Georgia. Clay won in Ohio, Kentucky, and Missouri. Jackson, who received the largest number of electoral votes – ninety-nine to Adams' eighty-four – was the only candidate whose following cut across regional boundaries. He divided the Western states with Clay and the South with Crawford, pulled in the Scotch-Irish of Pennsylvania, the Middle States, and the upland South, but his vote was not enough to secure a majority. The election went to the House of Representatives, where Adams, with Clay's support, won. Clay became Secretary of State in Adams' cabinet, drawing charges of 'bargain' and 'fraud' from the Jacksonians.

Adams' narrow victory foreshadowed a new alignment in American politics. Jackson became the symbol of the common man, those who opposed him symbolized aristocracy. Jackson's supporters frankly appealed to the democratic elements in American society for a broadening of government – held too long, they said, in the hands of New England and Virginia dynasties. The Western farmer, the Eastern labourer, and the Southern yeoman, dimly conscious of their potential political power, surged to Jackson's support and bitterly attacked the 'stolen' election. Shrewd political leaders like Martin Van Buren of New York and Thomas Hart Benton of Missouri capitalized on the groundswell of opinion to begin building a new party, called without subtlety the 'Democratic' party. The remnant Federalists, the industrialists and shippers of the Northeast, and the planters of the South formed an unstable alliance behind Adams and Clay, calling themselves 'National Republicans'. The lines of cleavage were drawn immediately after the vote in the House, and Adams' administration became one long campaign for Jackson in 1828.

'I am a man of reserve, cold, austere, and forbidding manners', wrote John Quincy Adams in his diary. Self-contained, arrogant, quite unaware of the arts of blandishment, Adams was constitutionally unable to win personal friends or popular support. His four years in the White House were unhappy and embattled ones, yet the way he handled events proved him an intelligent, foresighted, and statesmanlike President. He refused to play cheap party politics or to dally with boodle; Thurlow Weed of New York exclaimed hotly, 'Mr Adams . . . failed to cherish, strengthen, or even recognize the party to which he owed his election; nor so far as I am informed with the great power he possessed did he make a single influential friend.' He offered cabinet posts to his political enemies if they were able men, attempted to evolve a just and honest Indian policy, agreed with Clay on co-operation with the South and Central American nations, and tried on every political and foreign issue to pursue the wisest and most objectively advantageous policy. Whatever he did, Jacksonians and men from his own party frustrated him at every turn, discredited what little he did accomplish, and attacked him for not doing more. No President was ever more thoroughly sabotaged than J. Q. Adams.

Adams' first annual message outlined a programme of canal, harbour, and road improvements; military schools and a stronger militia; and a national university – all Federally financed. This was attacked as a 'spendthrift programme' even by the nationally-minded Jacksonians, and much was made of the fact that the fourteen million dollars spent by his administration represented the nation's highest peacetime budget. With his long experience in international affairs Adams might have been expected to produce some improvements in foreign policy; however, his appointment of Clay and the accusation of 'corrupt bargain' hurt Adams' prestige at home and nullified much of Clay's effectiveness abroad. The British Foreign Secretary, George Canning, the Monroe Doctrine in mind, won his government over to recognition of the Spanish American republics and refused to open the West Indies to American commerce except under conditions unsatisfactory to America; thus Adams noted Canning's death in his diary with some relief, for Canning outwitted him badly. In the same way Adams' attempt to guarantee just treatment to the Indians alienated the South. Southerners wanted the Cherokees, Creeks, Choctaws, and others moved west to open their lands to white settlement. Adams rejected the fraudulent Indian treaties and demanded new and better ones and thereby aroused Southern anger and cries of 'states' rights'.

The tariff was a particularly sharp thorn in the administration's side. The tariff of 1816 satisfied the West, but helped neither New England commerce nor Southern agriculture. The tariff of 1820, asking higher protection for manufacturing, failed by one Senate vote but passed in 1824, while one with still higher rates failed in 1827. The Jacksonians in Congress then evolved a devious plan to win support for Jackson and undermine Adams, without really committing themselves. A tariff bill would be introduced with such high rates on raw materials that both Northeast and South would join to oppose it: the Jackson men would vote down amendments to it, and thus claim credit in the North for having sponsored a high tariff and in the South for having helped vote it down. The bill had nothing to do with manufacturing, John Randolph of Virginia said, except ' the manufacture of a President', Andrew Jackson. Actually, enough support appeared for the bill to insure its passage, and Adams was blamed for it all.

Jackson's backers used the four years of Adams' reign to good advantage. By 1828 the harassed New Englander had lost the support of many of his own party leaders, while the public at large was regaled with gossip and innuendo. It was rumoured that Adams was a nasty aristocrat, a spendthrift, pro-British, that he kept a billiard table in the White House, that he had once sold a pretty American girl to a Russian. At the same time, the Jackson men spent four years building and perfecting their party machinery, adopting some of the methods originated by the revolutionary Committees of Correspondence. Using conventions, caucuses, committees, and clubs, they evolved an implacably efficient organization that reached down into townships and even rural school districts. They had also more voters to organize. Manhood suffrage increased from 1816 to 1828, as the older states lowered the requirements for voting and the new frontier states almost wholly eliminated them. By 1828 New Hampshire, Maryland, and Connecticut dropped property qualifications, while New York and Massachusetts retained only nominal ones. The ballot opened up to nearly a million new voters in the lower economic brackets, a potential that the Jackson's adherents recognized at once. They developed new techniques of party politics, promising this here and denying it there, playing interest against interest, prejudice against prejudice, weaving it all into a national party pattern. Adams stood very little chance against them.

That was the way it was. The campaign was an unusually malicious one, issues forgotten, rumour rampant, personalities smeared, with Adams' National Republicans winning the palm for scurrility. Jackson was called murderer (his military and duelling record), adulterer (his irregular marriage to Mrs Rachel Robards), corruptionist (his dealings with politicians) and worse. The bitterness of the campaign hurt and angered him and he held to the end that it caused the death of his wife a few months later. He never forgave Adams, who he believed could have stopped the stories but did not, nor did he ever again give quarter to his opponents. Memories of the campaign of 1828 were the driving force in Jackson's politics ever after, colouring his political relationships and some of his policies. Nevertheless, despite the mudslinging, 'aristocratic' John Quincy Adams was no match for 'democratic' Andrew Jackson, who swept into the Presidency with the electoral votes of all states except New England, Delaware, Maryland, and New Jersey. After Adams only one New Englander was ever President again, Calvin Coolidge, nearly a hundred years later.

How sharply American politics had changed, and how clean a break the election of 1828 made with the past, showed at Jackson's inauguration. Gone were the Federalist decorum of Washington and John Adams, the courtly Virginia democracy of Jefferson. Rough, rowdy, back-country people in homespun flooded Washington, shouting and carousing in the streets. Gentlemen drew aside from the jostling, motley crowds on Pennsylvania Avenue; 'It was like the inundation of northern barbarians into Rome,' remarked one of them. Jackson walked bareheaded and erect through the muddy streets to the Capitol for his oath-taking, and as he finished it, 'the peal of shouting that arose rent the air and seemed to shake the very ground'. At the reception after, hordes of enthusiastic Democrats jammed the White

House, muddied the rich damask furniture with their boots, broke crystal, ruined carpets, and drove Jackson into a corner where men linked arms to guard him from the crush. 'I never saw such a mixture', wrote Justice Story. 'The reign of King Mob seemed triumphant.'

CHAPTER 23

THE AGE OF JACKSON AND EMERSON
1828–52

THE conflict between Federalistic and Jeffersonian democracy characterized the first phase of American history after the Revolution. Jeffersonian principles dominated the 'era of good feelings', but Jackson's victory marked the beginning of a new trend, based on a political theory which combined elements of the older Jeffersonian strain with later developments in both Western and Eastern political thought. 'Jacksonian democracy' is in some ways a misleading term. It was part of a transformation of American society that appeared not only in politics, but in nearly every other area of American thought. The prevailing philosophy of the period can be called 'Jacksonian' only to the extent that Jackson represented the political phase of a larger movement. 'Old Hickory' himself was as much a creation of the movement as he was its spokesman; the democratic or 'Jacksonian' trend manifested itself in many other spheres of action with which he had little or no connexion.

The heyday of Jacksonian democracy came in the 1830's and 1840's, before it was broken by questions of slavery and union that it was not equipped to solve. Stripped of its external political apparatus, it was essentially a system based on an expanding agrarianism – a democracy of independent property owners. In Jackson's words, government existed for the benefit of 'the planter, the farmer, the mechanic, and the laborer' who 'form the great body of the people of the United States'. His party's concern, he said, was for 'the liberty of men owning independent means of livelihood', for the so-called 'common man' – meaning the small independent merchant, farmer, or artisan. Jackson had great faith in the uncommon ability of the common man to discharge all his functions in a democratic society. Any man of average intellectual substance could, in his opinion, handle the business of government; as he once said, 'The duties of public office are, or at least admit of being readily made, so plain and simple that men of intelligence may readily qualify themselves for public office.' As more and more farmers, workers, and debtors gained the right to vote, widening the base of popular political activity, the Jacksonian idea of 'mass politics' took root.

Jacksonian democracy held that government was the creature of the majority will. The whole purpose of National Republican and Whig politics, in Jackson's opinion, appeared to be to grant the wishes of the minority without consulting the majority. If the common man were so trustworthy and responsible, as the Jacksonian judged him to be, it was therefore necessary and right that government be under the direct control of the majority, sensitive to its demands and receptive to its desires. The constitutions adopted by the new Western states during the Jacksonian period reflected this belief. Their short-term governors, frequent elections, large grants of power to lower legislative houses, and restrictions on executive and judicial branches were all devices intended to make government dependent rather than autonomous. For this reason, among others, Jackson added so swiftly to the powers of the President that his enemies called him 'King Andrew I'. He regarded himself as the chosen representative of the people (understandable in terms of his smashing popular vote) and considered the powers of the President superior to those of both Congress and the Supreme Court. He battled Congress, dominated its legislation, vetoed more bills than all his predecessors together, and clashed constantly with John Marshall and the Court.

The Jacksonian belief in the adequacy of the common man to perform all political duties had its corollary in a belief in every man's right to equality of economic opportunity. The Jacksonian believed that if this right were safeguarded, some sort of equal sharing of economic goods would inevitably result. An integral part of Jacksonian politics was its opposition to any special interest, monopoly, or favouritism that might deny equality of opportunity. Jackson himself had been several times heavily in debt. As a debtor under the thumb of Eastern bankers he had already conceived before his election to the Presidency a hatred of concentrated economic authority that accurately reflected the attitude of others like himself, both East and West. The party slogan 'Equal rights for all, special privileges for none', had economic as well as political connotations; political power, said the Jacksonians, must not be used to gain economic privilege.

The Jacksonian view of economic life exactly fitted the needs of an expanding nation. With the opening of the West and the mushrooming of industry, opportunities were great in the thirties and forties. An important aspect of Jacksonian political philosophy was its desire to keep the door to wealth open by cancelling out any special privileges which gave economic advantages to the favoured few. Jacksonism was the classic philosophy of a rising middle class, aimed at encouraging creative individual enterprise, at developing a more fluid and open economic society. Daniel Webster caught the essence of the prevailing spirit in his statement, 'Society is full of excitement; and intelligence and industry ask only for fair play and an open field.' The Jacksonians believed deeply in *laissez-faire*, holding that an overdevelopment of governmental power, state or federal, crushed individual enterprise and smothered individual opportunity. They could not foresee, in the forties, that concentrated economic power might close the doors of opportunity as tightly as the most controlled bureaucracy. After the Civil War, from this cherished Jacksonian doctrine, came an economic oligarchy more potent than anything dreamed of by Hamilton or Fisher Ames or Nicholas Biddle. The Gilded Age had its roots in Jacksonism.

Jacksonian democracy was national-minded. Although Jackson and John Marshall were political enemies, they agreed that the power of the Federal government must be defended againt encroachment by the States. Old Hickory's famous toast, 'Our Federal Union – it *must* and *shall* be preserved!' was his own and his party's central principle, one never compromised in his long battle with the states-rights school of South Carolina's Calhoun. But at the same time, the Jacksonians vaguely realized that the consolidation of power in Washington might bring centralization, stratification, classification, and possibly special privilege and hierarchy. The Jacksonians therefore held a somewhat bifurcated view of federalism, involving on the one hand a profound attachment to the national government, but on the other a deep suspicion of the centralized or bureaucratic state. It was not that the Jacksonian really feared the State; he feared instead that the *control* of that State might some day be vested in a minority group of special interests.

The differences between Jacksonism and Jeffersonianism were fundamentally great. Both, it is true, were based on an agrarian economy. But Jefferson's system, founded on a static agrarianism, suited an era of relatively stable land values and of a unified agricultural system. Jackson built on a dynamic agrarianism; his political philosophy reflected an era of expanding land values, rich speculative opportunities, and a much more diversified agriculture. Its economic spirit was totally different. In another sense, the Jeffersonian and the Jacksonian differed in their concept of federalism. Jefferson, a child of revolution, taught that an increased centralized power was inimical to democracy; intent upon restraining government, the Jeffersonians concentrated on keeping it within carefully prescribed limits. To Jackson the federal government was not simply a policeman to keep order, but a parent who gave a helping hand when it was needed – but only when the citizen asked for it. The Jacksonian did not want the government to control his affairs except to the degree that he requested it do to so. He was never loth (nor were the Grangers and Populists later) to call on Washington for assistance, for roads, canals, credit, or subsidies; yet at the same time he fiercely resented any intrusion of federal power into his own domain of authority.

Jefferson and Jackson held quite different estimates of mankind. Jefferson's faith in the people was genuine and sincere, but it was the substance of things hoped for rather than achieved. He was not a believer in absolute equality, but in a graded equality, led by a natural aristocracy (as he told Adams) of education, talent, and worth. Jackson's faith in humanity was of another sort, an unequivocal confidence in the common man's innate natural wisdom and in his ability to cope with almost any problem – a belief shared alike by Western frontiersman and Eastern labourer. The temper of Jacksonian democracy was rude, vociferous, powerful, aggressive; Jefferson's democracy decorous, orderly, dignified. The Jeffersonians of 1800 looked hopefully toward the finer civilization to come. The Jacksonians of the 1830's gloried proudly in the civilization they had made, in their strength, their freedom, their aliveness.

Andrew Jackson, elected to the Presidency by 'ordinary men', was not one of them. The contemporary campaign picture of him as an illiterate, irascible, rabble-rousing radical was far from the truth. He was not learned, but he was by no means ignorant and his mind was sharp. He was a pragmatic man (like Lincoln and Franklin Roosevelt), who recognized and seized opportunities with an almost incredibly accurate sense of timing. He possessed, as one contemporary remarked, a scent for the trail of political opinion as delicate as a bird dog's; he was peculiarly adept at following when he seemed to lead. Social, economic, and political forces beyond Jackson's control really shaped the Jacksonian movement, and until he was elected to the Presidency he contributed practically nothing to it. Yet he stepped in at the head of the procession, became its symbol, gave it a name, and impressed it with his own powerful personality, a feat only a man of uncommon ability could achieve. The yeoman and small planter of the South, the Western farmer, and the Eastern urban worker constructed about him a political machine more compact and militant than even Jefferson built. The circumstances and the times combined to make Jackson what he liked to call himself, 'the tribune of the people', and few Americans have led political movements with greater skill or success.

The politics of the Jacksonian period, and for that matter of the antebellum decades generally, may be understood best in terms of the developing sectionalism that characterized the age. In the major land areas new social, economic and political relationships were in the process of formation, altering in turn the political attitudes men held on contemporary issues. It is always difficult to establish hard and fast boundaries for sections in American history; such demarcation lines have a habit of fading when too definitely drawn. But at the same time it is apparent that there existed in pre-Civil War America a Northeast, a Northwest, and a South.

In the Northeastern states of New England, New York, Pennsylvania, New Jersey, and Delaware, great changes took place after the turn of the century. Farming, once the mainstay of New England economy, decreased in importance as the rich lands of the West drained off the young men and outproduced the small farms of the East. More and more, as cities like New York, Philadelphia, and Boston grew in size and importance, the area turned to manufacturing. Cheap water power promoted the growth of a great textile industry, concentrated in Massachusetts and lower New Hampshire. Northeastern capital, once heavily invested in shipping, poured into factories. Old ports, such as Salem, Newburyport, and Marblehead, faded rapidly before the rise of new factory towns like Lowell and Lawrence. The great mercantile firms and the new industrial corporations linked themselves with banking and shipping interests to establish fairly complete urban control over the political and economic life of the area. And as New England shifted from an agricultural to an urban-industrial economy, conflict between capital and labour grew sharper, while the tremendous flow of immigrants into the cities created new economic and social problems. It was not accidental that the loudest contemporary cries for reform came from the Northeast, nor that labour unions, utopian communities, and humanitarian movements found their centre there. The clash between have and have-not, between conservative and radical, was strongest in the Northeast.

The Northwest embraced Ohio, Indiana, Illinois, Michigan, Wisconsin, Iowa, and the new territory of Minnesota. It grew rapidly in population during the Jacksonian era and continued to grow even more swiftly after the Civil War. Settlers from the upland South gave the Ohio river country a Southern tinge; in the Great Lakes region settlers from New York and New England predominated, mixed with numbers of German and Scandinavian immigrants. With its tremendous diversity of peoples, creeds, backgrounds, and interests, the Northwest was the least unified of the three major sections, less rigid, less cohesive in its social and intellectual patterns. The Northwest had cities like Cleveland, Cincinnati, Detroit, Chicago, and Milwaukee, but it was chiefly a land of farms, many of them not far from the pioneer stage. An aggressively democratic area, with a legacy of Jeffersonianism and a strong predilection for Jacksonism, the politics of the Northwest were self-interested, concrete, practical.

The South encompassed thirteen states with at least four subdivisions: the upland South of Kentucky, Tennessee, and Western Virginia; the tidewater South of Maryland, Virginia, North and South Carolina; the Gulf South of Georgia, Alabama, Mississippi, Florida, and Louisiana; the Southwest of Missouri, Arkansas, and later Texas. It was chiefly an agricultural section, with few important cities other than Baltimore, Charleston, Mobile, and New Orleans – a varied land of swamp, plain, mountain, forest, town, farm, and plantation, ranging from temperate cold to tropic heat. Virginia, Kentucky, Tennessee, and Maryland raised tobacco; the Carolina coast depended on rice, Louisiana on sugar cane. But the fundamental fact about the South was the huge cotton empire that stretched from Virginia to Texas, carrying slavery with it. The settling of the Gulf States and of the Southwest produced no break in the Southern pattern. Cotton culture simply moved west with the migrants, and the Southwest, unlike the Northwest, displayed no real sectional variations from the parent states.

Southern life, based on a definite social and economic order, exhibited far more coherence than that of either of the other two sections. At the top of the order, giving Southern civilization its distinctive complexion, stood the great planters who owned fifty or more slaves, one or more plantations, most of the South's best land, and three-quarters of its wealth. There were never many of them, probably fewer than fifty thousand out of the South's population of eight million. Only 300 planters held more than 200 slaves each; there were, of course, a few exceptions, such as Wade Hampton of South Carolina (who had 3,000) or Nathaniel Hayward of South Carolina (who had fourteen plantations and 2,500 Negroes). The plantations averaged perhaps 500 acres; a few planters owned as many as 15,000. These men provided the South with its intellectual, social, and cultural leadership. They built huge white-columned Greek revival houses, wintered on the Gulf Coast or in Europe, hunted foxes, attended balls, raced horses, served in the legislatures and the courts, in Congress and the Army.

The planter-aristocrat educated his sons and daughters with private tutors or at fashionable academies, the young men continuing at West Point, Yale, Harvard, Princeton, or abroad. He owned a good private library, respected his Anglican church, took the Grand Tour, and bought his family's clothes in London or Paris. His pride of family was strong and sensitive, his fondness for tradition legendary. Gallantry in gentlemen, purity in ladies, proper assumption of cultural and political responsibilities – these were his passions. At its best the class produced a humane, educated, courtly, cultured aristocrat. At its worst it produced the 'cotton snob' or the bullying, arrogant 'fire-eater', infected with what Mark Twain called 'the Sir Walter Scott disease' of chivalry. There was something in his life of the crisp rustle of crinoline, of magnolias in the moonlight, of court-balls and happy darkies tinkling banjoes in the dusk – but not much. He was above all a hard-working agricultural capitalist with a huge investment in the complex cotton business, facing difficult problems of crop prices, credit, export, labour, and worn-out land. Slavery, despite its cheapness, was neither an efficient nor an economically sound labour system, and slaves were a constant source of trouble.

Below the great planter in the scale was the small planter who owned from one to twenty slaves. He held less land and that less fertile, owned a frame house (or a log one) and lived a simple, unostentatious life of hard work. Though he often sweated in the fields beside his own slaves, ate the same fare, and (except on Sunday) dressed not much better, he was violently anti-Negro and pro-slavery. Culture, fashion, travel, the legislature, West Point, and magnolias in the moonlight were not for him, but his great dream was to acquire them by obtaining more land, more slaves, and entry into the upper stratum of aristocracy. Next to him came the yeoman farmer, the 'redneck' or 'woolhat boy' who made up more than 75 per cent of the South's population. He owned no slaves. His farm was small and poor, located in the mountains, the barrens, or on the margin of the rich cotton belt. His house was often a ramshackle cabin, and his days were spent in the backbreaking job of trying to scrabble a living from the obstinate red clay. Earnest, solid men, they too were violently anti-Negro and pro-slavery. They feared the Negro as a social and economic competitor; slavery provided their only means of keeping him under control. Lastly, in the lowest social and economic brackets were the 'crackers', 'poor whites', or 'sand-hillers', scattered on the poorest land, illiterate, shiftless, living on the bare edge of subsistence – not a large group, but an extremely vocal one in its hatred of the Negro, for its members realized subconsciously that the barrier of slavery alone kept them from hitting the bottom of the scale.

Such was the antebellum South, a varied yet peculiarly unified section, a state of mind as much as a geographical area, a pattern of life shaped always by cotton and slavery. During the first half of the nineteenth century the South became acutely aware of the fact that it was a section, with a culture, tradition, and interests of its own, and its leaders made strenuous efforts to preserve and develop them. It had a closely-guarded set of values, a way of life deemed worth protecting and defending; it had also an extremely difficult set of political, social, and economic problems, all tied up with slavery, the one-crop system, and a rigid social order. Its literacy rate was low (80 per cent as compared with the Northeast's 99·58 per cent and the Northwest's 97 per cent) and not all of its illiterates were Negroes. Some of its universities were excellent – Virginia, William and Mary, the College of South Carolina, several good state institutions – but its educational record was poor. Intellectually the South in the nineteenth century produced nothing to match the Northeast. Its great political leaders were too often dedicated to the single aim of defending the *status quo*.

Jackson entered office uncommitted to any specific platform, for part of the Democratic campaign strategy had been to make varied promises to various sections. His first message to Congress recommended 'cautious modification' of the tariff, the removal of the Indian population to lands west of the Mississippi, and a programme of such Federally-financed internal improvements as might be 'constitutional'. It was a conciliatory message, calculated to stir up no immediate reactions. Jackson's cabinet selections, however, boded little peace for the future. Major John Eaton of Tennessee, Secretary of War, had recently married Peggy Timberlake, a handsome young widow whose acceptance into Washington society seemed doubtful in the light of current gossip. Eaton, Attorney General Berrien, Secretary of the Navy Branch, and Secretary of State Van Buren were all friends of Jackson. Postmaster General McLean and Secretary of the Treasury Ingham were close to Vice-President Calhoun. When Peggy Eaton was soundly snubbed by the cabinet wives, Jackson, remembering his own dead Rachel, sprang to her defence, aided by Van Buren, a bachelor who had nothing to lose. Calhoun and his friends abetted the tea-table gossip, and for a time the battle over Peggy Eaton took on real political importance, splitting the cabinet wide open. When tempers reached the limit, Jackson persuaded his entire cabinet to resign. New appointments pointedly ignored Calhoun's friends, making the break between Jackson and Calhoun final and complete. Van Buren's insistent championing of the maligned Peggy brought him closer than ever to Jackson, who turned more and more frequently to the New Yorker for advice.

Jackson's first term was principally occupied with political manoeuvrings designed to consolidate his party. His lieutenants, working on the principle that spoils belong to the victor, demanded that 'the barnacles be scraped clean off the Ship of State' and that all offices held by Adams' appointees be redistributed among loyal Democrats. Actually, the shift was not so sweeping as the cries of dispossessed office-holders indicated; in Jackson's first term about 900 changes were made in a total of 10,000 positions, not always for political reasons. The 'spoils system' did, however, serve as a concrete illustration of the Jacksonian idea that one man was as good as another, and did prove to be a practical method of solidifying the party structure. Whereas earlier Presidents had been chary of removing incumbents, the Jacksonians quickly recognized the potentialities of political patronage and used it, opening the way for its abuse in later years.

Toward the end of Jackson's first term one issue appeared that he met squarely. The Second Bank of the United States, chartered in 1816, needed a renewal of its charter before 1836. Controlled by a group of Eastern financiers, the Bank had long been a target for the Democrats, who accused it of dabbling in politics and claimed that it existed for the primary purpose of enriching a few capitalists. Henry Clay believed the Bank to be a good political issue, and with the help of George McDuffie, a friend of Calhoun's, he fashioned a new pro-Bank political party. The National Republicans met in Baltimore in late 1831, declared themselves for the Bank, and nominated Clay as their candidate for the presidency in 1832. Meanwhile a bill for rechartering the Bank passed both houses of Congress and came to Jackson for his approval. The plan was to confront Jackson with an insoluble dilemma; he either signed a bill he did not like, or he took the blame for an unpopular veto. In either case Clay felt that he could make capital of the Bank issue in the forthcoming campaign.

Clay's guess could hardly have been more wrong. Jackson vetoed the rechartering bill and sent it back to Congress with one of the most astute veto messages ever penned. The Bank, said Jackson, was simply a huge monopoly, controlled by rich men like Nicholas Biddle of Philadelphia, a few wealthy Englishmen, and 'others of the richest class'. It plundered the poor and lined the pockets of the rich; constitutional or not, the Bank must go – Jackson, the poor man's friend, would not have it. The veto was shrewd politics, if not brilliant finance, for it vividly dramatized the issue of special privilege versus public interest. Working men in the cities sang in the streets, to the tune of Yankee Doodle,

> Yankee Doodle, smoke 'em out
> The proud, the banking faction –
> None but such as Hartford Feds
> Oppose the poor and Jackson.

Old Hickory's popularity skyrocketed, and his re-election in 1832 was practically assured.

The election of 1832 was briefly complicated by the appearance of the first organized third party in American history. In 1826 one William Morgan of western New York State published a pamphlet allegedly revealing the secrets of Freemasonry; his subsequent disappearance seemed to indicate he was a victim of Masonic reprisal. When public furor against the Masons and other secret orders reached a high pitch, Jackson's opponents attempted to divert it into political channels. An anti-Masonic party was quickly formed, appealing to the large Catholic immigrant population of the cities and eventually embracing all of Clay's 'American System' and most of the National Republican platform. The strange rag-tag party met in convention to nominate William Wirt of Virginia for President on an anti-

Jackson, anti-Masonic, anti-almost-anything platform. Since its views were practically indistinguishable from those of the National Republicans (except for its frank appeals to prejudice) it carried little weight in the elections. For that matter, neither did Clay and the National Republicans. The Jackson–Van-Buren ticket swept the nation. Even solid New England broke up, with Maine and New Hampshire voting for Jackson and Vermont for Wirt, while in the South only South Carolina failed to vote for Old Hickory. The result seemed to be a complete endorsement of Jackson, his party, and his principles.

But the silent intramural war between Jackson and Calhoun was by no means over. South Carolina, divided between back-country Jacksonians and seaboard Calhoun men, had long opposed a protective tariff. The mercantile interests of the state believed (with some justice) that its economy had suffered because of the tariff of 1828; Southern Congressmen worked ceaselessly against it while Calhoun, a brilliant political theorist, worked out an intricate and ingenious method of disposing of it. A state, he affirmed, might nullify an act of Congress within its borders by appealing to the principle of state sovereignty. If three-quarters of the states nullified it, then the act was void everywhere, although what happened if the Federal Government failed to agree seemed not to enter into Calhoun's calculations. When J. Q. Adams (now in the House) and Henry Clay engineered the passage of a new tariff bill in 1832, Calhoun judged it time for action. Late that year a state convention met in South Carolina, declared the 1828 and 1832 tariff bills inoperative, ordered non-compliance, and opened the state's ports to free trade. Calhoun resigned the Vice-Presidency and went home, where the voters promptly sent him back to the Senate.

To a devout nationalist such as Jackson South Carolina's act was intolerable. Seven revenue cutters quickly appeared in Charleston harbour with a battleship to protect them. Jackson bluntly proclaimed that 'the laws of the United States must be executed', that nullification of a federal law by a state amounted to disunion, and that disunion was treason. Only Henry Clay's compromise tariff bill, rushed through Congress in early 1833, prevented a head-on conflict, and Jackson, who was quite willing to hang Calhoun for treason, always rather regretted that he did not. Not quite thirty years later, as Lincoln prepared to write his inaugural address in the face of secession, he placed both the Constitution and a copy of Jackson's Nullification Proclamation on his desk before him.

Jackson assumed that his decisive victory in 1832 was a mandate to proceed against the Bank. 'I shall not shrink from my duty', he said, 'until I can strangle this hydra of corruption', and as soon as he had disposed of Calhoun and South Carolina, he turned his attention to Nicholas Biddle. By reshuffling the cabinet he obtained Roger Taney of Maryland as Secretary of the Treasury, who, at Jackson's orders, began to withdraw federal deposits from the Bank and to deposit new revenues in state banks, chiefly in the South and West. Biddle retaliated by reducing the Bank's discounts and call-in loans, and by presenting state bank notes for immediate redemption. New England suffered from a money shortage, while the state banks, encouraged by Taney's policies, happily returned to some of their old wild-catting practices. Credit tightened, businesses crashed, and a small panic started that snowballed with the passing months. Jackson blamed it all on Biddle. 'We have no money here, gentlemen', he told a delegation of worried businessmen who called at the White House. 'Biddle has all the money. He has millions of specie in his vaults, lying idle . . .' The pressure of public opinion was too great. Biddle gave in, railing at the 'gang of Banditte' in Washington, and began to negotiate for a charter from the state of Pennsylvania. His scalp joined Clay's and Calhoun's at Jackson's belt.

Fortunately Jackson encountered no real diplomatic problems in foreign affairs during his eight years in office. Lord Aberdeen, the British Foreign Secretary, was much easier to deal with than his predecessor Canning, and Jackson, despite his vehement Anglophobia, got along well with him. Jackson's administration wisely decided not to emphasize the Monroe Doctrine and allowed matters at issue with Britain to settle down. The United States reopened discussion of the West Indian trade, and with British co-operation evolved a workable though not wholly satisfactory compromise. Jackson's only real problem, largely of his own making, lay in American relations with France. For more than twenty years the United States had vainly attempted to collect redress from France for damages suffered by American shipping during the wars following the French Revolution. Eventually France in 1831 agreed to pay twenty-five million francs in six annual instalments, but in 1833 the French defaulted, and in 1834 they flatly refused to pay at all. Jackson, who disliked France only a trifle less than he did England, threatened to expropriate French property in the United States if the instalments were not paid, salting his threat with a few hot-tempered remarks on Gallic perfidy. The French government took immediate offence and replied in kind. The exchange of notes continued, until in 1835 the two nations very nearly broke off diplomatic relations. A year later Jackson, on advice from his State Department, offered a rather stiff-necked apology, and with the British government serving as mediator, France arranged a satisfactory schedule of payment. The affair underlined Jackson's great weakness as a diplomat. A man of strong anti-European bias, a believer in direct, soldierly action, he was neither trained nor equipped to handle foreign affairs with tact; on the other hand, his firmness and vigour in the French incident did help to arouse respect for the United States in foreign chancellories.

Jackson, old and tired, designated Martin Van Buren of New York as his successor in the election of 1836. A descendant of an early Dutch family of poor farmers, Van Buren was a slick little professional politician who built and controlled the Democratic organization in New York State, where he practised politics with such dexterity that he earned the name of 'The Little Magician'.

The National Republicans, who had absorbed most of the anti-Masonic, anti-Jackson elements, lacked the unity necessary to provide much resistance. Since one of their party's chief planks was opposition to Jackson's 'Tory' assumption of authority, they styled themselves 'Whigs'. The Whigs actually put four candidates in the field for the presidency, among them Daniel Webster and Indian-fighter William Henry Harrison, but four were hardly enough. The smooth-working Democratic machine swept Van Buren in by a respectable margin, and Jacksonian democracy seemed safe for another four years.

Van Buren's magic could not ward off the disaster that struck the Democrats almost at once. The loose finances of Jackson's time, plus inflated Western land values, wildcat banking, paper speculation, easy money, and heavy public debts (incurred for canals and roads) blew the lid off the national economy in 1837. By September, with Van Buren barely installed in office, nine-tenths of all the factories in the East were closed. Before the panic was over 33,000 business firms collapsed with losses amounting to 440 millions; it was estimated later that half the property in the United States changed hands within two years. Mobs of unemployed roamed the streets, and troops had to be called into New York City to protect stores and warehouses from plundering gangs. The manufacturing Northeast stopped dead in its tracks; the debtor West and South were hit almost equally hard. Van Buren, sticking to the *laissez-faire* principle that hard times wore themselves out, did little to relieve the situation, and indeed there was little that he could do. The brunt of the blame for the panic fell on him, and when the Whigs seized control of Congress in 1838 his days were numbered.

As the election year of 1840 approached the Whigs had victory practically assured if their party could only hold together. Henry Clay was willing and eager to run for the presidency, but the convention of 1839 picked William Henry Harrison, the hero of Tippecanoe. Harrison was a Westerner, a military man, and a comparative unknown who might be advertised as another Jackson to attract the 'common man' into the Whig party. John Tyler of Virginia, a close friend of Clay's, took second place on the ticket.

A chance remark by a disappointed Clay man gave the Whigs their campaign strategy. Harrison, he said, was so shiftless that if somebody gave him a barrel of hard cider and a log cabin he would rest content for the rest of his days. The Whigs pounced on the statement. General Harrison, a simple, kindly Westerner, would henceforth be the 'log cabin, hard cider' candidate, in contrast to the aristocratic Van Buren, who lived in elegance on his Kinderhook estate in New York, used gold spoons on his table, wore imported lace on his cuffs, and drank expensive foreign wines. The fact that Harrison was a courtly, dignified old man who lived comfortably on a 2,000-acre farm made no difference. It was coonskin cap against beaver hat, common man against aristocrat; the Whigs had no other platform and needed none. They made a circus out of the campaign. '6¼ cts. a day and sheep's pluck to the laborer under Van Buren – $2 a day and roast beef under General Harrison!' read the inscription on the banners. The Whig convention at Baltimore shouted, 'Tippecanoe and Tyler too!' and sang lustily,

> Make way for old Tip, turn out, turn out!
> 'Tis the people's decree, their choice shall be,
> So Martin Van Buren – turn out, turn out!

One Whig delegation rolled a huge ball from Alleghany, Pennsylvania, inscribed 'Farewell dear Van – you're not the man – to guide the ship – we'll try Old Tip'. Processions of Harrison men carrying smoking torches paraded the city streets at night to the beating rhythm of 'Van, Van, is a used-up man!' Harrison won by 234 to 60 electoral votes, although his popular majority was less decisive. So ended the dynasty of Jackson.

The period of Jacksonian political ascendancy lasted for only a little more than a decade. After its defeat by the Whigs, the Democratic party came more and more under

Southern control, until it turned eventually into a pro-slavery instrument. Jacksonian democracy, originally an expression of faith in the common man, became the political agent of the Southern planter. The new Whig party, until the break-up of the major parties in the fifties, remained dominant but never really unified. In the Northeast, in Daniel Webster territory, the Whigs attracted those manufacturing interests who favoured a protective tariff and those bankers and merchants who had suffered under Jacksonian fiscal policy. New England anti-slavery men and the remnants of anti-Masonry went Whig, by and large. In the South, some of the sugar and cotton planters, led by Tyler and Calhoun, went Whig, for only the Whig party seemed to offer protection against the rising political power of back-country dissidents and debtors. Even some of Clay's Western followers, resentful of Old Hickory's extreme nationalism and 'executive tyranny', joined the Whigs. The Whig party was in effect a party of 'cons', not 'pros', a party of talent, wealth, and conservatism, but an unstable alliance at best. It was impossible to find any common factor that would bind together Eastern manufacturing capitalist, slave-holding Southern planter, and prosperous Western farmer.

After 1830 both major parties were forced to recognize the existence of two increasingly important elements in politics – business and labour. The United States, like the rest of the world during the first half of the nineteenth century, saw the Industrial Revolution brought to completion by numerous new inventions which revolutionized communication, transportation, and industry. Morse's telegraph, which linked the nation together by 1860, made communication among far-flung settlements swift and efficient. Cyrus McCormick's improved reaper changed the economy of the wheat-growing West, while Lane's steel mouldboard plough (later improved by Oliver) provided a better means of breaking the tough virgin sod of new lands. Colt's revolving pistol, according to popular legend, 'civilized the West'. At the same time, the twin principles of standardization and interchangeability of parts, developed by the ubiquitous Yankee Eli Whitney, stimulated the rise and spread of the factory system. New British techniques of refining iron, joined with huge and accessible coal-fields, made Pennsylvania the centre of an expanding iron and steel industry. The clipper, unquestionably the most perfect ship of its kind, reached its highest development in the forties and fifties. Outspeeding the bluff-bowed British and Dutch merchantmen on the India or China run, the American clippers dominated world trade until driven out by steam. Railroads, especially important in a nation of tremendous distances, tied East and West closely together by the 1860's. The Baltimore and Ohio was incorporated in 1827, and shortly afterwards the first links were made in what became the great New York Central and Pennsylvania systems. From 3,000 miles of track in 1840, the railroads grew to more than 30,000 by 1860, chiefly in the North and Northwest.

The rise of industrialism created a new type of American businessman, quite different from the eighteenth-century colonial merchant or landed gentleman. It was the day of the entrepreneur, of the Lowells, Lawrences, Appletons, Vanderbilts, and others like them. There was an entire continent of illimitable natural resources to exploit, a constantly expanding market, and a rapidly growing industrial system to feed it. America was the businessman's oyster. After 1820 business became a national, transcontinental affair, so complex and so richly rewarding that it demanded a man's entire time and energy. The man of business no longer had the leisure to cultivate the arts or serve in Congress; he might miss something if he failed even for a moment to attend to his affairs. Yet the businessman had to pay close attention to politics to get what he wanted – tariffs, access to resources and markets, cheap and tractable labour, other favours and necessities. Without the time (and in some cases the skill) to play politics himself, he found it advantageous to establish a working relationship with those who did. The alliance between business and politics, which reached its climax after the Civil War, had its beginnings in the industrial expansion of the period 1830–60, and remains yet a vital constituent of American politics.

The growth of the factory system in the Northeast created a labour problem with direct political implications. The disappearance of the domestic labour system and of the older trade guilds, as workmen went into factories, created a new kind of labour-management relationship. Working conditions under the factory system were often less than desirable; a work day of thirteen to fifteen hours was common, health and safety rules usually non-existent, child and female labour shamelessly exploited. In the twenties a few labour groups, patterned after British models, formed to agitate for better conditions. A serious carpenter's strike in 1827 in Philadelphia emphasized the need for better labour organization and resulted in the establishment of the Mechanics' Union, a federation of several trades union groups. The federation principle spread, national labour conventions met annually, and some unity of purpose was imposed on the unions scattered through the Northeast.

Labour leaders saw at once the value of organization for bargaining purposes. They also discovered the strike and used it; one hundred and sixty-eight strikes occurred between 1833 and 1837. However, strikers were often prosecuted under the laws of conspiracy and the strike never became a really effective weapon until the courts reinterpreted the statutes after 1842. Most significant, however, was labour's gradual perception of its political potential; what could not be gained by bargaining or striking, its leaders realized, might be won at the polls. Working-men's parties appeared in several Northern states, while other labour groups endorsed candidates for office on the basis of their stand on labour problems – the principle of 'reward your friends and punish your enemies' subsequently followed by the modern American Federation of Labor and C.I.O. Political Action Committees. The Locofoco movement of the 1830's marked the actual entrance of labour into party politics, when the labour element attempted to gain a place in the Democratic organization. (The name came from the 'locofoco' matches once used to light a meeting after an anti-labour group cut off the gas.) Though the labour movement was temporarily broken by the panic of 1837, it forced the old parties, before the Civil War, to put into effect many of the reforms the working-men's parties desired, thus nipping in the bud a national political labour organization. Many industries established a ten-hour day; a few states adopted health and safety regulations; imprison- ment for debt, long a union target, was abolished in the North, though not in the South. Recognizing the potency of the labour vote, both major parties began to insert attractive planks in their platforms, with the result that after 1840 no party could afford to neglect the working-man's demands.

The American sense of nationality, born during the War of 1812, came of age during these pre-Civil War years. Americans speculated on what made a nation, and what made it great, deepening and strengthening their feelings of patriotism. 'Uncle Sam', who emerged in caricature during the War of 1812, became firmly fixed as a national symbol, a tall, loose-jointed, shrewd, good-hearted man who repre- sented the American spirit. Francis Scott Key's 'Star Spangled Banner', a product of the same war, held equal popularity with Samuel L. Smith's 'My Country 'tis of Thee', written in 1832 to the tune of 'God Save the King'. Monuments, beginning with one at Bunker Hill, were raised to commemorate national heroes and events, scatter- ing a rash of equestrian figures through the public parks. It was a time of national self-confidence, of zest for American living and thinking, of bombastic Fourth of July orations and flag-worship.

The exaggerated nationalism of the Jacksonian period produced a reaction against the wave of immigration that flooded the nation before the Civil War. Economic and political conditions in Europe, particularly in Ireland and Germany, sent nearly four and a half million immigrants across the Atlantic before 1860. The Irish left Ireland in their thousands during the 1830's and 40's because of political oppression (real or imaginary), overpopulation, depression, crop failure, and plain famine. Almost unanimously Catholic, clannish, usually uneducated, these Irish settled in the populous Eastern cities as a cheap labour pool. The Native American or 'Knownothing' movement was an attempt to put anti-foreign, anti-Catholic nativism into politics on an 'America for Americans' platform; the Knownothing Party even ran a presidential candidate, ex-President Millard Fillmore, in the election of 1856. Victims of both economic and social discrimination for a generation or more, the Irish meanwhile found American politics tailored to their talents, and drastically changed the entire pattern of urban political life, particularly in Boston and New York.

During the same period the number of German immigrants increased until nearly a million and a half had arrived in the United States by 1860. Those who came were usually somewhat higher in the social and cultural scale than the Irish. Some, such as Carl Schurz and Franz Sigel, were political refugees escaping the abortive revolutions of the forties; others hoped to avoid military service; factory hands left after the collapse of the German textile industry; cheap land in the West attracted land-hungry farmers. The majority of Germans went West, giving cities such as St Louis, Cincinnati, and Milwaukee a highly Teutonic flavour.

Stable citizens, good farmers, excellent businessmen, and skilful artisans, the German migrants were easily absorbed into the prevailing economic and social pattern and were rarely bothered by anti-foreign movements. Also, between 1840 and 1860, some 64,000 settlers arrived from the Scandinavian countries, most of them headed for the Middle West of Illinois, Wisconsin, and Minnesota.

The great migrations of the mid nineteenth century gave the tradition of nationalism its severest test. The influx of Catholic population into a traditionally Protestant society raised serious problems, not the least among them a reconsideration of the American principle of separation of church and state. Economically, the presence of a large cheap-labour market affected the status of native American labour

THE WESTWARD GROWTH OF THE UNITED STATES

ORIGINAL THIRTEEN STATES

FLORIDA PURCHASE (from Spain) 1819

Ceded by Treaty of 1783 and acquired during Revolution

LOUISIANA PURCHASE (From France) 1803

Ceded by Britain 1818

Ceded by U.S.A. 1818

TEXAS ANNEXATION 1845

OREGON CESSION (by Britain) 1846

MEXICAN CESSION 1848

Gadsden Purchase 1853

and encouraged industrial expansion. Social tensions and stresses appeared in older communities unaccustomed to foreign ways and ideas, eased only after several decades of adjustment. The 'melting pot' concept took hold slowly in American thought, until the initial conflict of foreign culture and native nationalism wore off.

Jeffersonian and Jacksonian democracy were primarily political re-statements of eighteenth-century doctrines of natural goodness and human perfectibility, already expressed in the Declaration and the Bill of Rights. Manifestations of the same faith in man appeared in nineteenth-century religious, social, and economic thought. William Ellery Channing, who in 1830 hailed the arrival of 'a great age of progress', saw evidence all about him of 'a tendency and a power to exalt a people'. The theme of the new age, he believed, would be 'devotion to the progress of the whole human race' by the religious emancipation of man's spirit, the amelioration of his social and economic ills, the removal of obstacles to his steady upward march toward a state of political perfection. The central themes of the Jacksonian epoch were trust in man and certainty of his progress. 'Progressive development does not end with us', wrote Theodore Parker. 'We have seen only the beginning; the future triumph of the race must be vastly greater than all accomplished yet.'

The democratic drive of the Jacksonian era generated tremendous activity in American intellectual life. Particularly in New England, the new spirit flowered in literature, which for the first time felt itself free of bondage to Europe. 'Our day of dependence, our long apprenticeship to the learning of other lands,' wrote Ralph Waldo Emerson in 1837, 'draws to a close.' During the next quarter of a century, as Emerson predicted, there emerged a native, indigenous, American literature, combined with the best of the European tradition. Oliver Wendell Holmes, John Greenleaf Whittier, Henry Wadsworth Longfellow, James Russell Lowell, Henry Thoreau, and Emerson himself, among a host of others, were all men who drew inspiration from their native environment, yet kept touch with the intellectual currents of the rest of the world. The South contributed fewer great names, but among them was Edgar Allan Poe, the Ishmael of American letters. New England's George Bancroft, a Jacksonian by preference, began to write the history of the United States in order to glorify American democracy as 'the culmination of God's wonder-working in the life of mankind'. Jared Sparks began his lifelong task of collecting all the significant documents of American history, pausing meanwhile to write glowing biographies of great Americans but so editing his materials that the founding fathers, as he put it, might never appear in public 'in *dishabille*'. William Hickling Prescott and John Lothrop Motley chose to write histories of Spanish America and the Dutch Republic, Francis Parkman those of New France and the Oregon Trail. Washington Irving, having exhausted Dutch New York and Moorish Spain, found fresh material in the West of Astor and Captain Bonneville. American science, like history and letters, gained greater stature. Benjamin Silliman and Asa Gray established world-wide reputations in geology and botany; Louis Agassiz, a transplanted Swiss, pioneered in zoology; Captain Matthew Maury of the Navy did excellent research in oceanography. Surveying all these accomplishments. Robert Breckenridge of Kentucky exclaimed that 'no mortal power could esti-mate the heights of grandeur waiting to receive us' as a nation.

The most dramatic affirmation of the prevailing belief in progress appeared in the religious ferment of the period, a series of upheavals already foreshadowed by the Unitarian triumph over Calvinism a decade and more earlier. Trans-cendentalism, a philosophico-religious system current in New England from 1830 to 1860, staked out the route of the new trend. Contrary to popular belief, transcendentalism was never an established sect or creed, but rather a some-what fluid agreement on certain religious matters arrived at by a relatively small group of intellectuals clustered about Boston and its environs. It did not play directly on the main stream of American thought, though through Emerson, Thoreau, and a few others it undoubtedly had a powerful indirect impact on contemporary ideas. What Emerson thought and said was what America, in cruder and less intellectual terms, believed; transcendentalism, on a high spiritual and intellectual level, caught and expressed the spirit of the age. The Jacksonian Democrat need not have read Kant or Coleridge to believe as Emerson did in the worth of the individual, in self-reliance, in the integrity of one's own mind – but transcendentalism buttressed his faith in such things and extended it into the realm of philosophical and religious speculation.

The guiding spirit of the transcendental movement was Ralph Waldo Emerson. Born in 1803, the descendant of several generations of Calvinist divines, Emerson, after studying theology at Harvard, entered the ministry as a Unitarian. Dissatisfied with the confinements of even his own liberal sect, he soon resigned his pulpit to travel in Europe. On his return to New England he began to evolve, through lectures and essays, the central doctrines of a new, free, individualistic religious philosophy, disdaining any organized philosophical system and ranging through the whole wide world of thought for his ideas. Emersonian thought, in fact, transcendentalism in general, rested on the single belief that every man had within him a spark of divinity. 'In all my lectures', Emerson wrote, 'I have taught one doctrine, namely, the infinitude of the private man.' In a series of essays and books Emerson built his system about the principle that all men possess both the power to discern intuitively God-given truth and the ability to govern themselves by it. *Nature* (1836), *The American Scholar* (1837), *Self-Reliance* (1841), and all their successors explored and expanded that principle. In effect, Emersonian transcendentalism was a mystical affirmation of the prevailing American belief in freedom and equality, a re-emphasis of frontier individualism, a nineteenth-century modification of the old Puritan doctrine of election and an assertion of the divine election of every man. His volumes were one great paean to

Jacksonian America, Emerson himself its lay preacher. 'We will walk with our own feet', he wrote, 'We will work with our own hands; we will speak with our own minds.'

Though Emerson was popularly regarded as spokesman for the transcendentalist group, it gathered in as well most of the freshest and most brilliant minds of New England. Most of all, Emerson's doctrines impressed young Henry David Thoreau of Concord, Massachusetts. Thoreau, fifteen years younger than Emerson, practised the doctrines of self-reliance and self-sufficiency that the older man preached. He retired to a rude cabin on the shores of Walden Pond, near Concord, to test to his own satisfaction the values of an independent existence. 'I went to the woods', he wrote in *Walden*, 'because I wished to live deliberately, to front only the essential facts of life, and to see if I could learn what it had to teach, and not, when I came to die, discover that I had not lived.' An arch-individualist, Thoreau attempted to carry the moral idealism of transcendentalism to its logical conclusion in a sort of philosophical anarchism.

Thoreau's emphasis on individualism brought him into open conflict with organized society, which he found sadly lacking in moral and spiritual values. His experiment in living at Walden Pond he intended to serve both as protest against and proof of the inadequacy of contemporary American society's materialistic, anti-individualistic goals. By the same token his doctrine of the absolute freedom of the individual led him to reject the authority of government; he changed Jefferson's concept of 'that government is best which governs least' to read 'that government is best which governs not at all'. The individual, thought Thoreau, possessed an absolute and inherent right to nullify laws made by ignorant, wrong-headed majorities, if those laws conflicted with his own inner convictions. If the State follows an immoral policy, reasoned Thoreau, the moral individual must perforce disobey it: 'Any man more right than his neighbors constitutes a majority of one.' Thus he preferred to go to gaol rather than pay a tax to support a State engaged in what he regarded as immoral actions – in particular, the Mexican War and the continuance of slavery. His reasoning, as explained in *Civil Disobedience*, was simple and direct. 'If the alternative is to keep all just men in prison, or give up war and slavery, the State will not hesitate which to choose', he wrote, thus implementing a doctrine that was later to influence Gandhi and other exponents of passive resistance. Emerson stressed the nobility of the individual, the innate authority of the average man. Thoreau emphasized the duties and capabilities of that man in society.

Transcendentalism was an integral part of the American Romantic movement of the early nineteenth century, originating primarily in the discovery by New England intellectuals of German and British romantic philosophy. It derived from Coleridge and Carlyle, from Kant and his followers, from Cousin and French eclecticism, from Oriental sources, from native Calvinist and Unitarian and Quaker roots, all bent to nineteenth-century Yankee uses. It was at bottom a manifestation in philosophy and religion of the same optimistic, individualistic, egalitarian spirit that produced Jacksonian democracy, although Emerson could never quite bring himself to unqualified approval of Old Hickory. Transcendentalism really meant, as one of its followers phrased it, 'that men are free, and claim the right to think for themselves in religious as well as in political matters'. It emphasized the worth of the individual and the principle of self-reliance; it admired the man of action and original thought, not the man bound by tradition or formal creed; it believed in the values of instinctive and individual judgement, rather than in those of authority and convention. It said, in Emersonian terms, 'God is in every man', which in the final test was not far removed from what Jackson meant.

Transcendentalism, however, was a highly specialized philosophical system, its appeal limited to a small group of cultivated New Englanders. The average American applauded the transcendentalists' conclusions about his indisputable worth and inherent ability, but the Kantian-Coleridgean-Platonic background of the Emersonian system was well beyond his ken. Neither Emerson nor his followers were able to translate their beliefs into familiar terms, whatever their Jacksonian implications. On the popular level, the translation was accomplished by a different kind of movement, 'come-outism'.

'Come-outism' was the name applied to those dissident, unorthodox sects that dotted America during the pre-Civil War period. It meant, roughly, establishing one's religious independence by 'coming out' of the orthodox churches. The 'come-outer' sects stressed individualism, self-expression, equalitarianism in religion, thus affirming transcendental-Unitarian principles on a lower, more common, direct level. Dozens of these new religious societies, some of them on the lunatic fringe, appeared during the later eighteenth and earlier nineteenth centuries. The Shakers, more properly titled The United Society of Believers in Christ's Second Coming, gathered about 'Mother' Ann Lee, an Englishwoman influenced by Quakerism and evangelism. Mother Ann built up a small American following that increased after her death in 1784 to a sizeable body of believers. The Shakers rejected most of the traditional Calvinist doctrines, condemned marriage, practised celibacy, and retired from the world into a number of self-sustaining communities in Pennsylvania, Ohio, New England, New York, and Kentucky. In 1831 William Miller of western New York, who preached the imminent second coming of Christ, established the sect of Millerites, whose churches were soon scattered from Maine to Wisconsin. According to Miller, Christ would appear in the year 1843, at which time there would be a second judgement, a terrible condemnation of the sinful, and the founding of a literal Kingdom of God on earth for true believers. By 1843 Miller claimed nearly a million followers, many of whom that summer waited vainly on hilltops for Christ's arrival. Extremist though the Shakers and Millerites were, the numbers of adherents they were able to attract indicated how strongly the promise of utopia appealed to the common man.

Another facet of 'come-outism' appeared in the religious communities which were established in the United States between 1820 and 1850. The Rappites, led by George Rapp, settled in Pennsylvania and later Ohio and Indiana; William Keil established his Bethel Community in Mississippi and moved it to Oregon; the German Separatists settled at Zoar, Ohio; the Amana Society of New York was transferred to Iowa; Eric Janson's Bishop Hill Colony chose Illinois; the transcendentalist-inspired Brook Farm community in Massachusetts owed its leadership to Emerson's friend George Ripley. All of these religious communal groups were bent on making religion a personal, individual matter, bringing it into the daily social and economic life of the average man. They were socialistic or communistic by necessity rather than intent. Many of the sects, it is true, originated in the pietistic movements that flourished in Europe after the French Revolution, but their transplantation to the American scene coincided with the democratizing spirit of the times.

Mormonism provides perhaps the best illustration of the religious ferment of the period. Its membership was drawn almost wholly from those lower and lower middle classes that Unitarianism and transcendentalism never touched. Joseph Smith, a shrewd, semi-literate young man from upper New York State, announced in 1827 that he had received an angelic visitation which led in turn to his discovery of some golden plates inscribed with sacred scriptures. Translated and published, these appeared in 1830 as *The Book of Mormon*. That same year Smith established the Church of Jesus Christ of Latter Day Saints under a state charter. Converts flocked to him. A few years later the Saints moved to Ohio, where the revivals of the Second Awakening had already ploughed fertile recruiting grounds. When his church numbered several thousand members, Smith moved its headquarters to Missouri and later to Nauvoo, Illinois, which had a population of nearly 15,000 by the mid-forties. However, neighbouring 'gentiles' and Mormons frequently clashed (over commercial as well as religious matters) and during an armed attack on Nauvoo Smith and his brother were killed.

After Smith's death leadership of the Mormons passed to Brigham Young, an intelligent, authoritative man who immediately imposed unity and purpose on the church. Despairing of ever finding peace and security in Illinois, Young led the Mormons in 1846 and 1847 on a great migration across the plains to the promised land of Deseret, where they might live in isolation on the shores of Great Salt Lake. Certain members of the Smith family broke off from Young's group to create the Reorganized Mormons, while another faction followed 'King Jesse' Strang to a chain of islands in upper Lake Michigan. Mormonism, unlike many other 'come-outer' sects, was a strong and disciplined movement with powerful and purposive leadership. It appealed to the common man and especially to the poor one, stressed an orthodox and old-fashioned Calvinistic morality, established an almost Puritanic theocracy, and furnished its followers with a simple, easily grasped, and highly effective socio-economic code. Mormon leaders placed great emphasis on group co-operation and attempted to develop in their society a strong sense of social responsibility. The practice of polygamy, which caused most of the Mormons' troubles, was never really an important part of Mormon faith, being intended instead as a sensible solution to certain practical problems of frontier life.

The most important influence on the religious thought of the period was the 'perfectionist' movement of the thirties and forties. Despite the Unitarian triumphs in New England and the transcendentalist revolt against Unitarianism, orthodox Congregational, Presbyterian, and Methodist churches still dominated the religious life of the West. Neither Congregationalism nor Presbyterianism was especially well suited to Western life, since both possessed views of human nature and hierarchical organization that failed to agree with either frontier equalitarianism or Jacksonian democracy. The Methodists' evangelistic doctrine of 'momentary sanctification' and their loose church structure always met greater approval in the new settlements. As a result, western Congregational and Presbyterian churches soon found Methodist ideas creeping into their creeds. In 1825 reports reached the Eastern church bodies of a wave of revivals sweeping western New York under the leadership of a young Presbyterian named Charles Grandison Finney.

Investigation revealed that Finney, some five years earlier, had committed himself to a doctrine of 'free and full salvation', quite similar to Methodist doctrine. After some difficulties in getting ordained, Finney then began preaching his theory that sin was selfishness and virtue benevolence. Conversion, he said, is a normal experience, accomplished by the sinner himself under the stimulus of emotional excitement; conversion simply meant exchanging sinful selfishness for virtuous selflessness. Any human being can, said Finney, attain a state of perfection by his own efforts, but salvation alone was not enough. The 'perfected' one must make his religion directly active; he should, said Finney, 'have the determination to aim at being useful in the highest degree possible'. Salvation was not the end, but the beginning of a useful life.

Finney's doctrine violated practically every tenet of orthodox Congregational and Presbyterian creed – sin, salvation, election, good works, free will. Equally disturbing were the 'new measures' of worship that he adapted from traditional Methodist and Baptist camp-meeting techniques. Finney, it was claimed, held 'protracted meetings' lasting from three to ten days; permitted women to pray publicly; encouraged 'groaning and posturing' among the congregation; instituted an 'anxious seat' for sinners; and used new converts as lay preachers.

Despite opposition from the Eastern churches, Finney's doctrines swept the West and later the East. He penetrated into strongly Congregational New England, gathering thousands of converts; in New York City the wealthy Tappan brothers built a huge church, the Broadway Tabernacle, especially for him. Oneida Seminary in New York turned into a training school for Finneyite preachers, and Lane

Seminary in Cincinnati and later Oberlin in Ohio (where Finney himself was professor of theology) trained perfectionist ministers for the West. Though denounced as heresy by the orthodox Congregational and Presbyterian churches, perfectionism was successful.

Finney's beliefs had more than a religious significance. Like transcendentalism and Unitarianism, perfectionism stressed individual ability, equalitarianism, and self-reliance couched in terms that the ordinary man could easily grasp. The perfectionist ideal was in essence another affirmation of the contemporary belief in optimism, progress, and democratic individualism. It was 'come-outism' with a vengeance, a sharp break with authoritarianism in religion, a theological restatement of Jacksonism. In particular, Finney's idea of 'usefulness' reinforced the numerous humanitarian-reform movements of the time. Many of Finney's followers were attracted to the abolition movement, which was gaining ground in the thirties, simply transferring Finney's revivalistic techniques to this new and different crusade. It was no accident that Lane Seminary produced thirty-two agents for abolition societies (among them Theodore Weld, who trained nearly all the anti-slavery lecturers in the West) or that Oberlin College became the Western centre of abolitionism. The abolitionist movement in its early phases had a strong religious cast that was a direct result of perfectionist influences.

The religious upheavals of pre-Civil War America were merely parts of a wider search for economic equality and justice. The period proved to be a happy hunting ground for utopian experiments in living, particularly for those patterned after the theories of Robert Dale Owen in England and Charles Fourier and Étienne Cabet in France. Twelve communities based on Owenite socialism were established in 1825 and 1826, among them the New Harmony, Indiana, colony supervised by Owen himself. Owen, who bought out a Rappite group for $140,000, at one time had nearly a thousand persons in his colony, though it dissolved in dissension within a few years. Fourierism, popularized by

Arthur Brisbane (who studied in Paris under Fourier) fared not much better, though it attracted support from such prominent men as William Ellery Channing, Horace Greeley, Parke Godwin, George Ripley, and Charles A. Dana. Twenty-seven Fourieristic communities were founded between 1843 and 1853, some as far west as Michigan and Wisconsin. Brook Farm Colony, near Boston, was supervised by Ripley and patronized by Nathaniel Hawthorne, Margaret Fuller, and others from the Massachusetts transcendentalist group. It operated with indifferent success for six years until it was destroyed by fire in 1847. The North American Phalanx in New Jersey, the most prosperous of the Fourieristic colonies, lasted for thirteen years and was able to pay off its stockholders at 65 cents in the dollar when it dissolved. A total of sixty-one utopian communities were established in the United States between 1825 and 1860, some religious in origin, some socialistic after the manner of Owen, Fourier, or Cabet, and others simply independent. 'Not a man you meet', Emerson wrote in his journals, 'but has the draft of a new community in his pocket.'

The search for perfection took other forms as well. Horace Mann, convinced that if the average American were to assume his social responsibilities he must be properly educated, worked tirelessly for free, tax-supported public schools. The educational theories of Pestalozzi, Fellenberg, Froebel, and other European innovators were transplanted to American soil; kindergartens, teacher-training schools, and public high schools appeared everywhere. German-trained scholars like Edward Everett, George Ticknor, George Bancroft, and Joseph Cogswell introduced new methods into higher education, while Mary Lyon founded Mount Holyoke in 1837, the first women's college to be planned as a true equivalent of men's education. In the western states, state universities were established almost as soon as the states themselves were ready for admission to the Union – Ohio (1804), Indiana (1820), Michigan (1821), Missouri (1839), Iowa (1847), Wisconsin (1848), and others.

Meanwhile the Sunday School, the Lyceum, the subscription library and the literary or debating society served as educational media on the popular level.

At the same time, the plight of the criminal, the deaf, blind, and poor attracted attention. Jefferson redesigned the Richmond gaol on more humanitarian principles, while in 1816 New York commissioned two new prisons at Auburn and Ossining, using the new cell-block system. Connecticut, which used an abandoned copper mine as a state prison, followed suit, and by 1840 eight other states completed new ones. In the prisons themselves routine and discipline became less dreary and harsh; flogging, stocks, and solitary confinement were gradually abandoned. Samuel Gridley Howe of Boston and T. H. Gallaudet of Philadelphia pioneered in the education of the blind and deaf. Gallaudet opened the American Asylum in Connecticut in 1815, and before 1851 thirteen states founded similar institutions. Poor relief in 1800 was handled in a manner not much different from that of 1600. The fact that in early America land was cheap and labour scarce gave currency to the persistent American idea that poverty must be the result of indolence, but after the growth of cities and the emergence of industrial economy, thinking on the matter slowly changed. A few states passed poor relief laws, usually inadequate, while some of the larger cities established charity houses, as in New York (1825), Boston (1826), and Philadelphia (1828).

Not until the third decade of the nineteenth century did the insane attain the status of human beings, to be treated as individuals worth saving. Agitation for the elimination of the traditional Bedlam came after the work of Philippe Pinel in Paris became known in America through the writings of Dr Benjamin Rush. The most effective reformer was a young Boston girl, Dorothea Dix, a friend of William Ellery Channing's. With the support of Samuel Howe and Charles Sumner, she began in 1841 a two-year survey of gaols, asylums, and reform schools in the state of Massachusetts. Her report to the legislature in 1843 shocked the nation and touched off an immediate reform programme.

She made similar surveys in Rhode Island, New Jersey, and Pennsylvania, leaving behind her new and better hospitals for the insane wherever she went. By 1854 Dorothea Dix had travelled 30,000 miles and had reported on the institutions of every state east of Indiana; by 1860 she had covered the rest.

The temperance movement stemmed from several sources. Evangelistic revivalists of the early nineteenth century, believing in Finney's doctrines of perfectibility and usefulness, viewed alcoholic beverages as a major obstacle to social progress. Interest in the creation of an enlightened electorate, stimulated by the spread of manhood suffrage, provided another impetus toward temperance reform. At the same time, social workers interested in eliminating poverty and crime in the cities found overwhelming evidence that excessive drinking was a major cause of both. The great temperance crusade came after 1810, under the leadership of the clergy. The Presbyterian Church took an official stand on the use of alcohol in 1811, followed by the Methodists in 1816; earlier, in 1813, the Congregationalists and Presbyterians joined to form a state temperance society in Massachusetts. By 1825 more than a million were enrolled in state and local church-sponsored societies throughout the nation, and in 1826 the American Society for the Promotion of Temperance began work on a national scale. It established a missionary system, published pamphlets, sent out speakers, employed professional organizers, and in general copied the revivalist methods of the evangelical churches. The Washington Temperance Society, formed in 1840, used the same techniques even more successfully, carrying on its campaign against drink by camp-meetings, songs and stories, 'Cold Water Parades', and travelling lecturers – Timothy Shay Arthur's *Ten Nights in a Barroom, and What I Saw There*, was perhaps its best-known product; a novel against liquor which as a best-seller ranked just behind *Uncle Tom's Cabin*, and which, in dramatized form, was a favourite tent-show for another generation. But the societies soon split over the question of whether drinking was immoral or simply economically wasteful. Nor could they agree on method, some believing the solution to drinking lay in education, others in prohibitive legislation. Somewhat ineffectual laws governing the sale of liquor appeared in thirteen states before 1860, but not until the twentieth century did the movement seem to attain its objectives in the eighteenth Amendment to the Constitution.

Both the frontier necessity for equal treatment of women, and the eighteenth-century emphasis on the rights of individuals were contributing factors to the movement for women's rights. It was also apparent to any onlooker that women in America had but few more legal, political, and social rights than the Negro slave – as the abolitionists continually pointed out. The question of female participation in contemporary religious revivals brought the issue up in another connexion; could not women testify and be saved too, thus finding equal status with men in salvation? Strong-minded women like Catherine Beecher, Emma Willard, Lydia Maria Child, and Margaret Fuller, began to agitate in earnest for the recognition of women's legal and personal rights. Lucy Stone spent a lifetime on the lecture platform; Amelia Bloomer campaigned for dress reform and immortalized her name in an unlovely article of feminine apparel; Harriet Hunt and Elizabeth Blackwell graduated from medical schools to become the first women physicians; Sarah Joseph Hale edited *Godey's Lady's Book*; Abby Kelley, Elizabeth Cady Stanton, and the Grimkè sisters went into the abolitionist movement. Their first victory came in 1848 with the passage of New York's Married Women's Property Law. Their real accomplishments, however, came after the Civil War, culminating in the nineteenth Amendment, which became part of the Constitution in 1920.

In practice, all the reforms of pre-Civil War America, however disparate their aims, merged into a single great reform – to make America perfect. With political equality seemingly achieved by Jacksonian democracy, and with the dominance of an authoritarian theology threatened by a variety of new faiths, the nation turned its attention to the removal of all possible obstacles from the path of national progress. The democratic and the humanitarian-reform movements melted together, pooling their methods, efforts, objectives. 'Every possible form of intellectual and physical dyspepsia brought forth its gospel', wrote James Russell Lowell in retrospect. 'No brain but had its private maggot.' But Lowell recognized that there was in them all 'a very solid and serious kernel, full of the most deadly explosiveness. It was simply a struggle for fresh air . . ., this life which the reformers demanded, with more or less clearness of consciousness and expression, life in politics, life in literature, life in religion'. Jackson, Emerson, Cooper, and Garrison were products of the same drive.

Reform was of course not a uniquely American phenomenon. On both sides of the Atlantic philanthropic men and women were seeking out and striving to cure social and economic ills. The Reform Bill of 1832, the Chartist movement, the Factory Act of 1833, and the repeal of the Corn Laws in 1846 reflected British attempts at reform; in continental Europe there was a general trend toward a recognition of human rights and the reality of human duties, culminating in the widespread revolutions of 1830–48. Americans learned a great deal from European reformers, who for a long time had wrestled with the same problems in a much older society. The reform movement of the earlier nineteenth century in the United States was not an evangelism of the underprivileged, a class bootstrap lifting of the oppressed, but a movement in which rich and poor, cultured and uneducated, radical and conservative joined. Neither was it a mass revival, like the two Awakenings, but a sincere and rational effort (with the eccentric, it is true, showing at the edges) to realize fully for once and all the innate capabilities of man.

Emerson summed up the trend best with the remark that the cause of reform lay in the belief 'that there is an infinite worthiness in man, which will appear at the call of worth, and that all particular reforms are the removing of impediments'. The reformers were all simply interested in removing impediments. They trusted the individual and believed in his ability to better himself. A good digestion, a ten-hour working day, sensible apparel and a vote for women, temperance, better gaols, labour unions, utopian economics, and a state of spiritual communion with God were each of them steps that might advance humanity a few paces farther towards the ideal. But above and beyond all American efforts to secure social and political and economic justice, above all lesser humanitarian reforms, stood the question of slavery, which eventually overshadowed and embraced them all.

The anti-slavery movement began as part of the whole great stirring of nineteenth-century humanitarianism. It was a reform motivated by the same drives that produced Jacksonian democracy, utopian communities, and other humanitarian and social experiments. Until the mid-forties anti-slavery was simply one of many reform enthusiasms, one frowned on, in fact, by the more stable and conservative-minded reformers. Gradually it rose to eclipse the others, because its appeal was wider, its leadership more skilful, its relation to politics more direct, its relevance to the future of American democracy more unmistakable.

In the opinion of many Americans, chattel slavery was a clear violation of and a direct threat to the traditional concept of American democracy. The slavery question became eventually a question of whether the nation would continue to exist, and if so, of whether it would exist as a democratic nation. There was a compelling danger, as Lincoln pointed out, that it might continue as an undemocratic nation, completely given over to slavery. Slavery existed near enough to touch the orbit of every individual's future, yet geographically far enough removed from some to allow it to be judged and evaluated more or less impersonally. It was also confined to a portion of the nation whose political and economic interests differed sharply from those of the non-slave-holding portions. In addition, the slavery system was politically accessible, subject to state and federal law.

Neither slavery nor its abolition became an important

issue in America until 1830. Opposition to slavery was common in colonial days, but it was not until after the formation of the Republic and the enunciation of eighteenth-century doctrines of liberty and equality that a serious examination of the institution began. The prohibition of the slave trade in 1808 aroused little real opposition. After that date anti-slavery sentiment grew, especially in the South. In 1827 Benjamin Lundy, the Quaker reformer, listed 130 anti-slavery groups, 106 of them in slave-holding areas. State societies, beginning with Pennsylvania's in 1777, were working in nearly all the states outside the South before 1830. But with the increasing importance of cotton as the basic Southern crop, Southerners perceived that slavery was absolutely essential to their economic and social welfare. Thereafter anti-slavery talk abruptly stopped south of the Mason-Dixon line; in 1837 Lundy could find only a very few of the 106 societies still in existence.

At the same time the temper of Northern anti-slavery sentiment changed. What had once been mild approval of some sort of emancipation, or at best mild disapproval of slavery in principle, became an aggressive, forthright, sometimes intemperate demand for the instant abolition of the entire institution. William Lloyd Garrison, the New England firebrand, struck the keynote of the new crusade in the first number of his abolitionist paper, *The Liberator*. 'I am in earnest', he wrote. 'I will not equivocate – I will not excuse – I will not retreat a single inch – AND I WILL BE HEARD.' Under the leadership of Garrison and others, newly organized societies carried abolitionist doctrines through the North and Northwest. Garrison and a few friends founded the New England Anti-slavery Society in Boston in 1832. Within the next year similar groups appeared in New York City, Providence, Philadelphia, and Ohio. In 1833 representatives of these societies met in Philadelphia to organize a national body, the American Anti-slavery Society, which remained under Garrisonian control throughout most of its existence. In 1840, however, a large number of moderates withdrew to form the American and Foreign Anti-slavery

Society. Both societies sent out speakers and organizers, published newspapers and tons of pamphlets and books, founded state and local branches, and publicized the abolitionist cause with unflagging zeal. By 1840 the entire complexion of the argument had changed; compromise or agreement among anti-slavery, abolitionist, and pro-slavery adherents was no longer possible.

The arguments on both sides of the slavery question were extremely complex, nor were pro- and anti-slavery groups always able to agree among themselves. The anti-slavery societies intended to appeal to the nation by fact and argument, to change public opinion, and thus to build a great body of Northern and Southern anti-slavery sentiment that would eventually (by legal and political means) abolish slavery. Their attack on slavery rested on several principles, any one of which might be stressed to the exclusion of others.

First, said some, slavery was wrong, on moral grounds. Slave breeding, and the refusal of slave-holders to sanction slave marriages or to recognize the slave family as a unit, struck at the very foundations of morality. Relations between slave and master encouraged immoral behaviour in Negro and white alike. The system was also cruel, barbaric, and inhuman; Theodore Weld's study, *American Slavery As It Is* (1839), Mrs Stowe's *Uncle Tom's Cabin* (1852), and countless other studies and novels appeared to document the accusation with stories of whippings, tortures, confinements, bloodhounds, slave marts, and separated families.

Slavery, said others, was unchristian and irreligious, a clear violation of Scripture. Chattel slavery arrogated to one man a power which belonged rightfully only to God; it violated both the Christian ethic of brotherhood and the law of Christian charity. It was impossible, in the Garrisonian view, for a man to be a slave-holder or a slavery sympathizer and a Christian; it was equally impossible for an American church to remain Christian while condoning or supporting slavery. Such views naturally aroused argument within the Protestant Churches, leading the Wesleyan Methodists to withdraw from the Methodist convention of 1843 in protest against its failure to take an official anti-slavery stand. Two years later the Southern Methodists, objecting to anti-slavery talk in the churches, separated from the Methodist organization to found the Methodist Episcopal Church, South. The same year the Southern Baptist Convention split on the issue. Presbyterians managed to postpone the break until 1857, when their Southern congregations seceded.

In addition to being unchristian, slavery was also believed to be undemocratic, irreconcilable with other American institutions and with the American tradition. It produced a small, powerful, minority class of aristocratic landholders who, it was claimed, had entered into a secret 'slave-power conspiracy' to extend slavery everywhere and to impose their rule on the nation at large. After 1850 the progress of this 'conspiracy' was carefully charted by the abolitionists; as some Northerners pointed out after the Dred Scott decision of 1857, it needed but one more favourable Supreme Court decision to make slavery a national rather than a Southern institution. 'Reflecting men', wrote Henry Wilson, 'saw that there must be some malignant and potent agency at work . . ., a commanding power in the land . . . before which all other interests were compelled in greater or lesser degree to bend.' If the Southern 'slaveocracy' joined forces with the Northern industrial capitalists, abolitionists pointed out, the two oligarchies together could and would control the nation. Only the abolition of slavery itself could forestall the combined tyranny of 'The Lords of the Lash and the Lords of the Loom'.

Slavery, it was argued, was economically unsound, wasteful, and inefficient. The poor white man in the South could not compete with unpaid slave labour; neither could he break the political and economic domination of the slave-holding aristocracy over the South. Last of all, some anti-slavery men claimed that slavery was simply illegal. The Declaration of Independence, they said, banned slavery by its enunciation of the natural rights philosophy. If the Declaration were not considered as part of constitutional law, then the Constitution, by outlawing the slave trade, also implicitly outlawed slavery. If the Constitution were neutral on the subject, as some assumed it was, the abolitionists reasoned that since the Declaration had abolished slavery prior to 1787, the framers of the Constitution had not considered it necessary to label as illegal an institution already outlawed. If the Constitution did actually sanction slavery, as certain commentators believed it might under the guaranteed property clause, the Christian must then obey 'a higher law' of morality and reject the authority of the Constitution. Thus William Lloyd Garrison publicly ground a copy of the Constitution under his heel, exclaiming, 'It is an agreement with Death and a covenant with Hell!'

Anti-slavery sympathizers, whatever their reasons, agreed generally that slavery was wrong and that it must be abolished, but they found great difficulty in agreeing on how and when to abolish it. The question of 'when' caused especial trouble. One faction favoured instant emancipation and 'immediate enfranchisement of our slave population', the policy generally approved by the New England societies. The 'gradualist' school of thought favoured piecemeal emancipation, extended over several generations, with gradual absorption of the Negro into the social and political structure – a policy attacked by Garrison as 'gradualism in theory and perpetualism in practice'. The so-called 'New York doctrine', adopted by the New York Society, compromised on 'immediate emancipation, gradually accomplished', a theory difficult to understand and equally hard to publicize. In the West the Lane Seminary group evolved a theory of 'gradual emancipation, immediately begun'. The Garrisonian and Lane factors found most supporters, but never reached agreement.

The 'how' of abolition proved no less troublesome. One group, basing its opposition to slavery on moral and religious grounds, believed that a national campaign for moral regeneration – an evangelical religious crusade – would result in the abolition of slavery by unanimous consent,

North and South. Appeals to the national conscience, thought Theodore Weld, would soon convince slave-holder and non-slave-holder alike that the system was against God and Christianity. Another school of thought believed that slavery could best be abolished by legal action within the existing political framework, either through existing parties, which could legislate slavery out of existence, or through a third party, which might gain control of the Federal government to accomplish the same end. For this reason abolitionists founded the Liberty Party and nominated James G. Birney for President in 1840 and 1844. The political phase of the abolition movement, culminating in the Liberty, Freesoil, and Republican parties, rested primarily on the Lane doctrine, though it held Democratic-flavoured ideas on the tariff, bank, and internal improvements issues. A third group, believing that the Constitution legalized slavery and that there were no proper legal means of abolishing it, advocated either abandoning the Constitution for a new one or seceding from any government based on it. If the Constitution sanctioned a system which violated 'higher laws' of morality and natural right, a man must follow his conscience and refuse to remain in the Union. Garrison's *Liberator* carried on its masthead for years the slogan, 'No union with slave-holders!'

The 'colonizationists' proposed to extirpate slavery by transporting the Negro elsewhere, either to Africa or to some unsettled portion of the West. The American Colonization Society, founded in 1816 and counting among its members such men as Bushrod Washington, James Madison, Charles Carroll, and Henry Clay, established the colony of Liberia in West Africa for this purpose in 1822. After 1830 the abolitionists attacked the colonizationists both for their lack of success and for their refusal to face the problem directly; understandably, the colonizationists never found much support in the West. In forty years of activity the Society shipped about eleven thousand Negroes to Africa at a cost of more than a million dollars – a number replaced within a month by the birth rate. Various other methods received some notice. Quaker groups argued that a boycott of slave-state products would force the South into emancipation. Some recommended paying wages to slaves so that they might buy their own freedom. Others proposed an appropriation of state and federal funds to purchase slaves for expatriation.

Freesoilism, a doctrine developed in the forties in the Northwest, was less a scheme for the abolition of slavery than for its containment within existing Southern boundaries. The Northwest farmer, who could not afford slaves and who found slavery unadaptable to his type of agriculture, did not want the fertile land of the plains states given over to slavery. Frontier equalitarianism mitigated against the system, while Western rural society was formed on a much more fluid and less stratified pattern than Southern slave society. The free-soil farmer had little humanitarian concern for the Negro and great unfamiliarity with slavery, but he definitely did not want the Negro as an economic competitor. Gradually the free-soil position moved closer to the legalistic, humanitarian, natural-rights theories of the abolitionists. By the mid-fifties the Freesoil and Liberty parties, both opposed to slavery but on different grounds, joined with the new Republican party. 'Immediate' abolitionism eventually killed off or engulfed its opponents, until by 1860 the single great issue became – not if, how and when slavery must be abolished – but one of freedom versus oppression, right versus wrong, Christianity versus evil.

The pro-slavery forces from the outset presented a much more united front than the anti-slavery groups. There were, however, some disaffected areas in the South (western Virginia, western North Carolina, parts of upland Georgia, eastern Tennessee and Kentucky) which refused to co-operate. Anti-slavery thought in the South was in general very well controlled, either by legal intimidation or by social pressure, and the pro-slavery cause was so efficiently propagated that by 1850 the slave-holding states formed a solid bloc of opinion on the issue. In order to obtain solidarity Southern leaders were forced to make clear infringements on freedom of press, speech, thought, and education, to condone and encourage mob action, and to appeal to distinctly anti-democratic political, social, and racist theories.

The pro-slavery argument was both defensive and offensive in nature. In rationalizing the existence of slavery in a democratic nation, its proponents encountered stumbling blocks in the great Virginia liberal tradition and in the Declaration of Independence it had produced. The only alternative was to discredit both the tradition and the document, which Southern writers proceeded to do. Jefferson was ridiculed as an unstable reformer, infected with French radicalism and New England venom; Washington was drawn as a good-intentioned but politically naïve man taken in by Northern propaganda. The Declaration of Independence, said Calhoun, represented an admirable theory but no guide for practical life. Of Jefferson's phrase, 'All men are created equal', he remarked, 'Taking the proposition literally, there is not a word of truth in it', a view to which many other Southern leaders agreed. 'The universal law of nature is force', Thomas Cooper wrote. 'By this law the lower animals are subdued to man, and the same law governs the relations between men.' Slavery, from a Southern point of view, had deep roots in natural law, the Declaration notwithstanding.

Replying to Northern critics, the exponents of slavery retorted that men were actually born neither free nor equal. Liberty is not an inheritance granted to every man, they said, but only to those who are equipped to deserve it. *Natural* rights to liberty do not exist. Men possess only such rights as society grants to them; that which society gives it can also take away. As Calhoun summarized the argument, men are born into a political and social state, subject to its laws and institutions. A Negro, being socially, mentally, and anthropologically inferior to white men, has no natural rights, deserves none, and could not make responsible use of them if he had them. 'The Negro', wrote J. B. D. DeBow, 'cannot be schooled, nor argued, nor driven into a love of freedom.' Southern preachers scrutinized the Bible for arguments justifying slavery as carefully as Northern divines examined scripture for arguments against it. Both Jesus and the apostles exhorted slaves to obedience and fidelity to their masters; the sons of Ham were cursed to eternal servitude by divine decree.

Having once established slavery on religious and political grounds, its supporters proceeded to prove that its continued existence was both necessary and desirable. Slavery was best for the Negro, since he needed the care and guidance that only some system of servitude could provide. 'Providence has placed him in our hands for his good', wrote Governor Hammond of North Carolina, 'and has paid us from his labor for our guardianship.' The fact that the Negro failed to appreciate this simply proved his lack of intelligence. Economically the pro-slavery writers continued, slavery was absolutely necessary to the South and to the world. The Negro represented a huge investment in property, whose loss would mean financial ruin for one-third of a nation and probably for the nation itself. David Christy, in *Cotton is King* (1860), reasoned that since cotton depended on slavery, and the world economy depended on cotton, therefore the world economy depended on slavery.

Slavery was, said the South, an absolute social necessity. Only by declassing and subduing the Negro could the white race keep itself racially pure; if the black man gained social status, miscegenation inevitably followed. Freeing the Negro meant reprisals on white masters, murder, pillage, rape, and destruction. A slave revolt in 1831, led by a free Negro named Nat Turner, costing the lives of sixty-one white men, women, and children, served to emphasize the point. The argument from plain personal safety was a powerful one, and the spectre of the 'Black Terror' hung always over and behind pro-slavery talk.

As time passed the South produced a flood of pro-slavery literature proclaiming slavery not only necessary and justifiable, but the best possible system – a 'positive good' – that should be extended to the North and West, perhaps to white men everywhere. 'Free society', editorialized the

Richmond *Enquirer*, 'is in the long run an impracticable form of society.' John C. Calhoun pointed out that inequality is essential to progress, which is possible only when individuals desire to better their condition. A real democracy, like the Athenian, could exist only in a clearly stratified society; slavery therefore was 'the most safe and stable basis for free institutions in the world'. Furthermore, the conservatism of the established master class guaranteed social stability, since its interests lay in maintaining the status quo, while the classes that could make revolutions had no power to do so. The 'demoralized, insurrectionary' free society of the North contrasted ill with the 'harmony, union, and stability' of the slave-holding states. In the South there were no starving paupers, no 'wage slaves' to foment strikes, no 'free love' colonies. Senator Downs of Louisiana, echoing Carlyle's sneer at British abolitionism, challenged anyone 'to prove that the white laborers of the North are as happy, as contented, or as comfortable as the slaves of the South'. George Fitzhugh of Virginia, in *Sociology for the South* (1854) and *Cannibals All!* (1856) carried the 'positive good' argument to its ultimate conclusion. One sentence penned by Fitzhugh – 'Slavery is the natural and normal condition of the laboring man, whether black or white' – probably did more damage to the pro-slavery cause in the North than all that Garrison ever did or wrote. When war came Fitzhugh's words were used as concrete evidence of what a Southern victory might mean – white slaves in the North, as well as black ones in the South.

The pro-slavery argument achieved its purpose. One anti-slavery editor printed two quotations side by side in 1855. The first, from the Richmond *Enquirer* for 1832, called slavery 'a dark and growing evil'. The second, from the same paper for 1855, called it 'a natural and necessary and hitherto universal, hub, element, or institution of society'. The contrast, representing more than twenty years of agitation, illustrated the effective work of the Southern pro-slavery forces.

The Whigs elected Tippecanoe in 1840, but they got

Tyler too. When Harrison died suddenly, only a month after his inauguration, the succession passed to Vice-President John Tyler, a Democrat who happened to be in the Whig party chiefly because he hated Jackson. Tyler was a pro-slavery Virginian, a strong opponent of federal centralization, the tariff, the Bank, federally-financed internal improvements, and the rest of the Whig programme. A proud, stubborn man, Tyler immediately ran headlong into Henry Clay, the Whig leader. Since he either opposed or vetoed nearly every bill Clay and the Whigs supported, Tyler's entire cabinet (except for Secretary of State Webster) soon resigned in disgust. Clay himself left the Senate and retired to Kentucky to prepare himself for the presidential election of 1844, while Tyler was formally ejected from the Whig party. With the Whigs split, their congressional strength divided, and a President without a party in the White House, legislation on domestic issues came to a dead stop. The only real accomplishments of Tyler's administration were those of Daniel Webster.

Webster became Secretary of State at a time when relations with England were in a delicate state of balance. Lord Palmerston was always difficult for Americans to handle; it was a tribute to Webster and to Lord Ashburton, Palmerston's emissary, that Anglo-American relations remained relatively peaceful. But Webster had his hands full. The northeastern boundary between the United States and Canada had been in dispute since the Treaty of Paris; over it, in 1837, some Maine and Canadian lumberjacks fought the abortive 'Aroostook War', and the entire American-Canadian boundary was still vague in places, especially in the Oregon country. Ashburton came to Washington in 1841 to open negotiations for a settlement, finally fixing a satisfactory boundary as far west as Lake of the Woods.

But there followed immediately another incident. During the Mackenzie rebellion in Canada many Americans sympathized with the insurrectionists, sending them both volunteers and supplies. In 1837 the British seized and burned a small supply ship, the *Caroline*, and in the process killed a crew member. The *Caroline* affair stayed quiescent for three years, until a drunken Canadian named McLeod boasted in a New York saloon that he had been with the boarding party and had killed a seaman. McLeod was immediately arrested for murder, whereupon Palmerston in his usual forthright fashion informed the United States that since the boarding party had acted under official orders, hanging McLeod meant war. Again Webster spread oil on the waters, while McLeod, fortunately, was acquitted.

Less than a year later Webster was involved in another dispute with Britain. The slave trade had been illegal since 1808, but a good many 'blackbirders' still ran slaves into Southern ports. The British Navy took the lead in attempting to suppress them, stopping and searching suspicious-looking vessels. When some American ships were searched, protests poured into Washington. Though Webster and Ashburton worked out an agreement whereby both British and American squadrons shared the African coast patrol, the United States Navy never fully lived up to its agreement and many slave-runners filtered through. Much more serious was the *Creole* case. When American ships were forced into British West Indian ports by storm, any slaves aboard were usually declared free under British law. In 1841 the *Creole*, carrying slaves from Virginia to the Louisiana canefields, was seized by the slaves and sailed into Nassau, where they became free. Since the *Creole* case involved both mutiny and murder on the high seas, it became a complicated diplomatic issue. Webster and Ashburton could work out only an unofficial solution, but in 1853 the United States was awarded $110,000 in damages.

The Texas problem, however, overshadowed all else on the foreign and domestic fronts. The Texas country had been settled as early as 1821 by Americans attracted by free, fertile lands and by the liberal colonization policies of the Mexican government to which it belonged. Westward-moving Southerners from Missouri, Kentucky, and Tennessee swarmed into it in the late twenties, carrying cotton-culture and slavery with them; a few Germans, French, and

Northerners came too. However, friction between Texans and the Mexican government developed swiftly. Texas was not even a separate Mexican state; it had practically no political representation in Mexico City; it was a Protestant island in Catholic Mexico. In 1830 Mexico stopped immigration from the United States into the Texas area, armed the border, and suspended trade relations with the United States. Several times the American government unsuccessfully attempted to purchase Texas or parts of it.

In 1835 the Texans, smarting under Mexican rule, began a revolution which ended in 1836 with the proclamation of the Texas Republic. Santa Anna, Mexico's dictator, wiped out a small group of Texans at the Alamo, but the main body of the Texas army defeated him decisively at San Jacinto and made good their independence. The Washington government maintained a sympathetic neutrality throughout the revolution, although many Americans, including Andrew Jackson, favoured immediate annexation of the Republic to the United States. After some delicate diplomacy, since Mexico threatened war if Texas were annexed, Jackson on his last day of office recognized Texas as a Republic. There was a great deal of sentiment, nevertheless, for admitting it to the Union as soon as possible. The prospects of fresh land for cotton and new markets for American products were attractive, and it was assumed that absorbing Texas was simply part of America's 'manifest destiny' to expand to the Pacific.

'Man and woman were not more formed for union, by the hand of God, than Texas and the United States are formed for union by the hand of nature', wrote one newspaper editor. Since Texans were, after all, Americans by blood and heritage, they belonged under the American flag. There was also fear in official circles that if America did not annex Texas, Great Britain might accept it as a protectorate in defiance of the Monroe doctrine, thus establishing a second outpost on United States borders. On the other hand, others believed the entry of Texas into the Union meant another step in the extension of slave territory westward, with a corresponding shift in the congressional equilibrium between free and slave states. Texas, an area as large as Germany, might be divided into several states, all of them slave, completely upsetting the balance of power in Congress.

From 1836 to 1838 Texas, constantly threatened by Mexico, repeatedly requested annexation to the United States. In dire need of loans, trade agreements, and military protection, Texas emissaries travelled to Europe, where the British welcomed them, anticipating a lucrative trade in cotton. Tyler, under pressure from both Congress and the State Department, in 1842 again encouraged Texas to apply for admission, and the issue of Texas became important in the 1844 campaign, with the Northern Whigs in general opposing Texas' entry and the Southern Democrats favouring it. Tyler approved the annexation treaty, only to have the Senate reject it, but in his last weeks of office another resolution of annexation passed. Before the end of 1845 Texas became a state, but troubles with Mexico were only beginning.

The westward march of the 1830's and 40's brought 'manifest destiny' to other western lands. The Santa Fe Trail, running from Missouri to the Far Southwest, opened in 1822 and soon developed into a lively trade route, though the desert lands of Arizona and New Mexico attracted few permanent settlers. Americans began filtering into Mexican California in 1822, where millions of acres lay open around Sutter's Fort on the Sacramento river. Both Jackson and Tyler, recognizing California as a potential Texas, offered to buy the area from Mexico but met a flat refusal. The British too were interested in California, with a fair-sized colony established there by 1840. Although Lord Aberdeen ordered British agents in California to be 'entirely passive' in their conduct, the State Department feared that the British had designs on the west coast area. In 1842, in fact, Commodore ap Catesby Jones and a naval squadron captured Monterey and claimed California for the United States, under the mistaken impression that a war with Mexico had broken out and that the British Navy was about to seize California for the Crown. Jones had to give it back, of course, but the fate of California remained closely bound up with the United-States-Mexican-British relations until after the Mexican War.

The most difficult problem of westward expansion during the forties concerned Oregon. The Oregon Trail was an important trade route early in the century, after Lewis and Clark and the Astors once opened the area. The United States acquired the Oregon Territory from Spain in the Florida Treaty of 1819, while Britain acquired an adjoining area from Russia in 1825. The United States and British claims overlapped, but since there was no immediate necessity of settling the boundaries, the two countries made provisions for joint occupancy. During the 1830's friction appeared among American and British settlers, fur traders, and missionaries. There was excellent farming land to be had in the Oregon country, and in the early forties thousands of emigrants left Independence, Missouri, for the long trip over the 2,000-mile trail, leaving a plainly marked road of wagon ruts that can still be seen on the prairies. The Conestoga wagon of the Cumberland Road turned into the 'prairie schooner', a huge covered wagon built of three-inch planks, with wheels six feet high, drawn by four to twelve horses. A moving fort, capable of carrying complete households, strong enough to ford rivers, withstand rocks, and deflect Comanche or Kiowa arrows, the covered wagon carried America west.

The growth of population made it necessary to settle the boundary line quickly, for as early as 1843 an Oregon convention petitioned Congress for territorial status. The South favoured the petition, since the North might be placated by admitting Oregon as free territory in exchange for Texas as slave. With the Oregon and Texas questions thus tied directly to both 'manifest destiny' and political sectionalism, one great issue of the campaign of 1844 became, in Democratic phraseology, 'The reoccupation of Oregon and the reannexation of Texas.' The Oregon boundary must be 'fifty-four forty or fight!'

While the emigrants were pushing into the Far West the settlement of the Mississippi Valley was nearly completed. Ohio, Indiana, and Illinois, bordering the Ohio river, all entered the Union before 1818. Michigan came in in 1837, and the rest of the Northwest Territory followed rapidly. Iowa became a state in 1846, Wisconsin in 1848, and Minnesota achieved territorial status in 1849, entering in 1858. Florida, admitted in 1845, and Arkansas, added nine years earlier, filled in the area east of the Mississippi. West of the river the land sloped gradually upwards into a great plateau, ending abruptly at the barrier of the Rockies. This was dry and forbidding country, considered until the 1850's to be uninhabitable and impossible to farm. Iowa, it was generally believed, was the westernmost boundary of tillable land; beyond Iowa the country was good only for Indians.

Westward expansion, of course, met vigorous opposition from the Indian tribes, who saw land, forests, and game disappear before the white man's advance. The frontiersman usually considered the Indian simply something to be pushed aside; a savage, cruel, pagan, unreliable barbarian, the only good Indian was a dead one. The Indian, on the other hand, was often cheated, defrauded, and maltreated by the white man, who had little understanding of his civilization and less respect for his rights. There was constant frontier warfare between Indian and American throughout the nineteenth century, with scalpings, torture, pillage, and massacre common to both sides. The only solution to the Indian problem, as the Eastern tribes were slowly pushed toward the Mississippi, seemed to be to resettle them west of the river on the great plains, a move agreeable neither to the Eastern nor the Plains tribes. Monroe initiated the Indian removal policy, while Jackson continued it more energetically. Congress authorized the exchange of lands west of the Mississippi for Indian lands east of it, and the great resettlement began in the 1820's, not without bloodshed. The Seminole War in the Gulf South, which lasted nearly ten years, ended only when the Seminoles retreated into inaccessible swamps. The Black Hawk War of 1832, culminating in the merciless slaughter by militia of hundreds of defenceless Sacs, Foxes, and Winnebagoes, marked the last serious Indian resistance in the Mississippi Valley. By 1850 nearly all the tribes east of the river had been moved into a vast Indian Territory, stretching from the Dakotas to Texas, created for the purpose. After the Civil War, when the Plains territory beckoned to settlers, the conflict began all over again.

The election of 1844 hinged on the Texas issue. At the outset it seemed certain that Martin Van Buren would be the Democratic candidate and Henry Clay the Whig; neither, however, wished to declare himself unequivocally on Texas. Both issued vague letters on the subject early in the year; both advised against undue agitation of either the Texas or the slavery issues. Clay's refusal to take a stand did him no harm in the North, but Van Buren's caused consternation among Southern Democrats. 'I would to God I had been at Mr V. B.'s elbow when he closed his letter!' exclaimed old Andrew Jackson. A few days after his letter appeared, Clay received the Whig nomination. Later in the month the Democrats, however, rejected Van Buren in favour of James Knox Polk of Tennessee, a 'dark horse' unknown to most Democrats, and adopted a platform calling for the immediate occupation of both Texas and Oregon. The anti-slavery Liberty Party offered James G. Birney for the second time. Ironically, in the election that followed, Birney drew enough Whig votes to throw the victory to Polk, a slave-holder himself and the nominee of the Southern-dominated party.

James K. Polk was a political unknown, but he had served seven terms in the House as representative from Tennessee and he knew politics from the inside. He was a conscientious, hard-working man with a definite programme, and before he left office his entire programme had been completed. First of all, the Walker tariff of 1846 abandoned the protective principle, despite the efforts of the manufacturers to defeat it, and pacified the South. The Oregon boundary settlement of 1846 redeemed another campaign pledge, although the United States accepted the forty-ninth rather than the fifty-fourth parallel, and did not fight. At the same time Polk began negotiations to acquire California from Mexico, a transaction completed by the Mexican War.

As soon as the resolution annexing Texas passed Congress in the closing days of Tyler's administration, the Mexican minister left Washington in protest. Nevertheless, Polk appointed John Slidell of Louisiana as Ambassador to Mexico with orders to adjust the Texas boundary, to settle Texas claims against Mexico, and to purchase both New Mexico and California. Since the Mexican government had virtually broken relations with the United States, Slidell found no response whatever to his proposals; in fact, anti-American feeling ran high in Mexico City and the Mexican press talked loudly of war. To complicate matters further, Texas and Mexico had never settled an old boundary dispute – Texas claimed the Rio Grande as its southern boundary, while Mexico claimed it lay at the Neuces river. Polk, hoping to precipitate a settlement, ordered General Zachary Taylor and his army to occupy the north bank of the Rio Grande, an action regarded by the Mexicans as an invasion of their territory. On 24 April 1846 American dragoons and Mexican patrols clashed along the Rio Grande. Polk notified Congress that 'Mexico has passed the boundary of the United States, has invaded our territory, and shed American blood on American soil'. Congress immediately declared war.

The war with Mexico was not popular with all Americans. Northern Whigs charged the Democrats with fomenting war to gain popularity for the 1848 elections. Anti-slavery Northerners, bitter over the annexation of Texas, claimed the war was a slave-holder's conspiracy to extend slavery. Texas, wrote James Russell Lowell, was simply 'a bigger pen to cram slaves in'. Many Southern Whigs supported the war while denouncing Polk for starting it. Western Whigs and Southern Democrats welcomed it; more than half of the army volunteers came from the West, and some

Westerners in Congress urged the annexation of Mexico itself when the war was won. Nor was the war easy to win. The American armies were inexperienced, badly supplied and equipped, and inadequately trained.

Fortunately the Mexican armies were worse, so that General Taylor's little army, advancing into Mexico, defeated the Mexicans in quick and decisive engagements at Palo Alto and Resaca de la Palma. Within five months he occupied the important city of Monterey. Two other armies, under General John Wool and Colonel Doniphan, marched from Texas and New Mexico to join Taylor. Another, under the brilliant Colonel Stephen Kearney, captured Santa Fe in New Mexico and struck across the desert to California, joining the marines who had landed near San Diego. Once there, they found that American settlers under John C. Frémont had already seized control of California and had set up an independent 'Bear Flag Republic', which lasted only until Commodore Sloat and the Navy took formal possession of California for the United States.

The swiftness of his victories made Zachary Taylor a national hero. Taylor had no visible political affiliations, but there was Whig talk that 'Old Rough and Ready' was good presidential timber. Polk therefore decided to shift the plan of attack on Mexico with a drive at Mexico City by way of Vera Cruz. When a new commander was chosen for this expedition, Taylor was passed over, and since there were no really successful Democratic generals available, the choice fell on General Winfield Scott, a Whig but a dependable one. Scott's forces took Vera Cruz in early 1847. After six months of extremely hard fighting they captured Mexico City and hoisted the American flag over 'the halls of Montezuma'. By the terms of the Treaty of Guadaloupe Hidalgo, accepted in February of 1848, Mexico agreed to recognize the Rio Grande boundary and to cede New Mexico and California to the United States, including all lands between. The United States agreed to pay fifteen million dollars for the territory and to assume slightly more than three millions in claims.

California proved an immediate treasure. Before the Treaty of Guadaloupe Hidalgo could be ratified, a few flakes of gold were discovered in a mill-race on John Sutter's California ranch. The news spread swiftly, turning California from quiet ranching country into a roaring, crowded, hell-raising paradise for fortune hunters, singing

> Oh, Susanna, don't you cry for me,
> I'm off to California with my washbowl on my knee.

President Polk himself confirmed the reports of gold strikes in his annual message to Congress in 1848, while men raced by land and sea to wash millions out of the gulches and dig more from the hills. By May 1849 there were 5,000 wagons on the California trail; one observer on the Missouri river reported that 12,000 wagons had already passed the fords. Cholera, Indians, starvation, and the freezing cold of the mountain passes killed hundreds, but thousands got through. California grew from 12,000 population to 92,000 by late 1850, when it was admitted as a state, and by 1860 it had grown to 380,000. In the towns hastily thrown up – Poker Flat, Hangtown, Skunk Gulch, Red Dog, and others with unprintable names – eggs cost $10 a dozen, bread $25 a loaf, beds rented for $500 a month, and law meant nothing. Gamblers and prostitutes found easy prey in men who could make $100 a day with a shovel and a pan. The wealth that flowed out of California during the next few decades can be compared only with the flow from South America to sixteenth-century Spain; the Pacific Mail Company alone carried 122 million dollars worth of gold dust and bullion in its first four years of operation.

Northern anti-slavery men, who had bitterly opposed the Mexican War, determined that slavery must not be allowed to profit by it. As early as 1846 David Wilmot of Pennsylvania, an anti-slavery Democrat, added, to a bill appropriating money for the purchase of Mexican lands, an amendment designed to exclude slavery from any territory so acquired. In effect the 'Wilmot Proviso', even before the war, linked the slavery question with politics and westward expansion. It lost, but the issue was hotly debated for several years. Some, like Polk, suggested extending the old Missouri Compromise line of 36° 30′ to the Pacific Coast. Calhoun, speaking for the slave South, argued that the new West belonged to the federal government; since slavery was constitutionally legal anywhere in federal domain, it could not be banned from any new federal territory. Webster, speaking for New England, claimed that since California and Oregon had never had slavery, they were automatically free territories. Others, like Lewis Cass of Michigan, thought that the new territories themselves should be allowed to decide – a doctrine called 'squatter sovereignty', later dignified by the title 'popular sovereignty' and espoused by Stephen A. Douglas. After long debate, Oregon was admitted as a free state in early 1848. Iowa and Wisconsin, free states admitted in 1846 and 1848, were balanced by Texas and Florida, both slave states admitted in 1845. Southern leaders viewed the future, however, with trepidation. The North was fast outstripping the South in population, Minnesota and California were nearly ready for admission, and the rest of the Mexican cession was approaching territorial status. Would the new states be slave or free?

At the close of the Mexican War the United States experienced a tremendous outburst of national pride. The westward march to the Pacific was over. Within the short space of three years the nation gained Texas, Oregon, and huge areas from Mexico, a total of more than a million square miles. In foreign affairs, especially after the military triumphs in Mexico, diplomatic relations with Europe were marked by an aggressive self-confidence combined with an ill-concealed contempt for the 'effete monarchies' of the Old World. During the 1850's American ministers abroad were ordered to abandon the gold braid, lace, and other trappings of diplomatic livery and to appear in black evening clothes, 'the simple costume of an American citizen'. Twisting the tail of the British lion, or making sport of the 'perfumed lacqueys of France' became favourite political practice. Bellicose speeches in Congress, breathing defiance of Europe, were commonplace. Europe, it was assumed, was done for; there was a new world power on the scene.

The most important aspect of American foreign affairs during the Mexican War period involved the struggle with Britain for supremacy in South and Central America. The idea of a canal across the Isthmus of Panama was not new, but recent acquisition of great areas of land fronting on the Pacific made a short water route to the West a matter of great importance to the United States. In 1846 New Granada (Colombia) granted the United States transit rights in the Panama region, an agreement viewed with suspicion by the British Colonial Office. Since England had important colonial stakes in Jamaica, Honduras, and elsewhere in the area, American control of a vital canal meant not only American dominance over trade routes but an invitation to further Yankee expansion. British land and naval forces accordingly moved into the region to seize both the Pacific and Atlantic terminals of the proposed canal route. Conversations between the British Foreign Office and the State Department ended nowhere; neither nation would ever consent to a canal controlled by the other. 'These Yankees', Palmerston remarked, 'are most disagreeable Fellows to have to do with about any American question', a feeling heartily reciprocated in Washington.

After protracted discussions the Clayton-Bulwer Treaty of 1850 provided a grudging settlement. The two nations, it was agreed, would co-operate in constructing a canal and would neither fortify nor assume exclusive control over it; in addition, Britain promised (though in somewhat ambiguous terms) to stop its attempts to expand in Central America. Many Americans were dissatisfied with the settlement, since it seemed to block prospects of American expansion as well, but on the other hand, it did place an obstacle in the path of British imperialism and it did imply a tacit recognition of the underlying principles of the Monroe Doctrine. Nevertheless, clashes of interest between Britain and the United States continued to occur in Central

America, since both (whatever the implications of the 1850 Treaty) obviously did have imperialistic aims. Eventually Britain's attention was diverted by events in Europe, especially after its declaration of war on Russia in 1854. By 1860 British policy in Central and South America was much more pacific and less expansionist.

But the island of Cuba remained a tender spot. Spain, after the disastrous Central and South American revolutions, retained only Puerto Rico and Cuba among its once great Western possessions. The latter island, because of its wealth and strategic location, Spain was anxious to keep, although the United States had looked at it with interest since Jefferson's time. Not only did Cuba appear to be a highly desirable possession, but its occupation by France or Britain would be a major threat to American security. Spain received several assurances that the United States would assist her in resisting any attempt by another power to take Cuba, as well as several offers of purchase. Southerners were anxious to obtain the island as new slave territory to balance the free territories of the West; Democrats made frequent references to it in various campaign platforms. By the 1850's the Cuban question agitated politics considerably and relations with Spain were somewhat strained. The intervention of the Civil War distracted attention and possibly prevented open conflict.

The triple-headed question of slavery, sectionalism, and territorial expansion dominated the elections of 1848. The Democrats who nominated Lewis Cass of Michigan carefully avoided any mention of it in their campaign. The Whigs were even more careful. They adopted no recognizable platform whatever and nominated General Zachary Taylor on the basis of his military record, but as it happened, Taylor lived in Louisiana and owned slaves. For Vice-President they chose Millard Fillmore of New York State, an old-line Whig. With both major parties silent on the matter of slavery and its extension, a convention representing seventeen states met to found a third party, the Free

Soil Party, and to nominate Martin Van Buren. Although the new party was by no means predominantly abolitionist, its chief issue was the prevention of slavery in the new territories, expressed in its slogan, 'Free Soil, Free Speech, Free Labour, Free Men!' The election itself was not an exciting one, since only Free Soil candidates seemed willing to discuss the real issues. As it happened, the Free Soilers polled 300,000 votes, sent thirteen men to the House and two to the Senate, and by robbing Cass of votes in New York, threw that pivotal state into the Whig column and helped give Taylor the Presidency. The results showed no popular mandate on slavery. Cass carried eight free and seven slave states, Taylor seven free and eight slave, although Taylor's popular vote was less than Cass' and Van Buren's combined.

Zachary Taylor, born in Virginia but raised in Kentucky, took over the leadership of a disturbed and troubled nation in 1849. He had spent nearly his entire life in the army, had no real party ties, and little political experience. His cabinet, which contained three Southerners and no abolitionists, satisfied the South, which assumed that he would somehow keep political peace on the slavery question. Taylor, however, did not live up to expectations. The pressing question of whether or not slavery should be admitted into the new territories acquired from Mexico was still unsettled, and the application of California (and later Utah) for admission to the Union as a free state presented his administration with difficult problems. Taylor's answer was simple – allow the new states to decide for themselves – a solution that seemed to the South to be simply the Wilmot Proviso in new form.

The Congress that met in December 1849 to wrestle with these problems was so evenly divided between Whig and Democrat that the handful of Free Soilers actually held the balance of power. It was an able Congress, including such men as Clay, Calhoun, Webster, Douglas, Jefferson Davis, Salmon P. Chase, William H. Seward, and Alexander Stephens. Sectional feeling was intense. Taylor's stand on slavery in the West aroused immediate, bitter opposition from the Southerners. Into the breach stepped aged Henry Clay of Kentucky, 'the Great Compromiser', to attempt once more to adjust the differences between North and South.

In January of 1850 Clay introduced into the Senate a series of eight resolutions (later packaged into an omnibus bill) designed to effect a reasonable solution to the problem of slavery and its extension. Among these resolutions the most important involved admitting California as a free state, placing no restrictions on slavery in the rest of the Mexican cession, assuming the pre-annexation debts of Texas, and instituting a new and more stringent Federal fugitive slave law. It was this, said Clay, or dissolution of the Union, possibly open war, for he believed that the states were 'twenty-odd furnaces in full blast', ready to erupt. Disunion was closer than Congress knew. Everyone should 'conjure at the edge of the precipice before the fearful and disastrous leap'.

In the eight months of debate over Clay's resolutions that followed, the entire problem of slavery – of its continuation and expansion, of sectional versus national interest, of federal versus state power – was thoroughly explored, not without heat. Calhoun of South Carolina, as usual, spoke for the South. Too ill to stand and less than a month from his grave, Calhoun sat glowering in the Senate while Mason of Virginia read his last great speech, an uncompromising demand for concessions from the North. The only way to mollify the South, he said, was to cease agitating against slavery, allow the Southern states equal rights in territorial expansion, recognize slavery as a permanent, national institution, and enforce the fugitive slave laws to the hilt. Failing this, 'Let the States . . . agree to separate and part in peace.'

Three days later Daniel Webster, the foremost statesman of New England, rose to defend the North against Calhoun's charges and to plead for union, compromise, concession, sanity, peace, a speech that shocked and angered the abolitionists who had long considered him their champion.

William Seward of New York and Salmon Chase of Ohio, representing the anti-slavery forces, quickly replied, answered in turn by Jefferson Davis of Mississippi, whose stand was as bitterly uncompromising as Calhoun's. As the debate wore on, the tide gradually turned toward Clay. Tempers cooled; Calhoun's death removed the leader of the South; Taylor's death (probably from typhoid) in July of 1850 brought Millard Fillmore, who favoured compromise, into the presidency. Clay's bill failed, but the essential issues it contained were finally incorporated in another bill presented by Stephen Douglas of Illinois, passed, and signed by Fillmore. California came in as a free state. The matter of slavery in the Mexican cession was left for the territories themselves to decide. Slavery was abolished in the District of Columbia. A drastic new federal fugitive slave law was approved. The Compromise of 1850 was over. It settled nothing, satisfied neither North nor South, and widened the sectional breach, but it did delay the 'inevitable conflict'.

Southern leaders found little to cheer about in the settlement. In exchange for an unpopular and unworkable fugitive slave law they lost the West and the balance of power in Congress, for the free states now outnumbered the slave, sixteen to fifteen. Georgia, Alabama, Mississippi, and South Carolina called state conventions to consider the advisability of secession, led by hot-headed men like Davis, Toombs of Georgia, and Yancey of Alabama. In South Carolina the secessionists actually had a majority, but the dispute simmered down without decisive action.

At the same time the new fugitive slave law angered many Northerners who hitherto had been cool to abolitionism and gave the abolitionists a real propaganda weapon. The law denied jury trial to the escaped slaves, barred their testimony, ordered Federal and state officials to aid in their capture, and provided stiff fines and imprisonment for those who aided escaping slaves. The harshness of the law seemed a taunt and an ultimatum to the North. 'It turns us all into slave catchers', cried one Ohio newspaper, and even mild-mannered Ralph Waldo Emerson was moved to exclaim, 'I will not obey it, by God!' John Ramsdell, a New Hampshire tanner, phrased it in doggerel:

> What, bend the knee to Southern rule?
> What, cringe and crawl to Southern clay?
> And be the base, the simple tool
> Of hell-begotten slavery?

One of the irritations felt most strongly in the South was Northern aid to those fugitive slaves who successfully escaped into free territory. Not only was the loss of a slave financially serious in itself – a good strong slave might be worth $2,000 – but his flight was a direct refutation of the claim that slaves were happy and contented labourers for kindly masters. Since the Constitution and the Fugitive Slave Law of 1793 both required the return of fugitives, assistance to an escaped Negro was punishable by law. But Northern abolitionists and anti-slavery sympathizers, appealing to the 'higher laws' of morality, retorted that the violation of existing state and federal fugitive slave laws was a Christian duty. Southerners, understandably sensitive about runaway Negroes, searched constantly for ways of plugging loopholes in the border-state areas. The 'patrol' system, whereby organized groups patrolled Southern roads and towns looking for wandering slaves, was only a partial answer to the problem. The only solution seemed to be more stringent and carefully-enforced Federal laws.

Northern free Negroes had helped runaway slaves since the mid eighteenth century, but it was not until after 1830 that Northern white abolitionists joined them. Pennsylvania Quakers founded the first more-or-less organized white group pledged to aid fugitives, and after the formation of abolitionist societies in the 1830's and 40's a network of routes and stations for an 'underground railway' appeared in Indiana, Illinois, and particularly in Ohio, with Canada as the terminal. In New England another system centred on Boston, where stowaway slaves arrived on boats from Southern ports. After 1850 abolitionist agents, white and black, worked in the South, organizing slaves into groups and furnishing them with maps and instructions. Josiah Henson, Mrs Stowe's model for Uncle Tom, escaped with his family to Canada in 1830 with just such instructions, and on later forays of his own into the South brought out 118 Negroes through Ohio. Those who were caught assisting runaways and who were prosecuted under the new Federal law were hailed as martyrs in the abolitionist press, while government officials in several Northern states deliberately disobeyed or impeded its operation. Despite the harsh provisions of the 1850 statute, the 'Underground Railroad' expanded swiftly. Abolitionist societies boasted in 1851 that a slave could be run from any Southern border state to Canada in forty-eight hours or less; several newspapers openly published route maps, travel instructions, passwords, and locations of over-night stops. It is impossible to estimate accurately the number of Negroes who escaped by the underground route, but it is clear that while the 'railroad' probably did not materially weaken slavery, it did a great deal to create ill-feeling in both North and South. In the North it made the runaway slave an object of public sympathy and his 'con-ductor' an heroic fighter for liberty. In the South the existence of a well-organized conspiracy to defeat the Federal Law seemed simply another proof of the North's determination to destroy the South's vitally important labour system.

Yet the Compromise of 1850 represented quite accurately the temper of American public opinion. The nation at large was tired of argument, accusation, and acrimony. Business was good, farming profitable; wages high, industry pros-perous, and those who profited from good times wanted no apple carts upset. In the elections of 1852 the air was full of olive branches. Early in 1851, before the party conventions met, fifty-four Congressmen of both major parties signed a pledge to oppose any presidential candidate who refused to accept the Compromise of 1850 as the final statement on the slavery question. At convention time the Democrats, after a deadlock among Cass, Douglas, Marcy of New York, and

George Buchanan of Pennsylvania, compromised on Franklin Pierce of New Hampshire, an undistinguished but respectable candidate; not even Nathaniel Hawthorne, who wrote the official campaign biography, could make Pierce a great man. The Democratic platform hopefully promised to 'resist all attempts at renewing in Congress or out of it, the agitation of the slavery question'. The Whigs felt much the same. After pledging the party to a 'discountenancing' of the slavery question, their convention nominated General Winfield Scott, who said that he personally agreed to the Compromise but who was known to have powerful friends in anti-slavery circles. The Free Soilers, who roundly condemned the Compromise, nominated John P. Hale. The campaign was lethargic and uninteresting, since both Scott and Pierce avoided embarrassing questions. The election, a fairly close one in terms of the popular vote, gave Pierce a large margin in electoral votes.

The result seemed to show that the nation preferred Pierce and quiet to Scott and uncertainty or to Hale and agitation. The new President, in his inaugural address, put it very well by saying, 'I fervently hope that the question (*of slavery*) is at rest, and that no sectional or ambitious or fanatical excitement may again threaten the durability of our institutions or obscure the light of our prosperity.' It was a false hope. In 1852 Harriet Beecher Stowe's *Uncle Tom's Cabin* appeared, selling 300,000 copies in ten months. When Anthony Burns, an escaped slave, was captured in Boston and marched to the train in irons, the streets were lined with stony-faced, silent Yankees, flags at half-mast, church bells tolling. The North knew what the fugitive slave law meant. Politicians might 'discountenance' the slavery question, but it was there, and the people knew.

CHAPTER 24

THE EMERGENCE OF LINCOLN

FRANKLIN PIERCE declared in his inaugural address that the Compromise measures of 1850 were 'strictly constitutional' and 'unhesitatingly to be put into effect'. In an attempt to divert public attention from the slavery question, he suggested the 'acquisition of certain possessions not within our jurisdiction', that is, the Caribbean and South American regions. Pierce's cabinet, composed chiefly of Southerners, was as favourable to imperialistic expansion as it was to slavery, while Pierce apparently wished to make the purchase of Cuba the outstanding achievement of his administration. However, the only result of his programme was the purchase of a small slice of Mexican land south of the Gila River, the 'Gadsden Purchase', to provide a better route for a future railroad to California. In the Far East, American expansionism was more successful. Commodore Perry visited Japan in 1854 with the largest fleet ever gathered by the U.S. Navy in the Pacific, and the Japanese, impressed by the display, agreed to open two ports to American ships, beginning what soon became a highly lucrative trade.

Despite all the efforts to find a substitute issue, the slavery problem would not die. Northern abolitionists attacked the expansionist policies of the Democrats as further evidence of a Southern plot to add more slavery territory to the Union. Fugitive slaves, captured under the provisions of the 1850 Compromise, made headlines in Northern newspapers; churchmen hotly sermonized on the morality of slavery; the 'underground railroad' grew in size and efficiency; several Northern states passed 'personal liberty laws' designed to nullify the Federal acts. It was evident too that initiative in politics was passing to new leaders who had little of the spirit of compromise that marked the old. Van Buren was retired, Calhoun dead, Clay and Webster both to die in

1852. In the North, men like Seward of New York, Charles Sumner of Massachusetts, Salmon P. Chase and Joshua Giddings of Ohio went to Congress, all uncompromising anti-slavery or free-soil men. From the South came men like Jefferson Davis of Mississippi, Robert Toombs of Georgia, and Barnwell Rhett of South Carolina – pro-slavery, states' rights, anti-Northern firebrands. There were, of course, peacemakers (usually called 'doughfaces') such as Marcy of New York and Cass of Michigan, but their influence was never strong.

The responsibility for reopening the slavery question in Congress must rest on the shoulders of Stephen A. Douglas, the Democratic Senator from Illinois. Douglas, known affectionately in his home state as 'The Little Giant' or 'Steam Engine in Britches', was a New Englander who came West to seek and find his political fortune in Illinois. An ambitious, shrewd, audacious little man, Douglas accurately represented the rough and aggressive democracy of the frontier country. He was especially interested in developing the West; he had already won large land grants for railroad building and had helped to make Chicago the chief Western rail centre. What really appealed to him, however, was the prospect of a railroad linking Chicago with the Pacific coast; but before it could be built the Indian lands west of Iowa had to be organized into territories, surveyed, and put up for sale.

Douglas boldly determined this should be done. In January 1854, after receiving promises of support from Pierce, Douglas introduced into Congress a bill to organize the area west of the Missouri and Iowa into territories in which 'all questions pertaining to slavery' would be 'left to the decision of the people residing therein' – the old 'squatter sovereignty' principle, now called 'popular sovereignty'. The area, to be divided into Kansas and Nebraska, lay north of the Missouri Compromise line of 1820 and was therefore not open to slavery. Douglas appended to his bill an amendment declaring the Missouri Compromise inoperative, superseded by the principles of the Compromise of 1850. He knew exactly what he was doing. He did not particularly like slavery, nor did he have much sympathy for abolitionists or free-soilers. At the same time he believed sincerely in the people's right to decide matters for themselves, and he believed even more strongly in western expansion. Reopening the slavery question was in his opinion a small price to pay for a transcontinental railroad. What Douglas did not understand was the tremendous emotional charge generated by the issue of slavery and its extension.

The Kansas-Nebraska bill passed Congress in March 1854. Pro-slavery Southerners were overjoyed, seeing in it a magnificent opportunity to add one or possibly two slavery states to the Union. Anti-slavery Northerners and Northwest free-soilers regarded it as a deliberate betrayal of the Missouri Compromise and an open attempt to introduce slavery into the Northwest. The bill split the Democratic party sharply into pro- and anti-Nebraskans and left the Whigs hopelessly divided. Douglas was bitterly denounced in Northern pulpits as a modern Judas; angry mass meetings formed in major Northern cities, while Douglas admitted that he could probably travel from Washington to Chicago by the light of fires built to burn him in effigy. The South had won again, and as Horace Greeley wrote in his *Tribune*, Douglas made more abolitionists overnight than Garrison could have made in fifty years. Southern Congressmen in their jubilation paid no attention to old Sam Houston croaking from Texas that the bill was 'the worst thing for the South that has ever transpired since the Union was formed'.

The passage of the bill simply moved the struggle over slavery from Congress to Kansas; nature and the Missouri Compromise might have intended the area to be free, but the pro-slavery men had no intention of allowing it to stay free. Settlers from Missouri, Kentucky, Mississippi, and Tennessee poured into Kansas, and by 1854 they had organized it as a territory. In early 1855 they held elections for the territorial legislature, with armed bands stationed at key centres to see that the winning candidates were slavery sympathizers. Although the territorial governor declared many elections fraudulent, no anti-slavery men were elected and the new legislature immediately enacted laws protecting slavery in Kansas.

In the meantime settlers from abolitionist New England arrived, financed by the New England Emigrant Aid Society and church groups. Henry Ward Beecher, the great Massachusetts preacher, urged that all emigrants be equipped with rifles (henceforth known as 'Beecher's Bibles'), and the New Englanders were ready for a fight. Late in 1855 the anti-slavery men called a convention at Topeka, drafted a new state constitution forbidding slavery, and elected a new governor and legislature. A few months later a band of pro-slavery men sacked the town of Lawrence, anti-slavery headquarters. In retaliation John Brown led a raid on the settlement at Ossawatomie, murdering five pro-slavery men in cold blood – a deed which made him a hero in New England. With Kansas teetering on the brink of civil war, Pierce finally appointed a new governor, John Geary, who called in Federal troops to restore order, but not before more than two hundred lives were lost.

The Topeka constitution was submitted to Congress for ratification in 1855, with a petition for statehood which Pierce angrily rejected. The ensuing debates over the admission of Kansas were perhaps the most rancorous ever heard in Congress. The climax came in 1856, after Senator Charles Sumner of Massachusetts completed a violent tirade against the South, bristling with insults and personal allusions. Two days later Congressman Preston Brooks of South Carolina approached Sumner, who was seated at his Senate desk, and brutally beat him into insensibility with a heavy cane. Sumner's injuries kept him out of the Senate for two years, during which time Massachusetts proudly refused to replace him. Brooks resigned from the House, was promptly re-elected, and was showered with gifts of canes from applauding Southerners. Many Southern moderates immediately disowned him, but to the North he remained 'Bully' Brooks.

Douglas' assertion that his legislation would take the slavery issue out of national politics could have hardly been more wrong.

After the passage of the Kansas-Nebraska bill the pattern of politics changed with amazing swiftness. With both the Whig and Democratic parties irrevocably split, the way was open for a new anti-slavery party. In February of 1854 an anti-Nebraska meeting at Ripon, Wisconsin, recommended the organization of a party opposed to the extension of slavery, suggesting that the name of Jefferson's old party, 'Republican', be appropriated for it. In July the Republican party actually came into existence at Jackson, Michigan, asking for repeal of the Kansas-Nebraska bill, abolition of slavery in the District of Columbia, and repeal of the federal fugitive slave law. 'Republican', 'Independent', and 'Anti-Nebraska' parties showed considerable strength in the elections of 1854, carrying the state of Ohio and sending forty members to Congress. Old Free Soilers and Liberty men flocked to the new party in the West and Horace Greeley's powerful New York *Tribune* supported it in the East.

The Republican party was unusual in that it originated almost spontaneously. No single leader or set of politicians formed it, as Jefferson shaped the first Republicans, Jackson the Democrats, or Clay the Whigs. The solution was there, and Douglas' bill chilled it into crystallizing. Although abolitionists joined the party in droves, they never constituted a dominant element in its councils; as Woodrow Wilson later observed, the Republican party got 'its radical and aggressive spirit from the abolitionists, whom it received without liking'. The extension of slavery, not its abolition, was the Republicans' real issue, based in turn on the deeper problem of the disposition of Western lands. That the party outlived slavery so long is good evidence of the fact that the slavery issue was less important to it than the aim of keeping the 160-acre western homesteads safe for free farmers, not for huge plantations. Republican issues were Free Soil issues, not Whig. At the same time, labour contributed a substantial amount of support to the new party. The fear of nationalizing slavery, and the necessity of maintaining a free labour system in the North, attracted many elements from labour's ranks.

Political waters were further muddied by the appearance of the American or 'Knownothing' party, a nativist, anti-Catholic movement originating in Eastern urban centres, strong wherever Irish and German immigrants were numerous. An odd mixture of secret society and political organization, the party got its name from the reply supposedly given by its members to questioners, 'I know nothing'. It drew a great deal of support from Eastern Whigs, and except for its appeals to racial and religious prejudices, looked much like the old Whig party. Knownothingism also had a fair following in the South, where it was assumed that since immigration strengthened the Northern industrialist system, it therefore constituted a secondary threat to slavery.

Whigs and Democrats alike watched the election year of 1856 with interest. The Whig party was hopelessly split and rapidly dying; the Democratic party, controlled by the South, was steadily losing Northern support; the bigotry of the Knownothings repelled intelligent men both North and South. The new Republican party seemed to offer a haven for homeless anti-Nebraskans; Seward of New York (an anti-slavery Whig) and Chase of Ohio (a leading Democrat) both swung over to it. With the border warfare in Kansas and Brooks' assault on Sumner fresh in the public mind, the young party met to evolve a platform and choose a candidate for the forthcoming campaign.

They picked John C. Frémont, soldier, explorer, politician, popular hero, a man who possessed, remarked one contemporary, 'all the qualities of genius except ability'. Their platform called for the admission of Kansas as a free state, denounced the Kansas-Nebraska bill, opposed the extension of slavery, advocated a railroad to the Pacific, and asked appropriations for internal improvements – a good Western platform. The Democrats passed over Pierce to choose James Buchanan of Pennsylvania, a conservative old-line politician who had been absent as minister to

England during the Kansas-Nebraska argument and therefore was not on record about it. The Knownothings nominated ex-President Fillmore, a choice with which the pitifully small remnant of the Whigs concurred.

The Republicans campaigned in 1856 almost solely on the issue of 'Bleeding Kansas' and the extension of slavery. George Fitzhugh's remark that slavery was the 'natural condition' of the labouring classes received due emphasis, and in hundreds of enthusiastic rallies Republicans sang (to the tune of *The Marseillaise*):

> Arise, arise ye brave
> And let your war-cry be,
> Free speech, free press, free soil, free men –
> Frémont and liberty.

The Democrats stressed the necessity of soft-pedalling slavery, holding the Union together, preventing a division of section against section, keeping peace between North and South. Despite internal dissension, the Democrats won. With a middle-of-the-road candidate they could still win an election, but what of the future?

Frémont polled a million votes, carried all but five of the states north of Mason and Dixon's line, and showed considerable strength in the five he lost. Actually the Republicans came closer to uniting Northeast and Northwest than ever before – and this in less than two years of party activity. The million Frémont votes, in Southern eyes, posed a direct threat to Southern interests; a Frémont victory, wrote Rufus Choate, would have meant 'a hostile government' representing 'a vast region of States organized on Anti-slavery'. 'Almost as a mass', said one Southern editor, 'the North has gone for him, and gone for him too on a platform the carrying out of the principles of which would inflict immeasurable degradation upon the Southern people . . .' After 1856 there was real fear in the South and much talk of secession if the election of 1860 should go against them.

Neither the doctrine of secession nor its corollary doctrine of states' rights were new to American political history. Their genesis lay in the theory that the states have certain rights preserved to them by the Constitution, which defines the spheres of power belonging to the nation and to the states. The base of the Southern argument rested on the proper construction of the language of the Constitution, particularly that of the Tenth Amendment, which 'reserved to the States respectively or to the people' those powers 'not delegated to the United States by the Constitution, nor prohibited by it to the States'. The problem was, simply, the old political puzzle of aligning unified Federal control with state sovereignty. The Revolutionary War was fought in part because the British government failed to find a satisfactory solution to the same problem; the Articles of Confederation provided only a temporary and unsatisfactory answer; the Constitution attempted to solve it in a different manner, but no more clearly. Leaders of both states' rights and Federalistic schools of thought could (and still can) find evidence in the Constitution to support their opposing views. The question was, in 1861, is the nation a confederation of states, with certain sovereign rights guaranteed to each; or is it a sovereign union of states, with the central government holding final authority over its disparate units? The Civil War decided by force of arms what the Constitution meant; in a broad sense it was fought between two interpretations of that document.

The question of states' rights and secession frequently appeared in American politics before 1861. The Virginia and Kentucky Resolutions of 1798–9, aimed at the Alien and Sedition Acts, affirmed that the Union was a compact of sovereign states whose rights could not be contravened by a federal government that exceeded its constitutional limitations. The Hartford Convention of 1814, as we have seen, in protest against the War with Britain, reaffirmed the states' rights tradition and flavoured it with talk of secession from the Union. The Georgia legislature of 1827, during its dispute with the federal government over Indian policies, ordered state officials to refuse to honour any mandate of the Supreme

Court that violated Georgia's 'sovereign rights'. Calhoun refined and developed the doctrine during the nullification troubles of 1832–3, though the result of his tangle with Jackson seemed to indicate that an aggressive Federal government would always be able to prevent a state from exercising its sovereignty in conflict with federal law. But the South Carolina legislature in 1831 uncovered the kernel of the secession idea with its announcement that 'this is a confederacy of sovereign states, and each may withdraw from the confederacy when it chooses'. The next logical step was to substitute secession for nullification as a last-resort answer to Federal 'tyranny'. From 1830 to 1861 justifying this substitution became the primary task of the Southern proponents of the states' rights doctrine.

For twenty-five years before his death in 1850, the chief political philosopher of states' rights was Senator John C. Calhoun of South Carolina. Calhoun, like John Marshall, was a product of the Southern frontier, born in the same county that produced Daniel Boone and Andrew Jackson. He was no planter aristocrat, but he respected the institution of slavery, considered it an absolute necessity for the South, and was convinced that it could not be abolished without utterly ruining Southern life. After 1830 he apprehensively watched the spread of abolitionism in the North, the rapid growth of Northern wealth and population, and the increasing difficulty by which a balance of political power between slave and free states was maintained. The day might come, and soon, Calhoun prophesied, when Northern and Northwestern free states obtained a congressional majority and destroyed slavery by federal action; indeed, Northern abolitionists frankly admitted that such was their aim. The problem became then, to Calhoun, how to protect the Southern minority against the Northern majority within the framework of the American political system.

Calhoun's *Disquisition on Government*, published in 1850, together with his numerous speeches in Congress, contained his answer. The majority, he reasoned, must inevitably control the minority in any democratic state; the minority, consequently, must have some method of safeguarding its rights and interests. Only by appealing to the states'-rights doctrine could the South protect itself against a Federal government controlled by a Northern majority. By conceding the sovereign rights of states, the Federal government therefore lost the power to encroach on these rights; the states'-rights doctrine gave the state the power (as it had in the nullification controversy) to declare an act of the Federal government inoperative. But what if the Federal government refused to recognize the state's right to void such an act, as it had in the nullification argument? Then, in Calhoun's view, there remained only the final step of secession from the Union. The parting might be peaceful or not, but it must be a parting. Thus, in 1850, Calhoun addressed the North, 'If you are unwilling we should part in peace, tell us so, and we shall know what to do, when you reduce the question to submission or resistance.'

Calhoun's theories were expanded and augmented after his death by an articulate and militant South, conscious of its minority status and fearful for its rights in a world that seemed to be running against them. As the tempo of the argument over slavery quickened, more and more Southerners were forced to stand with South Carolina and Calhoun. Southern 'fire-eaters' like Rhett of South Carolina, Yancey of Alabama, and Ruffin of Virginia hammered at secession, emphasizing the confederate nature of the Union and the absolute right of any state to secede from it; they envisioned a new Confederacy of seceded states, where they might construct an empire on the pattern of Calhoun's Athenian democracy and Fitzhugh's aristocratic society, founded on cotton and slavery. As early as 1856 Preston Brooks advised the South to 'tear the Constitution of the United States, trample it underfoot, and form a Southern Confederacy'.

The economic and political implications of slavery had much to do with the South's position. There was, however, always a racial factor involved – fear of the Negro as a social, political, and economic competitor; miscegenation, revolt, riot; destruction of a whole traditional pattern of race relations – which partially explains the willingness of a non-slave-holding majority in the South to consider slavery as absolutely essential and to secede from the Union if it were threatened. The South must be kept a white man's country, the Negro kept in his place. Slavery, it must not be forgotten, was among other things a device to guarantee white supremacy.

The South held the conviction after 1850, true or false, that sooner or later the North and Northwest intended to use the power of the Federal government to destroy its peculiar institution and to ruin its social and economic system, regardless of Southern rights. States' rights and secession were the last shots in the Southern locker, last defences against Federal authority. By 1861 the South agreed that the time had come to use them; only Kentucky, a border state, chose a neutral course. The Mississippi convention that voted that state out of the Union summarized admirably the Southern position:

We must either submit to degradation and the loss of property worth four billions of money, or we must secede from the Union framed by our fathers to secure this as well as every other species of property. For far less cause than this our fathers separated from the Crown of England.

James Buchanan was ill-equipped to take over the leadership of a confused and divided nation. Sixty-five years old, he was a weak and uncertain man, firmly convinced that the Union must be preserved but that the only way to preserve it was to give the South its way. He spoke optimistically in his inaugural of a quick settlement of the slavery issue – let the people speak, and the majority will prevail – and evinced vague hopes that a solution might soon be worked out 'speedily and finally'. Two days after his inauguration the Supreme Court provided a solution, but one that threw a whole new light on the controversy.

The Dred Scott decision, finally handed down after years of litigation, gave the Republican party a new issue. Dred

Scott, a St Louis Negro, had been sold in 1833 by one Elizabeth Blow to an army surgeon, Dr John Emerson. Emerson took Scott with him during brief residences in Illinois (a free state) and Wisconsin territory (where slavery was forbidden under the Missouri Compromise) and returned to Missouri (slave territory) in 1838. On Emerson's death Scott became Mrs Emerson's property, but she remarried and moved to Massachusetts, whereupon Scott, an apparently shiftless worker, fell back upon the charity of the Blow family. At the insistence of the Blows Scott sued for his freedom on the ground that his residence in free territory ended his status as a slave. He lost the first case and won a second. Meanwhile Mrs Emerson (now Mrs Chaffee) transferred Scott's ownership to her brother, who wanted to use him as a test case. Scott therefore claimed Missouri citizenship and sued his new owner, a citizen of New York, for his freedom. Eventually the case came to the United States Supreme Court.

The majority decision, written by Chief Justice Roger Taney, declared that Scott as a Negro slave was not a citizen of Missouri nor of the United States; hence he could neither sue nor be sued in federal courts. Scott's visits to free territory north of the Missouri Compromise line had not made him free; the Compromise was, in Taney's opinion, unconstitutional in that it denied protection to property (and slaves were property) in that part of the Louisiana Purchase. Though Justices Curtis and McLean dissented, Southerners could hardly have asked more from the Court, for Taney and the majority accepted the Southern position completely. The entire nation was open to slavery; though the decision was denounced as 'wilful perversion', 'an atrocious doctrine' and 'the last victory needed by the Slave Power', still it stood, with a President to enforce it. The Dred Scott decision appalled the North. If the Missouri Compromise, a law of Congress, could not exclude slavery from a territory, how then could a territorial legislature, which derived its authority from Congress, exclude it? What became of 'popular sovereignty'?

Shortly after the Scott decision Buchanan sent a new Governor, Robert Walker of Mississippi, to bring order out of chaos in Kansas. Walker called an election of delegates for a constitutional convention, but the free-state settlements, suspicious of a Mississippian, refused to participate. As a result, the overwhelmingly pro-slave convention at Lecompton drafted a pro-slavery constitution and submitted it to the people for ratification. However, taking no chances, the convention had the ballots marked in such a manner that a vote *yes* meant Kansas would definitely be a slave state and a *no* meant that slavery *as it existed* in Kansas 'would in no manner be interfered with'. Recognizing the ruse, the free-staters refused to vote and the pro-slavery constitution passed. However, the free-state men did vote in the following elections for the legislature and elected a majority. This legislature resubmitted the Lecompton constitution to the people, but this time the pro-slave men refused to vote.

Buchanan, convinced that elections and votes solved nothing in Kansas, recalled Walker and submitted the pro-slavery Lecompton constitution to Congress, urging its acceptance. It passed the Senate, but failed in the House. Meanwhile, Buchanan's course of action in the Kansas affair was more than Stephen Douglas could swallow. He believed deeply and sincerely in the principle of popular sovereignty. The mishandling of it in Kansas, added to Buchanan's obvious pro-slavery favouritism, angered him. Breaking with the administration took courage, since it also meant loss of favour in the Democratic South, but Douglas took the step. 'By God,' he said, 'I made James Buchanan, and by God, I will unmake him!' Douglas therefore opposed the Democratic hierarchy with all the vigour he possessed, and for his stand on Kansas he was promptly read out of the party. Since he was up for re-election in 1858, his entire political future was in jeopardy.

Yet at the same time Douglas found many allies among Northern Democrats and even among Republicans. Horace Greeley in the East, alert for leaders, considered Douglas a potential Republican and advised party leaders in Illinois that it might be wise not to oppose him for re-election; others spoke guardedly of him as a Republican presidential candidate in 1860. But Illinois Republicans regarded Douglas as a congenital Democrat and did not like his 'popular sovereignty' principle at all. As one of them said, it was asking too much 'to now surrender to Judge Douglas . . ., to quietly let him step foremost in our ranks and make us all take back seats'. So the Illinois Republicans prepared to enter the campaign, choosing Abraham Lincoln of Springfield to run against him. Lincoln was a worthy opponent and Douglas knew it. 'He is the best stump speaker, with his droll ways and dry jokes, in the West', said Douglas when he heard of Lincoln's candidacy. 'He is as honest as he is shrewd, and if I beat him, my victory will be hard won.'

Abraham Lincoln was well known in Illinois. Born in 1809 in a crude log hut in Kentucky (a few miles from Jefferson Davis' birthplace) as a boy he moved with his improvident father to Indiana and later to Illinois, growing up on the hard, rough, poverty-stricken frontier. Self-educated, primarily by thorough reading of the Bible, Shakespeare, Blackstone, Euclid, and the English classics, he had behind him when he entered politics an undistinguished career as farm-hand, storekeeper, flatboatman, and clerk. Lincoln's family, like most poor frontier families, favoured Jackson, but young Abraham, an admirer of Henry Clay, came into politics as a Whig. Shortly after his arrival at New Salem, Illinois, he ran for the state legislature and lost, but won at a second attempt and served several terms. At the age of twenty-seven he became Whig floor leader in the Illinois House. Meanwhile he read law, entered the bar, and married Mary Todd, an ambitious and comparatively wealthy young woman with a strong belief in his talents. In 1847 he was elected to Congress for one term as a Whig.

From 1849 to 1854 Lincoln lived in virtual retirement, practising law, searching unsuccessfully for a way back into politics. For him it was, without doubt, a period of deep frustration, for he had set his mind on a political career and as his law partner Herndon said, 'His ambition was a little engine that knew no rest.' During the debates over slavery Lincoln laboriously threaded his way through the issues and puzzled out his solutions, disentangling the strands of argument with his clear, precise mind. An avid reader of newspapers and an inveterate keeper of scrapbooks, he constantly traced and tested public opinion on the streets, in the press, in the courts, on the law circuit. By the mid-fifties Lincoln was probably one of the best-informed men in the nation on political matters.

It took Lincoln a long time to make up his mind on slavery. In the early fifties he adopted a position much like that of the Free Soilers. 'The whole nation', he wrote at the time, 'is interested that the best use shall be made of these Territories. We want them for the homes of white people. This they cannot be, to any considerable extent, if slavery shall be planted within them.' He was not an abolitionist, and took pains to say that he was not; he recognized the constitutional right of slave-holders to hold property, and never advocated the abolition of slavery in areas where it existed. But in his careful analysis of contemporary issues he became convinced that slavery, unless its spread were prevented, would become nation-wide, and, as Calhoun and Fitzhugh prophesied, eventually engulf the white labourer. Not until 1854 did Lincoln publicly denounce slavery on moral grounds, condemning it as 'a monstrous injustice'. Not until then did he decide that the institution threatened the democratic tradition he believed in, that the alliance between cotton capitalism and industrial capitalism was close at hand. For Lincoln the slavery question was tied closely to the questions of Union and democracy. In every recorded speech from 1854 to 1861 he repeated the warning that slavery might become national, and that if it did, free America was doomed. His classic 'House Divided' speech of 1858 expressed it clearest and best:

I do not expect the Union to be dissolved – I do not expect the house to fall, but I do expect it to cease to be divided. It will become all one thing or all the other. Either the opponents of slavery will arrest the further spread of it, and place it where the public mind shall rest in the belief that it is in the course of ultimate destruction; or its advocates will push it forward, till it shall become alike lawful in all the States, old as well as new, North as well as South. Have we no tendency to the latter condition?

The oft-omitted last sentence, with its implied affirmative answer, is essential to the meaning of the passage.

The acrimonious debates over the Kansas-Nebraska bill brought Lincoln back into politics as a 'Conscience' or 'Anti-Nebraska' Whig, and his first real opportunity came at the Illinois Anti-Nebraska convention in 1856. Here he dominated the proceedings, welded the motley assembly of delegates into something resembling a political unit, and practically created the new Republican party in Illinois. But Lincoln was cautious. He went to the national Republican convention of 1856 as a Whig, and although he made fifty campaign speeches for Frémont, he refused to call himself a Republican. Not until 1858, when he accepted the party's senatorial nomination, did he really affiliate with the party.

The congressional elections of 1858 were fairly quiet throughout the country, except in Illinois where the attention of the nation was focused on Douglas, fighting for his political life. Lincoln knew that he could not hope to battle with Douglas, a powerful orator, on his own level, and as the two men stumped the state it became apparent that of the two, Lincoln seemed to make the more sense. Torchlight processions and rhetorical flourishes meant little in cold newsprint; Lincoln's dry, sharp, informal talks sounded better and better as time wore on. He asked questions, hard ones, and when Douglas answered them, Lincoln asked more. Cleverly shifting tactics, he then challenged Douglas to a series of public debates, a challenge the Little Giant could hardly refuse. The situation was all to the advantage of Lincoln, probably the ablest jury lawyer in the West.

The debates that followed represent a high-water mark in American political history. They also made Abraham Lincoln a national figure, and killed Stephen A. Douglas'

chances for the Presidency. In the second debate at Free-
port, Illinois, Lincoln forced Douglas' hand with the question, 'Can the people of a United States Territory, in any
lawful way, against the wishes of any citizen of the United
States, exclude Slavery from its limits prior to the formation
of a state Constitution?' If Douglas answered yes, he repudiated the Dred Scott decision, lost the South, and stood on
'popular sovereignty'. If he answered no, he repudiated his
own principle and lost Illinois and the North. Douglas
answered yes, won Illinois, and won the Senate seat. But
Lincoln's question brought the real issue into the open –
might not slavery become the national system?

The 'lame duck' session of Congress that met after the
1858 elections was badly split on sectional lines. Except in
Illinois, the elections had gone against the Democrats, and
it was clear that the next session would be under Republican
control. Southern Congressmen, hoping to accomplish as
much as possible before it met, supported but lost a bill to
purchase Cuba (as probable slave territory). Congressmen
from the Northwest demanded a homestead bill, opening up
the western public lands, but Buchanan vetoed it. A Pacific
railroad bill, supported by the Northwest, lost to the
Southern bloc, and so did the tariff bill much desired by New
England manufacturers. Southern congressmen orated bitterly about Northern aid to escaped slaves, while Northern
congressmen accused the South of slave-running in violation
of the 1808 embargo. It was an unpleasant session, and after
its close something happened to make the next one worse.

John Brown of Ossawatomie fame had been travelling
freely through the North, though under indictment for
murder in Kansas. Deeply religious, by 1859 Brown had
developed his abolitionism to a point well beyond fanaticism. In New England he collected money from a number of
prominent abolitionists to finance what he vaguely outlined
as some sort of scheme to free numbers of slaves. In May of
1859 he met with a handful of followers in Canada, held a
'constitutional convention', adopted a new 'constitution'
for the United States (providing for a Negro president) and

DIVISION OF THE STATES OVER SLAVERY

Union States
1st Group of Seceding States
2nd Group of Seceding States

returned to lease a farm near Harper's Ferry, Virginia, the site of a Federal arsenal. He planned to call on all Negroes to revolt against their masters, arm them from the captured arsenal, and spread a wave of terror through the South.

On 16 October 1859 Brown and his band of eighteen men descended on Harper's Ferry, captured thirty prisoners in the sleepy and surprised little town, and barricaded themselves in the arsenal while emissaries went abroad to arouse the slaves. But Harper's Ferry was far removed from the heavily slave-populated plantation area, and his raiders found only a few confused Negroes whom they brought back by force. Within two days a detachment of Federal marines arrived, commanded by Colonel Robert E. Lee and Lt J. E. B. Stuart; after a short, sharp engagement, in which Brown's two sons were killed, his raiders surrendered. In less than a week a grand jury indicted Brown for treason and for waging war against the Commonwealth of Virginia.

News of Brown's raid swept through the South. The 'Black Terror' of slave insurrection had eaten for years at Southern hearts. Was John Brown a sign of things to come? Was this abolitionism in action? The fact that Brown's raid was a senseless failure, engineered by a half-insane zealot, was lost on a frightened South. And it was difficult to explain away the abolitionists who backed Brown, and those Northerners like Emerson who hailed him as a martyr to a just cause, or like Louisa May Alcott, the gentle author of children's books, who called him 'Saint John the Just'. In the weeks that followed Brown, convinced of his righteousness, comported himself with calmness and dignity, but on 2 December he was hanged while church bells tolled in the cities of New England. 'I, John Brown,' he wrote before he went to the gallows, 'am now quite *certain* that the crimes of this *guilty land*: *Will* never be purged *away*; but with Blood.'

The new Congress met under the shadow of Brown's dangling body. The statement of Hammond of South Carolina that every congressman came 'armed with a revolver – some with two – and a bowie knife' was an exaggeration, but it reflected the temper of both houses. Douglas' quarrel with Buchanan had cut the Democrats in half. The balance of party power lay with Buchanan and the Southern wing, controlled by Jefferson Davis, who set about to drive out Douglas and to make of the Democrats a Southern party. At the same time machinery was in motion in the Southern states for the same purpose. In 1858 state Democratic leaders like Yancey, Rhett, and Ruffin organized the League of United Southerners to 'fire the Southern heart, instruct the Southern mind, give courage to each other', and to agitate for Southern political rights. In December 1859, as Congress convened, the South Carolina legislature sent delegates to other Southern states to organize for action. Virginia held back, but Alabama, Louisiana, Mississippi, Florida, Texas, and Arkansas agreed to co-operate.

The wide rift in the Democratic party immediately appeared at its presidential convention, which met in Charleston, S.C., the centre of Southern extremism. Douglas, backed by the Northern Democrats, was a logical candidate, but Davis and the South would have none of him. When the Douglas Democrats succeeded in getting through a compromise platform, the Southern delegates stalked from the convention and called for a rump meeting in Richmond. The remaining delegates, after fifty-seven futile ballots, adjourned to meet in Baltimore. There the Northern Democrats nominated Douglas; the Richmond meeting named John Breckenridge of Kentucky. Thus the division of the party into Northern and Southern wings was made complete.

In the meantime two other parties were holding conventions. A sizeable group of Whigs and Knownothings met in May 1860 to form the Constitutional Union party, pledged to recognize 'no political principles other than the Constitution of the country, the Union of the States, and the enforcement of the laws' – meaning the laws governing slavery. To attract unionists and moderates in both sections of the country, they chose John Bell of Tennessee as their candidate and Edward Everett of Massachusetts as his running mate, both middle-of-the-roaders.

The Republicans, jubilant over the Democratic split, met in Chicago. A good ticket and a good platform, the practical politicans felt, stood an excellent chance of winning. The platform they evolved was a masterpiece of multi-group appeal, based on old Free Soil and Whig issues with anti-slavery interpolations. It denounced disunion and secession, which could offend no one outside the South. It opposed the extension of slavery into the territories, but pledged non-interference with the system where it already existed, thus attracting free-soilers and anti-slavery moderates. For the New England businessman it promised protective tariffs; for the Western farmer it promised a railroad to the Pacific, a quarter-section of land to settlers, and federally-financed internal improvements; for the foreign-born it promised more liberal naturalization laws. It denounced John Brown, and approved the Declaration of Independence. There was, in effect, something in it for everybody. The choice of a candidate was harder. Seward of New York or Chase of Ohio were logical choices, but their records looked too radical. Abraham Lincoln of Illinois, considered a moderate, won on the third ballot.

Nearly every plank in the Republican platform favoured something that the South had fought against for years. The strong nationalism of the party meant that if it won states' rights was dead. Its opposition to the extension of slavery meant that the new Western states would all be free, making the slave-holding states a permanent minority in Congress. Both Lincoln and the party's proclaimed platform promised not to interfere with slavery where it existed, but was this an honest promise, and was Lincoln the real leader of his party? The presence of known abolitionist radicals in the party councils was not reassuring. The Republicans offered everything to the Northeast and Northwest; to the South they promised nothing. Davis' old prediction that the aim of the North was to dominate and vassalize the South seemed about to come true, and Southern leaders in general agreed that the election of Lincoln would constitute cause for secession.

The campaign itself was strange. In the North the contest lay between Lincoln and Douglas; in the South between Breckenridge and Bell. 'Honest Abe, the Railsplitter', 'The Man of the People', polled 1,800,000 votes, all from the North. Douglas and 'popular sovereignty' polled 1,300,000 in both sections. The radical candidate, Breckenridge, received 850,000, practically all from the South. Unionist John Bell polled less than 600,000, from both North and South. Lincoln's popular vote was smaller than the combined total of votes against him, but he was not elected by the Democratic split. His majority in the electoral college was decisive, and even if the votes against him had been given to a single candidate, still he would have won. The key to the election lay in the Northwest. As late as 1858 the Democrats had recorded large votes in that area, but in 1860 it swung to the Republicans, completing the alliance of Northeast and Northwest so much feared by the South. Slavery helped to cement it, but it was not that issue alone; the sections were tied together by bonds of economic and political interests – unionism, railroads, water routes, business commitments, markets, migrations – that were stronger than a common aversion to slavery and secession. When Lincoln was elected the whole North was united and the house finally divided.

'The people are run mad,' wrote Alexander Stephens of Georgia. 'They are wild with passion and frenzy . . . Men will be cutting one another's throats in a little while.' Allowing for hyperbole, there was some truth in his view of the South at the news of Lincoln's victory. Many in the South feared 'Black Republicanism' as deeply as those in the North feared the 'Slave Power', but cool-headed Southerners agreed with the Tennessee editor who counselled that secession was 'no remedy for the South's wrongs, or only a madman's remedy'. Others disliked the turmoil created by hot-heads and believed that the South could best achieve its purposes within the Union, that Lincoln's election was perfectly legal, and that the democratic process must be trusted. Economic circumstances, too, favoured patience, for the South was prosperous. The panic of 1857 had touched the slave-holding states but lightly; the cotton crop was good and prices satisfactory.

The secessionists, however, were determined and organized. They set to work quickly in Alabama, Mississippi, and South Carolina. In South Carolina a convention met a month after Lincoln's election and on 20 December 1860 it adopted an Ordinance of Secession, dissolving 'the Union now subsisting between South Carolina and the other States under the name of the United States of America'. Commissioners were immediately appointed to visit other Southern legislatures, urge secession, and propose a new union of seceded states. Before the close of January 1861 Mississippi, Florida, Alabama, Georgia, Louisiana, and Texas followed South Carolina out of the Union. The conventions which voted for secession met quickly and acted speedily; lacking unity and organization, Southern unionists had little chance to resist. But still from the list of departed states there were notable absentees: all the border states of the upper and western South, where Union sentiment was strong.

While Lincoln waited in Illinois for his inauguration day Buchanan followed a do-nothing policy that undoubtedly encouraged secessionism in the South. In his annual message to Congress he denied that a state had a right to secede, but he also admitted that the Federal government had no real power to force a state to remain in the Union, and to calm Southern excitement, he recommended a constitutional amendment recognizing slavery in areas where it already existed. He allowed the seceded states to take over all Federal property within their borders, including all arsenals and forts except Fort Pickens in Florida and Fort Sumter in Charleston Harbour. On 8 January 1861 a supply ship approached Sumter, only to be turned back by the shore batteries, but Buchanan preferred to ignore what was really an act of war.

Congress at once set about finding a compromise. Com-

mittees in both House and Senate discussed several proposals, of which two received special attention. Andrew
Johnson of Tennessee submitted a plan for electing Senators
directly (instead of by legislative appointment), alternating
the Presidency between North and South, dividing Northern
and Southern representation on the Supreme Court, and
providing for a run-off election in case no future presidential candidate received a majority. Crittenden of Kentucky,
another border state, submitted a milder proposal to extend
the Missouri Compromise line, define Congressional power
over slavery, and provide compensation to owners of runaway slaves. Against solid Republican opposition both sug-
gestions collapsed. In desperation the Virginia legislature
called for a 'peace convention' under the chairmanship of
ex-President Tyler, and delegates from twenty-one states
met at Washington in February 1861, but again to no avail.
Neither the seceded states nor the Republican-controlled
states of the West bothered to send representatives. As
Salmon P. Chase declared, 'Mr Lincoln was the candidate
of the people opposed to the extension of slavery . . . Do you
think we who represent this majority will throw it away?'

While the 'peace convention' met in Washington, dele-
gates from the six seceded states met in Montgomery,
Alabama, to establish a new nation, and on 8 February
this meeting adopted a provisional constitution for the
Confederate States of America. Next day it chose Jefferson
Davis of Mississippi as President of the Confederacy and
Alexander Stephens of Georgia as Vice-President. Then it
remained in session for several weeks, acting as a national
legislature and drawing up a constitution, modelled on the
Federal document but differing sharply from it in several
respects. The importation of slaves was banned, but slavery
was protected in the territories and the Confederate Congress was specifically forbidden to deny or impair the right
to hold property in slaves. The President was limited to one
term of six years, the rights of states carefully noted, and
cabinet members given seats (but not votes) in the House
and Senate. The provisional legislature also voted a bond

issue of fifteen million dollars to support the new government, and authorized the creation of an army of 100,000 men.

As inauguration day approached, the divided nation watched Lincoln. He said nothing, spending his time selecting a cabinet chiefly from among the disappointed presidential candidates of his own party. Seward went in as Secretary of State, Chase as Secretary of the Treasury, Cameron of Pennsylvania as Secretary of War (soon ousted), and Bates as Attorney General. While the 'peace convention' floundered and the Confederacy met in Alabama, Lincoln began a leisurely trip to Washington, stopping for frequent speeches that were eagerly scanned for intimations of his policy. For the most part he repeated safe generalities – the Union must be preserved; he would execute all laws in all parts of the United States; no force would be used unless to meet force. But his inaugural address was a calm, clear statement of policy, cautious, conservative, conciliatory.

The apprehension seems to exist among the people of the Southern states that by the accession of a Republican administration, their property and their security are to be endangered. There has never been any reasonable cause for such apprehension.

No state had the right to secede; therefore none had. The Union remained whole. 'I hold that in contemplation of universal law and of the Constitution,' said Lincoln, 'the union of these states is perpetual.'

It is safe to assert that no government ever had a provision in its organic law for its termination. No State upon its mere motion can lawfully get out of the Union. I therefore consider that the Union is unbroken and shall take care that the laws of the Union are faithfully executed in all the States.

'The government will not assail you,' he told the South. 'You can have no conflict without being yourselves the aggressors.' Thus Lincoln shifted responsibility for secession to the Confederacy, leaving the South no alternatives but to remain in the Union or make war to stay out.

In all of this there was little satisfaction for the South, where, even in the border states, the unionists accepted the right to secede, if not its wisdom. Nor were the Republican leaders in the North mollified by Lincoln's statement of principles. Seward, in fact, believing Lincoln confused and incompetent, offered to take over the reins of government, leaving Lincoln a figurehead, an offer that was politely refused. Again Seward came forward with a plan to unify the nation by a quick declaration of war against France and Spain, but with the same result. For nearly a month Lincoln did nothing.

The problem that eventually forced his hand was the question of Federal property in the seceded states. Post offices, mints, customs-houses, arsenals, and forts belonging to the United States had been occupied without incident by Confederate state officials and forces (except for Pickens and Sumter); and as soon as Lincoln was inaugurated, Confederate commissioners called on Seward to ask for the surrender of Fort Sumter, commanding Charleston harbour. Seward quite properly refused to receive them, but Major Anderson, commanding the Sumter garrison, reported that he was running desperately short of supplies. Feeling that the prestige of the Federal government was at stake, Lincoln, over the objections of most of the Cabinet, determined to send relief expeditions to both Pickens and Sumter. The ship to Fort Pickens arrived safely and the fort remained in Federal hands.

Sumter, however, was a different matter. When news reached Charleston that the fort was to be provisioned, Brigadier General Pierre Gustave Toussaint Beauregard of the new Confederate army placed batteries along the shore, consulted Governor Pickens of South Carolina, and asked for instructions from the Confederate Secretary of War. The Confederate Cabinet discussed the matter carefully. The issue was perfectly clear. The relief of Sumter would constitute a direct challenge to the new Confederate government. On the other hand, while resistance meant open war, it might also serve to tip the balance in the

hesitant border states. Beauregard was instructed, therefore, to demand the evacuation and surrender of the
Fort.

On 11 April 1861, Beauregard formally requested the
possession of Sumter. Major Anderson, a Kentuckian himself, refused, and on the morning of the 12th the first gun
fired in the Civil War was touched off. Through the day the
shore guns boomed while the Federal relief squadron stood
off the harbour. On the 13th, with food and ammunition exhausted, Anderson surrendered 'with colors flying and drums
beating . . ., saluting my flag with fifty guns'. One man was
killed, he while firing the final salute, but there would be
more before it was over. Lincoln, on the 15th, called for
75,000 militia for ninety days to subjugate rebellion and to
restore the authority of the Union.

The first post-war generation of historians almost unanimously agreed that the Southern states seceded because of
slavery, and that the North fought secession as treasonous
rebellion. Later historians have found the causes of the
Civil War much more numerous and complex. Was it caused
by slavery? Was it caused by the aggressions of a 'slave
power conspiracy', or by a 'Northern plot' to vassalize the
South? Was it a constitutional conflict between states' rights
and nationalism? Was its cause chiefly economic, the clash
of an agrarian with an industrial civilization? Was it a
failure of leadership, the work of hot-headed agitators and
irresponsibles on both sides? There is reason to accept some
or all of these as factors, at least, in the precipitation of the
conflict. At any rate, it had been brewing for a long time.
Madison, at the Constitutional Convention of 1787, even
then noted signs of friction between Southern planters and
Northern merchants. After the War of 1812, the underlying
clash of sectional interests grew sharper, complicated not
only by slavery, but by changing economic conditions, the
opening of the West, political rivalry, and other points at
issue. American history from 1814 to 1861 was a record of
constant compromise and concession on sectional issues,
until the final break. Whether the war could have been

avoided, or whether it was truly an 'irrepressible conflict' – in Seward's phrase – are insoluble questions.

Despite abolitionist claims, there is no evidence to support the existence of an organized 'slave power plot' to subvert national liberties and nationalize slavery. The South was never so completely unified as the abolitionists assumed, though there was obviously a tacit agreement among slave-holders and non-slave-holders that slavery was a good system, perhaps the best, one most certainly to be retained and extended. Nor is there evidence to support the Southern accusation that Northern interests were allied in an attempt to crush the South and reduce it to economic and political bondage, despite the warnings of Calhoun, Davis, and Rhett.

The cause of the war cannot be laid solely to an economic clash between the sections, though such conflict undoubtedly played a major part in initiating it. It is quite possible that if slavery had not been an issue, secession might have come about from economic rivalry alone. Almost from the beginning of the Republic sectional leaders differed sharply on economic policy, over the tariff, public lands, western settlement, internal improvements, financial measures. According to Toombs, 'The instant the Government was organized . . . the Northern States evinced a general desire and purpose . . . to pervert its powers for sectional advantage, and they have steadily pursued that policy to this day.' By the 1850's it seemed to Toombs and others that the North was steadily winning the race for economic advantage. The Northern states, as successive censuses showed, grew rapidly in wealth, population, and industry, while the South, despite the general prosperity of its staple crop system, became more and more dependent on the North. The conflict between a static, agrarian, cotton-producing, slave-labour economy and an expanding, commercialized, industrialized economy was deeply rooted. Secession obviously meant economic loss for the Northern merchants, manufacturers, property owners, shippers, middlemen, and creditors, but it is doubtful if such loss alone would have precipitated a war to prevent it.

There was also the issue of state sovereignty versus federalism, at bottom a contest over control of national policy in regard to such things as banking measures, tariffs, internal improvements, and especially slavery. If the Union were a voluntary federation of sovereign states, with the important powers residing within them, the whole course of national policy followed the Southern channel. If the Constitution created a perpetual, tightly-bound union with a strong national government, the Southern cause was lost. To Alexander Stephens, for example, secession and war were necessary to prevent the subversion of the rights of states; the 'constitutional compact', said the South Carolina legislature, 'has been deliberately broken and disregarded by the non-slave-holding states . . ., and the ends for which this Government was instituted have been defeated'.

Lincoln's first inaugural, presenting the other side of the case, affirmed that 'the Union of these States is perpetual', and that the power of the whole remained always superior to the power of the parts. In effect, the war was truly a civil war, fought to decide which theory of government should become the basis of future national policy. There was in the North (and especially in the Northwest) a strong and deep-seated belief in a strong Union as the best instrument for maintaining freedom and democracy. This belief was powerful enough to tie together abolitionists and non-abolitionists, New Englanders and Westerners, city workers and pioneer farmers in a struggle, as Lincoln called it, 'for maintaining in the world that form and substance of government whose leading object is to elevate the condition of man'. Believing this, men who had never seen a slave were willing to fight a war to preserve a union without which their democratic way of life could not continue.

The seizure of leadership in both sections by agitators and propagandists influenced the final break. The generation of Clay and Calhoun was willing to compromise, to delay, to temporize, but the generation of Davis and Seward and Garrison was not. Both sections were subjected for nearly thirty years to a thorough propagandizing that oversimplified and distorted the real issues. Northern abolitionists launched vicious attacks on the morals, religions, personal character, and family life of slave-holders. Southern fire-eaters replied with vitriolic abuse of Northern civilization, fanning a hatred of 'damyankees' that struck deep into Southern life. Politicians eager for votes played on popular fears and emotions until a reasonable approach to a solution of the sectional conflict became nearly impossible. A majority of sober Northerners disapproved of the fanaticism of Garrison, Sumner, and John Brown, quite as strongly as intelligent Southerners disagreed with the extravagances of the Fitzhugh-Brooks school of thought. But bitterness and misapprehension grew nevertheless.

And of course there was slavery, heavy with economic, moral, political, social, and emotional connotations. The abolition of slavery, a symbol as well as a system, meant the overthrow of the whole Southern way of life and all that it stood for – the killing of the dream of a chivalric civilization, of Calhoun's vision of a new Greece. Though moderates on both sides held no strong feelings on slavery (Douglas said he did not care if it were 'voted up or down') thousands viewed it as either a national disgrace or the best possible social and economic institution. There was moral idealism on both sides. To the South slavery meant much more than the simple issue of free versus slave labour. It involved the social and economic status of five and a half million white men and three and a half million black. It involved a whole concept of race relationships within a traditionally fixed social system. It involved a legitimate, sincerely-held belief that the minority had rights that must not be subject 'to the tyranny of an unbridled majority'. To many in the North, slavery represented a blot on the national escutcheon, a moral blight. 'No man is free', wrote one Northern moderate, 'so long as another is held in bondage.' War was, then, to some an act of national purification, a terrible and last resort.

The Confederate government, from the moment of its organization, carried within it the seeds of its own destruction. For nearly four years Jefferson Davis and his cabinet faced the impossible problem of imposing unity upon an area that was by no means a social, political, or economic unit. Only a minority of Southerners held slaves; large segments of the population were lukewarm towards secession. The conflict within the Confederacy between moderates (such as Stephens, Walker of Alabama, Mallory of Florida, and others) and radicals (such as Rhett, Toombs, Yancey, and Howell Cobb) was never completely resolved. The Rhett faction was almost completely overlooked in Davis' government and constantly criticized it.

Southern leaders were divided in their opinion of what the Confederacy was. Some thought of it in terms of a Southern nation; others assumed that it was to be a loose confederation of sovereign states. Jefferson Davis was a Southern nationalist. Robert E. Lee, who did not resign his commission in the Federal Army until his own state of Virginia left the Union, was a states' rights man, and was later charged with neglecting the rest of the South in Virginia's favour. Late in the war Davis was soundly berated by his state governors (all of whom were states' rights men) for his 'despotism'; Georgia even threatened to recall its troops from the Confederate armies. Born in war, plagued throughout its existence by the harsh necessities of war, the Confederacy never had a chance of normal development. Urgent military and diplomatic problems left no time for internal adjustments, no time for discussion and compromise, no time for politics.

Eleven states left the Union, twenty-two remained within it. In the division of population, wealth, and resources the North had far the greater potential. The Confederacy totalled nine million people, one-third of them slaves. Since Southerners were naturally reluctant to place rifles in Negro hands, Davis' armies never had a pool of more than a million men available for military service. The North had a total population of twenty-two million, four and a half million of military age, and a steady stream of immigration pouring into its cities. But at the same time the South possessed a strong military tradition, for Southerners had long dominated West Point and the Federal Army. Almost one-third of all Federal officers resigned their commissions to go with the Confederacy, among them Lee, Jackson, Albert Sidney, and Joe Johnston, Bragg, Stuart, and others who represented the cream of the American military. The Southern aristocrat, accustomed to leadership and command, possessed in common with the Southern middle class and lower class soldier a belief that he could 'lick any five Yankees' singlehanded. The Southerner was used to caste lines and adjusted himself more quickly to military life than did the independent individualists from the Northeast and Northwest. That the outmanned Confederacy held out as long as it did is a tribute to its courage and military skill.

The Confederacy was always harassed by shortages of material, supplies, and transportation facilities. By seizing the Federal arsenals its armies gained 135,000 stands of arms, only a small portion of them modern; the Southern soldier was always poorly armed, often dependent on rifles captured in battle. Only two main railroad lines linked the Eastern and Western halves of the Confederacy, slowing down movements of supplies and men. There was no place in the South to manufacture a locomotive. Since the available supply of iron was needed for munitions, neither rolling stock nor rails could be easily replaced; rails on secondary railroads had to be torn up for use on vital lines. The Confederacy had only a small merchant marine to obtain supplies and arms from abroad, and no navy to protect its shipping. The Federal blockade hurt it badly.

Yet the South had a virtual monopoly of the world's cotton, comprising both tremendous potential wealth and a useful diplomatic weapon. Had the Confederacy been able to export its cotton freely, in exchange for goods manufactured abroad, it might have been a different story; as it was King Cotton figured importantly in Confederate foreign relations. The South was a predominantly agricultural area with a large and dependable supply of slave labour, the great majority of which remained loyal. The Confederacy never really suffered from a shortage of foodstuffs, although both military and civilian populations were consistently bothered by lack of facilities for its transportation.

Jefferson Davis, in his first inaugural, said that 'our future policy is peace' and that he would appeal to arms only if 'the integrity of our territory and jurisdiction be assailed'. From the beginning, therefore, the Confederacy had the psychological and military advantages of a defensive war, believing that it need only fight until the North tired and sued for peace. Except for two or three forays into Northern territory (notably Lee's invasion of Pennsylvania) the Confederacy fought the entire war on its own terrain, in familiar territory where the location of every creek and bush was known, where shorter inside lines of communications and supply gave it a distinct advantage. Furthermore the Southern soldier had the moral stimulus of fighting against an invader in defence of his home, his independence, and his right of self-government.

The North possessed by far the greater share of the nation's manpower and resources. Nearly all known American deposits of coal, iron, copper, and other minerals lay within Northern boundaries. Ninety-two per cent of the nation's manufacturing facilities was located in the North; New York and Pennsylvania alone produced each year more than twice the amount of goods manufactured in the entire South. Lincoln had a Navy, and the bulk of the American merchant marine belonged to Northern owners. The North had 30,000 miles of railroad, connecting all parts of Northeast and Northwest, as well as lake, river, and canal routes. It had raw materials, a good supply of skilled labour, efficient transportation, and growing factories.

The Northern soldier, although more difficult to train and discipline than his Confederate counterpart, was educated, resourceful, and mechanically inclined. He suffered through the early years of the war from indecisive and often downright incompetent leadership, since the North had no established military tradition and no officer caste. McClellan, Burnside, Rosecrans, Pope, Hooker, and even Meade were not the stuff of Lee and his lieutenants, but the Federal armies developed leaders under the stress of war – Grant, Sheridan, Thomas, Sherman – who learned to think in new terms and unorthodox patterns. And always, as Southern ranks thinned, the Federal armies could draw on their tremendous reserve of manpower.

The regular Army of the United States in 1861 numbered about 16,000. Lincoln's first request for 75,000 additional troops was based on an old militia law which required each state to furnish a certain number of militia regiments to the Federal government in time of need. No Northern state, however, had a sufficient number of organized militia units to answer Lincoln's call. Each state governor, therefore, called for volunteers to enlist in the state militia. Companies were recruited and enlisted locally, each town contributing its quota to be formed into regiments and brigades at the state capital. Companies and regiments as a rule elected their own officers, with the governor retaining the right to appoint those of regimental command grade; in practice he often simply ratified the election results. General officers were commissioned by the President.

Theoretically the states were responsible for training and equipping their own militia. Arms and uniforms were sometimes furnished by the men themselves or by the town, for few states had either proper equipment or training facilities to add much to the volunteer's accoutrement or military education. As a result, Northern troops reported to training camps in an astonishing variety of uniforms, with arms ranging from flintlocks to squirrel rifles and in various stages of disciplinary disorder. There were established outfits like the New York Fire Zouaves (wearing red fezzes and baggy trousers); the socialite New York Seventh; the old Philadelphia Light Artillery; New England militia companies whose names appeared on the rolls at Saratoga and Bunker Hill; Wisconsin and Iowa farm-boys in homespun and butternut; the proud Michigan Rifles; Unionist Kentuckians whose grandfathers had fought at New Orleans with Jackson. War Department policy kept volunteer and regular army units apart, although regular army officers were usually chosen for training purposes and higher command posts.

Lincoln's request for ninety-day men was followed by a second for 42,000 troops on a three-year enlistment, and by a third for a volunteer army of 400,000 three-year men. Liberal cash bounties were offered for enlistment and re-enlistment, but in early 1863, after two years of heavy fighting, Lincoln asked for and received a conscription law which, combined with enlistments, kept the Federal forces at full strength, though it caused serious riots in New York and a few other cities. The volunteer system had certain military advantages. It kept home-town boys together in units, served to lift morale, and capitalized on local enthusiasms. Soldiers knew their own officers and shared their responsibilities. However, it had its disadvantages too. Soldiers knew their officers sometimes too well and took discipline lightly. The concentration of troops from the same community raised havoc with home-front morale; battles like Shiloh and Antietam swept away at one blow all the young men from some small towns. Democratic election of officers did not necessarily produce the best ones, for popularity and political skill too often overshadowed other and better qualifications.

Shortly after Lincoln's first call for troops, Jefferson Davis sent a similar request to the Confederate states for 100,000 volunteer militia. Many organized and equipped militia companies were ready, and the Confederacy mobilized somewhat faster than the Union. Like the Northerners, the Southern troops reported in all manner of uniforms and states of discipline. Wade Hampton, the wealthy South Carolina planter, brought his Hampton Legion, in which it was rumoured, even privates had Negro body servants; the Louisiana Zouaves came up from New Orleans to join the Richmond Greys and the Life Guards of Virginia, men whose grandfathers had ridden with Marion the Swamp Fox and Light Horse Harry Lee; hundreds of Southern farmers joined line regiments that had fought at Cowpens and Kings Mountain. The Confederacy had no standing army, of course, but it had a large number of well-trained officers who established an excellent system of recruitment and training that quickly produced an efficient fighting force. The manpower shortage, however, forced the Confederate Congress in 1862 to pass a conscription law that was strongly resisted by some states' rights men. Nevertheless, neither resistance to conscription nor desertion was ever a factor in Confederate military affairs, even toward the end of a losing war.

Lincoln seemed to possess at the outbreak of the war neither the skilled political advisers nor the military leadership that Davis had at his side. His cabinet contained several able men, all of whom at the outset considered Lincoln an inexperienced man of mediocre talents. One of his major problems was to impose unity on his party and his cabinet, and to find competent subordinate leaders, both civilian and military.

In the Cabinet, Cameron of Pennsylvania, the Secretary of War, proved to be so untrustworthy that Lincoln removed him within a few months, replacing him with Edwin Stanton of New York. Stanton, an Ohio-born Quaker and a famous lawyer, was an old-line Jacksonian who shifted to Republicanism over the slavery issue. A master of knife-in-the-back politics, he had served briefly in Buchanan's Cabinet, and his appointment to Lincoln's caused considerable comment; a man with a violent temper and an insulting tongue, he held little respect for Lincoln and had already attacked him privately and publicly. Yet he was a brilliant organizer and administrator, and a man of boundless energy. Seward of New York, Lincoln's Secretary of State, still entertained some bitterness over his failure to gain the Republican nomination in 1860. He had little respect for Lincoln's ability, but he gradually acceded to Lincoln's will and became one of the nation's better Secretaries of State, threading his way carefully and expertly through the tangled diplomacy of the war years. Salmon P. Chase of Ohio, Secretary of the Treasury, was the only authentic abolitionist in the cabinet. With Seward and Sumner he led the anti-slavery contingent in Congress during the fifties, and like Seward he was a disappointed presidential hopeful at the 1860 Republican convention. Chase left behind him a good record in wartime finance and later served as a distinguished Supreme Court Justice, but he never really liked or trusted Lincoln.

Lincoln had few competent military advisers or officers at the beginning of the war. The best of the officer crop went South, leaving only a handful of second-grade commanders. Major General Winfield Scott, a Virginian, stayed behind as chief of the Union armies, but while his brain was as sharp as ever, he was so old and fat as to be almost completely inactive. Brigadier General Irvin McDowell, who commanded the armies in the field, was an able organizer but no match whatever for anyone on the Confederate staff; McDowell's highest troop command at the outbreak of the war had been as lieutenant of artillery. At first Lincoln pinned his hopes on young George McClellan, who replaced Scott in late 1861. McClellan, a West Pointer with a good Mexican War record, had resigned his commission some years before to enter the railroad business in Illinois, where he was eminently successful, but at the outbreak of the war he re-entered the army, took over the training of troops in Ohio, and performed brilliantly in the early West Virginia campaigns. McClellan, however, suffered from a Napoleonic complex and from political ambition. Cursed by an inherent lack of aggressiveness, obnoxiously arrogant, unable to adapt himself to new situations, McClellan eventually clashed once too often with Lincoln and was removed. The real military leaders in the North were buried in the army during the early phases of the war, and emerged only after Lincoln's patient search for someone he could depend on.

William Tecumseh Sherman was an Ohio-born West Pointer who, like McClellan, had retired from the army to enter business. In the West, where he re-entered the service, he held gradually increasing responsibilities under Halleck and Grant until Grant's departure, when he took command of the Western armies and drove to the sea. A short-tempered, nervously energetic man, Sherman recognized war as a violent and unlovely business and never tried to make it anything else. George Thomas, another Virginian who remained loyal to the Union, was placid, dignified, and courtly, a perfectionist in war and an excellent foil for Sherman, with whom he worked well, although his lethargy irritated both Grant and Sherman no end. Philip Sheridan, a handsome, volatile Irishman, viewed war much as Sherman did. A fine infantry commander, Sheridan eventually became one of the great cavalry leaders of all time, and with Gregg, Kilpatrick, Buford, Custer, and others made the Union cavalry into a powerful weapon.

Ulysses (Hiram) Simpson Grant, like Sherman an Ohio-born West Pointer, was in 1861 an admitted failure both as a soldier and a civilian. After a poor record at West Point and undistinguished service in the Mexican War, Grant served at an Oregon frontier post and drank himself out of the army just ahead of a court-martial. Unsuccessful at farming and real estate, he entered his father's hide and leather business in Illinois, where he was known locally as 'Cap' Grant, a shiftless ne'er-do-well. At the outbreak of the war he offered his services to the War Department and received no reply. Fortunately he was appointed colonel of an Illinois volunteer regiment, and from that point on his star rose steadily. Grant was made for war; war gave him the stimulus alcohol had once provided, and his cold and emotionless nature, as Henry Adams noted, exactly suited the business of fighting. He had two qualities lacked by nearly every other commander in the North – he never made the same mistake twice, and he avoided politics like the plague. He was no military genius like Stonewall Jackson, nor a god-like leader of Lee's stamp, yet the stumpy man with the rumpled uniform and the dead cigar had a common sense, a directness of mind, and a tenacity that set him apart as a great military commander. It is significant that Sherman and Sheridan, the two finest combat officers in the North, idolized him, and that Lee held him in highest respect.

Abraham Lincoln remains the greatest enigma of them all. It is clear that he was the most skilful politician in American history; no man ever out-intrigued or out-manœuvred him, though many tried. Nothing but politics really interested him, and even as a lawyer he was happiest in that kind of practice that most resembled politics. His law partner, Billy Herndon, who knew Lincoln as well as any man could, wrote, 'It was in the world of politics that he lived. Politics were his life . . .' His conduct of the military aspects of the Civil War was not notably effective, but more than anyone else, North or South, Lincoln recognized the importance of the politics of war. In making his moves and counter moves he faced a cabal within his own party, organized opposition from without it, a constant threat of foreign interference, a divided and arrogant cabinet, and shifting public opinion at home and abroad – all within the framework of a war whose fortunes rose and fell with every report from the field. Yet his mistakes were few, quickly rectified, his political sagacity unquestionably dominant.

But to think of Lincoln only as a skilled politician is to falsify him. He was an extraordinarily complex, compelling figure, of contradictory qualities, the despair of biographers and historians. His political philosophy, an eclectic thing, was drawn from many internal and external sources. The Union was the central fact of his political life, an almost mystic belief colouring all his ideas and acts. He stated many times his view of the slavery controversy and of the war – his objective was to preserve the Union, to guarantee its continuation on democratic principles, and nothing else. The Union must be saved, he repeated, for he believed it to be the chief instrument of democracy. Without union there could be no democracy; without democracy there could be no union. The spread of slavery doomed democracy; the threat of secession doomed the union. This was the inspiration of Lincoln's mature career, that he saw, as no other man of his time, that slavery and secession struck at nationality and democracy. There was no cheap and easy solution.

His belief in democracy was deep. His frontier backgrounds, his contacts with people and events, his political
experiences, and most of all his innate admiration for the
Jeffersonian tradition, combined to produce in him a profound faith in it. He accepted the Declaration of Independence literally and completely, not as a theory but as a
practical manner of life. 'I have never had a feeling politically', he once said, 'that did not spring from the Declaration of Independence', and his memorable phrase, 'government of the people, by the people, and for the people' is still
as much a part of the texture of American political life as
Jefferson's preamble. Yet like Jefferson he too faced the old
question of centralized versus decentralized political power;
in his considerations of practical politics and war he was
capable of using strong Hamiltonian measures to preserve
Jeffersonian and Unionistic ends. As he once wrote, 'Must a
government, of necessity, be too strong for the liberties of its
own people, or too weak to maintain its own existence?' – a
question he tried to answer with his whole political life.

Certainly part of Lincoln's strength sprang from his own
feeling of averageness, from an inner awareness of his own
commonness. Until 1858 there was nothing about him to
lift him above the crowd. He was a good lawyer, but others
were better known; he was a fairly successful politician on a
small scale, but no success like Douglas; and as his wife and
friends pointed out, he had like his pioneer father a lamen-
table tendency toward laziness. He could laugh at coarse
jokes with his friends, call a soldier from the ranks with
'Hey, bub!' and lounge in the capitol in his shirt-sleeves,
all with perfect genuineness and not as a political act. Never
happy alone, he had a sense of sharing life with his fellows.
Men recognized this. He drew men to him and was drawn
to men with some irresistible force. This quality led worldly-
wise John Hay to think of him as 'the greatest figure since
Christ' and made tough-minded men like Stanton and
Seward worship him. The 'man of the people' theme has
been strummed too often by his biographers, yet it has
undeniable truth in it. His feeling for people enabled Lincoln

to understand his times and his contemporaries more clearly than others could. Few men in American history ever had so precise a grasp of the meaning of events, or a clearer sense of the drift of public opinion. It was this, possibly, that helped to make him the supreme politician he was, that led him with an unerring sense to weigh the situation, make up his mind, and do the right thing at the right time. He gambled – in the Douglas debates, at Sumter, on Grant, on emancipation – but it was a calculated risk with the odds on his side.

With all his averageness, Lincoln possessed an uncommon mind and never lost a chance to sharpen and improve it. He was flexible, alert, intelligent. The hours spent with the Bible, Shakespeare, and Blackstone were hours of mental training; he used geometry as a sort of mental exercise long after he laid Euclid down. The erudition of Douglas or Everett was far beyond him, but one need only to read Lincoln's speeches – clear, concise, terse, with underlying echoes of the King James version – to realize that Lincoln's was by far the greater and better-trained intellect. His mind cut through the confused welter of ideas and issues like a surgeon's knife. But with this clarity of intellect there was a strain of melancholy that at times almost unfitted him for action. Dreams, forebodings, black moods of depression dot his life with shadows. He had an unmistakable sense of the irony of life, of the operation in human affairs of 'certain irrefragable and irresistible laws . . ., that what was to be would be inevitable'. 'I must . . . confess plainly', he once said, 'that events have controlled me' – yet as Herndon wrote, 'he was always calculating and planning ahead', supremely capable of decisive and perfectly timed action.

The cabinet selected by Jefferson Davis included several able men, none of the calibre of Stanton or Seward. Alexander Stephens of Georgia, Vice-President, was a unionist with an instinctive distrust of military men and secessionist politicians. Secretary of Navy Mallory, a Floridian, agreed with Stephens. Christopher Memminger of South Carolina, a strong secessionist, was Secretary of the Treasury, and nowhere near Chase in ability. Regan of Texas, Postmaster General, was a hard-headed realist, no admirer of Davis. Walker of Alabama, Secretary of War, was an aristocratic lawyer who so disbelieved in the possibility of war that he once offered to 'wipe up with his handkerchief every drop of blood spilled by secession'. Judah P. Benjamin, the Jewish lawyer from Louisiana who was Attorney General (later Secretary of War and Secretary of State) was by all odds the most brilliant man in the cabinet, but he was highly unpopular, a theorist, and an opportunist. Robert Toombs of Georgia, a fire-eating secessionist and a financial expert, was Secretary of State, probably the one post for which he was least fitted. Thus the Confederate Cabinet was filled with men in the wrong positions; half of them were lukewarm towards secession, only one or two depended on slavery for a livelihood, and only one represented the radical point of view. Davis was never able to impose any unity on it or to get complete co-operation from it.

A great deal of the fault lay in Davis himself. A Kentuckian by birth, Davis lifted himself out of the lower middle class to the Mississippi planter aristocracy by his own bootstraps. A West Pointer with a fine Mexican War record, he entered politics during the forties as a friend of Franklin Pierce and an ardent admirer of Calhoun. From that point on, he became one of the leaders of the militant corps of Southerners in the Senate, and after 1857 was generally acknowledged as the foremost Southern statesman. Davis was really a Southern nationalist who saw the Confederacy not as a loose aggregation of states but as a strong, centralized, slave-holding nation. A powerful and sincere speaker, a shrewd reasoner, a good administrator, Davis had at the outset of the war the support of both radicals and moderates in the South, but he did not have the political skill to keep it.

Jefferson Davis was an honourable man, but he had more than his share of arrogance and a vain respect for his own opinions. As time passed he personally identified himself more and more with the Southern cause, refusing advice, losing himself in theory, wishful thinking, and administrative detail. He had no real concept of the human element in politics and little understanding of the common people of the South. In the end, his aloofness and rigidity undid him. He lost touch with reality, and while the Confederacy collapsed about him he busied himself with records, orders, and querulous arguments with his advisers. He never fully understood the arts of war and politics; after the war he remained a tragic, proud, and puzzled figure, writing his life away explaining a lost cause.

In military personnel Davis had all the advantages. He had a good grasp of military problems and avoided much of the inefficiency and entanglement that plagued Lincoln's War Department in the early years of the war. He created five generals immediately – Cooper, Albert Sidney Johnston, Lee, Joe Johnston, and Beauregard – set up a full army staff of experienced military men, and soon had a functioning military machine. In the two Johnstons, Stuart, Hood, and Longstreet, he had leaders of undoubted talent; in Lee, Jackson, and Nathan Bedford Forrest he had men of genuine military genius. Davis himself, however, had a propensity for meddling with commands and a strong but misplaced confidence in lesser men like Cooper, Braxton Bragg, and Beauregard.

Lee was the South's greatest asset. A scion of the great Virginia dynasty, son of the famous 'Light Horse Harry' Lee, a patrician cast in the perfect mould of the Southern gentleman, he was the embodiment of all that was admirable in the Southern tradition. He had served as Scott's chief of staff in the Mexican War, won three brevets for personal gallantry in the field, and was regarded by Scott as the ablest officer in the service. Lee was, above all else, a Virginian, who believed neither in slavery nor secession, yet who saw it his duty to serve Virginia when war came. As a military commander he was blessed with brilliant subordinates whom he allowed to exercise considerable latitude, but the overall plan was always Lee's. His tactical skill was unsurpassed (though Longstreet always thought him 'overcombative') and he had an uncanny knack of judging his opponent's weaknesses with devastating accuracy. Five Union generals broke themselves on Lee, who outgeneralled and outmanoeuvred each in turn, until the appearance of Grant, whom Lee could never fathom. Under Lee the Army of Northern Virginia emerged as the finest fighting force of the war, possibly matched only by Sherman's Army of the Tennessee; it was 'Marse Robert's' personal army, bound to him by something stronger than a chain of command. Significantly, it was to Lee that the South in its death throes turned for leadership.

Thomas Jonathan Jackson, another Virginian, was something else. Jackson came from a poor back-country family of rigid Scotch-Irish Presbyterians. A silent, grim, godly man, brusque and introverted, Jackson seemed a throwback to the Cromwellian Roundheads, in whose army he would have felt perfectly at home. The romantic appellation of 'Stonewall', attached to him after First Bull Run, never suited him. His infantrymen called him 'Old Tom' or 'Old Jack' and would follow him anywhere he rode on his white horse, the Bible, Napoleon's *Maxims*, and a lemon in his saddlebags. After Jackson died at Chancellorsville at the end of one of his most brilliant movements, the Army of Northern Virginia was never the same again.

James Ewell Brown Stuart was Jackson's exact opposite. Called 'Beauty' Stuart for his handsome face, tall trim figure, and curling yellow hair, half the women of the South were in love with this *beau ideal* of a soldier, who kept an Irish banjo player named Sweeny on his staff for music in the lighter moments of war. Nathan Bedford Forrest, a bearded giant from Tennessee who entered the Confederate army as a private, later formed and commanded his own battalion of cavalry, or 'critter company' as he called it. A crude, profane, semi-literate slave-trader, Forrest knew nothing of war as West Point taught it, but he developed into perhaps the finest irregular cavalry leader of all time. Eventually he became a lieutenant-general, but the war was already lost and Forrest's untutored military genius was largely wasted. His statement 'I git thar fustest with the mostest' is still the classic definition of the first principle of attack.

Thus the forces gathered for a civil war over issues for which Americans could find no compromise. From the early tentative attempts to gain a foothold on the continental edge of the wilderness, through two wars and all the internal racks attendant to an experimental government, the United States succeeded, by concession and adjustment, in establishing a nation. Now it was threatened, split in two; possibly it might be divided again (if the breach were not closed) into five, or a dozen, or more. The struggle now was not against Indians, or the wilderness, or foreigners, but between irrevocably divided ideas – to determine whether its government, or any government so conceived and dedicated, could long endure.

CHAPTER 25

YEARS OF BLOOD
1861–5

LINCOLN's call for volunteers, added to his announcement of a blockade of the Confederacy, crystallized opinion in the wavering border states. Kentucky, Arkansas, Maryland, and Missouri had close commercial ties with the North, while the mountain counties of Virginia, Tennessee, and North Carolina were anti-slavery and unionist in sympathy. Since Virginia was the pivotal border state, others watched to follow its lead. The planters of the seaboard Virginia counties, where slavery was economically important, favoured secession. The farmers of the western hill country, bordering on Ohio and Pennsylvania, were against it, but the secessionists controlled the state legislature. Two days after Lincoln's call for volunteers, the Virginia state convention passed an ordinance of secession (to be ratified by popular vote) over the protests of the delegates from the forty-six unionist counties, who immediately retaliated by threatening to secede from Virginia. Votes from this area were not counted in the tally on the secession ordinance, which passed. Virginia therefore formally seceded from the Union on 7 May 1861; the loyal counties later applied for admission to the Union as a separate state and were eventually admitted as West Virginia in 1863.

Arkansas preceded Virginia into secession by a few days, but in Tennessee and North Carolina opinion was sharply divided. The secessionists, however, seized the initiative and quickly rushed through bills of secession. Plans for eastern Tennessee to follow western Virginia's course were scotched by the quick entry of Confederate troops into unionist areas. Maryland and Missouri were similarly kept in the Union by the speedy dispatch of Federal militia to secessionist centres. Kentucky proclaimed itself neutral, and when Confederate troops entered the state unsuccessfully protested at the violation of its neutrality and declared itself loyal to the Union.

Meanwhile, ninety thousand volunteers poured into the Union training camps. The largest number went to Washington, for Confederate outposts had already appeared across the Potomac and the secession of Maryland, which seemed imminent, would cut the Federal capital off from the North. Other training posts were placed at St Louis, Cincinnati, and Chicago. In the West, the dashing, wavy-haired explorer and ex-presidential candidate, John C. Frémont, took over leadership of the raw troops. At Cincinnati young George B. McClellan drilled the Ohio volunteers. At Washington General Irvin McDowell, in command of the entire Union forces, tried to make an army out of daily trainloads of whooping militia – St Louis Germans, singing songs of '48; Irishmen from Boston and New York; New England and Pennsylvania farm-boys clutching flintlocks. Not far to the South the Confederates faced the same problem. Beauregard, the conqueror of Sumter, held one army along the Potomac, threatening Washington, while Joe Johnston gathered his forces in the Shenandoah Valley of Virginia near Harper's Ferry.

While the troops drilled, Lincoln's council planned strategy. It was clear that the North must invade, the South defend. The Appalachian mountains, running north and south, split the Confederacy into two battlefronts, while the Mississippi, Cumberland, and Tennessee rivers, as well as the East–West rail lines converging on Atlanta and Chattanooga, formed the major lines of Confederate supply and communications. Old 'Fuss and Feathers' Scott still had a keen brain. He advised Lincoln to follow an 'anaconda' policy: first blockade the entire Southern coast with the Navy, then drive two armies into the Confederacy, one in the East and one in the West, to capture the river and rail systems that linked it together. Then while the Navy squeezed the Confederacy from without, the armies within might cut it up into smaller and smaller pieces.

First, however, the fighting front had to be stabilized.

After Virginia had threatened to move Lee into the area to hold it in the Confederacy, the loyal West Virginia counties sent appeals for help to Washington. Lee, busy near Richmond, dispatched General Garnett and 8,000 men into the mountains toward Wheeling and the Ohio river, and Scott therefore moved in McClellan's Ohio troops, now fairly well trained. McClellan's campaign was a brilliant success. Partly by skill and partly by luck, he completed a difficult flanking movement that caught the Confederates napping, appropriately at Philippi, and drove them back toward Richmond; then he succeeded in encircling the main Confederate force, cut it off, and captured most of it in July 1861. The Northern newspapers exulted at first blood and 'Little Napoleon' McClellan made headlines.

While McClellan chased Garnett in the mountains, Lincoln called a council of war to discuss a movement against Richmond, the Southern capital city. McDowell thought his troops still too green for an attack in force, but so were the rebels. Ninety-day enlistments were running out, and Congress demanded action; the Confederates, it was pointed out, might move first. Beauregard sat with 23,000 men near Harper's Ferry while in the Shenandoah Valley was Johnston with some 20,000 militia. So McDowell, with some misgivings, agreed to move on Richmond with 28,000 men of his own and 22,000 militia under General Patterson. The Union march was slow, disorganized, and remarkably well publicized; Washington newspapers published McDowell's plans in full, including good maps, before he began to move on 16 July 1861.

McDowell's advance was a weird parade of undisciplined troops, some still in civilian clothes, accompanied by congressmen and their families in buggies and by dozens of newspapermen. Johnston and Beauregard had no intention of waiting for him. Johnston left a force to confuse the timid Patterson and marched double-quick to join Beauregard. On 20 July the Union advance guard pushed in Confederate pickets near Bull Run Creek, twenty-five miles from Washington, and on the next morning McDowell began his attack. It was a good attack, and the Confederate lines wavered, except for those troops under General Thomas Jonathan Jackson, who, it was said, 'stood like a stone wall'. By afternoon Johnston's army swung into line after their hard march and the picture changed. Once the raw Union volunteers began to fall back their retreat turned into a panic-stricken rout. All night the beaten Union army flowed into Washington, leaving behind its artillery, equipment, and even a few frantic Congressmen. In the dark hour of panic Scott and Lincoln called for McClellan, who arrived in a crisp new uniform, exuding confidence, put regiments of regulars to work reorganizing the shattered commands, and began the long task of rebuilding the army.

Bull Run had a salutary effect on both sides. No one now believed that the war would be a ninety-day affair. 'On to Richmond' and 'On to Washington' headlines disappeared from the papers while both armies settled down to learn how to fight a war. McClellan marched and countermarched his troops on the Washington flats. Joe Johnston, who replaced Beauregard, drilled his not far to the South. By autumn, McClellan had increased his army to 90,000 troops and had more than doubled his ego. 'By some strange magic', he wrote to his wife, 'I seem to have become the power of the land.' Old General Scott resigned in November and Lincoln, remarking that he would hold McClellan's horse if he would only win victories, gave complete command to 'Little Mac'.

The western theatre of war was divided between General Buell, commanding the department of the Ohio, and General Halleck (Frémont's successor) commanding the Mississippi-Missouri area. Facing them was General Albert Sidney Johnston, commanding the Confederate Army of the West. Buell's first march was across Kentucky to relieve the unionist sympathizers in eastern Tennessee, a slow and indecisive advance that ended in a stalemate at the battle of Mill Spring in January 1862. Under him in the Department of Missouri Halleck had a brigadier-general named

THE CIVIL WAR

Line of 1861
Line of 1862
Line of 1863
Line of 1864
Southern Bdy
of Free States
Mason-Dixon Line
Sherman's March

Grant who had shown some promise. In command at Cairo, Illinois, Grant, acting on his own initiative, moved down the Mississippi, surprised the Confederate garrison at Belmont, and captured it; next he swung across Kentucky to seize Paducah and Smithfield at the junctions of the Tennessee and the Cumberland.

Grant now besieged Halleck with requests for permission to proceed up these rivers against Forts Henry and Donelson, both strong emplacements controlling the waterways. Halleck finally gave in, and in early February of 1862 Fort Henry fell to Grant's army and gunboats. Donelson, a much stronger fort, was a harder nut to crack, but on 13 February Grant encircled it. Two days later Confederate General Buckner and 17,000 men accepted Grant's terms of 'unconditional surrender'. With Henry and Donelson gone, Johnston's carefully-planned western defence line collapsed. Kentucky fell into Buell's hands, and Nashville too; Johnston was forced to draw in his troops down the Mississippi River to Corinth, Mississippi.

Grant's growing reputation worried Halleck, who did not like competition in the headlines. Halleck asked for and received control of three armies – the Missouri, under Pope, the Ohio, under Buell, and the Tennessee, under Grant, who was swiftly pushing on down the Mississippi after Johnston. His overall plan called for Grant and Buell to combine at Corinth for a show-down with Johnston, while Pope executed a holding action in Tennessee. Therefore he ordered Grant to stop at Pittsburg Landing on the Tennessee to wait for Buell's army to join him. Buell moved slowly, and Albert Sidney Johnston was nobody's fool; this was his chance to chop up Halleck's armies in sections. While Grant's forces lay unsuspectingly at Pittsburg Landing, Johnston gathered his full army of 40,000 men and fell on him at dawn on the quiet Sunday morning of 6 April, catching the Union soldiers half-asleep. Grant, seven miles away, hurried back to the battle to find his disorganized army engaged in a bitter struggle around Shiloh Baptist Church and losing ground fast; that night the

Confederates camped on the Union lines. But Buell arrived in the dark with 20,000 fresh troops and on the next day pushed the Confederates back toward Corinth, leaving Johnston dead on the field and Beauregard in command. Shiloh was a drawn battle, with a loss of 10,000 on either side, its most decisive feature that Grant was never surprised again.

Shiloh broke the back of Confederate resistance along the Mississippi. Halleck, who rushed down to take personal command after Grant's fiasco, inched his armies toward Corinth and finally took it, only to find Beauregard gone. At the same time, a joint army-navy expedition under General Ben Butler and Admiral Farragut took New Orleans and closed the river's mouth. The Mississippi was open now from north to south, except for Vicksburg, the last remaining Confederate stronghold. Kentucky and western and middle Tennessee were in Union hands. East Tennessee was still under Confederate control, including Chattanooga, the junction point of three railroads connecting with Memphis, Atlanta, and Richmond.

In contrast to the unsuccessful campaigns in the East, Halleck's western manoeuvres were a welcome relief to the North. He was promoted to Washington, leaving Grant in command of the armies west of mid-Tennessee and Buell of the Army of the Ohio. Halleck did not think well of Grant; his reputation for drinking preceded him; he had acted precipitately in the Henry-Donelson campaign and was likely to do so again; he had been badly surprised at Shiloh. But Lincoln said, 'I can't spare this man; he fights.' Grant stayed.

In April 1862, while Grant rested at Shiloh, McClellan finally responded to Lincoln's urgings and began his long-delayed march towards Richmond. The 'Little Napoleon' did not like Lincoln's plan for an overland attack on Richmond, preferring to circle it and attack from the sea. He also had an inherent tendency to overestimate the strength of his opponent, and what Lincoln wryly called 'the slows'. Nor was the eastern theatre of war unified. Lincoln had moved

Halleck east as supreme commander, placed Pope in command of a new Army of Virginia and McClellan in command of the Army of the Potomac, thus dividing both armies and leadership. Though General Joe Johnston could gather only about 70,000 Confederates to oppose him, McClellan moved cautiously across the tangled swampy terrain, writing ill-tempered notes back to Lincoln, arguing, temporizing, and demanding more men and supplies. Nevertheless some progress was made, and by May 1862 McClellan's main army was encamped only twenty miles from the Southern capital, with another force proceeding toward it up the James river from the sea. On 31 May Johnston's army hit McClellan at Seven Pines, hurt the Union forces severely, and stopped McClellan's careful advance dead in its tracks. When Johnston was wounded, his command passed to Robert E. Lee.

Lee's mastery of battle was evident at once. Realizing that McClellan's slow, siege-like tactics might eventually take Richmond, Lee evolved an audacious counter-attack. Stonewall Jackson had a small army of 19,000 men to the west in the Shenandoah Valley; Lee sent him Ewell's division and turned him loose. This was Jackson's kind of war. Leaving Ewell to hold his bases, he set off with his 'foot cavalry' in an amazing march of fifty miles in three days, struck one Federal force, demolished it, swung back in a three-day sixty-mile march, hit another, and drove it clear back to the Potomac. Halleck, in consternation, began recalling troops from McClellan's army to protect Washington, but Jackson slipped between the Federal forces and hit again at Port Republic and Cross Keys. Then, after having tied down nearly 100,000 Federal troops and frightened Washington half to death, he swung back into Virginia to join Lee.

While the Union troops vainly chased Jackson in the Valley, Lee shook loose J. E. B. Stuart's cavalry. Stuart rode north and then turned east, circled McClellan's army, cut the railroad lines, destroyed seven million dollars' worth of supplies, and returned with a complete map of McClellan's positions and forces. As the Northern generals reeled, Lee consulted with his staff – Jackson, Longstreet, D. H. and A. P. Hill – and attacked. In the Seven Days' Battle that followed, ending at Malvern Hill, Lee lost 16,000 men, but Richmond was saved and the 20,000 Union casualties left on the field sent a wave of gloom through the North. McClellan's campaign had failed. Lincoln left him on the James with a few troops and called on John Pope to command a new army to march from Washington to Richmond.

Pope took over with complete confidence. 'I have come from the West,' he said, 'where we have always seen the backs of our enemies.' He scraped together a dispirited army, while McClellan sat at Fortress Monroe and sent angry explanations of his failure to Washington. Pope was not brilliant, but he was stubborn. His orders were to march on Richmond, and as soon as he had his forces organized he set out so to do. But Pope was easy for Lee. While Jackson's swift-marching infantry swept around his flank and Stuart's cavalry slashed across his supply lines, Lee hurried the Confederate army over the mountains into position near the old Bull Run battlefield. Hopefully Pope prepared to attack and on 30 August he sent his men at the Confederate lines. When this attack was spent Lee released Longstreet and Hood with the Virginia and Texas infantry. The Union lines wavered, broke, and fell back, while the Confederates cut isolated regiments to pieces. It was not a rout like First Bull Run, for McClellan trained his men well, but it was a decisive defeat.

Second Bull Run produced bitter disappointment in Washington. The demoralized Army of Virginia was broken up, Pope sent back to the West, several staff officers relieved of duty, and one court-martialled. Halleck, at his wits' end, seemed able to do nothing, so, much against his better judgement, Lincoln recalled McClellan to command the armies based on Washington. He managed to instil new spirit into the reconstituted Army of the Potomac but, still cursed with that military under-confidence which seemed to deny his personal conceit, McClellan waited for Lee to move first.

And Lee, after his resounding successes over McClellan and Pope, now dominated Southern military thinking. In the North, he knew, there were mutterings of discontent over the string of Union defeats. If he could inflict one great blow, such as the capture of Washington (which the Federal government expected momentarily) the Northern public might tire of the bloody business and force Lincoln to sue for peace. It was time, in Lee's opinion, to shift to the offensive, and an invasion of Maryland seemed the best move. The Army of Northern Virginia was short of rations and recruits. The barns of Maryland farms bulged invitingly. There were in Maryland a great many Southern sympathizers and they, Lee hoped, would flock to the Stars and Bars.

Lee marched northward through the mountain gaps with 40,000 men, intending to advance toward Hagerstown, Maryland, and then to turn east toward Baltimore and Washington. The Marylanders, unimpressed by his ragged army, neither flocked to the colours nor loaded the Confederates with supplies. At the same time the Federal cavalry probed sharply at Lee's columns, harassing his movements and even capturing a copy of his orders. Armed thus with complete knowledge of his opponent's plans, McClellan marched on him with 70,000 men, reorganizing his army as he came. Since Lee had detached Jackson and 20,000 men to clear the Federals out of Harper's Ferry and Martinsburg to the west, McClellan hoped to catch him with his army divided.

McClellan's move was as always ponderously slow, while Stuart's cavalry brought in periodic reports on the Federal advance. Jackson hurried back on one of his famous forced marches, but even so Lee's army was not at full strength when the Army of the Potomac made contact with it at Sharpsburg, near Antietam Creek, on 15 September. Had McClellan attacked at once, he might have crushed Lee with overwhelming numbers, but his desultory tactics betrayed him again. On the 16th Jackson's men arrived and went into the line. And then McClellan attacked.

At dawn on the 17th, 'Fighting Joe' Hooker's corps hit the Confederate left in the first phase of McClellan's plan; a hard, vicious assault that almost cracked Jackson's defence line, followed by attacks from Mansfield's and Sumner's corps that should have been better co-ordinated with Hooker's. This bad timing enabled Lee to draw troops from his centre and right to hold on, while Burnside's delayed attack on the Confederate right came too late to do any good. As it was, the Army of Northern Virginia lost 10,000 men; the Army of the Potomac lost 12,000 men, but they had replacements on the way. Lee, knowing he could ill afford further losses, drew back along the mountains to reform his shaken army while McClellan, having bungled a battle, called Lincoln for more men. 'Sending that man reinforcements', remarked Lincoln, 'is like shovelling flies across a room.' Instead he removed McClellan from command and substituted Ambrose E. Burnside, a man with little to commend him except imposing whiskers and abolitionist sentiments, but a man who knew his own limitations, did not want the command, and took it only after some persuasion.

When Burnside accepted he found 113,000 men on the rolls of the Army of the Potomac, the majority of them seasoned troops with battle experience. Lee, reorganizing his Army of Northern Virginia at Fredericksburg, now had 80,000 (the result of the new Confederate conscription law) commanded by Longstreet, Jackson, D. H. Hill, and J. E. B. Stuart. With commendable energy Burnside began the customary overland march toward Richmond, planning first to crush Lee at Fredericksburg and then to sweep into Virginia. His army moved so slowly in the rainy autumn weather that it was not until early November that it reached Fredericksburg. Lee, of course, guessing Burnside's intentions perfectly, had fortified the city to the teeth. In an agony of uncertainty, Burnside waited three weeks before deciding on a direct frontal assault, probably the most insane scheme of the war. His plan meant throwing his men across a river under the direct fire of good artillery, storming a steep, well-fortified hill, and then fighting hand-to-hand with 80,000 well-trained troops. Hooker's men, after receiving their orders on the evening of 12 December 1862, quietly divided up their possessions and wrote farewell letters home. The next morning they charged up Marye's Heights and returned, leaving behind 15,000 dead and wounded.

That night, under cover of the artillery, the Army of the Potomac withdrew while Burnside sobbed in his tent. Not long after, heeding the requests of Burnside's entire staff, Lincoln removed him and gave the command to Joe Hooker. That there was still an Army of the Potomac to command at all was a wonder. Beaten at First Bull Run, decimated in the Seven Days' Battle, mishandled at Second Bull Run and Antietam, slaughtered at Fredericksburg, the army still had fight and spirit, and still hoped for the right leader. Perhaps Joe Hooker was that man.

The first effect of the Civil War was to throw the North and Northwest into a sharp economic depression that shortly gave way to a tremendous boom of prosperity. The demands of a huge army for food and supplies more than compensated Northern merchants and farmers for the loss of Southern markets. The need for increased crops led to the opening of two and one-half million new acres in the West, while Congress obligingly passed the Homestead Law of 1862 (long opposed by the South) granting virtually free land to all comers. Loss of manpower to the services was more than offset by the increased use of farm machinery that enabled the farmer to extend his acreage without requiring more labour. Throughout the war growing conditions were ideal, market prices high and steady, and export demands consistently good. At the close of the conflict the farmer was more prosperous than he had ever been before.

Northern industry, stimulated by military needs and protected by ever-higher tariffs, profited more than agriculture. Old factories expanded and new ones sprang up wherever the new railway lines stretched. Government contracts could be had almost for the asking. Cloth manufacturers profited above all, selling uniforms to the army, while the war changed the clothing habits of the American male by accustoming him to ready-made suits, shoes, hats, caps, and other clothing. Unfortunately, much of the business done with the army was shot through with graft. 'Shoddy' uniforms sometimes dissolved in a hard rain; casks of sugar turned out to be half sand; coffee bags held rye; purchasing agents took bribes and accepted favours. Business in general developed an attitude of 'get-rich-quick' cynicism that carried over undiminished into the post-war period. Yet despite the waste and inefficiency, things somehow got done. Chicago's meat packing industry expanded swiftly; Pittsburg strengthened its position as a steel-production centre; Pennsylvania's new oil industry (from deposits discovered in 1859) went through the first stages of its development. The North's natural resources were exploited as never before – lumber from the Great Lakes region, gold and silver from the west, copper and iron ore from Michigan and Minnesota, coal from the great Pennsylvania fields. Railroads, the key to Northern industrial expansion, did increasing amounts of business; Erie stock, for example, jumped from seventeen to 126 in three years.

War-born industrial activity created a whole new class of *nouveaux riches*, but labour complained that prosperity was not evenly distributed. While the cost of living went to 125 per cent of pre-war levels, real wages rose by only about 20 per cent. Trade union activity increased and there were numerous strikes, nearly a hundred in 1864 alone. Industry, in a favoured position, showed marked tendencies towards centralization. Monopoly was on the way.

The financing of the war had lasting effects on American financial history. The classic method of financing the nation – a higher tariff – proved to be inadequate. To augment the Federal income Secretary Chase resorted to loans, and by 1865 the Treasury had issued 2,000 million dollars' worth of bonds, often sold through private bankers who collected for themselves a comfortable commission. Taxation during the war was the heaviest yet recorded – income taxes, excise taxes, use taxes, every conceivable kind, nearly all of them repealed after 1865. But since neither taxes, bonds, nor tariffs provided sufficient revenues, Congress therefore legalized several issues of paper money, called 'greenbacks'. (About $430,000,000 in greenbacks still remained in circulation in 1865.) Early in the war the Federal government suspended payments in specie, so none of the greenback issues were worth their face value in gold. Their value fluctuated with the fortunes of the Federal armies, reaching their low point of 39 cents in the dollar in early 1864, during Grant's hammering campaigns in the Wilderness.

To the South the war brought nothing but dislocation and adversity. The blockade turned Southern economic life upside down. Before the war the Southerner exported two main crops, tobacco and cotton, importing not only his manufactured goods but also a substantial share of his food-stuffs from the North and abroad. The blockade cut off his exports and imports; he had no market, no credit, and no means of getting either. Blockade runners got through a little cotton and returned with a minimum supply of manufactured goods. Southern farmers substituted wheat and cattle for cotton, but there was never enough. Lack of railroads hampered distribution of the few supplies there were; corn raised in Georgia sold in Virginia for fifteen times its Georgia price and flour cost $300 a barrel in Richmond. The Confederacy was forced to shift almost overnight from a one-crop to a diversified agricultural system, an impossible task in the face of blockade, loss of markets, and inadequate transportation.

For four years the agricultural South struggled futilely to develop an industrial machine capable of supplying its military and civilian needs. Munitions, shoes, clothing, iron and steel, salt, and other necessary industries had to be developed without the aid of technically skilled men and adequately trained labour. Since private capital was hardly equipped to develop huge industries swiftly, the Confederate government took over the establishment of firms producing salt, guns, powder, and medicines. But while Northern factories mushroomed, the South was forced to turn back to pre-Industrial Revolution methods of hand industry, making clothes, shoes, and other necessities whenever possible in the home. Great as was the effort of the South, it was never enough. In need of nearly everything, Southerners were forced to draw on accumulated wealth or to provide make-shifts. Church bells reappeared as guns; window weights were melted down for bullets; rings and jewellery were needed for currency. Old clothes were remade into 'Sunday best'; burnt corn or rye served for coffee, molasses for sugar, carpets for blankets. Newspapers appeared on wallpaper or wrapping paper, books almost not at all; *Tannhäuser*, wallpaper edition, sold for $7.

Wartime financing in the Confederacy was a tangled maze. Heavily in debt to Northern and European creditors in 1861, the South was unable to obtain sufficient credit from abroad. Both state and Confederate governments floated bond issues at home and in Europe, but they sold only passably well. Like the North, the South soon resorted to direct taxation and levies, though few in the Confederacy had money with which to pay. Early in the war the Confederate government flooded the South with paper money, eventually to the extent of a thousand million dollars, backed only by promises. As the amount of paper increased and military reverses continued after 1863, Confederate money depreciated swiftly – 25 cents in the dollar in late 1863, 5 cents in early 1864, nothing at the time of Appomattox. 'I used to go to market with money in my pocket and bring back my purchases in a basket,' one Southerner said in 1864, 'now I take my money in a basket and bring home what I buy in my pocket.'

Social life in the North, reflecting the frantic uncertainty of wartime, turned into an extravagant pursuit of pleasure for those who could afford it, and many could. Theatres played to crowded houses, prize-fights and horse-races were jammed. Baseball, a comparatively new game in the army camps, grew in popularity. Tiffany's, the New York gem dealers, reported an unprecedented demand for diamonds and pearls, while urban merchants everywhere were swamped with orders for expensive clothes and furnishings. Wealthy socialites held ostentatious balls and saloons. The sale of alcoholic beverages tripled. The stock market spiralled dizzily, while trading on the New York Exchange went from twenty-five to one hundred millions a day and was still rising at the war's end. The majority of Northern citizens remained as steady and hard-working as before, caught in a whirl of wartime inflation, trying to make ends meet. Yet it was apparent that a brassy new tone, frenetic and often vulgar, appeared in American life.

In the South the picture was different. War tore up the established ways of life by the roots. Cut off from Europe and the North, Southern cultural life came to a dead stop. Schools and colleges closed; students enlisted and teachers followed them, while those scientists, writers, artists, and scholars who were ineligible for service turned to war work. Publishing houses shut their doors and the great Southern magazines, like *De Bow's Review* and *The Southern Literary Messenger*, closed their files for ever. Its society and economy disrupted, its manpower depleted, food and supplies short, and money almost non-existent, the culture of the Old South disappeared under the stress of war, never to return.

When Halleck went to Washington he left Grant in charge of the Armies of the Mississippi and the Tennessee, with Don Carlos Buell commanding the Army of the Ohio. Facing Buell was the Confederacy's Braxton Bragg, and Generals Van Dorn and Price held Grant's armies at Corinth, Mississippi. It was Halleck's plan that Grant should capture Vicksburg, thus opening the Mississippi river to the Gulf, while Buell drove through Tennessee and beyond, dividing the eastern from the western Confederacy. Bragg, however, confused the plan by slashing northward across Kentucky clear to the Ohio river, and Buell, in hot pursuit, finally caught up with him at Frankfort, Kentucky, in the autumn of 1862. Grant meanwhile set a trap for Van Dorn and Price, sprang it a little too late, and then soundly beat them at the battle of Corinth in October 1862. Disappointed at the defeat, Jefferson Davis sent General John C. Pemberton, a Pennsylvanian gone South, to take over Van Dorn's and Price's combined armies.

As the Confederates retreated from Corinth, Bragg and Buell made contact in Kentucky near Perryville. After an indecisive engagement, distinguished by the brilliant action of young Philip Sheridan, a newly-made general, Buell allowed Bragg to escape to Murfreesboro, in middle Tennessee. Both Halleck and Lincoln were dissatisfied with Buell's performance – he was a good tactician, but unable to handle troops in the mass – and offered his command to his able lieutenant, George Thomas, who turned it down. On the strength of his deportment at Corinth and Iuka, the post went to William Rosecrans of Grant's staff, who took over the Army of the Ohio (soon to be renamed the Army of the Cumberland) in the closing months of 1862. Corinth and Perryville caused similar dissatisfaction in the South. Since some of the Confederate difficulties in the West seemed to arise from divided authority, Davis assigned Joe Johnston to full command of the area, with Bragg and Pemberton under him. But Davis neither liked nor trusted Johnston, argued with him, and occasionally countermanded his orders, making matters if anything worse than before.

Bragg, resting with his army at Murfreesboro, and Rosecrans, in winter quarters at Nashville, pecked at each other for weeks while Richmond and Washington demanded action. In December 1862 both armies finally began movements that brought them together at Stone's River, Tennessee. A bloody two-day battle sent Bragg reeling in retreat to Chattanooga, leaving behind him 14,000 casualties. Rosecrans' Army of the Cumberland, with 11,000 dead and wounded, was too battered to follow, but Bragg's invasion of Kentucky and Tennessee was over. No Confederate army in the West ever marched so far north again.

In early 1863 the war in the West seemed a virtual stalemate. Bragg was beaten back, but he still held Chattanooga,
the key to Tennessee and Alabama. Grant had repelled
Van Dorn and Price, but Vicksburg still blocked the Mississippi. Here was Grant's task, and a hard one. Heavily fortified and garrisoned, the city was protected on the north side
by swamp, on the west or river side it bristled with guns, and
on the east and south the approaches were heavily entrenched and manned. Grant, in the autumn of 1862, hoped
to send Sherman's army down river to try the fortifications
on that side, while he was to march overland from his base
at Memphis to attack from the east and north. Both movements were failures. Snatching at ideas, Grant tried digging
canals so that the river guns could be by-passed, but this
failed too. By April 1863 he was still stuck in the swamp
bottoms, and questions were being asked in Washington.
Soldiers died of fever; rations were short; five assaults on
Vicksburg left only fields littered with dead.

But Grant's cold brain was working hard. Capture of
Vicksburg from the river side was impossible, nor could an
army go through the swamps to the north of it. The only
way to capture Vicksburg was from the south and south-
east, on dry ground. To get there meant marching from
Memphis in a great circle to the east, leaving his supply
lines extended and vulnerable to the Confederate cavalry.
But he could march in a circle down the west bank of the
Mississippi past the city, cross to the south of it, and get at
Vicksburg from the rear; a movement that might cut his
army completely from its Memphis base. If it failed it meant
probably complete annihilation of his army and certainly
for him court-martial and dismissal from the service.

In mid-April Grant made his move, crossed the Mississippi, and marched down the west bank with 40,000 men.
'What is your plan now?' asked Sherman. 'Cross here and
reach high ground', said Grant. 'But your communications?'
asked Sherman. 'You can't get supplies down the river past
the guns.' 'No communications', replied Grant. 'The troops
can live off the country.' Sherman was thunderstruck. It

was impossible. But Grant did it. On the last day of April the Federal troops began to stream across the river and a week later his army was moving on Vicksburg from the south and southeast, travelling fast. Ten days later he had it surrounded – Pemberton and 30,000 Confederates trapped inside – with the right wing of his army touching the river north of the city and his left wing touching the river to the south of it. He tried a few assaults, then settled down to wait. Johnston, rushing north to Pemberton's aid, met Sherman's 40,000 and turned back. In June mule-meat and rats began to appear on Vicksburg menus, and on 3 July Pemberton asked for terms. On 4 July he surrendered, and the Army of the Tennessee, buttons polished and flags flying, marched into the city with its bands playing 'John Brown's Body'. Grant was master of the Mississippi, which, Lincoln said, 'once more flows unvexed to the sea'.

The 'anaconda policy' of slowly strangling the Confederacy called for a complete naval blockade of the South. Early in 1861 Jefferson Davis authorized privateers to prey on Northern commerce, and two days later, on 19 April, Lincoln retaliated by declaring a blockade of all ports in the seceded states. The task of making this effective fell to the new Secretary of the Navy, efficient Gideon Welles of Connecticut.

The problem was by far the most difficult yet faced by the small Federal Navy. The Confederacy had 3,000 miles of coastline dotted with hundreds of good natural harbours. The Navy, at the outbreak of war, consisted of some ninety ships, about half of them fit for blockading purposes. On the other hand, since the Confederacy possessed no navy and no facilities for building one, almost any vessel that could carry a gun was useful. Before the end of 1861 about one hundred auxiliary ships were in blockade service, with more building in Northern shipyards. Furthermore, ninety per cent of the American merchant marine was in Northern hands, providing a pool of trained seamen and officers to man the new ships.

The blockade was almost immediately effective, and was

in the long run a prime factor in the defeat of the Confederacy. By the close of 1861 the Navy had sealed off most of the South Atlantic coast and the big Southern ports of Savannah and Charleston. In early 1862 it extended the blockade to the Gulf Coast, capturing New Orleans in May and gradually closing off lesser ports by 1863. After the first few months of war, shortages of tea, coffee, sugar, cloth, soap, manufactured goods, and particularly medical supplies were obvious in the South, and remained throughout the course of the conflict. The Confederacy had plenty of cotton and foodstuffs, but neither the facilities nor the technical skills to produce much else.

The Confederacy quickly resorted to the building of blockade-runners to pierce the Federal naval line with cargoes from foreign ports. These swift ships successfully eluded the Navy for four years, bringing in a minimum amount of the supplies needed to keep the Southern armies in the field. The Confederacy also commissioned raiders to attack Northern commerce, swift, heavily-armed ships built and outfitted chiefly in British ports. Nineteen of these *Alabama*-class raiders were built; they raised havoc with the Northern merchant marine, sinking more than 200 vessels during the war. To engage the Federal Navy directly, the Confederacy planned a fleet of powerful rams, remaking the captured *Merrimac* into an ironclad that in 1862 struck a unit of the Navy at Hampton Roads and nearly destroyed it – until it was stopped by the famous *Monitor*, the 'cheesebox on a raft', in the first major naval battle between ironclads. The Northern blockade was never again seriously threatened.

Inland, particularly in the West, the Federal Navy played an important rôle. In May 1861 Captain John Rodgers armed three river steamers and sheathed them with heavy timbers for use in river war. Shortly afterwards James B. Eads, a famous ship designer, built nine flat-bottomed paddle-wheel gunboats, plated with iron, which were placed under the command of Flag Officer Foote. The 'Eads gunboats' and the 'timberclads' provided the Western armies with effective floating artillery. Wisely and bravely used, the 'webfoot navy' performed an essential function in the capture of fortifications on the Mississippi, Tennessee, Cumberland, Red, and other rivers in the Western campaigns. 'Wherever the ground was a little damp', said Lincoln, 'they left their tracks.'

Hooker wintered the Army of the Potomac along the Rappahannock River in Northern Virginia. He had a reputation as a hard fighter (and as a hard drinker) and his soldiers responded to him well. In April 1863, when Lincoln came to review the troops, Hooker could show him an army of 110,000 infantry and 11,000 cavalry, organized into eight well-drilled corps. Lee had only about 65,000 effectives at Fredericksburg, and when Hooker heard that Lee had sent Longstreet's forces to worry the Union garrison at Fortress Monroe, he believed it time to act. He planned to send the Union cavalry sweeping to the west around Lee to divert his attention, while he pushed around Lee's left to block his path to Richmond. Late in April Hooker crossed the Rappahannock toward Fredericksburg.

His flanking manoeuvre fooled Lee for the moment, but the tangled wilderness country made Hooker's march difficult. His army slowly gathered itself near Chancellorsville, a few miles east of Fredericksburg, where Lee moved his forces to intercept it. By the evening of 1 May 1863, Lee and Jackson held strong positions between Chancellorsville and Fredericksburg, while Hooker's huge army thrashed about in the forest, forming battle lines. That night Lee and Jackson discussed the next day's plans. Their position was not wholly favourable, but while they talked in the firelight, Stuart's cavalry rode in to report that Howard's division, on the right flank of Hooker's army, lay exposed west of Chancellorsville. Lee and Jackson talked excitedly, drawing diagrams in the dirt with a stick. Then Jackson, his face set, walked away.

Lee's plan was as dangerous as it was brilliant. Jackson was to take his whole wing, nearly half of Lee's army, and

in a swift night march swing in a wide eight-mile circuit to
Hooker's right, cutting in on the exposed right flank. This
left Lee with the other half of the army facing Hooker's
centre and left. When Jackson hit the right, Lee was to
attack and hold. The manoeuvring meant dividing the
smaller army directly in the face of the enemy; it required
perfect timing and depended on swift, secret movement. If
Hooker attacked while Jackson was on the march, the Army
of the Potomac could easily crush Lee and then turn on
Jackson.

It worked like a charm. Jackson's men were on the march
at midnight of 2 May and into position early the next morning. Von Gilsa's Germans of Howard's corps were quietly
cooking their noon meal when 30,000 yelling rebels swept
out of the woods. In half an hour Howard's corps was in
complete rout, the Union right disintegrating fast. Only
tough artillery resistance kept the whole Union front from
collapse, and by nightfall the Army of the Potomac was
bent double like a horseshoe. Jackson extended his lines,
made contact with Lee, and pulled A. P. Hill's division into
line, ready to close the open end of the horseshoe and spring
the trap. Eagerly Jackson rode forward into the dusk, looking for a weak spot to hit the next morning. The 33rd
North Carolina, firing at shadows in the darkness, shot him
down.

Joe Hooker was a brave man, but the first day of Chancellorsville required more than bravery. Helplessly tangled
in the maze of a nearly disorganized army, Hooker struck
back the next morning as best he could. He tried to move his
army towards Fredericksburg, but Lee and Stuart (A. P.
Hill was wounded) beat him back. Soon the Army of the
Potomac held nothing but the river ford behind it, the only
way of retreat. Hooker, dazed by the concussion of a cannon-
ball that struck near him, in great pain and in complete
confusion, ordered the retreat. Sickles' and Slocum's men
held off the Confederate army for hours until the beaten
Federals were safely disengaged. Lee's masterpiece was
complete. He had outgeneralled and outfought a superior

army, had very nearly closed a trap that would have anni-
hilated it, and had inflicted 16,000 casualties to his own
12,000. If Jackson had been there on 3 May it might have
happened as Lee planned it. But Jackson, lingering on his
death bed, fought out in his delirium some old action, mut-
tering, 'Tell Hill to bring up the guns, bring up the guns!'
On 10 May he spoke again: 'Let us cross the river and rest
under the shade of the trees.' So died Thomas Jonathan
Jackson, the long right arm of Lee.

The news of Chancellorsville brought despair to Washington and jubilation to Richmond. Hooker, it seemed clear,
must go, but Lincoln could find no one to replace him. To
the South, the Confederate government felt sure that one
more such battle should bring peace feelers from Lincoln.
Both Davis and Lee believed it absolutely necessary to continue aggressive action in the East, though General Longstreet wisely argued for sending reinforcements at once to
the West, where Grant gnawed at Vicksburg. Longstreet
was overruled. Lee needed rations – let him get them in
Pennsylvania. Lord Russell in London wrote to Lord
Palmerston; in view of the string of Union defeats, would it
not be wise to offer England's services as peace mediator?

On 3 June 1863 Lee's army began to move northward,
reinforced to 75,000, a sharp-honed fighting force that had
never been defeated. By 12 June Confederate cavalry was
reported in the upper Shenandoah Valley, while Hooker
called on Lincoln (shades of McClellan) for reinforcements.
There was no doubt about it; Lee was coming north, swing-
ing in a wide circle west of Washington, sending Longstreet's
infantry and Stuart's cavalry ahead of him, ranging through
the valleys of Maryland and southern Pennsylvania. Hooker
moved the Army of the Potomac in a smaller inner circle,
keeping between Lee and Washington. Panic hit Philadelphia; business suffered in New York; Pittsburgh organized
home guards and dug trenches; the papers called for Mc-
Clellan again. 'Old Jubilee' Early's Confederates captured
York, Pennsylvania, then ransomed it for $100,000 and a
thousand pairs of shoes. Stuart's cavalry appeared on the

outskirts of Washington, then again near Harrisburg; Ewell turned up in Chambersburg, Pennsylvania, then left to join Lee. Meanwhile, with the Confederate forces approaching mid-Pennsylvania, Hooker called for more men, threatening to resign unless he got them. Lincoln surprised him. He accepted the resignation, and in Hooker's place put George Gordon Meade, untried in battle but a brilliant engineer and good tactician.

Hooker's counter to Lee was sound enough, but he never had a chance to put it into execution. His idea was to concentrate somewhere between the head and tail of Lee's advancing army, strike it in the middle, divide it, and defeat it by halves. The concentration had barely begun when Meade, aroused from sleep, took command. Lee remained uncertain as to the location of the main body of Meade's army, and when he discovered the Union forces massing south-east of Chambersburg, he began to pull back his advance units and to concentrate his own army. A fight was in prospect, and after winning it, Lee intended to move straight on to Washington. On 1 July 1863 General Heth's division of A. P. Hill's Corps ran into resistance at Gettysburg, Pennsylvania. 'Don't worry,' said Heth, 'it's only Pennsylvania militia.' He was wrong, for this was Buford's cavalry and the famous Iron Brigade of the Army of the Potomac, sweeping out of the woods in a bayonet charge. The battle of Gettysburg had begun.

At Gettysburg the two armies, both at nearly full strength, suddenly stumbled together. Lee's main force lay somewhat to the north and west of the sleepy little farming town, Meade's to the east and south. When the news came of contact at Gettysburg, both men knew instantly what had happened, but Meade was fortunate in having General Reynolds on the scene. Reynolds quickly surveyed the terrain, chose a long low hill, called Cemetery Ridge, south of the town as suitable ground, and fell dead from a sniper's bullet. Ewell's Confederate II Corps came rushing in from the north, while the Federals, fighting fiercely against three to one odds, slowly fell back towards Cemetery Ridge.

By the evening of 1 July Lee had two-thirds of his army at Gettysburg, with Longstreet on the way. The Union army was still outnumbered on the field, but Meade was hurrying his main force toward the town. Lee arrived at midnight, talked to Hill and Ewell, and laid his plans. Longstreet was to hit the Union left, entrenched along the Ridge; then Hill was to attack the centre, while Ewell circled the Union right and cut in behind it. Meade arrived that night too, exhausted and sleepless. He knew Lee's favourite trick of breaking down a wing and poured troops into line until dawn.

Cemetery Ridge is shaped like a fish-hook, two miles long, the curved end on the north, the shank on the south. On the morning of 2 July Longstreet sent McLaws' Carolinians and Hood's Texans at the south end of the Union line, while Ewell struck at the north end of the hook. But Sykes' and Sedgwick's Corps came rushing up to stave off Hood and McLaws, while Gregg's cavalry beat back Ewell. Hood noted something that no one had seen – at the south end of Cemetery Ridge stood two small hills, Big Round Top and Little Round Top. If the Confederates controlled those, artillery could enfilade the entire Union line. At the same time Meade's Chief of Engineers, Warren, saw them too. Acting without authority he called up the 20th Maine and a New York regiment, in time to meet the first wave of Hood's assault. Outnumbered two to one, the Federals fought hand-to-hand with clubbed rifles and held the hills.

That night Lee believed he had victory firmly in his hands. Two days of fighting, he was sure, had badly shaken his enemy, and he proposed on the third day to drive straight through the centre of the Union Line, a plan Longstreet did not like. Meade, during the night, shifted his troops about, sending Gregg and Custer with the cavalry to hold off Stuart, whose tired men had just ridden in. Hancock's II Corps Meade placed in the centre to relieve the battered XII and III. For the assault at the Union centre, Lee chose Pickett's fresh Virginians, prepared a tremendous concentration of artillery to support it, and waited for morning.

On the morning of 3 July Stuart's attack failed; Custer

and Gregg soundly whipped his cavalry for the first time in his career. Noon came. Pickett's division formed ranks, bayonets in line, while Colonel Freemantle, the British observer, admired them. Artillery opened thunderously on the Union centre. Federal artillery fire slackened, then stopped – to let the guns cool, though Lee thought otherwise. Then, at Lee's word, Pickett's division burst out of the woods into the rolling fields, lines dressed, flags waving, the flower of the Army of Northern Virginia.

Longstreet was right and Lee was wrong. Meade had simply out-thought Lee. Guessing that Lee's assault would strike the centre, he reinforced it with fresh troops, concentrations of artillery backed by cavalry in case of a breakthrough. Hancock's II Corps, lying behind a low stone wall, was the best in the Union army, and Pickett's charge headed straight at it. The Union artillery opened up again, tearing huge holes in the advancing line, but Pickett's men came on while the Federal artillerymen pulled their guns up with the infantry, switched to canister, and then to grape at point-blank range. The Confederates came up to the wall and over it, into the guns, and for one brief moment the Union line was pierced. Then Hancock, lying wounded, saw two Pennsylvania and Maine regiments sweep by, bayonets low, to plug the hole. That was the end. Pickett's column, torn to bits, fell back, fell back farther, and finally reached the Confederate lines. Fifteen thousand of them went out. Five thousand came back. Lee watched them come, and broke into a sob. 'It's all my fault,' he said. Gettysburg was over.

The Army of Northern Virginia lost 22,000 men at Gettysburg, the Army of the Potomac 18,000. On 4 and 5 July Lee's men took up the long weary retreat southward into Virginia, a defeated army but by no means a broken one. Meade's army was too badly hurt to follow. The battle proved nothing, except perhaps that Lee could not successfully invade the North. It did not establish that Meade was a better general than Lee; it did prove that Meade was capable of excellent staff work and knew how to use efficient subordinates, whereas Lee no longer had a Jackson to help him carry out his plans. The fall of Vicksburg on 4 July and of Chattanooga in November had much more to do with the final outcome of the war. Yet Gettysburg was for Lee the turning point. From then on it was all down hill.

They gathered the dead from Gettysburg field, Union and Confederate, and buried them near Cemetery Ridge under row on row of white stones. It was designated a national cemetery, and on a cool November morning in 1863 the officials held the dedication ceremonies. Edward Everett, the great New England orator, spoke for two hours. Then Lincoln walked awkwardly forward on the platform to read in a high thin voice the sentences he had scribbled on a sheet of paper the night before. It lasted less than five minutes, followed by a spatter of applause. Seward whispered to Everett, seated beside him, 'He has failed, and I am sorry for it.'

War or not, politics went on as before. Within the Republican party one group (of which Lincoln stood as representative) believed that the war was being waged to preserve the Union, with slavery but a secondary issue. Another group of Republicans, the so-called Radicals, insisted that the emancipation of slaves was the chief objective of the conflict. The Joint Committee on the Conduct of the War, formed by Congress in April 1862, and controlled by the Radicals, hampered Lincoln's war efforts, tampered with military policy, favoured Radical Republican army commanders, and in general attempted to seize control of the party and the war. Meanwhile men like Ben Wade of Ohio, Zach Chandler of Michigan, and Thaddeus Stevens of Pennsylvania – Radicals all – loudly criticized Lincoln for his failure to free the slaves. Lincoln, however, in his reply to Horace Greeley of the New York *Tribune*, stated his position in clear language:

My paramount object in this struggle *is* to save the Union, and is *not* either to save or destroy slavery. If I could save the Union without freeing *any* slave, I would do it; and if I could save it by freeing *all* the slaves, I would do it; and if I could do it by freeing some and leaving others alone, I would also do that.

Eventually Lincoln's hand was forced. Convinced that free-ing the slaves would help to prevent foreign intervention in the war, would relieve abolitionist political pressure, unify his party, and clarify Northern war aims by injecting the issue of freedom into the war, he issued the Emancipation Proclamation on 22 September 1862, not long after his letter to Greeley.

The Northern Democratic party was also sharply divided over support of what seemed to some purely a Republican war. 'War Democrats' like Douglas (who died in 1861) and Stanton co-operated to the full with Lincoln and the Republicans. The 'Peace Democrats' (or 'copperheads') attacked Lincoln's war policies and clamoured, after every military defeat, for a negotiated peace. Extremist 'copper-heads' formed secret societies, such as the Sons of Liberty or the Knights of the Golden Circle, which attacked con-scription laws, discouraged enlistments, and covertly ship-ped supplies to the Confederacy. When the 'copperhead' movement reached its peak Lincoln moved swiftly to sup-press it. He suspended the writ of *habeas corpus* (actually illegally, since only Congress could so act) and arrested the 'copperhead' leaders, many of whom were summarily tried in military courts and quickly imprisoned. Ohio Congress-man Clement Vallandigham, leader of the western 'Peace Democrats', was banished to the Confederacy as a traitor. Lincoln's course aroused widespread criticism in the North. Defections from Republican ranks in the congressional elections of 1862, when six normally Republican states went Democratic, can be laid in part to dissatisfaction with Lincoln's handling of the 'copperhead' cases.

The proclamation of emancipation helped to bring some harmony to the Republican party, although the Radicals never ceased their criticism of Lincoln's conduct of the war. Meanwhile Lincoln attempted to formulate a workable policy whereby the seceded states might return to the Union. As soon as the Federal armies established control over some portion of a Confederate state, Lincoln appointed a provisional military governor for the area and prepared for the re-institution of civil government. In late 1863 he presented a more elaborate plan, one that he hoped might prove attractive to unionist elements in the South. Under this plan pardons were promised to all those citizens of seceded states (with some exceptions) who would take an oath to support the Constitution of the United States and all executive acts and presidential proclamations governing slavery. When 10 per cent of the voting population of 1860 subscribed to this oath, the state might then organize a civil government which would be recognized as the legal government of that state within the Union. Under this system minority governments in Arkansas, Louisiana, and Tennessee (all chiefly under control of the Federal armies) were organized and recognized in 1864. Such an attractive and convenient scheme for reconstructing the Union, however, failed to satisfy many Northern Republicans. It did not guarantee, obviously, that the reorganized governments would be Republican; the Radicals claimed that Lincoln's method would simply allow ex-secessionists, Democrats, or conservative Republicans to gain control within the returned states and in Congress. The Radical-sponsored Wade-Davis bill, which Lincoln killed by pocket veto in 1864, provided a much harsher substitute plan.

The 1864 election provided a serious test of Lincoln's strength. He faced the Radicals within his party and the 'Peace Democrats' without, as well as growing pessimism throughout the North over the long lists of casualties and defeats. Certain that his chances were slim, he prepared a memorandum promising to co-operate with his successor during the period between election and inauguration. Indeed, there was reason for his uncertainty, for a group of Radical Republicans met in May, condemned Lincoln and his war as failures, and declared themselves for John C. Frémont. Cooler Republican heads, however, thought the renomination of Lincoln better strategy. Frémont withdrew, and the Republican convention chose Lincoln and Andrew Johnson of Tennessee (a War Democrat) as its ticket; deciding, as Lincoln aptly phrased it, 'not to swap horses in the middle of a stream'. The Democratic convention ended in confusion. The 'Peace Democrats' pushed through resolutions declaring the war a failure and demanding an immediate peace. For President they chose General Mc-Clellan, who at once denounced the peace resolution on the ground that 'no peace can be permanent without Union'. Before the election Sherman captured Atlanta, and Sheridan ravaged the Shenandoah Valley, effectively refuting the Democratic platform. The result was a clear endorsement of Lincoln, 212 electoral votes to twenty-one for McClellan.

Jefferson Davis did not fare so well. In November of 1861 the Confederacy held its first elections, confirming Davis and Stephens in office for six-year terms and returning the majority of members of the provisional Congress. Yet there was growing dissatisfaction, despite the election returns. The blockade was beginning to hurt Southern economy, and Davis' government was soundly berated for shortages, high prices, and profiteering. The Confederate Congress passed a series of price-fixing and anti-profiteering laws, satisfying no one, and as prices rose and supplies dwindled criticism became sharper. The conscription law of 1862, filled with loopholes and exemptions, aroused resentment in certain states, especially in Georgia and South Carolina, which protested against it as an invasion of states' rights and counselled open resistance. At the same time Congress passed a number of acts suspending *habeas corpus* with much the same reaction that Lincoln met in the North.

The old political conflict between unionist and secessionist, small farmer and planter, states' rights man and nationalist continued unabated in the Confederacy. Against Davis stood his constitutional inability to conciliate men or to compromise opposing views. Southern newspapers, operating under heavy censorship, failed to provide a clear picture of events and policies, so that rumours floated freely and misunderstandings multiplied. Furthermore, the Confederacy was committed to a defensive war, and military victories – of which there were many – seemed to accomplish nothing as the war continued and casualties mounted. The bloody record of 1862 caused an upsurge of peace talk in the South. Davis, it was said, failed to take advantage of opportunities to end the war honourably; Vice-President Stephens openly accused him of refusing to send out peace feelers to Washington, and in 1863 Stephens went so far as to attempt to arrange a talk with Lincoln. In the same year the long-concealed opposition to Davis came to light in the election, which sent an anti-Davis majority to the Confederate Congress. After 1863 Davis was forced to deal with a hostile Congress and an increasingly hostile public. As the armies in the field won disastrous victories and later suffered equally disastrous defeats his leadership swiftly faded.

In the closing months of 1863 and the winter of 1863–4 both the Army of the Potomac and the Army of Northern Virginia remained inactive. The centre of action shifted to the West, where the Confederacy was in serious trouble: Bragg holed up near Chattanooga, the Mississippi open, Louisiana, Texas, and Arkansas split away from the rest of the South. Rosecrans held the Army of the Cumberland at Nashville and Murfreesboro, facing Bragg. Neither man had any especial taste for aggressive action, though both were under strong political pressure to do something quickly. In June 1863 Rosecrans began a slow advance towards Chattanooga, flanking Bragg out of his advanced positions in a series of minor actions. Rosecrans simply had more men, and by August he had cleared the Confederates out of eastern Tennessee, leaving Bragg holding only Chattanooga. Located at a gap in the Cumberland mountains made by the Tennessee river, Chattanooga was the control point for railroads radiating north, east, west, and south, and a city as important to the western Confederacy as Richmond was to the eastern. It was heavily fortified, but Rosecrans cleverly deceived Bragg by feinting an attack from the north and east while sending Thomas' corps to the south and south-east. Bragg suddenly woke up to find the major portion of Rosecrans' army marching behind him and Chattanooga almost cut off. Rosecrans occupied the city unresisted, and Bragg retreated into northern Georgia.

Success made Rosecrans overconfident. Bragg, he assumed, was in full retreat toward Atlanta, but instead Bragg was gathering his army for a stand, with reinforcements on the way from Mississippi and Longstreet's division en route from Lee's Army of Northern Virginia. By early September Bragg had 66,000 troops to Rosecrans' 57,000, and Rosecrans, realizing Bragg's intentions, began to pull his scattered corps together near Chickamauga Creek, a few miles south of Chattanooga. On 19 September, a foggy, wet morning, Bragg sent Polk's troops into the attack, followed by Hood's Texans, but the Federals under Thomas and Crittenden staved them off. On the 20th Bragg tried again with no greater success. Late in the morning, however, the break came when a muddled order left a huge hole in the Union line. Longstreet poured his 12,000 Virginians through it, swept down the line right and left, and shattered the Federal front. The Army of the Cumberland broke in panic, while Rosecrans fled to Chattanooga, wiring Louisville and Cincinnati to prepare defences immediately. Only slow-moving George Thomas and the Federal 14th Corps remained on the field, planted on the Union left, holding a low ridge called Snodgrass Hill.

Thomas knew nothing of what had happened. At noon he saw a cloud of dust on his right, looked with binoculars, and turned away, his face white. The approaching troops wore Confederate grey. He realized that somehow the rest of the Army of the Cumberland had been smashed, and that his 14th Corps covered the only escape route back to Chattanooga. He had three divisions, about 22,000 men; in front of him, and to his right and left, were 57,000 Confederates. A few minutes later the Confederates came boiling up the ridge. The 14th Corps threw them back, and a second and third time. They beat back Hood's Texans, and Longstreet's Virginians, later Longstreet again, and two more desperate charges. Water was gone; ammunition was gone; men crawled down the ridge to rob the canteens and cartridge boxes of the dead. Thomas' men soberly fixed bayonets in the deepening twilight; and the last charge they beat off

with bayonets and rocks. Longstreet, after this last unsuccessful attack, asked Bragg for reinforcements. 'I have none
to give', said Bragg. Chickamauga, the most murderous
battle of the war, was over, with 23,000 casualties. By nightfall Thomas and the remnants of the 14th were on the way
back to Chattanooga, where Rosecrans, dazed and weeping,
watched the stragglers come in. George Thomas, 'The Rock
of Chickamauga' had earned his name.

Bragg immediately surrounded Chattanooga and closed
the Army of the Cumberland in a trap. There were reper-
cussions in both armies. Bragg dismissed Polk and Nathan
Bedford Forrest for 'insubordination' (Forrest wanted to
pursue Thomas and cursed Bragg when permission was
refused) and Rosecrans, a broken man, was removed from
the Army of the Cumberland. Thomas took over for the
moment, until Lincoln, recognizing the need for a unified
command, called Grant to take charge of the entire West.
There was no doubt about the fact that Chickamauga was
a shattering Union defeat, but the tide was turning. Bragg
had all the advantages – superior numbers, the muddled
order, fine troops – yet the Army of the Cumberland still
existed as a fighting force, its morale high though its rations
were short. And Grant was there.

Grant rode into Chattanooga in the dripping cold autumn
rain, spattered with mud, 'an ordinary, scrubby-looking
man with a slightly seedy look', wrote the New York newspaperman, R. H. Dana. The situation was a bad one.
Behind Chattanooga lay a mountain chain, fine hunting
grounds for the Confederate cavalry, which had already cut
the single railroad supply line; 10,000 horses and mules died
of starvation while the troops ate acorns and parched corn.
In front of the city Bragg's troops held all the strong points,
waiting for the Army of the Cumberland to starve out.
Hooker came from the Army of the Potomac with two corps,
raising Grant's numbers to 40,000. Supply, reasoned Grant,
was the important thing, so he and Thomas set about opening a 'cracker line' on the Tennessee river. This was done
with almost ridiculous ease – Hooker's men slipped out of

the city, down a narrow valley, and in a surprise attack crossed the river and captured a bridgehead. Within a week wagonloads of food rumbled in and the army felt better. Next Grant called in Sherman with the Army of the Tennessee, raising his force to 60,000. Then he began to think about battle.

Chattanooga lies on the south-east bank of the Tennessee river, which curves in a narrow bight around it. To the south, south-west, and south-east of the city Lookout Mountain, Orchard Knob, and Missionary Ridge enclose it in a box. Bragg held them all, and the lines between. Grant planned to strike at the tip of Missionary Ridge, which protected Bragg's line of supply southward. On 23 November Sherman crossed the river and headed for the ridge, while Hooker was sent to demonstrate against Lookout to cover Sherman's movement. Sherman's maps were inaccurate: his men struck an unmapped ravine at the base of the ridge, and the Confederates had time to assemble defence. When Sherman requested aid, Grant sent Thomas' troops to him to help him hold on. Thomas' men paused at the foot of the ridge, above them three lines of rifle pits and sixty field guns. Then, without orders – no one yet knows why – they started up the steep cliff in the strangest charge of the war, straight into the guns, past the rifle pits, on over the ridge and down into Bragg's headquarters, yelling like demons. The centre of the Confederate line melted away, the right wing collapsed, and Bragg himself narrowly escaped capture; only a quick-thinking Confederate officer managed to hold his division in place long enough to cover the disorganized retreat. It was an absurd ending to a well-planned battle. Missionary Ridge was militarily impregnable to direct assault, and neither Grant nor Thomas would have dreamed of ordering a charge up its rocky sides. Yet it happened.

Chattanooga finished Bragg. He had beaten Rosecrans at Chickamauga, trapped an entire Union army in Chattanooga, and yet somehow he was now in full retreat. His friendship with Davis failed to save him. Joe Johnston took over command of the West and the fighting stopped for the winter, the Confederates resting in northern Georgia. Congress revived the grade of lieutenant-general, vacant since Washington's day, and at Lincoln's request gave it gratefully to Grant. So Grant went to Washington in March 1864 to take full command of all Union armies. Sherman replaced him in the West, while Halleck remained as chief of staff with nothing to do but fuss over reports. Lincoln's search for a general was finished. From now on Grant and Sherman would work together, stolid bulldog and wiry bird-dog, closing the ring about the Confederacy.

Grant, on his arrival in Washington, submitted to Lincoln his plan for the final defeat of the Confederacy. With the Armies of the Potomac, the James, and two smaller forces, he intended to advance on Richmond, pinning down Lee. At the same time Sherman, with the Armies of the Cumberland and Tennessee, was to move on Joe Johnston with Atlanta as his goal. Meanwhile, Grant brought Sheridan east to command the Federal cavalry, with orders to 'keep Stuart out of trouble'. Grant's plan was neither new nor brilliant, but it co-ordinated and concentrated the superior Union forces and settled on definite objectives in both eastern and western theatres, something that his predecessors had never managed. Lincoln approved, and with a sigh of relief turned the war over to Grant, rarely interfering again in military affairs.

On 4 May 1864, Grant, travelling with Meade and the Army of the Potomac, crossed the Rapidan River in the first step of his hammering campaign at Richmond. The Union armies moved blindly and slowly in the tangled underbrush of the wilderness country, while Lee, watching his cavalry reports, kept track of their progress. On 6 and 7 May Lee hit the Federals a few miles west of the old Chancellorsville field, while Stuart and Sheridan clashed in a sharp cavalry duel to the south in the hills. Caught in thick woods, with artillery useless, Grant's army lost 18,000 men in the two-day engagement. This was to Lee an old story: let them come on, strike hard, and send them reeling back toward

Washington, another Union general broken. The Army of the Potomac knew the script too. That night the Union troops waited for the familiar retreat order, but this was U. S. Grant. Instead the order came for a sliding advance to Lee's right, aiming at Spottsylvania Court House.

It was Lee's turn to be surprised. By all the rules Grant should have been backing away, but instead he acted as if he had won a battle. By the time Grant's armies arrived at Spottsylvania, the Confederates were there, dug in across the roads to Richmond. The results were the same – a field covered with dead, the Confederate lines intact. Again Lee waited for Grant to retreat, but Grant wired Lincoln, 'I propose to fight it out on this line if it takes all summer', and began his flanking advance once more. Thunderstruck, Lee hit the Federals again at North Anna; tremendous losses, the same inexorable flanking movement toward Richmond. Lee was worried, especially since Sheridan's cavalry was loose behind him, cutting at the Confederate supply lines. Nothing like this had ever happened before. Stuart, rushing back toward Richmond, caught Sheridan at Yellow Tavern only a few miles from Richmond and fought it out, but 'Beauty' Stuart fell with a bullet through his chest and the Confederate cavalry was leaderless.

On 26 May, in a swift march covered by wide-ranging avalry, Grant swung in a wide arc to Lee's right, straight at Richmond. By 2 June Lee had the move blocked at Cold Harbor, only six miles from the Confederate capital. The strain on both armies was heavy, almost a month of ceaseless movement, fighting, and slaughter. After a wrangle with Meade, Grant ordered a direct assault on the Confederate positions, a decision that he regretted for the rest of his life. In less than twenty minutes the Army of the Potomac lost 7,000 men. 'All day long', wrote General Warner, 'a perpetual funeral procession goes by my headquarters.' No army could stand such constant hammering, 55,000 casualties in three weeks to Lee's 19,000. People in the Northern towns read the daily death lists in silence and began to talk about 'Butcher' Grant. But Grant and Lee both knew that the end was not far off. Union losses could be replaced; Confederate could not. Boys of fifteen began to appear in the Confederate lines.

After Cold Harbor Grant shifted to McClellan's old plan of attacking the city from the rear, up the James River. Moving his army in a circle to the east of Richmond, he threw his forces about Petersburg, twenty miles south of the city on the Appomattox river, cutting off three of the five railroads into Richmond. After one unsuccessful attempt on Petersburg he settled down for a siege, Vicksburg-fashion, the kind of war he knew best. The fall of Richmond, in Lee's opinion, would be only a matter of time if Grant were allowed to squat thus on the city's outskirts, slowly closing in. The only answer was a diversion, a movement toward Washington that, Lee hoped, might so frighten the North that Lincoln would hastily pull Grant back to protect the capital. It had worked before, and should again. Therefore, Lee detached Jubal Early, gave him 30,000 men, and orders to swing up the Shenandoah Valley toward Washington. This was the type of action that needed Stuart, but Stuart was gone.

On 5 July Early crossed the Potomac and cut the Baltimore and Ohio railroad at Hagerstown, Maryland. Three days later he occupied Frederick, and Washington quaked. A motley force of 7,000 men met him at the Monocacy River and Early promptly engulfed them. On the 11th Early looked into Washington streets through his binoculars. But at that moment a corps of regulars from the Army of the Potomac disembarked from the ships, joined a few days later by a division from Sherman's army in the West. Early hesitated, turned away, and swung north to demand a ransom from Chambersburg, Pennsylvania, burning it to the ground when the half-million dollars he asked was not forthcoming.

Early's raid northward from the Valley had to be stopped. A new army was created, the Army of the Shenandoah, with more than 10,000 cavalry. For its commander Grant chose Sheridan, turning him loose with instructions to smash Early

and sweep the Valley clean. 'I will leave them nothing but
their eyes to weep with,' said Sheridan, and made his word
good. He struck Early at Frederick, Winchester, Fisher's
Hill, and Cedar Creek, defeated him decisively, and sent his
army retreating rapidly toward Richmond. Then for three
leisurely weeks Sheridan laid waste to the Shenandoah
Valley, leaving it so barren, his soldiers said, that 'a crow
flying across it had better carry his own rations'. His army
burned 2,000 farms, took every horse, cow, mule, and sheep
for seventy-five miles, and Lee got no more food for his
army from the rich farms of northern Virginia.

The 'municipal theory' on which Lincoln chose to fight
the war had certain advantages for the North, but it soon
proved unworkable in foreign affairs. The President could,
by the Constitution, suppress insurrection, but he could not
make war without the vote of Congress except in case of
actual invasion by a foreign power. Lincoln's position that
the seceded states had never left the Union placed the Confederacy in the position of an insurrectionary government
but did not recognize it as either belligerent, foreign, or
independent. However, in issuing his blockade order, Lincoln ran foul of a delicate technicality in international law.
Asserting on the one hand that there was no war, but rather
a rebellion, he yet proposed to seize ships of any nation
attempting to break the blockade. Instead of proclaiming a
blockade, which might be construed as recognizing the legal
belligerency of the Confederacy, Lincoln might well have
followed Jackson's lead and issued an order closing rebellious
ports, as 'Old Hickory' had shut up Charleston during the
nullification troubles. In the first case to appear in the prize
courts, involving a captured British blockade runner, the
Supreme Court decided that the conflict with the Confederacy must be a war with a foreign government, since
only such a war could justify blockade and search. Queen
Victoria, taking advantage of the legal point, immediately
recognized the Confederacy as a belligerent and accorded
Confederate ships the same status as Federal ships in British

ports, against the protests of the newly-arrived Minister, Charles Francis Adams, John Quincy's son.

Confederate diplomacy depended on 'King Cotton'. 'No, you dare not make war on cotton', remarked Senator Hammond of South Carolina. 'No power on earth dares make war upon it.' Southern leaders like Hammond were convinced that lack of raw cotton would soon force Britain and France to recognize the Confederacy as an independent nation and break the blockade, thereby precipitating war with the North. *Punch* pointed out in early 1861 that

> Though with the North we sympathize,
> It must not be forgotten,
> That with the South we've stronger ties,
> Which are composed of cotton.

The Charleston *Mercury* predicted that recognition of the Confederacy would come the day after British and French mills closed for lack of cotton; some Southerners, in fact, restricted cotton acreage and burned existing stores in order to hurry the shortage abroad. But there were large supplies of raw cotton in British and French warehouses, and although shortages in 1862 forced some British mills to suspend operations, the English working classes had great sympathy for the Union and for Lincoln – particularly when the Emancipation Proclamation placed the war on an abolitionist basis. New sources of supply, especially from India and Egypt, eased the scarcity in Britain, while Northern merchants shipped large amounts of captured Southern cotton abroad. Furthermore, Britain, suffering from crop shortages, began large importations of Northern wheat, and 'King Wheat' proved to be as diplomatically potent as 'King Cotton'.

In May 1861 Davis sent three commissioners to London to attempt to secure recognition of the Confederacy as an independent nation. Lord Russell, the Foreign Minister, gave them no promises, but two months later Victoria's proclamation recognized the Confederacy's belligerent status, followed by similar proclamations from other European nations. Regardless of the slavery issue, the attitude of the British ruling class was markedly pro-Southern, and Minister Adams faced the constant animosity of Lord Palmerston, the Foreign Secretary, who, he wrote, 'indulged in derogatory and insulting language rather than in conciliation'. Lord Russell, more flexible and astute than Palmerston, was less of a problem for Adams. Both mature, skilful, and brilliant diplomats, Adams and Russell staged a four-year duel that ended slightly to Adams' advantage: Britain did proclaim its neutrality and recognize the Confederacy as a belligerent, but it never recognized Confederate independence, the prize most coveted by the Southern emissaries. At the same time Adams found it necessary to check Secretary of State Seward, whose hot temper often led him into rash statements and dangerous policies. To add to his labours, Adams had also to watch Confederate agents in England, both diplomatic and commercial, to prevent if he could their purchase of war materials, ships, and manufactured goods.

Lord Russell at first received the Southern agents informally, but after Adams' protestations he closed his doors to them. In September 1861 the Confederacy decided to send formally accredited agents to both Britain and France, in the hope that they might gain an official audience. John Slidell of Louisiana, the commissioner for France, was an able diplomat and politician; James Mason of Virginia, the commissioner for England, was a skilful speaker and a personable man. After running the Federal blockade to Cuba both men took passage for Southampton on the British mail packet *Trent* on 7 November. But on 8 November the *Trent* was stopped by the Federal gunboat *San Jacinto*, Captain Charles Wilkes commanding, the ship searched, the commissioners removed, and both commissioners and their families carried to Boston for confinement.

The 'Trent affair' gave Adams a new headache. The Northern public was enthusiastic; Wilkes was hailed as a hero, flooded with dinners and presents, and congratulated by Secretary of the Navy Welles, though Lincoln doubted the wisdom of his act. At the same time resentment ran high in Britain. Palmerston, in a towering rage, demanded an apology and immediate release of the prisoners. Seward, who originally applauded Wilkes, soon began to have misgivings; a Northern war with Britain was exactly what the South desired, and furthermore there were obvious irregularities in Wilkes' conduct. Fortunately Prince Albert wisely toned down the ministry's angry note to the Queen, while Seward and Lincoln evolved a reply to the British that mollified public opinion at home. Mason and Slidell were released, sent to Europe on a British vessel, and everyone breathed a sigh of relief. As Adams remarked, 'The *Trent* affair . . . has proved somewhat in the nature of a sharp thunderstorm which has burst without doing any harm, and the consequence has been a decided improvement in the state of the atmosphere.'

In England Mason found considerable sympathy for the Confederate cause, especially among the upper classes who felt more kinship with Lee and the Southern aristocracy than with Lincoln and the class from which he sprang. After First Bull Run portions of the British press jibed at the 'drunken scum' put to rout by the Southern heroes, and even cool-headed Englishmen held the conviction that the South could not be conquered. The North's case was never fully clear to a large segment of the British public, which tended (at least until emancipation) to view the war less as an attempt to free slaves than to coerce a sovereign people into a Union they had already rejected. In 1862 when Confederate military successes followed quickly one after another, British sentiment for recognizing the Confederacy as an independent nation was at its highest. Gladstone declared in October that 'We may anticipate with certainty the success of the Southern States . . .', and pointed out that 'Jefferson Davis and the leaders of the South . . . have made a nation.' Russell, however, held Mason off politely, never committing himself, and after Antietam, in September of 1862, the Federal armies began to turn the tide. Lincoln's proclamation of emancipation enlisted the support of the

British working classes to the Union cause, strengthening the hands of pro-Northern liberals like Cobden and Bright. After the freeing of the slaves, Adams held a strong moral weapon that he used to good diplomatic advantage.

The most delicate of Adams' continuing problems had to do with the South's attempts to build a navy in British shipyards. Lacking both designers and construction facilities, the Confederacy sent Captain James Bullock to England in 1861 to let contracts for ships, the most important of which were to be a series of commerce-raiders built by the Laird Brothers at Birkenhead. In the spring of 1862 the first, 'Number 290', was launched while Adams protested to the Foreign Office over the delivery to the Confederacy of a ship obviously designed to attack American commerce. International law did not prevent a neutral nation from trading in war materials with belligerents, said Adams, but it did bar direct intervention or the use of the neutral country as a military or naval base. The Laird ships, claimed Adams, violated this latter rule. While British officials combed the books for an answer, 'Number 290' went to sea, was armed and equipped in the Azores with material sent from British ports, and, renamed the *Alabama*, began its depredations on Union shipping. The *Florida* followed shortly, under the same circumstances. However, Adams' violent protests stopped further construction of raiders. Years later, at the *Alabama* tribunal of Geneva in 1871, the British government officially expressed regret over the 'escape' of the raiders and paid fifteen and a half millions in damages.

The 'Laird rams', powerful ironclads built by the same Birkenhead firm in late 1862 and equipped with nine-inch rifles, provoked a similar crisis. At first the Lairds declared that the ships had been ordered by France, then by Egypt, both claims officially denied by the governments concerned. Confederate agents actually did have ownership of the vessels transferred to a French firm, a ruse that deceived no one. Though legally the Confederacy was on safe ground, Adams kept up such a volley of protests that Lord Russell ordered the rams to be held in the yards. They were never released, and with them went the last Southern chance to break the blockade.

John Slidell found considerably greater encouragement at the court of Napoleon III, who was quite willing to penetrate the blockade with French ships and to recognize Confederate independence, if only Britain would agree to co-operate with him. During 1862 Slidell and Mason held hopes of consolidating a Southern alliance with both France and England. In April 1862 Napoleon proposed a joint naval expedition up the Mississippi, a plan that Russell refused to consider; and in July, at Slidell's insistence, Napoleon sent another proposal to Russell for recognition of the Confederacy; again Russell refused. In January 1863, after Fredericksburg, Napoleon offered his services to Lincoln as a mediator, which Lincoln politely declined. Union victories at Gettysburg and Vicksburg in mid-1863 cooled British and French enthusiasm for intervention considerably, and Adams afterwards found his path much easier. Napoleon, however, had a deeper game to play.

The key to Napoleon's diplomatic manœuvrings during the Civil War lay in his desire to establish a Mexican empire, a venture made possible when Britain, France, and Spain decided that the Civil War gave them a chance to challenge the validity of the Monroe Doctrine. Frequent and bloody revolutions in Mexico, resulting in defalcation on debts and extensive destruction of foreign-owned property, led the three nations to agree in October 1861 on a joint military expedition into Mexico to protect investments and collect debts. Seeing little advantage in the scheme, Britain and Spain shortly withdrew, but not Napoleon, who had visions of establishing a puppet empire in Mexico.

In 1861 and 1862, with its hands full and military reverses following in quick succession, the Washington government could do little to thwart him. French troops entered Mexico, scattered Juarez's native army, and easily occupied Mexico City in June 1863. By that time, however, Union military prospects were considerably brighter, and Secretary of State

Seward could turn his attention toward Mexico. He had no desire to push France, already friendly to the Confederacy, into an outright alliance. At first he contented himself with carefully worded notes defining the American position and reaffirming the Monroe Doctrine, but never by name. In 1864, when Maximilian accepted the throne of Mexico, the tone of Seward's notes became sharper; after Appomattox, with the Confederacy no longer a factor in diplomacy, he strengthened his demands that French military forces leave Mexico. The North had 900,000 men under arms, and Grant had already ordered Sheridan with 50,000 veterans to the Texas border. In 1866 Napoleon abandoned Maximilian to his fate before a Mexican firing squad, and the French dream of a new American empire vanished.

After Gettysburg the sands of Confederate diplomacy began to run out. Crises in Italy, Poland, and Schleswig-Holstein turned Europe's attention away from the American conflict; Adams wrote that 'America is not much talked of here, never so little since I first came.' Early in the war Lincoln resolved to send prominent unionists abroad as unofficial ambassadors – men such as Thurlow Weed the politician, the Catholic bishops of Ohio and New York, and Robert Walker of Mississippi – who had strong influence on public opinion in Europe. Northern appeals to British workers proved extremely effective; though Lincoln's insistence on the preservation of the Union as his chief war aim meant little to the working man, the emancipation of the slaves completely changed his picture of the war. The war brought unemployment to 400,000 cotton mill workers, but Bright and others urged them to support 'the holy war' against slavery, and mass meetings of workers responded by passing resolutions favouring the North. The mill-hands of Manchester, among others, vowed to support the Union cause and congratulated Lincoln on his 'erasure of that foul blot on civilization and Christianity – chattel slavery'. While Southern propagandists vainly attempted to enlist British support and hoped that unemployment would force the British working classes into acquiescence, their hopes were shattered both by the determination of Bright and by the shrewdness of the Federal Congress which mitigated the worst horrors of idleness in the mills by sending to Britain shiploads of wheat.

By 1864 the Confederate agents had lost the battle for Britain. Sherman marched to the sea, Grant penned Lee in Richmond, and Davis observed that the French and British both treated his emissaries with cold formality. Davis' last desperate manœuvre – an offer to abolish slavery in the Confederacy in exchange for British recognition – fell on deaf ears, and Lee's surrender closed the books. At the news of Lincoln's assassination the British press excelled itself in praise of the man it had once bitterly reviled. Adams' work was done. As James Russell Lowell said, 'None did more for the North than he in his forlorn outpost at London.'

When Grant moved on Richmond in May of 1864, Sherman, the other arm of the pincers, left Tennessee. He had nearly 100,000 men; between him and Atlanta, the stronghold of the western South, stood Joe Johnston with 72,000. Johnston and Sherman were closely matched antagonists; in Thomas and Hood both had able lieutenants; both armies were experienced, disciplined, confident. There was only one feasible route to Atlanta – a city filled with heavy industry, iron-works, and storehouses – straight down the railroad from Chattanooga, and both Sherman and Johnston knew it.

An expertly-executed series of flanking movements, beginning in the spring of 1864, took Sherman's army into middle Georgia, and by early July he was only fifteen miles from Atlanta. Mutterings in the Southern press grew louder as he came closer, and there were angry debates in the Congress at Richmond. Joe Johnston's Fabian tactics – draw Sherman farther and farther away from his base in Chattanooga, and then strike him one shattering blow – were not popular in a South accustomed to Lee's victories. The Georgia delegation in Congress railed at Davis; he in turn railed at Johnston, who quietly told him that there was no way of stopping Sherman short of Atlanta itself. On 11 July Davis removed Johnston and gave the command to John B. Hood, a giant one-armed Texan with a flair for attack. Sherman, who respected and feared Joe Johnston, highly approved of the change.

Atlanta, built on a plateau surrounded by hills, ravines, and creeks, was expertly fortified with a ring of entrenchments. There Johnston felt he could have held Sherman off indefinitely. Hood, however, was no defensive warrior. He promised action, and on 2 July he attacked Sherman at Peachtree Creek north of the city. The brunt of the blow fell on Thomas' Army of the Cumberland, veterans of Snodgrass Hill and Missionary Ridge, and Hood lost 4,000 men in less than two hours. To make matters worse, Sherman sent McPherson and the Army of the Tennessee slipping around Hood's right, threatening Atlanta and cutting two of the four railroads into the city. The Texan pulled back his army, and the next day hit McPherson east of the city, losing 10,000 more men. Sherman immediately drew the ring tighter. Facing Atlanta from the north-west, north, and south-east, he slowly pushed the right wing of his army around Atlanta to the west. Hood struck at the circle again on the 28th – 5,000 casualties. 'They no longer come on so boldly as before', noted a Union commander, and shells from Sherman's artillery began to drop in the city streets.

For nearly a month Sherman held on, shelling the city, testing its defences, probing for a weak spot. Meanwhile, Wheeler's Confederate cavalry cut at Sherman's long supply lines, stretching north along the railroad to Chattanooga. Election time was approaching in the North, and after Grant's bloody Wilderness campaigns, the anti-Lincoln politicians shouted that the war was a failure. Finally, on 27 August, Hood's cavalry brought in reports that Sherman's army was abandoning its positions north of Atlanta, obviously preparing to fall back along the railroad lines toward northern Georgia. Hood was overjoyed, but while Atlanta's church bells rang in jubilation, the wind brought the sound of heavy artillery from the south. It was Sherman, who had

cut loose from his supply lines, swung his main army around
Atlanta, and at the moment was hammering at Jonesboro,
fifteen miles to the south of the city. The next day he took
Jonesboro, severed the last rail lines into Atlanta, and turned
on Hood with his full force. Two nights later, sitting on a
stump in the dark, Sherman heard guns to the north:
Slocum's artillery booming salutes as his men marched into
Atlanta's deserted streets; and he ordered a dispatch to
Lincoln, 'Atlanta is ours, and fairly won.' Atlanta's fall,
said Seward, 'knocked the planks out of the Democratic
platform' and practically assured Lincoln's re-election.

Hood, after escaping from Atlanta, reformed his army at
Macon. Sherman's position, despite his successful capture of
Atlanta, was precarious. He was deep in enemy territory,
dependent on a single railroad line connecting him with his
bases; Confederate cavalry cut it so often that the Union
army was almost constantly on short rations. Hood's army
was intact, though weakened, and Hood still perfectly able
to mount a strong offensive. Hood, furthermore, had plans
of his own to slip behind Sherman, march on Tennessee,
and force Sherman to rush back from Georgia to defend his
bases. With this in mind, Hood began to edge his way north
and west, aiming at Tennessee.

Sherman, having come thus far, refused to be forced back.
He detached Thomas and two corps, and sent them back to
Nashville with orders to hold Hood at all costs. This was
hardly enough to defeat Hood, but Sherman trusted Thomas
to weld an army that could out of the replacements and
minor forces scattered through Tennessee and Mississippi.
Let Hood move on Tennessee, Thomas could hold him. As
for Sherman, he had an audacious plan of his own. Why not
break away from Atlanta, live off the country, and head
straight across Georgia to the sea, thus severing what remained of the Confederacy and isolating Georgia, Alabama,
and Florida? Dangerous the plan might be. Lincoln was
fearful and even Grant uncertain. Against it stood so many
chances of misadventure. If Hood defeated Thomas and
took Tennessee, then the war in the West had to be fought

over again. Suppose Sherman's army could not live off the country, or met such resistance that it never reached the sea and the naval supply ships? Grant temporized, but Sherman prepared for his march with complete confidence. All sick, convalescent, and older troops he sent back to Thomas, stripping his own army down to young, battle-seasoned veterans. He reorganized his 60,000 remaining troops into two big wings, with a powerful cavalry force to sweep along at their sides. Then, in early November he received from Washington grudging permission to begin what the newspapers immediately labelled 'the wild adventure of a crazy fool'. On 12 November, after the last train left the city, Sherman tore up the railroad and headed for Savannah and the sea, while Atlanta, a useless hulk, burned fiercely behind him. 'I will make Georgia howl,' he said.

For three weeks neither Lincoln nor Grant had news of Sherman except from Southern newspapers. There was nothing in front of him except Wilson's cavalry and a motley collection of militia and home guards who scattered before 'Uncle Billy's bummers'. His troops ripped up railroads, twisting the rails into 'Sherman hairpins'; they pillaged stores and barns, burned towns, and left blackened chimneys where plantation houses once stood. They swept through Milledgeville, the state capital, and pressed on to the sea, leaving behind them a swath of destruction fifty miles wide. Negroes, convinced that 'de day ob Jubilo' had come, marched happily behind them, while cavalry raiders cleared plantation smokehouses of hams and filled their knapsacks with the family silver. It was almost a picnic; sixty years later old men vividly remembered that march in the cool Southern autumn as they sang exuberantly,

> How the darkies shouted when they heard the joyful sound!
> How the turkeys gobbled which our commissary found!
> How the sweet potatoes even started from the ground –
> While we were marching through Georgia!

Meanwhile, at Richmond, trains from the deep South no longer arrived, and one by one the telegraph lines went dead.

THE CIVIL WAR IN VIRGINIA

PENNSYLVANIA

✝ Gettysburg

MARYLAND

✕ Antietam
✕ Harper's
Ferry

○ Baltimore

WEST
VIRGINIA

Potomac

○ Washington

○ Front
Royal

✕ Manassas &
Chantilly

Shenandoah

Chancellorsville
Wilderness ☐ ✝ ✕ Fredericksburg

VIRGINIA

James

Richmond ○ ☐ Cold Harbor

☐ Appomattox

Petersburg ☐

○ Yorktown

Battles		Lee's advance to the North, 1863
✕	1862	
✝	1863	Grant's final campaign in the South, 1865
☐	1864-5	

On 10 December a Federal gunboat standing off Savannah saw gun-flashes in the dusk. It signalled the shore, 'Who are you?' The light winked back, 'Sherman'. That was the end of the march to the sea. At a cost of 400 men Sherman had slashed the Confederacy in two, destroyed fortunes in food and equipment, closed the next to last major Southern seaport, and stood with 60,000 fresh troops directly behind Lee. Behind him too, in the ruined Southern heartland, he left anger that still rankles.

While Sherman sliced through Georgia, Hood and his 50,000 men, preceded by Forrest's cavalry, marched across northern Georgia toward Thomas, who was hurriedly moulding an army from the casuals, sick, and unfit that (added to the 22,000 from Sherman) he had for the defence of Nashville. Hood moved surprisingly fast, and Thomas sent Schofield south of Nashville to hold him off. In a sharp clash at Franklin, Tennessee, Schofield slowed Hood's advance and inflicted heavy casualties, but still Hood pressed on toward Nashville. Thomas, a slow-moving perfectionist, refused to act until everything was in order; his cavalry lacked mounts, an ice-storm made roads slippery, he needed arms and ammunition; while Grant in the East fumed at his inaction. Finally, on 15 December, Thomas declared his army ready.

It was over in a few hours. In one of the most perfectly planned and executed battles of the war, Thomas completely smashed Hood's entire army. Of his original 55,000, a week later Hood was able to gather together only 9,000 men; 13,000 captured, 10,000 dead or wounded, the rest scattered beyond recall. It happened so suddenly that it was hard for men to realize that the war in the West was over; that there was no longer an effective Confederate army west of Richmond. Jefferson Davis now governed only three states, Virginia, North Carolina, and South Carolina, and only Lee was left to defend them. A month later a group of Confederate Congressmen called on Lee to offer him the Presidency. He refused, but Jefferson Davis never again had any real power in the Confederacy.

The loss of Savannah and the annihilation of Hood's army brought affairs in the South to a crisis. Lee, placed in complete command of all Confederate forces, called on Joe Johnston to stop Sherman, who turned north from Savannah and swept into South Carolina. Johnston was able to muster only 34,000 troops, drawn from the South's last reserve of manpower and no match for Sherman's veterans. Pushing the Confederates before him, Sherman lashed across South Carolina ('Here secession began', said one Union soldier, 'and here, by God, it will end') into Columbia, the capital, while the Navy closed off the South's last seaport at Charleston. By March Johnston's position was desperate. Retreating slowly into North Carolina, losing heavily at every engagement, outnumbered two to one, he asked Lee for reinforcements.

Lee had none to give. Grant waited near Petersburg, never attacking in force, wearing down Lee's army. The Confederate lines were dangerously thin; replacements were non-existent; no more supplies came in from the Shenandoah Valley or the deep South, no more arms or medicines from the blockade-runners. In March Lee gathered all his forces for a single desperate blow at Grant's centre, hoping to break out of Richmond and join Johnston for an attack on Sherman. The Union army beat it back, and Grant kept pounding at Richmond, hitting here and there, keeping Lee's tired and hungry divisions running back and forth within the circle to ward them off. It was a magnificent defence, ably and bravely done, but it was 60,000 against 120,000, and there was not enough to eat. Wherever Lee turned Grant was there, double in numbers. Richmond and Petersburg had only two rail lines running to the west; if Grant circled the city and cut these, Richmond and Lee's army were lost. On 1 April Lee attacked Sheridan's forces at Five Forks south of Petersburg in an attempt to break out of the circle. Sheridan beat him back, but Grant reasoned that if Lee could mount an attack at Petersburg, his lines must be dangerously thin somewhere else. He ordered an immediate attack on all fronts.

On Sunday, 2 April, Jefferson Davis went to church. In the middle of the service a man tiptoed down the aisle and handed Davis a note. He read it, flushed, and left. Lee was evacuating Richmond, dropping back along the railroads to the west. Richmond refused to believe it; but the next afternoon there was a sound of bugles and the Union cavalry rode into the city, followed by a crack Negro infantry regiment, its flags flying, band playing, uniforms creased and brass shining. Lincoln, walking in the quiet Virginia dusk, knocked at a door and asked for his old friend George Pickett. He was not at home.

Lee's troops marched westward along the rail lines to Danville, the Union army moving parallel, knifing into the tired columns. At Danville Lee found nothing but Federal blue. He turned toward Lynchburg. Sheridan's cavalry, a cloud of superbly mounted horsemen carrying repeating rifles, barred the way. The Army of Northern Virginia wearily prepared to attack, but almost with contempt the cavalry lines parted to show massed behind them the solid blue mass of Ord's infantry, spread out in battle order, artillery in place. On 7 April Grant called on Lee to surrender, shifting to him 'the responsibility of any further effusion of blood'. 'Then there is nothing left for me to do but to go see General Grant,' said Lee, 'and I would rather die a thousand deaths.' On 9 April he sent for Grant and met him near Appomattox Courthouse; Lee, dignified and impassive in a handsome gold-braided full-dress uniform; Grant, with the inevitable cigar stump, in a faded blue private's uniform with five tarnished gold stars on the shoulder straps. The two men talked for half an hour of old friends and Mexican War days, until Lee, recognizing Grant's diffidence, reminded him of the purpose of their meeting. The terms were easy and honourable: surrender of all men and equipment, but the Confederates might keep their horses and the Army of the Potomac would provide immediately full rations for 28,000 men. So the Army of Northern Virginia surrendered.

Five days later, at Ford's Theatre in Washington, Lincoln

watched *Our American Cousin*, a broad satire on British society. John Wilkes Booth shot him in the head, mouthed his inappropriate Latin phrase, and was gone.

News of Appomattox reached Johnston and Sherman by 18 April, and on 26 April Johnston surrendered. On 4 May the small Confederate forces isolated in the deep South gave up, followed in a few days by the scattered troops west of the Mississippi. Fleeing southward, Jefferson Davis joined Johnston, but Johnston refused to continue the hopeless struggle and Davis left for Mexico. Federal troops captured him in southern Georgia on 10 May and sent him to Fortress Monroe, where Vice-President Stephens and other Confederate officials were already imprisoned.

The long dying was over.

CHAPTER 26

THE GILDED AGE
1865–96

THE issues of post-war reconstruction were both sectional and national, so interlocked as to make them virtually inseparable. The Southerner's problem was threefold: to adjust to a new set of social and economic conditions; recreate a new political society; and pick up the pieces (if he could) of a life shattered by war. The North meanwhile was concerned with consolidating victory, retaining control of the Federal government, and establishing economic and political authority over the conquered Confederacy.

No period of American history saw such a drastic revision of the character of American life as the decades 1860–90. War and reconstruction, first of all, settled the old controversy between nationalism and states' rights. Even in the South the nationalizing process continued in wartime; the Confederate government laid taxes, conscripted troops, seized private supplies and facilities, ran industries – or in other words displayed all the qualities of a centralized state. Particularly in the North-west, where provincial loyalties were never strong, wartime nationalism continued undiminished. Proud of having survived its first test, more conscious than ever of its 'destiny', post-war America possessed, as one editor said, 'a new sense of free, quickened, national existence'.

The Civil War resolved the conflict over slavery, but in doing so created new conflicts. By eliminating chattel slavery, the war cut away the whole underpinning of Southern life. When slavery went the aristocratic leader-class went too; not for a generation could the South develop another set of leaders to replace them. Political power in the South had been vested since the founding of the Republic in a relatively small group of planter-aristocrats whose authority rested on slavery. The war swept them out of power and left the majority of Southern white men without leadership, side by side with four million new Negro voters. Without slavery the South's whole labour system required revision. Ex-slaves, almost all of them unskilled agricultural workers who owned no land, dreamed of owning 'forty acres and a mule'. Planters no longer had a supply of chattel labour nor money to hire their former slaves. 'Sharecropping' provided a substitute. Instead of wages the worker accepted a share of the crop, or (in the case of a tenant farmer) the landowner furnished tools, land, horses or mules, and the farmer furnished the toil. The system, at first a device to attract Negro labour, was shortly extended to whites, creating labour problems as difficult as any that ever existed under slavery.

The abolition of slavery upset the traditional system of race relations carefully worked out in the South over the space of a century. Readjustment was hard for both white and Negro. Deep-rooted prejudices simply carried over into post-war Southern life without noticeable change. The new Northern masters made no attempt to change the Southern pattern of race relationships; the Southerner could not. The Negro had his freedom, but with it he gained precious few rights. This was perhaps the most tragic aftermath of the Civil War.

His sudden freedom confused and bewildered the Negro, and for a year and more after the war thousands of ex-slaves wandered over the South while the Freedman's Bureau tried to make some order out of reconstruction. The freedman's first hope was for economic equality, either as a wage worker or as a farmer, but since slaves were taught few skills or trades, his prime usefulness was as a simple labourer. His 'forty acres and a mule' never came, and Thaddeus Stevens' suggestion that large plantations be confiscated and the land distributed to Negroes was quickly quashed. Congress instead left the matter in the hands of states or private agencies, with the result that the majority of Negroes went into share-cropping, which served as an effective way

of keeping them under social and political as well as economic control.

The place of the Negro in American life was fixed during
reconstruction by Northerners as well as by Southerners.
Opposition to slavery as a labour system did not always
imply acceptance of the ex-slave as a social, economic, or
political equal. Prejudice against the Negro was strong in the
post-war North; and the main body of Northern opinion
believed as the South did, that the Negro was an inferior
being, that he could never be fully assimilated into the
American system, that he was best kept subordinate to the
white man. Segregation, discrimination and 'jim crow'
customs received the tacit approval even of such Northern
liberals as Godkin of *The Nation*.

Negro leaders were cruelly disappointed at the failure of
Northern reconstruction to keep its promises. Frederick
Douglass commented bluntly that the Civil War simply
changed the form of slavery. Booker T. Washington, who
built Tuskegee Institute into a leading American Negro
educational institution, developed a policy, however, that
became the pattern for Negro life until well into the
twentieth century. The Negro, said Washington, must not
attempt to become a white man. He should learn to be a
skilled workman and business man, avoid conflict with white
men over civil or social rights, and earn the respect of the
nation through thrift, industry, courtesy, and morality. Not
all Negroes agreed. Some of Washington's contemporaries
and many of the leaders of the next generation believed that
a more aggressive struggle for Negro rights might hasten
their acquisition. Shortly after the turn of the century the
National Association for the Advancement of Colored People
organized to press for the observance of all Negro social and
civil rights as guaranteed by the Constitution and its amendments. Both philosophies of action still exist within the ranks
of Negro leaders.

War had an incalculable effect on American economic
life. The Civil War put the finishing touches to the Industrial Revolution, and when it closed, industrialism was

firmly fixed as the primary fact of the national economy. This would have happened had there been no war, but the military conflict speeded up the process and hastened the shift from agriculture to business as the nation's business. Industrial interests took full advantage of the magnificent opportunities provided by the War to gain almost everything they could possibly desire: protective tariffs, easy access to natural resources, lowered taxes, government subsidies, near-monopoly of certain economic areas. After 1865 'captains of industry' replaced farmers as the sovereign political class. The philosophy of business – the ideal of self-help, business leadership, beneficent industrialism – became the dominant ideal of American life. The agricultural interests of the North-west were neither strong nor well organized enough to challenge the leadership of business; Southern agrarians, defeated and discredited, could no longer offer the resistance they had maintained for fifty years. So 'big business' arrived. 'The leading capitalists', wrote John Sherman to his brother the General, '. . . talk of millions as confidently as formerly of thousands.'

Devastated though it was by war, the South's recovery was amazingly swift. Railroad tracks twisted by Sherman's armies were relaid and new lines built into the South-west; the old harbours of Norfolk, Charleston, Savannah, Mobile, and New Orleans hummed with trade. Where credit could be had a few enterprising manufacturers opened old factories or built new ones. Instead of shipping cotton North, Southerners began to develop their own textile industry. Coal and iron deposits in Alabama and Tennessee, neglected since the eighteenth century, were soon producing one-fifth of the nation's iron and coal, while the soft pine forests of the hill country became the basis of a new lumber industry. Tobacco crops flourished; twenty years after Appomattox North Carolina alone produced ten million pounds of tobacco a year.

Yet the South, despite its industrial advance, remained a predominantly rural and agricultural section; only one city in the South, New Orleans, exceeded 100,000 population.

Its tobacco, lumber, and textile industries were closely linked to its farms. Small farmers, poor whites, ex-slaves, and city-dwellers, shut out from the land by the planters for generations, bought up farm-plots when the cotton kings were forced to sell, eliminating the old-style thousand-acre plantation. In pre-war Mississippi few farms were less than ten acres in size; in 1870 there were 11,000 of ten acres and less, carved out of the feudal holdings of the great planters. Out of all this emerged a rising Southern class of merchants, farmers, artisans, business men, bankers, and small industrialists, the middle class the South lacked under slavery.

War stimulated Northern economy into wild activity. Congress and the states financed the construction of railroads to the tune of nearly a hundred million dollars; ten years after the war 20,000 miles of new track stretched through the West and South. In the same ten years the number of Northern manufacturing firms increased 80 per cent. More coal was dug, more iron produced, more steel made, more metals mined, more cotton milled, more of everything manufactured than in any previous period in American history. Names like Vanderbilt, Stanford, and Gould in railroading; McCormick in farm machinery; Carnegie, Hewitt, and Morgan in steel; and Rockefeller and Frick in oil, filled the headlines. The rewards of such industrial enterprise (and of plain luck) were fantastically large. Wealth influenced state and Federal legislation, founded colleges and universities, financed churches and foundations, bought art collections and filled museums. Wealth was the key to almost any kind of success, and wealth came from business and industry.

The farmer profited by the war, though never so much as the business man. The Republican-sponsored Homestead Act opened up new land areas to the small farmer, though some of it was virtually stolen by land companies and speculators. Wartime demands for wheat and corn and beef pushed farm production to new heights; millions of acres of virgin soil made it possible; thousands of miles of new railroads brought it to market. Agricultural production doubled between 1865 and 1875, most of the increase coming from the North-west, where Nebraska, Iowa, Kansas, Minnesota, and the Dakotas became the centre of grain and corn production. The post-war boom introduced into the national economy new and extremely complex agricultural problems of markets, credit, over-production, and tariffs that led directly to the agrarian uprisings of the nineties. But in the immediate post-war years the outlook for the farmer was rosy.

The working man probably gained least from the war. Wages rose, but prices rose faster. The return of a million veterans, added to the millions of immigrants admitted during wartime, upset the post-war labour market. As corporations grew in size and wealth the bargaining power of the individual worker (and of his union, if he had one) decreased. During the war a few skilled groups, such as shoemakers, printers, and bricklayers, organized into unions to protect themselves, without much success, against cheap labour, new machinery, and falling wages. The Republican party, anxious to pass legislation for business and industry, neglected the needs and wishes of the labouring man for the next twenty years, but not until near the turn of the century did labour become a real political force.

Post-war chaos carried within it the seeds of moral laxity and public dishonesty. Wartime spending encouraged speculation, lavish expenditures, and a consequent loosening of political morality. Money greased the ways while those profiteers and shady politicians who reaped harvests from wartime graft had no intention of going poor in peace-time. Political fortune-hunters ('carpetbaggers', because they came with a few spare clothes packed in carpet bags) rushed Southward to take advantage of new opportunities for pocket-lining. Uneducated, without political experience, dazzled and puzzled by his new responsibilities, the Negro was ridiculously easy prey for the grafter. There were also millions of Southern poor whites who, long before the Civil War, had been virtually disenfranchised; added to these were millions of Europeans who poured into the country under loosened immigration laws. Unaccustomed to political processes and with little understanding of governmental administration, the Negro, poor white, and immigrant provided during reconstruction perfect tools for unscrupulous politicians, North and South.

The war temporarily destroyed the two-party system in American politics. The Republican Party emerged from it strong and triumphant; the Democrats ended it discredited as 'rebels', divided in the North, suppressed in the South. When the war closed and some of the seceded states began to prepare to return to the Union, the Republicans faced the prospect of losing control of state and Federal governments. Reconstruction, therefore, had to be undertaken in such a manner as to insure Republican party supremacy for years to come. At stake were all the gains the Republicans had made during the war – policies of tariff, subsidy, taxes, currency, disposal of land and natural resources – and Republican leaders had no desire to see Southern and Northern Democrats allied with the North-west farmer, in a position to oppose them on any of these policies in Congress. The post-war plan of the Radical Republicans, therefore, was to prevent if possible the return to the Union of any Southern state under anything but Republican control.

To accomplish this it was first necessary to disenfranchise Southern Democrats and to enfranchise the only group that could be so controlled as to guarantee a Republican vote, that is, the Negro and the poor white. The Republican plan was clever, but it failed to consider the explosive nature of the racial issue in the South. The poor white (and his middle class brother) so feared the Negro that a political coalition of the two was impossible. As soon as Union military forces withdrew from the South, its whole political pattern was rearranged. Southern Democrats quickly found effective ways of disenfranchising the Negro; the poor and middle class white man simply followed his old leaders and voted with them. The Republican party, built on Negro votes and supported by Northern armies, virtually disappeared from the South after 1876.

The Republican organization itself was less unified than appeared at first sight. Under stress of war the abolitionists, War Democrats, old-line Whigs, and North-west Freesoilers who made up the party evolved an unstable unity on one principle only, opposition to slavery. Lincoln attempted to bind it together on the issue of union, but even his consummate political skill could not keep his party entirely unified. Fissures had appeared in its structure long before Appomattox. By 1863 it was clear that within the Republican party there existed a deep cleavage between Radical and Conservative Republicans, between the Wade-Stevens-Sumner group and the faction led by Lincoln. The Radicals angrily resented Lincoln's attempts to interfere with the process of wartime reconstruction and scoffed at the hope he expressed in his Second Inaugural that the Union be restored 'with malice toward none and charity for all'. Lincoln's assassination, declared one Radical, was apparently 'God's will'.

After Lincoln's death Republican leadership quickly passed to his opponents. The Radical Republicans in Congress, representing Northern industrialism, took charge of the party and of reconstruction, remaining in almost absolute control of the national government for twenty years. Meanwhile the Democratic party slowly and painfully developed into an opposition party of non-industrial, agrarian, and labour interests. Then and only then did the two-party system re-establish itself.

The scars of war healed very slowly, and encouraged intensely emotional political partisanships – 'the Solid South', and 'rock-ribbed Republican New England', among others. Sherman's march to the sea and Sheridan's ravages in the Valley are remembered yet in parts of the South; the horrors of Libby Prison and Andersonville stockade stuck in Northern minds for years. Veterans of both armies formed solid voting blocs that influenced the strategy of politics for at least two more generations. The Union veterans' organization, the Grand Army of the Republic, became a sort of unofficial wing of the Republican party. In the South, candidates wooing the Confederate vote needed only to refer to Lee, or Jackson, or Stuart, and wave the bloody shirt of the gallant dead. There was little hope of solving intersectional political problems so long as politicians fostered animosity and bitterness. It was twenty years after the war before a Democrat entered the White House, almost fifty years before a Southern-born candidate could be elected President, nearly seventy years before a Southern state gave its electoral vote to a Republican.

The real political meaning of the Civil War is that it was a war between governments representing sections. It was not a 'rebellion' nor 'a war between the states', but a war between the United States of America, a *de jure* government, and the Confederate States of America, a *de facto* government representing eleven states of the Federal Union. The result of that conflict determined that one set of sectional interests would dominate another, that one sectional political group would direct the national policy according to its own particular theories. The Northern victory meant that Northern industrial and business interests, long held in check by a coalition of South and North-west, were free to run the nation as they wished. Questions of land, taxes, internal improvements, industrial expansion, finances, tariffs, and the like, which had been hotly debated in Congress for years, were quickly settled as the Northerner wanted them settled. For a decade the South simply ceased to exist as a political force. The North-west, not yet organized as a political unit, was for the time being allied with the North-east. But in combining with the North-east to crush the South the North-west lost its old agrarian ally. When the South was rebuilt, and the North-west emerged as a sectional unit with its own set of political and economic interests, the sectional conflict resumed.

When Grant and Lee met at Appomattox the trans-Mississippi West was still an empty wilderness of mountain and plain, covering almost half the total area of the United States. California, of course, was a full-fledged state, and in the Pacific North-west a hundred thousand settlers clustered on the rich coastal lands of Washington and Oregon; but between the Pacific and the eastern rim of settlement in Iowa, Kansas, Nebraska, and Minnesota there was only an immense expanse of rolling plain, the land of Sioux and Crow, Cheyenne, Arapahoe, Ute, Kiowa, Blackfoot, and Apache. In 1890 all this was changed. That year the Census Bureau declared that the 'frontier of settlement . . . cannot any longer have a place in the census reports'. After three hundred years of westering, the frontier line was gone.

The opening of the last West was delayed by problems of climate and geography as well as by war. The farming line stopped at the 98th meridian, beyond which lay a high, arid plateau of sparse grassland reaching to the Rockies. There was little rainfall and long droughts, rivers were shallow, muddy, and unpredictable, there were no forests for timber, and the climate (from 110° in summer to 30° below zero in winter) was among the most inhumane known to man.

The most important factor in the settlement of the trans-Mississippi West was the railroad. A transcontinental railroad had been discussed in Congress since the fifties, but was blocked annually by the Southern delegates. When secession removed their opponents, Congressional supporters of a cross-continent rail line passed an act giving the Union Pacific a charter to build westward from Iowa and the Central Pacific, a charter to build eastward from California, the two to meet at some unspecified point between. By the terms of the act the construction companies received land and timber grants and Federal loans to cover costs; in 1864 a new act increased the grants and eased the credit terms. In all the railroads received twenty-four million acres of land and sixty-five millions in loans.

Construction began in 1863, although the major portion of the work had to wait until the end of the war. The Union Pacific imported thousands of Irish labourers; the Central Pacific used Chinese coolies, hence the remark that the eastern half of the line was built on whisky, the western half on tea. The labourers lived in shanties and tents, going to work each morning on 'track trains'. When the track was down for sixty miles the crews moved to 'end of track' and set up again, with a central 'Big Tent' (100 feet by 40 feet) housing a bar, dance floor, and gambling equipment. Each new 'set-up' was surrounded by tents and shacks housing more bars, more dance halls, more gambling quarters, and 'houses' for the women who followed the crews – some 3,000 people who formed a movable Gomorrah designed to separate the labourer from his wages every Saturday night. Today, a string of towns spaced roughly sixty miles apart, still marks the path of the Union Pacific. But the men laid track, four rails a minute. Racing with time, the crews battled over desert and mountain, dredged rivers, built bridges, fought off Indians, weathered forty-foot snows, and blasted through mountains; in one stretch of sixty miles the Central Pacific bored fifteen tunnels. On 10 May 1869 the two tracks met in Utah and the continent was spanned. Chicago celebrated with a procession seven miles long, Philadelphia rang the Liberty Bell, and the New York City Council ordered a 100-gun salute. Other lines soon pushed across the plains, the Santa Fe, the Southern Pacific, the Northern Pacific, the Great Northern.

The presence of the railroad, which sometimes preceded the settler, changed the character of the last frontier. For the pioneer there was no longer the painful, lonely period of isolation before settlement caught up with him, for the rails linked him with civilization, with markets, newspapers, magazines, politics, ideas. The whole process of evolution from empty land to territory to state was hastened by decades. The roll of states admitted to the Union after the war illustrated the speed with which this was accomplished. Nevada, admitted in 1864 when the Republicans believed its electoral vote might be needed, was first. Nebraska followed in 1867, Colorado in 1876; in 1889 and 1890 North Dakota, South Dakota, Wyoming, Montana, Idaho, and Washington entered, followed by Utah, Oklahoma, Arizona, and New Mexico, the last three after 1900.

The first break into the South-west came with the cattleman's invasion of the plains. The Spanish had raised cattle there for centuries, but Texas ranchers after the Civil War built an empire on beef. Selective breeding produced a tall, tough animal with enormous twisting horns, until there were five million such longhorns in Texas by 1865. The ranchers' biggest problem was transportation, since rail lines had not yet reached the area, but Texas cattlemen solved it in 1866 by simply driving the hardy stock across the dry lands to the Kansas railheads. By 1872 a half million cattle, destined for the stockyards of Chicago and Omaha, had made the trip via one of four trails, the Western (to Dodge City, Kansas), the Chisholm (to Abilene, Kansas), the Sedalia (to Missouri), or the Goodnight-Loving (to Cheyenne, Wyoming Territory). By the eighties the cattle kingdom reached into Colorado, Montana, Idaho, and the Dakotas, but the spread of railroads, the fenced range, and industrialized methods of stockfarming changed the character of the old-style 'cow country'. The beef boom collapsed. The golden era of the rancher and the cowboy lasted only twenty years, though it left behind a legend that still remains in American mythology – the old romantic West of tumbleweed and cowtowns, hard-shooting punchers and rascally rustlers, chuck-wagon camp-fires and sad songs of the cowboy's lonely lot.

While longhorns roamed the plains the farmer pushed his way into the last undeveloped areas of cheap land in the West. The invention of barbed wire in 1873 and the widespread use of the windmill helped to solve some of the problems of plains agriculture; in the mid-seventies the Federal government broke the land monopoly of the cattlemen and threw open the arable grasslands to homesteaders. Railroads, with millions of acres of land to dispose of, flooded the East and Europe with propaganda for the West, promising easy credit, reduced rail rates, good land, and every possible form of assistance. Land speculators, steamship companies, banks, and state and territorial governments advertised relentlessly for settlers. The Union Pacific described the Platte Valley as 'a flowery meadow of great fertility clothed in nutritious grasses and watered by numerous

·streams'. Minnesota bought space in Irish newspapers, hired agents in Germany, and printed pamphlets in six languages. Germans, Irish, Scotch, Scandinavians, and Russians responded in droves. In less than twenty years the population of the plains states leaped from one to four millions.

A second factor in the settlement of the plains West was the post-war mining boom. Gold was discovered in Colorado before the war, though the veins ran out fairly soon and those adventurers who stayed settled into farming. In 1859 prospectors located the great Comstock lode in Nevada, which produced 340 million dollars' worth of gold and silver before 1890; the Tonopah and Goldfield strikes brought another rush, immortalized by Mark Twain, who was there, in *Roughing It*. Deposits in these areas, and in Idaho and Montana, gave out quickly, but the huge copper mines of Montana, opened shortly afterwards, kept the mining boom alive. Eighteen seventy-six saw the last real gold rush, to the Black Hills of South Dakota. Yet the mining frontier, like the cattle frontier, left its stamp on the American past. Mining camps like Hangtown Gulch, Red Dog, Silver City, and Deadwood attracted the most adventurous and desperate elements in society. As the song expressed it,

> Oh, what was your name in the States?
> Was it Thompson or Johnson or Bates?
> Did you murder your wife, or fly for your life?
> Say, what was your name in the States?

Wide-open, lawless, spilling over with riches, drunkenness, and violence, the mines created a West of dance-halls and stud games, hurdy-gurdy girls and cheap whisky, stage-coach robbers and sudden hangings, a West that still lives in the legends of 'Wild Bill' Hickok and 'Calamity Jane' Canary.

The pioneer farmer, the rancher, and the miner intruded into the last major area left to the Indian, transferring to the plains the same Indian-white conflict that marked the settlement of the East a half-century earlier. Originally intended to serve as a huge reservation belonging to the

Indian tribes alone, the plains-land, the Department of the Interior decided, must be opened to settlers and the Indians herded into smaller, separate reservations, one for each tribe or family of tribes. Friction immediately developed. Sioux uprisings in Minnesota in 1862 and Arapahoe and Cheyenne massacres in 1864 brought the problem to the attention of Congress, which appointed an investigating committee in 1865. Indian affairs had been handled since 1849 by the Bureau of Indian Affairs in the Department of the Interior, but as a result of the investigation, which revealed a shocking amount of inefficiency and graft, Congress in 1869 created a Board of Indian Commissioners to advise the Department. In succeeding years the Department assumed greater and greater responsibility for the Indian, though his treatment was often far from merciful. The Dawes Act of 1887, intended to break tribal ties, teach the Indian agriculture, and educate him in the white man's culture, inaugurated the modern policy of merging him into American society.

The major points of contention between Indian and white were land and buffalo. The prospect of nomadic tribes holding thousands of tillable acres was too much for land-hungry settlers to bear; successive treaties, purchases, and grants gradually stripped the red man of his land, pushing him into desolate, sub-marginal areas. The buffalo was the staple of plains-Indian economy, providing the tribes with food, shelter, clothing, and fuel. But fifteen million buffalo were a constant menace to farmers and ranchers. The spread of railroads restricted the buffalo grazing grounds, while professional hunters like Buffalo Bill Cody killed thousands for meat, hides, and fertilizer. After 1872 hunters killed two million buffalo a year, and by 1885 the Western herds were almost completely gone.

It was not easy to make peaceful, reservation-dwelling farmers out of a savage race of hunters. Detachments of army regulars, charged with pacifying the tribes, found them formidable opponents, poorly armed though they were. Mounted on tough Spanish ponies and led by such expert warriors as Sitting Bull, Crazy Horse, Chief Joseph, Black Kettle, Red Cloud, and Geronimo, the Indians were a match for any cavalry in the world. The last serious fighting followed the Black Hills gold rush which sent thousands of miners and settlers into Dacotah Sioux territory. Here Custer, lured into ambush by Sitting Bull, lost his life and his command at the Little Big Horn. Sporadic outbreaks occurred until the eighties, when Geronimo, the Apache, was captured and exiled to Florida. Few Americans, reviewing the history of American-Indian relations, could disagree with President Hayes' statement of 1877: 'Many, if not most, of our Indian wars have had their origin in broken promises and acts of injustice on our part.' The lot of the Indian in the United States has been hard. Full legal rights and citizenship were not granted to him until 1924, and his assimilation into the pattern of American culture is still a problem. Some tribes, clinging to the old customs, remain alien islands in a white sea; others have adopted white ways without appreciable difficulty and have achieved full equality.

The settlement of the last West left permanent marks on American life. The pioneer plainsmen, reinforced by tradition of ranch and mining camp, were and are men of an individualistic turn of mind. Their rowdy politics, noted by every foreign observer since Bryce, was the source of every major radical or liberal movement up to 1924. Life on the prairie was a hard and challenging experience, with no place for the faint-hearted. The fertile soil could make a man rich in a few years, if all went well, but grasshoppers, drought, Indians, storms, and a murderous climate tried the soul. Like all pioneers, the plainsman had an eagerness for change, an unshakable faith in himself, and great hopes for his future. This was the heritage of the farmer's frontier. There was another West that left another heritage, the West of action and adventure, of violence and romance. This West too has become firmly established in American folklore as a native tradition of the Round Table, in which the Lone Ranger, Hopalong Cassidy, and Roy Rogers (before them 'Deadwood Dick', Tom Mix, and William S. Hart) perform as gallantly as Lancelot or Robin Hood.

'I shall do nothing in malice', wrote Lincoln. 'What I deal with is too vast for malicious dealing.' Lincoln's plan for Southern reconstruction was based on his contention that since the Confederate states had never really left the Union, reconstruction was simply a matter of readjustment rather than re-entrance. His Amnesty Proclamation of 1863 and his handling of the loyal West Virginia and Tennessee governments revealed that the general principles of his policy were to make the readjustment as rapid and easy as possible, and to reconstitute the Union as it was before secession. If one may judge from Lincoln's acts and speeches during the war, his method of reconstruction involved three basic ideas: the Southern states themselves should make their own rules for re-entering the Union, within reason; re-establishment of the Union should be accomplished as swiftly as possible; there should be a minimum of disenfranchisement of the Southern white man and a slow, gradual extension of suffrage to the freed Negro, who was, however, to have other civil rights at once. This programme should be Presidentially directed, cautiously, conservatively, humanely administered. 'We must extinguish our resentments,' said Lincoln, 'if we expect harmony and union.'

The Radical Republicans had a wholly different concept of reconstruction. In contrast to 'Mr Lincoln's policy of tenderness', men such as Thaddeus Stevens of Pennsylvania, Zack Chandler of Michigan, Charles Sumner and Ben Butler of Massachusetts, Boutwell and Wade of Ohio, Davis of Maryland, Colfax and Julian of Indiana, and Stanton, Secretary of War, favoured a harshly punitive programme for the seceded states. Their aim was threefold: punish ex-Confederates and destroy their political power; place reconstruction under the control of Congress; devise the machinery of reconstruction so that Republican dominance of the South might be permanently maintained. The Radicals protested that the Confederate states had 'committed suicide' by secession and had lost all rights as states; they were to be treated, as Stevens said, simply as 'conquered provinces'. Thus a Massachusetts abolitionist meeting resolved in 1866, 'The true doctrine of reconstruction is, that defeated rebels have no civil or political rights, which loyal men are bound to respect . . .' Harsher by far than Lincoln's Amnesty Proclamation, the Radically-sponsored Wade-Davis bill of 1864 provided that fifty per cent of a seceded state's inhabitants must take a loyalty oath before a civil government could be established within it. When this figure was reached the state's constitution must then be amended to repudiate any Confederate debts, abolish slavery, and refuse the vote to any Confederate official or officer of colonel's rank or above. Lincoln's pocket veto of this bill called forth Congressional cries of 'studied outrage' and 'insult'. With the death of Lincoln, the last barrier to complete Radical control of reconstruction was removed, or so they believed.

Historians have often explained Reconstruction as an effort by violent, vindictive men to humiliate a gallant, beaten opponent. Yet the Radicals and their supporters were incited by something more than simply the desire for revenge and political power. Some Radicals may so have been motivated, but to generalize thus is to forget the blazing fervour of the anti-slavery crusade and the deep faith in freedom that buttressed it. Some Northerners believed that the war had been fought to abolish slavery; the terms of peace must be such that the old master class that lived by slavery could never again dominate the South. Fanatics and carpet-baggers, with graft in their hearts, went South after 1865, of course, but there were also schoolteachers, lawyers, doctors, ministers, and plain citizens who went with nothing more than an earnest desire to help make the Negro a man. Ostracized, hated by the Southern white, faced sometimes by real physical danger, these Northern idealists are all too often lumped with the self-seeking politician. Moral conviction and idealism sent as many Yankees South as did the chance for quick wealth.

Andrew Johnson, Lincoln's successor, came from a poor North Carolina family and grew up in Tennessee as a Democrat. A tailor by trade, Johnson was almost illiterate at twenty. His wife taught him to read and write, and by his own vigour and drive he hammered out a political career in Tennessee as Congressman, Senator, Governor, and Vice-President. A rough, obstinate, choleric man, the South he knew was the poor man's South and he hated the cotton aristocrats with undying venom. Although he considered himself a states rights' man in the tradition of Calhoun, he was also a strict constructionist who could find no Constitutional justification for secession, which he condemned as treason. Throughout the war Johnson breathed fire against the Confederate leaders, and the Radicals called on him a few hours after Lincoln's death to assure him of their support. 'By the gods,' said Ben Wade, 'there will be no trouble now in running the government.'

But Johnson soon made it very clear that he intended to follow his own personal plan of reconstruction and not that of Congress. His Proclamation of Amnesty of May 1865 was a blow to Radical hopes. Johnson called for the abolition of slavery in the South, the repudiation of Confederate debts, nullification of ordinances of secession, and disenfranchisement of certain classes of Confederate supporters including – significantly – all those worth $20,000 or more. Though he was as bitter as the Radicals in his denunciation of the Southern planter, Johnson envisioned a wholly different rearrangement of Southern society than they. The Radicals hoped to build on Negro votes an industrialized South, under Republican control. Johnson hoped to destroy the power of the old aristocracy and raise instead a middle-class agrarian South controlled by the small farmer, merchant, and artisan. War Democrat though he was, Johnson disliked Northern industrialists as much as he did slave-holding aristocrats. The Civil War, thought Johnson, gave men of his own kind a chance to take control of the South. He had no objection to Negro suffrage, but as a states rights' man believed that only the states could bestow the vote on the freed slave. His programme, therefore, was immediately attacked by the Radicals in Congress, who demanded that the Negro be enfranchised by Federal decree and that harsher punishment be inflicted on the seceded states.

Johnson's hot temper and obstinacy worked against him. He slowly lost public and political support until the Radicals, it seemed clear, could put through their own plan against his opposition. The Joint Committee of Congress on Reconstruction, controlled by Radicals, in 1866 proposed the fourteenth Amendment to the Constitution, rolled it through Congress, and sent it to the states for ratification. This amendment, conferring citizenship on Negroes and disenfranchising Rebel leaders, satisfied all Radical demands except immediate votes for the freedmen. When the elections of 1866 returned a Radical majority to Congress Johnson was doomed. Not only the fourteenth Amendment, but also the fifteenth (which gave the Negro the ballot) were passed and with them a new plan of reconstruction. The South was divided into military districts, each governed by a Federal general. In each district the military authorities registered elegible voters. Ex-Confederates and others of doubtful politics were rigidly excluded from the registration lists while Negroes were enrolled by day and tutored in Republican politics at night. In all the ex-Confederate states (except Georgia, where the numbers of each race registered were about equal) registered Negro voters outnumbered white.

By giving votes to obedient Negroes and withholding them from influential white men the Radical Republicans, supported by the Federal armies, exercised complete control of the new Southern state governments. Not only did they succeed in beating Johnson, but they very nearly threw him out of the Presidency. In 1867 Congress passed the Tenure of Office Act, making it a misdemeanour for a President to remove civil office-holders without Senate consent, a slap at Johnson's authority. Johnson put the law to the test by dismissing from the Cabinet Edwin Stanton, one of his most vicious critics, whereupon the Radicals in the House voted to impeach Johnson for 'high crimes and misdemeanours'. He was tried before the Senate, sitting as a court as prescribed by the Constitution. Conviction failed by one vote.

The 'carpet-bag' legislatures of the reconstructed Southern states were among the most corrupt that American history has ever known. Yet their corruption must be placed in focus with the general decline of political morality that followed the war, for what happened in the South was but one phase of what happened elsewhere. Carpet-baggers' graft paled into insignificance beside the thefts perpetrated by their Northern brethren. The Tweed Ring stole six million dollars in six years in New York City; similar political machines in Pennsylvania, Massachusetts, and elsewhere lagged not far behind. Political corruption was neither new nor confined to carpet-baggers or Negro legislatures.

The newly-enfranchised ex-slaves elected both Negroes and white men to Congress, filled the state offices, wrote and passed reams of new legislation. Some of them were intelligent and able men; others were ignorant, unaware of their responsibilities, lacking in any concept of public morality. The so-called 'black legislatures' passed vengeful laws against former Confederates, forbade racial segregation, organized and controlled state militia, legalized exorbitant taxes, and authorized fantastically wasteful expenditures. In these things the Negroes were skilfully guided by renegade Southerners ('scalawags') and Northern carpet-baggers who reserved for themselves the choicest plums. Out of seven Southern states four Governors, ten Senators, and twenty Representatives were Northerners.

Yet at the same time these 'reconstructed' state governments put good laws on the books. They abolished property qualifications for voters and widened the basis of suffrage; they established better free schools, provided new penal codes, and opened up new areas of social and educational legislation. The constitutions developed by the 'black legislators' remained unchanged for nearly twenty-five years after their adoption, and subsequent revisions amplified and expanded rather than changed their principles. A majority of Southern white men, of course, regarded Radical policies as a 'barbarization of the South' and found the Negro vote a bitter pill to swallow. Appeals to Congress and to the North fell on deaf ears; meanwhile the Republican party, depending on its captive Negro vote, wrote and ratified the new state constitutions and petitioned Congress for the reentry of the seceded states. By mid-1868 seven of the ex-Confederate states were back in the Union. Only Virginia, Mississippi, and Texas remained outside.

After Johnson's impeachment the Radical Congressmen ran the nation without much regard for 'the dead dog in the White House', as Thad Stevens gleefully called him. In preparing for the presidential campaign of 1868 the Republicans made a deliberate appeal to the veterans' vote, denouncing Johnson as a traitor and the Democrats as the party of secession. Their convention unanimously chose U. S. Grant as its nominee, with Schuyler Colfax, a dependable Radical, as his running mate. Grant was a wise political choice. His name and record were on every tongue, his popularity with veterans was obvious, he had never touched nor had he been touched by politics, he was a man of simplicity, directness, and commonsense. The phrase 'Let us have peace' in his letter of acceptance was platform enough for a nation weary of bickering. The Democrats endorsed Johnson's programme of reconstruction but not Johnson. For President they chose Horatio Seymour of New York, an able conservative, and keyed their campaign to an attack on Republican corruption.

In spite of Grant's popularity his margin of victory was much smaller than the Republicans' leaders anticipated, a popular majority of only 300,000, and the success of the radical reconstruction programme lay in the fact that the Negro vote in the South contributed 600,000 to Grant's total. Radicals remained in control of both houses of Congress by small majorities, though the death of Thad Stevens robbed them of their most capable leader. With Congress and the Presidency firmly under control, the Radical

Republicans in 1868 set out to establish their supremacy so completely that it could never again be challenged.

Grant was utterly unaccustomed to civil responsibility and temperamentally incapable of providing the nation with the leadership it needed during a critical period. The army taught him that loyalty to subordinates was to be highly valued; in politics, party loyalty made Grant dependent on second-rate men and often he found himself defending crooks and thieves. He left office as he entered it, a silent, unassuming man who never understood that he had been the instrument of the worst elements ever to appear in American government. After his first year in office he relied almost exclusively on the advice of his Radical Republican friends who ran the party and the nation much as they pleased.

Not long after his inauguration Grant approved the re-entry into the Union of Texas, Virginia, and Mississippi, once they had endorsed the fifteenth Amendment and the Negro ballot, but it is hard to find any other positive accomplishment in his first administration. The Republican party, committed to the support of industry and business, passed all the legislation it wanted. Investors who had purchased war bonds with depreciated wartime currency saw Congress vote to pay them off in hard money. The wealthy were happy to see the income tax disappear. Railroad and land corporations took the pick of available public lands. Congress repealed all wartime taxes on industry but kept the high wartime tariffs. Financial legislation, written at the behest of Eastern banking groups, favoured a hard-money policy over the protests of debtor and agrarian interests. Business and industry, seeking favourable legislation on local, state, and national levels, spent millions for lobbies, gifts, bribes, and 'influence'. Grant's administration was shot through with corruption. The Navy Department accepted bribes from crooked contractors; speculators bribed Department of Interior officials out of millions of acres of public lands; Treasury department officers overlooked tax bills for a fee and took gifts from tax delinquents; customs-houses were full of shady characters. 'The Republican party', said one Republican with a conscience, '. . . is today the most corrupt and debauched political party that ever existed.'

The carnival of corruption that marked Grant's first term disgusted many Republicans, who organized in 1871 as 'Liberal Republicans' to fight against 'Grantism'. When it became clear that the Radicals intended to nominate Grant for a second term so that they could continue as before, the Liberals decided to split the party. At their own convention in Cincinnati the Liberals disavowed Grant and his cohorts and nominated Horace Greeley. Although Greeley had been one of the most energetic pre-war anti-slavery editors and was a strong believer in high tariffs, the Democrats at their Baltimore convention endorsed him and the whole Liberal programme, realizing that only a coalition of Southern and Northern Democrats with the dissident Republicans could beat Grant. But their plans foundered. After a violent campaign, Grant remained in the White House with a large electoral majority.

When Grant took the oath of office in 1872 it seemed that the Radical Republicans had accomplished what they set out to do. They had complete control of the executive and legislative branches of the national government, absolute mastery of about twenty states, and a closely-held bloc of a half-million Negro votes in the South. Even the coalition of Liberals and Democrats had failed to unseat them; Grant carried all but two states in the lower South and swept the North-west. But the Liberal revolt was a sign that Grant and his friends misread. The American electorate could stand only a little more.

The second Grant regime gave the public more than enough. In rapid succession a series of scandals broke in Washington. A small group of stockholders in the Union Pacific railroad (including some Congressmen) organized a construction company called the Credit Mobilier, which systematically milked the railroad of huge sums. Exposed by the New York *Sun*, the 'Credit Mobilier affair' ruined a good many Republican reputations, and other exposures followed with unpalatable regularity. Congress voted itself a fifty per cent salary increase, retroactive for two years, that caused so much public indignation that it was hastily repealed. Grant's Secretary of the Treasury resigned after irregularities in his department were disclosed. The new Secretary uncovered a 'Whisky Ring' of distillers who had defrauded the government of millions in taxes, and the trail of graft led to Grant's own private secretary. No sooner had the 'Whisky Ring' been exposed than the Secretary of War resigned to escape prosecution for selling posts in the Indian Service. Grant himself was never touched by suspicion, although he accepted favours a more circumspect President would have refused. To the end Grant considered the disclosures of graft within his administration as political propaganda and attempts to persecute his friends.

The exposure of corruption in Washington and the returning strength of the Democratic party combined to undercut Radical power in the Congressional elections of 1874. A serious depression, beginning in 1873 and lasting nearly five years, convinced Republicans and Democrats alike of the danger of playing fast and loose with fiscal policy and did a great deal to undermine public confidence in business leadership. Using depression and corruption as their issues, Democrats captured a majority of seats in the House and control of the more important committees. The truth was that the Northern voter at large was beginning to understand that the Radical Republican policy of favouring business and punishing the South was costing the nation more than it was worth. Many Northerners hoped, after 1865, that the Reconstruction governments would open the South to economic and industrial development. Instead the Radicals seemed interested only in exploiting the South for political purposes. So long as organized corruption, supported by military force, existed in the South, the area remained a very poor risk for Northern investments.

Reports of the excesses of the carpet-bag legislatures crept into the Northern press, and Horace Greeley, after a Southern tour, wrote that the area was plagued with 'decayed

aristocracy and imported rascality'. Pressure on Congress
forced the passage of the Amnesty Act of 1872, which in
effect restored political rights to all but a few of the Southern
white leaders, on whom Northern investors relied for economic reconstruction. Southern politicians slowly reorganized
the Democratic party, took over control of state after state,
threw out carpet-baggers and scalawags, and passed laws to
prevent or discourage the Negro vote. By 1876 only three
states (Louisiana, Florida, and South Carolina) remained
in the hands of carpet-bag legislatures, kept in power by
Federal troops.

The Amnesty Act was one sign of the approaching end
of Radical Reconstruction. Negroes themselves, now learning to play politics, after 1870 showed increasing dissatisfaction with their Republican guardians, for it was noticeable
that white carpet-baggers and scalawags took the better
offices and the larger share of the loot. And both Democratic
and Republican leaders realized that they were playing with
fire in balancing white against Negro in politics. One
alarmed politician observed that if this 'vast mass of ignor-
ance' ever 'combined for any political purpose, it would
sweep away all opposition the intelligent class might make'.
Thoughtful men, he added, feared that 'the ignorant voters
will in the future form a political party by themselves as
dangerous to the interests of society as the communists of
France'. Labour unions were on the upswing in the Northeast, and dissatisfied North-western farmers were busily
organizing the Grange. If these 'ignorant masses' combined,
the political consequences would indeed be disastrous to
'the intelligent class'. Faced by this prospect, Northern
leaders were willing to modify the methods of Radical
Reconstruction.

Despite the shift of Northern public opinion, the dissolution of Radical dominance would have been impossible
without a revolt within the South. While the Negro showed
restlessness, the Southern middle class and poor white
showed more. Johnsonian reconstruction promised to turn
over the South to them, but instead the Radicals based

reconstruction on their traditional enemy, the Negro. Corruption in carpet-bag legislatures and rising taxes hurt the small property holder as well as the large; political offices and power went not to the native white farmer but to the scalawag or carpet-bagger. In desperation this large Southern group turned for leadership to the old aristocracy, not because it wished to re-establish pre-war class alignments in politics, but because it could combine neither with the Republicans on the one hand nor the Negro on the other.

Southern conservatives and ex-Confederate leaders learned their political lessons swiftly. They feared both Negro and poor white rule, and hoped to control the vote of both groups. Meanwhile the cost of Radical rule drove them to desperation. Virginia's state debt rose from sixteen to forty millions in five years; South Carolina's from six to twenty-five millions; Texas, from zero to four millions. Tax-burdened and disenfranchised planters therefore adopted extra-legal means to defeat Radical aims, control the Negro, and effect an alliance with the poor white and small farmer by appealing to his anti-Negro prejudice.

The instrument at hand was the Ku Klux Klan, a secret order formed in 1866 by a small group of Confederate veterans in Tennessee. Dressed in ghostly white costumes, Ku Kluxers frightened Negroes by appearing to them as the 'spirits of dead soldiers'. When the political advantages of the order were recognized, it quickly spread throughout the South, encouraged by planters and small farmers alike. General Nathan Bedford Forrest was appointed 'Grand Wizard' of the Klan 'Empire', while in each community armed Klansmen, riding at night, whipped unruly or 'uppity' Negroes, beat Union soldiers, and threatened carpet-bag politicians. By 1870 several similar organizations appeared, with the result that the pro-Republican white man or Negro risked real danger if he refused to 'keep his place'. Armed bands patrolled parts of the South day and night; the more violent elements of the organizations did not hesitate at torture, arson, and murder.

Far from being the 'holy crusade' drawn by later Southern novelists and historians, the Klan was a vicious and despicable organization. In using it to deprive the Negro of his rights and to regain political dominance of the South, Southern leaders deliberately set poor and middle class white man against Negro by appealing to the lowest form of race prejudice. Congress struck back at the Klan with drastic laws and Federal troops. After some eighty-two convictions in South Carolina much of the violence stopped, but the Klan itself continued to exist as a deadly means of controlling the Negro under the same banner of 'white supremacy' that had been the chief stock-in-trade of the old pro-slavery aristocracy. By supporting the Klan, conservative upper-class leaders were able to drive a political wedge between the Negro and the white man, but its legacy has been violence, race prejudice, and the development of intimidation as a fine art in parts of the South.

The Republicans prepared for the campaign of 1876 with some misgivings. At their Cincinnati convention they constructed a platform pledging the party to a thorough housecleaning and a sweeping reform of the Federal Civil Service. For its candidate the party chose Rutherford B. Hayes, Governor of Ohio, an honest though pedestrian politician who had given his state clean government for three terms. The Democrats, meeting at St Louis, attacked the Republicans at their most vulnerable points – corruption and carpetbag reconstruction. To oppose Hayes they chose wealthy Samuel Tilden, governor of New York, the very arch-priest of reformers. With Tilden the Democrats hoped to carry a majority of the large Northern states as well as most of the South.

Early returns indicated that Tilden had won, since he took New York, New Jersey, Connecticut, and Indiana in the North in addition to the South, although results in South Carolina, Florida, and Louisiana remained in doubt. Without these three states, Tilden had 184 electoral votes, one short of the number needed for election. But with the nineteen electoral votes of the questionable states, Hayes would have 185 or exactly enough. Since Republicans controlled the canvassing boards in these three states, it was not difficult to change Tilden majorities into Hayes majorities. Senator Zach Chandler of Michigan, the Republican national chairman, therefore announced that Hayes had won.

The Constitution, however, provides that the electoral vote shall be counted before a joint assembly of Congress. Democrats held a majority in the House, Republicans in the Senate. Both voted investigations that came to nothing. Democrats, convinced that Tilden had been legally elected President, threatened to filibuster and delay the electoral count if the matter were not settled by inauguration time on 4 March 1877. Many citizens, North and South, expected fighting to break out if Hayes were declared the winner. Some Congressmen carried sidearms, and Abram Hewitt, the Democratic national chairman, wrote later that Democratic war veterans in fifteen states were ready to march on Washington to instal Tilden by force. A Congressional commission, however, heard the arguments of contesting counsel in late February 1877, accepted the Republican electoral votes from the three doubtful states, and made Hayes the nineteenth President of the United States.

There was no violence. The fact was that a compromise had been arranged. Republican leaders agreed to withdraw troops from the South, to allow the two remaining carpet-bag governments (South Carolina and Louisiana) to expire, and to give up control of the Negro, all in return for Hayes' election. The Southern Democrats in turn agreed to abandon Tilden and the Northern wing of the party, accept Hayes, and open the South to Northern economic penetration, in X× return for complete political control of the South. This was not a quick bargain, hurriedly arrived at, but the result of negotiations started months before the election. Railroad and industrial interests in the North had already conferred with Southern political leaders on the substance of the compromise; the disputed election simply crystallized it. The truth was that the North was weary of the old crusade. The old leaders were dead or silent, Stevens, Garrison, Sumner,

Weld, and the rest. The new leaders, men like Hayes, Blaine, Conkling, Garfield, in fact the whole continuity of Republican leaders down to McKinley, were more interested in profitable, practical politics than in reconstructing a new South on the foundation of the Negro and poor white.

The result of the Compromise of 1876 was a 'Solid South' under conservative Democratic rule, and the re-establishment of white supremacy as the dominant principle of Southern life. Henceforth the South was to be under 'Bourbon' domination; 'niggers' and 'woolhat boys' were back in their ante-bellum place within the Southern system. President Hayes was as good as his word. In April 1877 Federal troops left South Carolina and Louisiana. Their carpet-bag governments collapsed and Radical reconstruction was ended.

The Radicals were successful in doing what they set out to do, to keep the Republican party in control of the Federal government for as long as possible after the close of the war. But they were successful in nothing else. In the long run Radical reconstruction solved none of the problems it had posed and created several new ones. It failed to provide a way for Negro and white man to live peacefully together as equals. The politically-motivated 'Negro policy' of the Radicals and the sincere but hasty activities of the abolitionists made racial antagonisms in the South if anything stronger than before. Some of the bitterness was an inevitable consequence of emancipation, to be sure, but much of it was the product of Radical reconstruction policy. The white Southerner found it impossible to plan constructively for the future so long as the Negro remained outside his control, and after reconstruction he spent so much energy on the task of permanently subjugating the Negro that he neglected the South's most pressing problems.

The industrialization of the South, blocked for years by the planters, was accomplished under Northern direction by Northern capital, reducing the South to colonial status and fastening on it a colonial psychology. The activities of the

Klan and other organizations made the South tolerant of rule by force and of disrespect for law. Respectable, intelligent Southerners for generations since have often found it difficult, in the face of this tradition, to discourage and punish violence. And no matter what agreements or gestures were made, the hard fact remained that antagonism between North and South was stronger in 1877 than it had been at Appomattox. Radical reconstruction accentuated the after-effects of war and delayed serious consideration of important national issues. For years Northern politicians found it more profitable to quote Lincoln and cry 'Rebel' than to face issues squarely and honestly. Southern politicians found it equally useful to shout 'Damyankee' and 'nigger' at election time. Solutions to fundamental national and sectional problems had to wait until the wounds left by war and reconstruction healed.

'The world after 1865', wrote Henry Adams, 'became a banker's world' of millionaires. The American continent offered more natural resources than any country except Russia, and for the man of ability and energy, the rewards for exploiting them were so huge as to stagger the imagination. Carnegie's annual income exceeded twelve and a half million dollars; his total fortune reached 1,000 million; the cheque that he received for the sale of his share of United States Steel totalled more than the entire value of the United States in Washington's day. Rockefeller amassed slightly more than fifteen hundred million. The Guggenheim interests took 2,000 million from the Montana copper ranges. Vanderbilt II inherited a hundred million dollars and added ninety million to it in six years. Morgan's fortune equalled Carnegie's, while those of Gould, Harriman, Stanford, and Huntington (railroads), Stewart (real estate and stores), Swift and Armour (meat-packing), and Duke (tobacco) were not far behind. In 1890 an economist calculated that about 125,000 men controlled at least half the national wealth.

The most significant and far-reaching development in

American business during the late nineteenth century, and the greatest factor in the amassing of huge personal fortunes, was the development of monopoly. Business men soon found, in the intense competition of business life, that the best way to treat a dangerous competitor was to combine with him. By combining instead of competing, businesses could cut production costs, control prices, fix profits, and suppress rivalry. 'To say that competition is the life of trade', remarked one business man in 1880, 'is to repeat a mouldy old proverb.' Manufacturers accordingly formed associations by gentlemen's agreement, apportioning production and setting prices, but unfortunately, as one industrialist remarked, the participants were not always gentlemen. The 'pool', a popular device in the seventies, was especially well adapted to railroads. By the time the Interstate Commerce Act of 1887 banned agreements and pools, they were already being replaced by the more efficient trust, a device by which the stockholders of competing or related firms agreed to deposit controlling portions of their stocks with a board of trustees in return for trust certificates. The Sherman Anti-Trust Act of 1890, despite the vigour of its language, was difficult to enforce and easily beaten in the courts. The trust reached its highest development in Rockefeller's Standard Oil Company, which eventually controlled four-fifths of the national oil output, while the combined Morgan and Rockefeller interests held control of 341 major firms. By 1904 there were 319 trusts capitalized at 7,000 million dollars or more.

To compete and survive in businesses of such imperial magnitude required a man's entire time, energy, and brains. Thus the 'captain of industry' emerged, a peculiarly American type, ruthless and savage in his business dealings, a daring, imaginative, aggressive entrepreneur. To him business made its own law. He felt no particular social responsibility, recognized no obligations inherent in his possession of tremendous economic power, yet to indict him by hindsight is to indict his age, for his aims and ethics were merely those of contemporary society.

No code had been developed by 1865 for business enterprise on a grand scale, since no necessity for one had ever existed. The sudden appearance of the transcontinental corporation with its huge maze of intricate relationships caught both business and the public unawares. The possibilities of reward were so great, the struggle for survival so intense, that traditional concepts of ethics were lost in the chase. Nor were there laws on the statute books to establish legal control over the industrial juggernauts. When such laws were written business itself, allied with politics, for a long time wrote them to its own advantage. The age itself not only condoned but admired the 'cuteness' and 'slickness' of the shrewd operator, as in earlier days buccaneering and piracy were considered semi-respectable and enviable occupations. What one might object to in the behaviour of the millionaire was equally a part of the *ethos* of the poor clerk, who hoped to be a millionaire himself.

The general public, while condemning its methods and decrying its ethics, admitted big business' accomplishments. Whatever the transgressions of the 'robber barons' (and they were many) some of them vastly improved the American standard of living by providing masses of goods at a reasonable price – as well as at enormous profit. Giant industries, by introducing what they called 'scientific management', effected great savings in manufacturing processes. The substitution of exact knowledge for trial-and-error, of intelligent planning for traditional know-how, of calipers for rule-of-thumb, changed the face of industry the world over. To the mass-production technology of Eli Whitney and his contemporaries, post-war industry added the last ingredient – organization and integration of factory methods – and put into the hands of the ordinary man the tools of better and more leisurely living. Along with the sins of nineteenth-century business this must be counted on the side of virtue.

Nor was there any reason in the light of contemporary opinion why wealth and economic power should not be concentrated in the hands of a few. *Laissez-faire* was ingrained

in the American way of life, inherited not only from eighteenth-century economics but from pioneer experience.
Franklin's 'Poor Richard' maxims expressed an indigenous
American tradition. Resourcefulness, self-reliance, the ability
to stand on your own two feet and carve out a fortune with
nothing but your hands and brain, these things Americans
admired in a man. Emersonian self-reliance was never meant
to produce captains of industry, but it helped to justify
them.

The wealthy men of the period did not consider themselves to be bad men or 'robber barons'. They believed that
if individuals of exceptional ability were encouraged to
develop the national economic resources the whole of society
would benefit, even though a few did enrich themselves
enormously in the process – otherwise, where was the incen-
tive? They assumed that it was the function of government
to aid and protect business, to guarantee an industrial prosperity that inevitably percolated down to all the people and
to some degree enriched them all. Great wealth was a divine
gift, a mark that God had chosen the recipient as a steward
for His worldly goods, to be used for the benefit of less
capable men – an echo of the Calvinist justification of wealth
a century earlier. 'Great private fortunes', remarked Senator Ingalls of Kansas, 'are inseparable from high civilizations. All the great enterprises that exalt and embellish
existence and ameliorate the conditions of human life,
come from the conception of money in the hands of the
few.'

The prevailing ideology of business, thus justified by
Calvinist theology, frontier tradition, and eighteenth-century individualism, found additional support from the
popular acceptance of Darwinism, especially as worked out
by Darwin's disciple Herbert Spencer, who exerted a tremendous influence on American thought. The struggle for
existence, said Spencer, was natural and good; social or
legislative action limiting or preventing it was unnatural
and bad. The survival of the fittest theory, operative in
nature, applied in the same way to economic life. The rich

man got his fortune because he had the abilities required for success in the competition for wealth; the poor man was simply less well adapted, less fit. Both deserved what they got. The millionaire, said William Graham Sumner, the Yale sociologist, was 'the finest flower of a competitive society'.

The Darwinian point of view seeped into the thinking of people who had never heard of Darwin, but who found in the popular conception of his theory a satisfactory justification of current practices. It was very clear, said Francis Walker in 1890, that competition was 'the force to which it is mainly due that mankind has risen from stage to stage intellectual, moral, and physical power'. The Spencerian philosophy of competition and survival was taught in the colleges, explained in the journals by respectable writers, accepted by the responsible and educated members of society. It was, in effect, the *raison d'être* of the age.

The mass of Americans accepted this attitude toward business, yet with a certain uneasiness. Social Darwinism, particularly in its economic manifestations, seemed to deny the basic tenets both of Christianity and the natural rights tradition of the Declaration. A good many citizens, looking at 'Diamond Jim' Brady or Jay Gould, doubted if they were really the 'flowers of society' that Sumner called them. It was hard to think of J. P. Morgan as a divinely chosen custodian of cash. 'Mister Dooley', Finley Peter Dunne's fictitious Irish commentator, pointed out in the Chicago papers that John D. Rockefeller was 'a kind iv society f'r the prevention of croolty to money. He looks afther his own money and the money iv other people. He takes it and puts it where it won't hurt thim and they won't spoil it.' The billionaires who constituted the 'fit' – had they won in an open, fair 'struggle for survival', or had the rules been rigged? Some of those who were 'eliminated' in the struggle for survival were unwilling to give up without a protest. Since they had ballots, they might win politically the victory they had failed to win economically. Others, like Henry Adams, viewing the shameless buying and selling of democracy in the market-place, thought that big business was digging its own grave. The 'Gilded Age' philosophy of business had its sceptics from the time of its inception.

Criticism of the prevailing pattern of business centred about two main arguments. First, its critics claimed, the captains of industry often failed to recognize their responsibilities to society and to assume definite obligations for its progress. Although a few, like Carnegie and Rockefeller, offered socially-conscious theories of wealth, their policies seemed to have little influence on the actual operation of business. Second, there was a growing fear that the divorce of wealth from responsibility might create industrial feudalism, a 'plutocracy' that could finally dominate American life. Thus Henry Ward Beecher wrote in 1871, 'We are today in more danger from overgrown pecuniary interests – from organized money – than we ever were from slavery.'

The influence of wealth on politics provided an illustration. Business men of the period asserted that the role of government in economic life was that of umpire, charged with enforcing the minimum rules of fair play to prevent embezzlement, thievery, and abrogations of contract. Price-fixing, minimum wage or maximum hour laws, or laws governing working conditions or labour relations, were unnatural interferences with the operation of *laissez-faire* forces. Yet at the same time business understood that it needed favourable legislation to operate as it wished: tariffs to reduce foreign competition, subsidies for railroads, franchises and contracts to control markets. In order to obtain the right kind of government, business men were forced into politics. They needed an ally who could handle affairs for them on the political front while they gave undivided attention to economic warfare and the political boss was their man.

The 'boss' was not new to American politics. He appeared before the large corporations and will probably outlast them, but in the late nineteenth century he found in the business man the perfect natural alliance. The boss needed funds and patronage for his machine; the business man needed expert

political assistance and was willing to pay for it. Both profited by the exchange. The great bosses served as middlemen
who collected contributions from business to see that the
right laws were passed (and the wrong ones were not) by
placing sympathetic legislators in office. As a matter of
insurance business men often contributed to both parties,
although by most the Republican was considered to be the
safer investment. The real danger lay, as critics pointed out,
that both the boss and the business man were working for
personal rather than for public interest. 'Our political system', wrote Charles Francis Adams in 1870, 'cannot much
longer sustain the conflict with corporations. Modern civilization has created a class of powers which are too strong for
the control of our government. How long can they develop
together?'

The business man needed not only the assistance of the
politician, but also the help of the courts. Interpretation of
the law was as important to him as the law itself. During the
late nineteenth century, and after, the fourteenth Amendment to the Constitution proved to be an invaluable aid.
'No State', the wording of the Amendment runs, 'shall
make or enforce any law which shall abridge the privileges
or immunities of citizens of the United States; nor shall any
State deprive any person of life, liberty, and property, without due process of law . . .' In the minds of one portion of
the committee that wrote the amendment the purpose was
to protect the rights of the freed Negro. Others saw in it also
a means of protecting business from attacks by hostile state
legislatures. The definition of the term 'person' was left
to the courts to decide. Over a period of some twenty years
the courts determined that the term included corporations
and any person connected with them; any state law that
deprived a corporation or stockholder therein of property –
that is, wealth or profit – was in conflict with the fourteenth
Amendment. With both government and law firmly on its
side, business by the nineties had entrenched itself into a
seemingly impregnable position in American life.

* * *

The pre-Civil War national labour movement, never strong, had disintegrated in the depression of the 1830's. A few craft unions, chiefly printers, bricklayers, and train-men, were formed in the fifties, and in 1866 representatives of a number of craft unions organized the National Labor Union, which opened its membership to anyone except 'gamblers, saloon-keepers, bankers, lawyers, and stockbrokers'. The NLU scattered its energies in a diffuse programme, and failed to weather the depression of 1873. Of the thirty unions it represented, only eight or nine survived. Despite the collapse of the NLU labour leaders were convinced that some kind of national labour organization was inevitable. As industry spread, labour spread with it, so that low wages or poor working conditions were no longer local, but national problems.

Prospects for a successful national union were not bright, for labour was confused and split, uncertain of programmes or principles. Under mass production labour had lost much of its class-consciousness and pride. The production line made the old craftsman obsolete, killed pride of workmanship, and fixed the workman himself as simply a step in an operation. Every labourer was sure that his job was only temporary, that he would soon make his pile and go into business for himself – and it happened just often enough to convince the workman of the truth of the 'shirt-sleeves to millionaire' myth fostered by Horatio Alger and Andrew Carnegie. With the development of the transcontinental corporation the worker, organized or not, found no one to whom he could carry his problems. He no longer knew his employer by his first name – or perhaps by any name – and had no bargaining power as an individual.

The need for a collective bargaining instrument that the NLU failed to provide was immediately filled by a new organization, the Knights of Labor. Founded in 1869 as a semi-secret society, the Knights, under the skilful leadership of Terence V. Powderly, hoped to establish 'one big union for all'. But like the NLU the Knights diverted their energies into a battle for public ownership of public utilities, co-operatives, and other popular reforms. In the mid-eighties they won one strike against the railroads, lost another, and in 1886 struck the McCormick Harvester Works in Chicago. A bomb, exploded by persons unknown, killed seven policemen at a mass meeting in Haymarket Square, Chicago. Seven suspects, all anarchists, were quickly apprehended and tried by the courts in an atmosphere of blind anger. Four were executed, one committed suicide, and two received life sentences, to be pardoned later by Governor Altgeld of Illinois. The Knights never recovered from the after-effects of the Haymarket riot and thereafter slowly declined in membership and influence.

The American Federation of Labor, founded the year of the Haymarket troubles and still in existence, followed a much more conservative policy than either of its predecessors. Rejecting the 'one big union' idea of the Knights, the AFL built a federation of separate, semi-autonomous craft unions, leaving the mass of unskilled workers unorganized. Samuel Gompers, a London-born cigar-maker who served as its president from 1886 to 1924, saw it grow to a half-million members by 1900. Gompers knew the work of British and German labour reformers by heart, believed strongly in the capitalist system, and was convinced that labour could make its greatest gains within its framework. Avoiding third-party politics, he committed the organization to the principle of 'Reward your friends and punish your enemies, regardless of party', a position that with a few exceptions the AFL has steadily maintained to the present day. 'We have', said one Federation leader, 'no ultimate ends, but only immediate ends.' Using collective bargaining techniques with the strike as a last resort, the AFL pressed for an eight-hour day, higher wages, health and sanitation regulations, and child-labour laws.

The decades 1870 to 1900 were turbulent, restless years, marked by violent conflicts between capital and labour. The working-man's attempt to organize on a national scale naturally aroused tremendous opposition from industry. The right of business to operate without hindrance on its own

terms, to form its own protective associations, and to organize lobbies to influence government went unquestioned; if
labour organized for similar purpose it was considered
'unAmerican, illegal, and indecent', in the words of one
industrialist. Corporations therefore proposed to 'pull up
root and branch the unAmerican institution of organized
labour as it is at present conducted', a movement culminating in the founding of the National Association of Manufacturers in 1895.

Organized labour had other problems besides the un-
remitting hostility of business leaders. The twenty million
immigrants who poured into the United States between
1870 and 1900 provided industry with a backlog of unskilled,
tractable labour, while at the same time thousands of freed
Negroes filtered North to the factory towns. The immigrant
and the Negro labourer were difficult to organize, poorly
educated, and usually happy to accept low pay, long hours,
and unsatisfactory conditions. The general effect was to
vitiate labour unions and depress working standards. Labour
problems were also inevitably tied to politics and law. The
power to regulate such things as wages and hours was, until
recent years, chiefly lodged in the states. With the legal
aspects of most labour disputes lying within the jurisdiction
of local and state courts, labour unions might gain significant
victories in one section of the country while losing in another.
Until the Federal government found ways to establish control over nation-wide industry, the labour union had to fight
the same battles over and over in the states against a powerful coalition of legislative, judicial, and industrial forces and
their whole arsenal of weapons – the lockout, the injunction, the strike-breaker, the blacklist, the 'yellow dog' contract. It is ironic that the Sherman Anti-Trust Act was used
first by the courts to break labour unions.

The farmer too had his troubles. Between 1860 and 1900
four million acres of new land went under the plough, trip-
ling farm acreage. Agricultural production boomed. The
yield of wheat, for example, went from 173 million bushels in
1860 to a spectacular 522 million bushels in 1900, a rate of

increase matched by corn, pork, beef, and other products. There were several reasons for this post-war agricultural revolution. The push of population West opened up vast areas of fertile plain, linked to the East by the railroads. As the production of cotton, corn, wheat, and cattle increased, the centre of agricultural production swiftly shifted westward, leaving behind in the East a dislocated farm economy. Farm boys and girls streamed to the cities, leaving many rural communities stripped of young people. One song of the period, protesting against the urban movement, went plaintively:

> The city has many attractions,
> But think of its vices and sins;
> When once in the vortex of fashion,
> How soon the course downward begins!
>
> Stay on the farm, stay on the farm,
> Though profits come in rather slow.
> Stay on the farm, stay on the farm,
> Don't be in a hurry to go.

The new Western farms had all the advantages of mechanization. New ploughs and harrows, reapers, twine-binders, corn-planters and huskers, threshing machines, cream separators, and other devices made it possible for fewer men to produce more on larger farms. The labour required to produce one bushel of corn, for example, declined from four hours to less than fifty minutes; one corn-sheller replaced fifty men; four men and a threshing machine did the work of four hundred. The introduction of the steam tractor, and later, the gasoline motor, simply carried mechanization further.

The agricultural revolution drastically changed the position of the farmer within the national economic structure. Though farm production expanded, industrial production increased faster, and agriculture, once the mainstay of the American economy, found itself rapidly pushed into second place. Expansion brought new problems, many with political implications. Farming became a commercial venture involving a large investment in land and machinery and a staple crop to sell in a competitive market. The self-sufficient yeoman, who raised everything he needed, disappeared; in his place came the agricultural capitalist, fitted into a complex national and international economic pattern, tied to banks, railroads, industry, markets, credit, money. After Britain repealed the Corn Laws in 1846 and Western Europe followed, the American farmer became an exporter of food for the world, swiftly affected not only by Eastern market fluctuations but by crop failures in India or a drought in Egypt.

The changing face of American society was reflected in the increased activity of urban life after the war. The expansion of industry, the flood of immigration, and the dislocation of rural society in the Eastern states accelerated the growth of cities. Mechanized farming released workers for the factories; factories tended to locate in populated centres; railroads encouraged the growth of factories and made distant markets accessible; consolidation of industry encouraged railroads, factories, and cities. The trend toward the city was not a uniquely American phenomenon, but a result of the Industrial Revolution; both London and Paris grew after 1850, but the growth of American cities was more spectacular. New York quadrupled its size before 1900, Philadelphia tripled, and the rate of increase in Mid-western urban centres eclipsed theirs. Chicago, the western rail centre, was twenty times larger in 1910 than in 1860. Cleveland, Detroit, St Louis, Minneapolis, Toledo, and other cities in the Lake area grew almost as swiftly. Smaller towns grew too, until by 1910 thirty per cent of the nation lived in towns of 8,000 or more. Urbanism introduced a new and sophisticated attitude into American culture and marked a sharp departure from the moral and social patterns of rural life. It produced, among other things, a change in the temper of American society, emphasizing the widening rift between classes, placing extremes of poverty and wealth, power and weakness, side by side; mirroring all the racial, social, economic, religious, and political conflicts that beset a new and complex industrialized society.

The surge of population to the cities strained the fabric of urban government. Successive waves of immigration, each larger than the last, threw into the cities large blocs of foreign peoples of widely varying national, racial, and social backgrounds and traditions. Uneducated, innocent, confused, the immigrant was often shamefully used. He provided easily controlled blocs of votes that gave the city boss a heaven-sent opportunity. Subjected to both economic and social discrimination, the new arrivals huddled in slums, until by the eighties New York City housed more than 200,000 people in sub-standard tenements. Diseases like cholera, smallpox, and typhus periodically struck terror into city society, and crime increased alarmingly.

The problems of the cities were not entirely insoluble. The humanitarian impulse, always strong in Americans, prompted a great many efforts at reform: clinics, orphanages, playgrounds, almshouses, settlement houses, social service agencies. Boards of charities in the populous Eastern cities attempted to co-ordinate charitable work for greater efficiency, and state boards of health, established after 1870, helped to control standards of food and housing. And there were certain profits to be gained from social concentration and co-operation: better schools, museums, art galleries, libraries, and theatres than small towns could afford. Most of all, the city provided an opportunity for women to escape some of the rules imposed on them by nineteenth-century *mores*. The number of women gainfully employed in cities more than doubled between 1870 and 1900.

From the first founding of the colonies Americans believed deeply in education as the cultural foundation, as Jefferson called it, of 'a happy and prosperous people'. New Englanders established Harvard almost as soon as they landed; Franklin and Jefferson founded universities; and in the early nineteenth century the United States committed itself firmly to free public education for children of any race, sex, or creed. The traditional faith of the American in education was nowhere better illustrated than in the tremendous educational expansion of the post-Civil War years. The number of schoolchildren rose from five million in 1865 to seven million in 1870 to fifteen million in 1900, illiteracy meanwhile declining from 17 per cent to 11 per cent. The advance was qualitative as well as quantitative. States established teacher-training institutions and certification requirements for teachers. The older private academy was rapidly replaced by the public high school, offering a wider variety of subjects and attracting more students. By the close of the century the pattern of public school systems, still customary in the United States, was established at eight years of elementary school beginning at the age of five or six, plus four years of secondary or high school.

There were also changes in higher education. Both state and private institutions underwent remarkable developments under the direction of a particularly able group of university presidents, among them Eliot of Harvard, White of Cornell, McCosh of Princeton, Porter of Yale, Angell of Michigan, Gilman of Johns Hopkins, and Bascom of Wisconsin. If universities were to be opened to the masses, then a university education must be charted in terms of its meaning to the masses. The rigid 'classical curriculum' gave way to a broader elective system that included 'bread and butter' as well as cultural courses. State universities, notably that of Wisconsin, stressed education for intelligent citizenship and emphasized service to the state. Technical and professional schools of mining, forestry, agriculture, metallurgy, and engineering appeared in profusion. The proliferation of courses in American universities and the willingness of those institutions to consider almost any skill as fair game stems directly from the ingrained American idea that education is a mass process.

Since the Civil War the United States has developed an elaborate and expensive system of public education, ranging from one-room country school to city high school of 10,000, and from tiny church college to urban university of 25,000 students. The influence of the public school at least equals that of the church in American society, and in some communities surpasses it. Rich men have given millions to the schools; states have poured tax moneys into them; the most imposing public buildings in the United States are those of the urban high schools and the great universities. While the American system of public education has not always lived up to the expectations of its most sanguine adherents, neither has it failed to attain some of its more important objectives.

The influence of the schools in the period was augmented by other means of education, notably libraries and the lyceum and Chautauqua systems. By 1900 eighteen states and many large cities had authorized the use of taxes for the support of libraries, while philanthropists such as Carnegie spent millions in building libraries in small towns and remote communities. The lyceum, a popular New England institution, sent lecturers into every state, where for a small sum an isolated community might hear the nation's best lecturers. The Chautauqua, a Methodist version of the lyceum, replaced it before the turn of the century and lasted until the twenties, when it was killed by the movies and radio.

Late nineteenth-century American religious thought was much affected by developments in the physical and biological sciences. Spencer's volumes found a relatively wide reading public in America; Tyndall and Huxley made lecture tours of the United States in 1872, 1873, and 1876, while Spencer himself arrived in 1882. The new scientific concepts, especially Darwinism, all tended to cast doubt on the validity of established religious beliefs. Theologians of every sect met them with determined resistance, until one by one, as the dispute continued, liberal ministers found a compromise between science and religion. Henry Ward Beecher of New York, a preacher of national reputation, summarized the liberal position by declaring that the Darwinian hypothesis was nothing more than 'the deciphering of God's thought as revealed in the structure of the world'. Nevertheless, despite general adoption of Beecher's point of view, some sects in rural and isolated areas refused to compromise. Within Methodist and Baptist ranks there were many who disliked the new trend. A sizeable number of 'fundamentalist' or 'holiness' groups, determined to keep the old faith pure, split off from the parent churches. Several states passed laws (still existent but inoperative) to prevent the teaching of evolution as fact in the public schools, and as late as 1925 the famous Scopes trial in Tennessee upheld the legality of such legislation.

The contest between science and religion was only one aspect of the unrest, uncertainty, and doubt that disturbed the spiritual equanimity of the age. The effects of a long war, of rapid shifts in social patterns, and of revolutions in industry and agriculture, unsettled the times. 'The props of society', wrote one commentator in 1889, 'all seem to be coming loose', while people searched for some pillar of emotional and spiritual stability. The number of churches increased at a rate far exceeding the growth of population; a Methodist hymn boasted

> All hail the power of Jesus' name!
> We're building two a day!

The Baptists, who did particularly energetic missionary work among Negroes, spread even faster than the Methodists. Presbyterians made steady gains, while in the cities large and wealthy churches housed famous preachers; Beecher drew three thousand every Sunday to his Plymouth Congregational Church in Brooklyn, Phillips Brooks of Boston's Trinity was known the nation over.

Yet the figures concerning the growth of church membership during the late nineteenth century were deceptive. Organized churches, some believed, did not meet real social and spiritual needs, and failed to provide a positive Christian philosophy of life for a materialistic, industrial age. They were 'afflicted with moral astigmatism', said one critic; they 'are social clubs pure and simple', said another, 'preaching a faith wholly unrelated to the problems of contemporary life'. One reaction against the established churches took the form of an evangelical revival (in reality a third Great Awakening) which swept the American middle and lower classes. Of the many evangelists of the period the most successful was undoubtedly Dwight L. Moody, who with his choir leader Ira Sankey left a trail of fire across the country in the seventies and eighties. Moody preached an old-fashioned theology applied directly to daily life, filling a popular need unsatisfied by either Beecher's fashionable theology or the hellfire preaching of the 'holiness' sects. Others followed Moody, notably Billy Sunday, an ex-base-ball-player whose career was brief but brilliant, and by 1914 the wave of emotionalism in religion had receded. The touring evangelist with his tent is still a familiar part of the American religious pattern, but no fourth Great Awakening has yet appeared.

There were, of course, other indications that the orthodox churches did not meet contemporary religious needs. Spiritualism, which had enjoyed some popularity in the pre-war years, revived in the seventies. Madame Helene Blavatsky organized the Theosophical Society in 1875, merging spiritualism with East Indian philosophy. The most powerful of the supernaturalist churches founded at this time was the Church of Christ (Scientist) established by Mary Baker Eddy in 1879, attracting thousands of converts from the urban upper middle class, where its strength still lies. An opposite reaction was represented by Colonel Robert Green Ingersoll, who in the tradition of Tom Paine declared himself a free-thinking agnostic. Known as 'Royal Bob' to his friends and 'Devil Bob' to his enemies, he preached a socialized Christianity, independent of churches, applied directly to contemporary problems. His speeches and writings, distributed widely by Haldeman-Julius 'Little Blue Books' (priced at ten cents) profoundly affected the thinking of his and the next generation.

The most important religious movement of all, however, was the trend towards 'socialized Christianity'. Floods of young men and women to the cities needed spiritual guidance. The Y.M.C.A., imported from England in 1851, expanded from 200 chapters in 1861 to 2,000 by 1900. Its sister, the Y.W.C.A., grew almost as fast. The Salvation Army, another British import, began work among the urban poor in

1879, while settlement houses appeared in the cities. In fashionable churches ministers leaned more and more toward what they called 'applied Christianity', later named the Social Gospel. Believing that the church must meet the problems of an urban, industrialized age squarely, Social Gospellers hoped to 'substitute the law of Christian love in the sphere of social and industrial relations for Spencerian competition'. Christianity, as the Reverend Charles Sheldon phrased it, 'is simply putting the teaching of Christ to work in everyday life'. The Social Gospel movement was not confined to any particular sect, although a majority of its adherents were probably Congregationalists and Methodists. Meanwhile, the American Catholic hierarchy, after offering resistance during the eighties, gradually swung toward the leadership of liberal Cardinal Gibbons, while Pope Leo's encyclical of 1891 gave official support to Catholic social reformers.

The shift of emphasis from theology to society that characterized religious thought from 1870 to 1900 had a lasting effect on American church life. It reactivated many Protestant sects, providing them with new energy with which to withstand the assaults of science, industrialism, doubt, and lethargy. The Social Gospel was both an effective counter to the business man's 'gospel of wealth' and an antidote to the popularity of social Darwinism. Socialized Christianity, with its demand for immediate Christian solutions to social problems, led ultimately to parallel demands for social legislation, and in turn to politics. Thus it was entirely appropriate that the supporters of Theodore Roosevelt's Progressive party in 1912 should choose 'Onward Christian Soldiers' as their campaign song and that prominent ministers should lobby for minimum wage laws. The character of the American churches themselves was also radically altered. Many large urban churches to-day, and some in smaller towns, are social as well as religious institutions, with bowling alleys, gymnasia, concert series, group discussion rooms, athletic and social programmes, nursery schools, and vocational classes.

There was in the post-war period a general lowering of the level of American culture. The thinkers of the Golden Day were dead, scattered, or baffled by an America they did not understand. Mark Twain's name for this new age, 'The Gilded Age', caught its spirit perfectly, a time when taste turned cheap, ostentation replaced dignity, quantity meant more than quality, and a brassy vulgarity permeated American life. Ambrose Bierce wrote gloomily in 1881, 'The frosty truth of the situation is that we are a nation of benighted and boasting vulgarians, in whom the moral sense is as dead as Queen Anne at her deadest.' But at the same time it was not all bad. The age had tremendous vitality – unharnessed as yet to ideals – but still a great reserve of undirected energy. Its heroes were the doers, the fighters, the men who did big things in a big way: Buffalo Bill, 'Diamond Jim' Brady, John L. Sullivan the 'Boston Strong Boy', J. P. Morgan Senior, and not the thinkers and artists of fading New England. As Emerson represented his era, so Walt Whitman and Mark Twain summarized theirs, an era of rough, vital, careless power.

The cultural atmosphere of the period is best illustrated by its literature. Emerson, Lowell, Longfellow, and Holmes still lived and wrote, and Emily Dickinson, shut up in a New England garden, scratched her cameo-like poems on scraps of paper. But life had passed by all of them. The younger poets – Aldrich, Gilder, Sill, Stoddard, Stedman, and others – carried on the old polite tradition with unanimous mediocrity, while Sidney Lanier in the South raised a small, pure poetic voice that went largely unheard. The single poet of vitality was Walt Whitman, whose self-announced 'barbaric yawp' could hardly be overlooked. Whitman came out of the Civil War with a vision of science, industrialism, democracy, and love linked into one mystic circle of poetry. 'I hail with joy,' he wrote in Democratic Vistas,

the oceanic, variegated, intense practical energy, the demand for facts, even the business materialism of the current age, our States. But wo to the age or land in which things, movements, stopping at themselves, do not tend to ideas.

Embracing the whole of life like a lover, Whitman set himself to the task of hitching the energy of his times to art, attempting to 'elevate, enlarge, purify, deepen, and make happy the attributes of the body and soul of man'. Writing new poetry for a new America, he slashed away conventions of form, versification, and language, trying to dig down (as Emerson and the British Romantics before him) to the bedrock of common humanity. From the arrogant self-confidence of *Song of Myself*, through the quieter mysticism of 'When Lilacs Last in the Dooryard Bloom'd' and 'Out of the Cradle Endlessly Rocking', to the maturity of 'Passage to India', Whitman worked out of the old poetic tradition into the new. He transformed some of the optimism and vitality of Emersonian transcendentalism into a credo fit for a machine age, which paid him little homage for doing it. The critics liked better the traditional sterilities of Bayard Taylor and Richard Watson Gilder; the crowd read the folksy rhymes of Will Carleton and James Whitcomb Riley.

The prospect in prose was different. A variety of good novelists appeared after the Civil War, many of them willing to strike off in new directions. The 'nay sayers' discouraged at the trend of the times, turned back toward a genteel tradition in poetry, prose, and criticism, tacitly admitting the failure of the intellectual democracy that Whitman celebrated. The land of Thoreau and Hawthorne could produce nothing more than a succession of minor poets and a few writers of gentle prose like Sarah Orne Jewett and Mary Wilkins Freeman, though it did contribute a distinguished body of critics like Barrett Wendell, C. E. Norton, and later Irving Babbitt and Paul Elmer More. But fiction elsewhere showed surprising energy. The war focused authors' eyes on the variety and richness of the materials available in the newly unified nation, leading to the exciting discovery of 'local color' regionalism. Bret Harte's stories of California opened the Far West to exploitation, Mary Murfree discovered the mountaineers, Edward Eggleston wrote of rural Indiana, George Washington Cable of Louisiana Creoles, Harriet Beecher Stowe of the 'Old Town Folks' of Maine.

Hamlin Garland, until he became lost in reminiscence, wrote powerfully realistic stories of Mid-western farm life, and Twain spun the finest local colour stories of them all in *Roughing It, Life on the Mississippi*, and the classic *Huck Finn* and *Tom Sawyer*.

The great literary argument of the period centred about 'realism' in the novel. The frontier tall tale and the humorous, crude folk literature it produced were in themselves forerunners of a native realistic tradition, while the influence of science, industrialism, and urbanism turned artists more directly to fiction dealing with 'actuality' or 'real life', both of them terms hotly debated by critics. Garland, an early convert to realism, proclaimed himself a 'veritist' dealing with truthful pictures of life, and Twain himself, as early as 1868, hoped to be regarded as an 'authentic' writer. Harold Frederic and Joseph Kirkland called for realistic exactness in the novel, but it was William Dean Howells who made realism respectable and who, from his vantage point as editor of the *Atlantic*, defined and encouraged it. Howells, an early admirer of Tolstoy, drew back from the less pleasant implications of realism, preferring what he called 'the realism of the commonplace', of the normal and decent, in his own numerous novels.

Another group of novelists, however, took their cues from contemporary science and industrialism as well as from Darwin, Spencer, Nietzsche, Zola, Hardy, and Haeckel. The 'naturalistic' novels they wrote portrayed a deterministic, fatalistic, pessimistic world in which brute Nature controlled the destinies of helpless men. Frank Norris seized on the epic of wheat and its interrelations with railroads, big business, and politics, and left behind him at his early death a truncated trilogy of *The Octopus* and *The Pit*. Stephen Crane, declaring that 'sentiment is the devil', shocked the nineties with *Maggie: A Girl of the Streets*, following with the superb *The Red Badge of Courage* and a collection of lean, terse, beautifully-plotted short stories. Theodore Dreiser, the youngest of the group, published *Sister Carrie* in 1900 only to have it immediately suppressed. Perhaps the purest naturalist of all, Dreiser kept the tradition alive until it was picked up nearly thirty years later by Hemingway and others.

The fundamental cleavage in the American literary tradition was most aptly illustrated by the two major novelists of the post-war period. Samuel Langhorne Clemens, 'Mark Twain', owed not only his literary theory but his entire attitude toward life to the American West. He was born in Hannibal, Missouri, on the Mississippi river, one generation removed from raw frontier, and as printer, soldier, miner, reporter, unlucky business man, steamboat pilot, and traveller, he sampled almost every aspect of the raucous life of his era. His early work, done in the 'tall tale' tradition of frontier humour, blossomed into the magnificent local colour novels of his middle years; then, shifting to satire in the nineties, he moved late in life toward Swiftian strictures such as *The Mysterious Stranger*. An uneven artist, with a strong sense of the poetic and the melodramatic, Twain created in Tom, Huck, Huck's pappy, Colonel Sellers, the Connecticut Yankee, and others a galaxy of characters whose place is secure in the native tradition. He was strongly nationalistic, reflecting his Western backgrounds; Europe he rejected as effete and feudalistic, lashing out at priests, kings, remnants of tradition, and anti-democratic tendencies wherever he saw them. The savagery of *Joan of Arc*, the bitter passages of *A Connecticut Yankee at King Arthur's Court*, and the aggressive Americanism of *Innocents Abroad* are items in a long tradition of anti-European bias in American culture.

Yet in American culture there has always existed a counter force, a strong pull back toward Europe, a retracing of steps towards the society just left. Mather, Byrd, and Edwards felt it in colonial times; Irving, Longfellow, Emerson, and the rest were drawn toward England and Europe in the nineteenth century; the magnet of the old countries drew Howells and others after the Civil War. Henry James represented the late nineteenth-century version of this return to an older civilization in search of values and codes not quite lost in the departure from the old and not quite established in the new. James was born into a wealthy New England family, his father a philosopher-friend of Emerson, his brother William a psychologist and philosopher. After the age of twelve Henry James made his home in Europe; he travelled and studied abroad, returning to the United States at ever-longer intervals for briefer stays. In 1876, at thirty-three, he settled abroad, first in Paris, then in London, where he remained to take British citizenship in 1914.

James felt the pull of Europe powerfully; it took 'an old civilization', he said, 'to set the novelist in motion'. His early work was concerned with an analysis of the contrasting cultures of Europe and America, as in *Daisy Miller* and *The American*, for after long exposure to cosmopolitan society, James felt American inferiority acutely. As time passed he became less and less American and more the conscious artist, ultimately perhaps the most consciously artistic novelist who ever wrote. Vitally interested in providing a sensitive and complete impression of life, he rejected contemporary naturalistic and realistic generalizations about literature and art. His later work was increasingly delicate and intricate, reaching its height in *The Ambassadors*, *The Wings of the Dove*, and *The Golden Bowl*. Though he eventually ended his life the complete cosmopolitan, the path he took was a native American one of expatriation. James simply followed it to the end, which lay beyond the Atlantic, not to the West.

The fluidity of post-war America's concept of civilization was apparent in other cultural areas besides literature. American philosophers, educated in the idealism of Emerson, stumbled like the theologians on the hard block of Spencerian naturalism, and like them attempted to find an epistemology suited to the world and society around them. William James typified the struggle of the new philosophy to bridge the gap between the old idealism and the new science. Working outward from an idea expressed by C. S. Peirce of Harvard, James evolved a philosophical system called 'pragmatism', whose sole aim was to provide a guide for action in an age that sorely needed guides. Active, practical, confident, pragmatism represented a distinctively American point of view. An intellectual position, said James, is true if it will work, and if it will work, it will be consistent with other workable theories. The philosopher therefore tests old or new theories against the standard of workability, retaining or rejecting them in a sort of naturally selective process. John Dewey of Columbia University extended pragmatism into 'instrumentalism', which he defined as converting ideas into useful tools by which men can achieve a practical end in life. The effect of pragmatism and instrumentalism, popularized by James's and Dewey's followers, was to drive philosophy out of a corner into a direct preoccupation with contemporary differences and antagonisms. The so-called 'practical cash-value' test of ideas fitted a materialistic age. Its pervasive influence on American thought and institutions is attested by thousands of instinctive pragmatists in contemporary business, law, education, and social affairs who found in James and Dewey the guides they searched for.

As realism was to literature and pragmatism to philosophy, so functionalism was to architecture. From the popular Greek Revival buildings of ante-bellum America architecture turned to a confused eclecticism. H. H. Richardson's Renaissance style briefly dominated the scene, while Richard Hunt's French chateaux, built for millionaires, appeared in the cities. McKim, Mead, and White, who designed more public buildings than any other firm in America, favoured massive classicism; libraries, railroad stations, university and government buildings the breadth of the United States reflected their influence for two generations. The functional trend developed when Louis Sullivan proclaimed in the eighties that a building should represent its purpose, that a structure was organic, adapted to its use and environment. Sullivan's ideas (themselves an adaptation of Darwinism) found numerous followers as time passed, among them Frank Lloyd Wright, and the classic, Gothic, baroque, and Byzantine structure began to disappear. One obvious result was the 'skyscraper', an exclusively functional structure necessitated by the rising cost of urban property and the need for office space in the cities.

Art and sculpture displayed no consistent trends during the period. Post-war painters moved away from the Germanized 'Hudson River' school popular in the fifties, strongly influenced by French impressionism on the one hand and by realism on the other. Whistler and Sargent, both expatriates, carried on the French tradition; Homer, Eakins, and others pointed toward the 'revolt' led after 1900 by John Sloan, George Luks, and George Bellows. The Civil War placed hundreds of statues in city parks, done in the popular sentimentalized classic style of the fifties. Not until the appearance of St Gaudens and French, late in the century (both influenced by Rodin) could American sculpture be said to have come of age. In neither art nor sculpture was there evidence of a native tradition or of an 'American school'.

The pattern of American politics after 1865 was profoundly influenced by three factors. First, the idea of evolution and development changed the concept of politics from static to dynamic. Government, it came to be assumed, was not a fixed but a shifting, ever-adapting institution. The Constitution and frame of American government had been shaped according to the eighteenth-century Newtonian concept of order, stability, and permanence, but the later nineteenth century reshaped it according to Darwinian ideas of evolutionary development. This was a violent and revolutionary change of emphasis that outmoded much of earlier American political theory and made politics a thing developed, rather than contrived. Woodrow Wilson, writing in the eighties, expressed the new concept clearly:

Government is not a machine, but a living thing. It falls, not under the theory of the universe, but under the theory of organic life. It is accountable to Darwin, not to Newton. . . . Living political constitutions must be Darwinian in structure and practice.

Secondly, Americans adopted a pragmatic approach to

politics. The point of politics, it was assumed, was to understand the actual operation of government, to study unwritten as well as written laws, to recognize the political importance of men and pressures and opinions. The results of this pragmatic approach are evident in the appearance of analytical bureaux, such as the reorganized Census Bureau, the Bureau of Labor Statistics, the Departments of Labor, Commerce, Agriculture, and others. Thirdly, the late nineteenth century began to recognize more fully the functions of power groups. This was not new. Hamilton, Jefferson, Madison, and others had long before considered the importance of 'factions' in government, but political thinkers of the post-war period saw more clearly than they the importance of special interest groups in deciding political questions. Politics, no matter the campaign name or party label, was no longer considered a battle between 'good' and 'bad' but a conflict of interests – private and public, have and have-not, agriculture and industry, East and West.

From 1776 to 1865 the term *democracy* connoted opposition to absolutism, personal power, personal privilege, institutionalized political inequality, suppression of free speech and thought. After 1865 the problem became how to define and interpret the formulas and ideals of an historical eighteenth-century democracy in terms of a new social and industrial order. Though it might be assumed that *democracy* still meant what it always had, what did it also mean in terms of the factory, the 'captain of industry', the labour union, the farmer, the trust? Answers to the question involved recognition of certain new trends in American life, of the entrance of social issues into politics, of the contest among capital and labour and agriculture for political control, and of all those changes wrought in America by urbanism, industrialism, prosperity, increased population, immigration, and the settlement of the West. Politics of the later nineteenth century, therefore (and of the early twentieth as well) settled down into a conflict among differing interpretations of the word *democracy*. It was a contest between a conservative theory of *laissez-faire* and closely restricted government powers, and a liberal theory of stronger government under broader control with a wider social programme. The contest involved certain tangential issues, including, obviously, an attempt to use Hamiltonian means to attain Jeffersonian ends. It involved a complete re-thinking of hallowed concepts of individualism and *laissez-faire*, and it meant, of course, reconsideration of the goals of American democracy.

The Republican party, committed to the *laissez-faire* theory of government, was from 1860 to 1912 almost continuously in control of the executive and legislative branches of the government. To maintain its position it formed close alliances with industry and business, identifying itself with high tariffs, hard money, stable currency and credit, and aid to industry by subsidy. The Republican party became, in effect, the political instrument of an expanding industrial capitalism. Moreover, it was the 'respectable' party of the North, supported by the farmer who gained his land under Republican-sponsored Homestead acts, by the veteran who fought the war under Republican leadership and who received his pension from a Republican administration, by the manufacturer who liked Republican tariffs. Republicanism to many in the North was a fundamental and self-evident thing, like the flag or the Union; how could one disown the party of the martyred Lincoln? Republican leaders of the period traded on the party's *esprit de corps*, developing it into a highly-organized, tightly-disciplined political machine. At the same time the party always had within it an independent element, a 'mugwump' or 'progressive' group that battled constantly with the party leaders and occasionally forced concessions from them. The Democratic party, despite its minority position, was far from weak or ineffective. It elected Presidents in 1884 and 1890, and for twenty years held intermittent control of one House of Congress.

Hayes' victory in 1876 marked the beginning of the closest balance of party strength in American history. The fact was that the voter found little to choose between the parties. The colourless platforms of the years 1876 to 1896 showed that both parties existed in a vacuum, unaware of the vast economic and social changes that had taken place in the nation after the Civil War. In a sense, parties became ends in themselves, with Democrats existing to battle Republicans, Republicans existing to oppose Democrats. Lord Bryce, in his shrewd analysis of the American political scene, concluded that 'neither party has any clear-cut principles, any distinct tenets. Both have traditions. Both claim to have tendencies. Both have certainly war cries, organization, interests, enlisted in their support. But those interests are in the main the interests of getting or keeping the patronage of government.' The basic issues of the period's politics are discoverable chiefly in the platforms of the multitudes of third parties that dotted the times: the Greenback, Independent, Reform, and labour parties in the states, which culminated in the Populist Revolt of the nineties.

The dynamics of the two major parties from 1876 to 1896 were provided by men, not issues, by organizations, not principles. This was the heyday of the boss and the machine, both of which operated best at the city level, where governmental processes were close at hand, and control easiest to establish. William Marcy Tweed of New York and his Tammany organization were almost the prototypes of bosses and machines, but dozens like them existed in Pittsburgh, Cleveland, Chicago, St Louis, and other cities. The organization of both parties rested on such local bosses. The national committee of each party interlocked with a party committee in Congress, so that congressional politics might be directly co-ordinated with political strategy; national committees also worked directly with state and city bosses, who delivered votes on demand. The boss himself was an interesting character – never quite socially respectable, shrewd, expert at his business, true to his own peculiar code of ethics. He stood at the centre of a web that was connected with vice (gambling, liquor, prostitution) on one side and special interest groups (utilities, labour, corporations, manufacturing) on the other, serving as intermediary between both and government. For delivering his votes he received fees from both, keeping a percentage himself and passing the rest down to lower levels of the organization. The machine was kept together by jobs passed out through political patronage; by direct contributions from special interests, big and little; by graft legislation allowing access to public moneys; and by a crude but powerful sense of party loyalty.

Surveying the succession of Presidents from 1868 to 1900 Henry Adams remarked, 'No period so thoroughly ordinary has been known in American politics since Christopher Columbus first disturbed the balance of American society.' The Republicans who occupied the White House during those years were respectable mediocrities, dedicated to party service, with little understanding of the vital forces transforming the nation. Hayes, a conscientious man, quickly fell out with his own party leaders because of his insistence on reforming the civil service. The Democrats, who called Hayes 'His Fraudulency, The President', harassed him at every opportunity, and since they had a majority in the House (in the Senate too after the elections of 1878) they made his administrative position almost untenable.

Before the presidential conventions of 1880 Hayes announced he was not a candidate, a wise decision since few Republican leaders wanted him. Some of the older party men talked of running Grant again, but more leaned to James G. Blaine, the 'Plumed Knight' from Maine. Neither Blaine nor Grant could gather sufficient support at the convention, which eventually picked James Garfield of Ohio, a young and undistinguished party regular. As a concession to the Grant backers the Garfield men chose Chester A. Arthur of New York as vice-president. The Democrats nominated General Winfield Hancock, a fine soldier but with no political experience. Garfield won by an extremely narrow margin, fewer than nine thousand votes out of nine million. Garfield, however, was shot in July 1881 by a disappointed, and probably insane, office-seeker. Since Arthur was known as a machine politician, the public feared a swift return to 'Grantism'. Arthur surprised everyone by carrying on Hayes' struggle for clean and efficient government and forcing the passage of a good civil service bill. Ironically, it was Chester A. Arthur, from whom no one expected much, who put the first real dent in the old Jacksonian spoils system.

In 1884 the Republicans jettisoned Arthur in favour of Blaine, who had a strong personal following in the party and a none-too-savoury reputation outside it. The liberal Republicans had no use for him, threatening to bolt the party if the Democrats chose a better man. The Democrats did: Grover Cleveland, Governor of New York. In a vicious campaign Blaine's past was thoroughly raked, and several shady but profitable deals with railroads were uncovered. Cleveland, accused of fathering an illegitimate child in his youth, did not deny it, while his supporters pointed out that he had honestly assumed proper responsibility for his by-blow. Democrats chanted

> Blaine, Blaine, James G. Blaine,
> The con-ti-nent-al liar from the State of Maine!

while Republicans shouted in reply

> Ma! Ma! Where's my pa?
> Gone to the White House – ha, ha, ha!

The campaign seemed about even until a New York clergyman, speaking in Blaine's behalf, assailed the Democrats as the party of 'Rum, Romanism, and Rebellion', alienating many Irish Catholic voters in New York. Cleveland won by 23,000 votes in a total of ten million cast. The first Democratic President to hold office since 1856, he also took in with him a Democratic House.

Cleveland fought a courageous battle against the influence of special interests in government and guarded the Treasury well. The Grand Army of the Republic lobbied numerous pension bills through Congress only to have Cleveland veto most of them. In direct conflict with the advice of his party leaders he attacked the high tariffs beloved by manufacturers and demanded a reduction in rates that was blocked by the Republican Senate. He also increased the effectiveness of the civil service system and ordered an investigation of railroad land grants. By the end of his term Cleveland had offended the Union veterans, industrialists, business men, and a good share of his own party leaders, including Tammany. But his concern for doing the right thing earned him the respect of the public, and the party somewhat reluctantly nominated him for a second term.

The Republicans chose Benjamin Harrison, grandson of William Henry Harrison and an Indiana lawyer of no particular distinction. The campaign revolved chiefly about the tariff issue, Cleveland basing his on a demand for a lowered tariff, Harrison supporting a high tariff to protect manufacturing. Business interests contributed heavily to Harrison's support; election-day activities of both parties, in fact, were so scandalous that the movement to adopt the Australian ballot-system gained great headway. Cleveland had the larger popular vote by nearly 100,000, but lost the electoral vote and the election. The Republicans also gained control of both Houses of Congress.

The Republican party, in the light of Cleveland's popular vote, could hardly assume a mandate from the people. Harrison therefore proceeded cautiously. He left party policy mostly to Blaine, his Secretary of State, and for a time the Republicans had things their own way. The G.A.R. pension bills passed. The McKinley tariff went through, with the highest and most peculiarly distributed duties yet recorded in tariff history. Civil service suffered when the Republicans went to work on it; the system probably would have been wrecked had it not been for the resistance offered by Theodore Roosevelt, a young New York Republican on the Civil Service Commission. The congressional election of 1890, in which the Republicans lost control of both Houses of Congress, reflected the prevailing opinion of the Republican record. But in 1892 the Republicans, standing on that record, nominated Harrison once more, while the Democrats countered with Grover Cleveland again, with Adlai Stevenson of Illinois as his running mate. Cleveland won by a respectable majority, carrying both Houses of Congress.

In the election General James Baird Weaver of Iowa, running on the third-party Populist ticket, polled a million popular votes and twenty-two electoral votes, all from the agrarian West. The political game of Tweedledum versus Tweedledee, played by Republican and Democrat alike for twenty years, was about over and signs of revolt were already visible in the West.

American diplomacy from Appomattox to the Spanish War faced no serious crises, nor did it have any consistent pattern. National interest centred on westward expansion, on rebuilding the shattered South, on consolidating the gains of industry, and on exploiting the nation's vast natural resources. The 'manifest destiny' of the pre-war years settled into a mild expansionism, tempered by strong public disapproval of imperialism. The most delicate diplomatic problems were those left over from the Civil War, especially those involving Britain, against which the United States had some long-standing grievances. The retirement of Palmerston and Russell from British foreign affairs and the substitution of Clarendon smoothed the path of diplomacy considerably. The American Secretaries of State during the period were less pugnacious than some of their predecessors, while Seward (under Johnson), Hamilton Fish (under Grant), William G. Evarts (under Hayes), and Blaine (under Garfield and Harrison) were exceptionally able men.

Fish's handling of British-American relations during Grant's administration was one of the few accomplishments to its credit. His most difficult problem concerned Canada, the traditional subject of a great deal of spreadeagle annexationist talk by American politicians. There was, to be sure, anti-British sentiment in Canada, and Britain countered with the North America Act of 1867, creating the Dominion of Canada as a means of unifying Canadians against American penetration. At the same time the Fenian Brotherhood, an Irish-American society, evolved a wild plan of invading Canada, hoping to precipitate a war with Britain that by some obscure reasoning might end in freeing Ireland.

In 1866 and 1870 Fenian bands crossed the border to clash with Canadian volunteers, but in both instances the Washington government swiftly arrested the leaders and seized Fenian supplies. Such energetic action won applause from both British and Canadians and encouraged good feeling toward the United States. Fish's real triumph came in 1871, however, with the signing of the Treaty of Washington, which provided for settlement by arbitration of all remaining points of friction with Britain: the Oregon boundary dispute, the *Alabama* affair, and the Newfoundland fishing claims. For the first time since the outbreak of the American Revolution the British-American agenda was not only swept clean, but negotiation and arbitration were firmly fixed into the pattern of Anglo-American policy.

Seward, an ardent expansionist, set about after the Civil War to establish control over the Caribbean, Latin America, and the Pacific, but found Congress and the public lukewarm toward his ambitions. When Russia appeared willing to sell Alaska, Seward persuaded Congress to snap it up in 1867 for a little more than seven million dollars; however, the isolationist Senate balked at his efforts to acquire Santo Domingo and the Danish West Indies. People paid little attention to the purchase of 'Seward's Icebox', nor did the American occupation of uninhabited Midway Island in the Pacific excite much interest.

Most of American diplomatic activity was concentrated on the Pacific and Latin America. The United States had enjoyed excellent trade relations with China since the forties, but the importation of Chinese labourers in the seventies raised a serious immigration problem. Plagued by recurrent depressions and unemployment, American workmen bitterly resented the presence of 'the heathen Chinee' (as Bret Harte called him) as a cheap labour pool. Pressure on Congress during Arthur's administration brought an 'exclusion bill' preventing the entry of Chinese, the first of a long series of immigration laws directed at specific groups of particular racial or geographical origins. With Japan, opened by Perry in 1854, American merchants had similar good relations. After the United States, Holland, Britain, and France joined in 1865 to put down internal dissension in Japan, Japanese-American commerce steadily increased.

The Hawaiian Islands in the South Pacific had long been a port of call for Yankee ships and the United States a fine market for Hawaiian sugar. American entrepreneurs controlled three-fourths of the sugar plantations; in 1875 Fish engineered a trade treaty that markedly improved their position. Queen Liliuokalani, who ascended to the Hawaiian throne in 1891, had a strong anti-American bias, whereupon a revolutionary group overthrew her government with the help of United States Marines and proclaimed a Republic which Washington soon recognized. There was, however, strong public and Congressional opposition to outright annexation, which was not finally accomplished until 1898 during the imperialist enthusiasm of the Spanish War period. Samoa, complicated by the presence of German and British interests in the islands, was much the same story. In 1899 Germany obtained most of the islands, Britain withdrew, and the United States took possession of Tutuila.

With the Southern agricultural imperialists gone from Congress, American interest in Latin America and the Caribbean waned. Cuba seemed no longer a lure, though Cuban revolutionaries, engaged in perennial uprisings against Spain, severely strained Spanish-American relations by using the United States as a base of operations. Segments of public opinion sympathized with the revolutionary leaders and there was some sentiment in Congress favouring interference in their behalf, but Washington remained doggedly neutral.

The seizure of power by Dictator Diaz in 1876 opened a period of good relations between the United States and Mexico. Diaz encouraged American investments, settled old claims, and welcomed American counsel. James G. Blaine further cemented relations with Latin America by founding the Pan-American Congress (later the Pan-American Union) to facilitate commerce, improve understanding, and encourage cultural interchange. The one disharmonious note was struck by Richard Olney, Cleveland's Secretary of State. Venezuela, after long argument with Britain over its boundary with British Guiana, appealed to the United States for arbitration. Olney sent an aggressive and almost insulting note to Britain charging violation of the Monroe Doctrine and claiming complete authority not only over the dispute but over all Latin American affairs. Lord Salisbury at first refused to arbitrate but later agreed, with the result that British Guiana won most of the disputed territory. While American willingness to protect Venezuela pleased the Latin American republics, its calm assumption of hemispheric authority was less happily received.

In total effect, American diplomacy during the period displayed tact and common sense: France quickly cleared from Mexico, the war claims settled with dispatch, the Monroe Doctrine reaffirmed without undue muscle-flexing. The close of the Civil War seemed to mark the beginning of a period of greater self-confidence and maturity in American foreign relations.

The American farmer gained from the Civil War, but did not believe that he gained enough. For a time he was prosperous, but the bubble of prosperity, blown large by the war, collapsed shortly after it. Farm prices wobbled crazily year after year, gradually sliding downward. Wheat, rye, corn, and cotton dropped 20 to 50 per cent twenty years after Lee's surrender, which meant foreclosed mortgages, increased debt, poverty and distress in the West and South. At the same time that the bottom dropped out of the farmer's market, prices on the manufactured goods he bought stayed up, protected by tariffs and trusts, and even went higher. During the same lean years the national currency underwent a gradual contraction (the aftermath of wartime currency inflation) that depressed market prices even more. All this the farmer could not understand. During the Civil War, when 'greenbacks' were plentiful, prices for farm products were high. Why not, then, increase the amount of currency simply by passing the necessary Federal laws? In the same way Congress might settle such other agricultural problems as freight rates, taxes, and interest on mortgages.

Neither major party paid much attention to the farmer's demands. Over a period of years his resentment mounted against the Eastern banker (who tampered with the currency), the city loan shark (who charged high interest), 'Wall Street' (which in some subtle way rigged markets and caused depressions), railroad kings (who collected exorbitant freight rates), trusts (which engineered high tariffs and prices), and politicians (Republican and Democrat alike) who connived to keep the farmer poor. The farmer was angry, very angry, at 'the system that clothed rascals in robes and honesty in rags'.

The seventies and eighties were alive with dissident farm groups. Some, purely social, tried to break down the isolation of life on the empty western prairies – what farm women called 'the lones'. Some were educational, since rural schools lagged far behind urban. Some, by consolidating buying and borrowing power, turned into co-operatives; the great American mail order houses, such as Montgomery Ward and Company, were first founded to deal directly with farmers and to eliminate the middleman. But wherever farmers met in the South and West the talk eventually turned to politics, to government control of monopolies (especially railroads), easier credit with lower interest, cheaper money and more of it, a lowered tariff, better tax distribution with an income tax for the rich man, the elimination of corruption and privilege in government. All these issues boiled down to three general demands that ran consistently through late nineteenth-century agrarian thinking; remove special interest from politics, make government more responsive to the needs of more people, broaden its concepts to include economic and social welfare.

The most comprehensive of the early farm organizations was the Grange, or Patrons of Husbandry, a semi-secret society founded in 1867. The Grange was especially strong in the South and West, claiming 750,000 members by the mid-seventies. It was avowedly non-political, but since it was virtually impossible to keep farmers out of politics the Grange became a party in everything but name. When neither major party seemed responsive to Granger demands, farmers in several midwestern states formed Independent, Reform, or Anti-Monopoly parties and put a good deal of legislation, aimed primarily at the railroads, into the statute books. The dominant Republican party stood off the Granger threat, however, and most of the third parties were dead by the late seventies, absorbed into the Greenback party. Since the cheap money of the Civil War years suited the farmer and debtor very well, the Greenbackers framed their organization on the currency issue. They ran a few state tickets with moderate success and in 1876, with Peter Cooper running as presidential candidate, polled a million votes and sent fifteen men to Congress. After 1876 the Greenback party declined rapidly, merged with the Anti-Monopolists, and finally died.

The Farmers' Alliance replaced the Grange and the Greenbackers as an outlet for rural discontent. The Alliance split into two branches, the Southern and the North-western (or Northern). It was modelled after the Grange with an important exception – it was an admittedly political organization, since there was no point, as one Alliance organizer said, 'in making a gun that wouldn't shoot'. The Southern Alliance, the larger of the two, excluded Negroes and preferred to work within the framework of the Democratic party. The North-western admitted Negroes and labourers, was much more politically aggressive, and hoped to establish a third party. Attempts were made in the eighties to join with the Knights of Labor to form a Union Labor party, but without much success. Nothing daunted, the North-western Alliance announced in 1889 that it intended to create a party dedicated to the task of 'obtaining for the farmer and laborer equal privileges with the manufacturing and commercial classes'.

Hard times helped the Alliance cause. There were several successive drought years; wheat dropped to fifty cents a bushel, cotton to six cents a pound, corn was cheaper to burn as fuel than to sell. Meanwhile Congress raised tariffs, voted millions in pork-barrel bills, and paid no attention to the cries of distress from the farms. What the farmer needed to do, said Alliance organizer Mary Ellen Lease, 'The Kansas Pythoness', was 'to raise less corn and more hell'. Nurtured on falling prices, Alliance-sponsored third parties made strong showings in the state elections of 1890 in Georgia, South Carolina, Kansas, Nebraska, Minnesota, and the Dakotas. The parties varied from state to state, but the People's Party of Kansas, one of the more successful ones, lent its name to the protest movement: 'Populist' and 'Populism' were its hardy derivatives. With a going organization and good leadership provided by Ignatius Donnelly of Minnesota, James Weaver (the old Green-backer) of Iowa, 'Sockless Jerry' Simpson of Kansas, 'Pitchfork Ben' Tillman of South Carolina, Tom Watson of Georgia, and others, the Alliance believed it was time to stroke a nation-wide blow.

Southern Alliance leaders opposed political action on a national scale, since the Democratic party meant white rule in the South and if the white vote were split by a third party the Negro might gain ground. North-western leaders went ahead, nevertheless, to call a series of conventions in 1891, ending with the creation of the National People's Party at St Louis. For its presidential nominee the Populists chose Weaver of Iowa, an experienced campaigner, and a Union veteran, and for vice-president James Field of Virginia, a courtly ex-Confederate general. Designed to attract any dissatisfied voter – Greenbacker, Union Labor, Granger, Anti-Monopolist, or anyone else – the Populist platform denounced Republican and Democrat impartially. 'We meet', it said, 'in the midst of a nation brought to the verge of moral, political, and material ruin.'

The fruits of the toil of millions are boldly stolen to build up collossal fortunes for the few, unprecedented in the history of mankind; and the possessors of these, in turn despise the Republic and endanger liberty. From the same prolific womb of governmental injustice we breed the two great classes – tramps and millionaires.

'Populism', said the New York *Herald*, 'spread like flame on a dry prairie.' Though Weaver's campaign was a good one, his million votes were not much compared to the combined total cast for Harrison and Cleveland.

Behind the Populist party lay the built-up resentment of years of hard times. It expressed the suspicion of the rural dweller toward an expanding urban America, toward banks and trusts, toward the two major parties which seemed to disregard his interests. Populist thinking on these issues was strongly conditioned by the work of three influential reformers – Henry George of California, Edward Bellamy of Massachusetts, and Henry Demarest Lloyd of Chicago. The paradox of poverty in the midst of plenty puzzled George, until the answer came to him, he said, 'in an ecstatic vision'. The cause of poverty was a land monopoly which deprived the majority of free use of the land and enabled the few to attach the earnings of the many in the form of rent. The remedy, he believed, was a 'single tax' on the unearned increment that accrued to the owner of land or natural resources from the simple fact of ownership. His ideas, first stated in *Progress and Poverty* (1879) and expanded in later books, attracted a large following among Southern and Western farmers. By 1900 five million copies of his book had been sold, Single Tax Leagues founded by his supporters appeared in the cities, and George himself was nearly elected Mayor of New York. He travelled and lectured in Ireland and England, where he had some influence on the Webbs, Shaw, and the early Fabians.

The same problem of monopoly interested Lloyd and Bellamy. Lloyd, a Chicago journalist, studied Rockefeller's oil empire and wrote a series of articles on it in the early eighties. Finally he published *Wealth Against Commonwealth* (1894), the most careful and complete indictment of monopoly ever written. Edward Bellamy tried to solve the problem of centralized industry in terms of state socialism, explained in his utopian novel *Looking Backward* (1888).

Monopolies, wrote Bellamy, undermined liberty by destroying competition; to give security and equality to all its citizens, the state should assume control of economic life, substituting co-operation for competition as its motivating principle. Bellamy, George, and Lloyd were best sellers in Granger and Alliance circles and had much to do with the political education of the Populists.

Grover Cleveland entered the White House at an unlucky time. Depression struck almost as soon as he was inaugurated. Before 1894 169 railroads went into bankruptcy, and in late 1893 the banks began to go, national, state, and private, 600 in all before it was over. Cleveland was not equipped to handle the crisis. Business recessions, he believed, were matters for business and not for government to solve; if let alone, depressions wore themselves out. But little by little the national economy slowed down, factories closed, machines stood idle, unemployed flocked the streets, and farm prices plummeted downward, until a Kansas farmer, speaking for the Populist states, summed their situation up by saying, 'We have reached the bottom, we cannot further reduce our rations and live.'

A more flexible politician might have tempered the winds of depression, but Cleveland could not. Serious labour troubles broke out, culminating in the bloody Pullman strike of 1894 in Illinois, led by Eugene Debs of the new American Railway Union. Cleveland's answer was to send in Federal troops and to encourage the courts to use injunctions against the strikers, putting Debs in gaol. In Ohio, 'General' Jacob Coxey, a Greenbacker and Populist, organized and led to Washington an 'army' of unemployed to demand relief. Coxey's arrest for walking on the Capitol lawn simply served to underline the Populist accusation that Cleveland's whole administration was part of an 'unholy alliance with monopoly'. In the offyear Congressional election of 1894 thousands of farmers and labourers deserted the old parties to send a bloc of Populists and Independents to Congress.

The sudden emergence of the issue of 'free silver' muddied

political waters considerably. There was nothing new about currency-reform schemes in American politics, but 'free silver' gave a new twist to the old Greenback principle. Though United States finances were set on a gold standard, in the seventies some argued that the lavish issue of government notes backed by silver would improve the nation's finances and smother depressions in an avalanche of money. So 'free' or unlimited coinage of silver took on, for the farmer and labourer, the attributes of a cure-all for economic ills. Few understood exactly how free silver might settle everything, but many were convinced that it would. By tying it to the Eastern banker, to Wall Street, to the 'money power' of monopoly, politicians developed a highly emotional charge from a dry-as-dust, complex currency issue.

'Silver wings' appeared in both Democratic and Republican parties, while pressure increased on the Populists to accept a free silver plank. Silver was not a legitimate Populist issue except as it related to monopoly and hard times – both Populist rallying points – but a good many agrarian leaders who had run the gamut from Grangerism to Greenbackism to Populism were willing to accept it as a means of drawing votes from the major parties and from labour. Others, like Lloyd, were suspicious of it as 'the cowbird of the reform movement, likely to push the other eggs out of the nest'.

The nominating conventions for the presidential election of 1896 met in an atmosphere of tension. The Republicans nominated Governor William McKinley of Ohio and announced a gold-standard policy, the signal for the 'Silver Republicans' to bolt. The Democrats, three weeks later, found the silverites extremely well organized, and after a brief battle, the Western 'free silver' men won control of the meeting. There was no favourite for president, until William Jennings Bryan of Nebraska, a comparative unknown, exploded the convention. Rising to speak on a hot afternoon in Chicago, Bryan stampeded the meeting into one of the greatest demonstrations in American political

history. Tracing the background of the silver question, recalling all the bitternesses and hatreds of discontent for
twenty years past, crying out to labour for support, he
climaxed his speech with an inspired image saved for the
occasion: 'You shall not press down upon the brow of labour
this cross of thorns, you shall not crucify mankind upon a
cross of gold!' When the last phrase of the 'Cross of Gold'
speech died in the air, no one else stood a chance. This was
the West speaking, the Granger, the Greenbacker, the
Populist, the farmer with a mortgage and the jobless worker
in the street. The shout of 'Bryan, Bryan, Bryan' began to
beat across the land. The great crusade had begun, the
'Great Commoner' at its head. The Populist party, meeting
in the shadow of Bryan's cross of gold, succumbed and
nominated Bryan too.

Bryan represented the protest of an old agrarian class
against the new urban-industrial America. And Bryan himself fired the imagination with his massive, barrel-like body,
leonine head with coal black hair, flashing eyes, voice of
almost hypnotic power. His mind was not deep and his
principles were the simple ones of the rural West – equal
rights, popular rule, hatred of monopoly, a life of Christian
virtue. Of all he said, only the closing peroration of the Cross
of Gold speech remains, yet he was one of the most powerful
political influences of his time, a man who captured and
held for nearly fifteen years two parties and six million
voters.

Bryan faced two opponents in the 1896 campaign, William McKinley and his Republican campaign manager,
Mark Hanna. Hanna, a millionaire from Cleveland, was a
shrewd, intelligent machine politician who firmly believed
that good government was Republican government, instituted for the benefit of business. McKinley, the last of the
Civil War veterans to fill the Presidency, was a smooth,
handsome party regular of more than average ability as a
politician. The two made a team, each supplying what the
other lacked – McKinley the speeches and personality,
Hanna the organization. Bryan travelled the length and

breadth of the nation, speaking sometimes a dozen times a day, but Hanna quietly collected funds and set the Republican organization to work. The party coffers held nearly twelve million dollars, which Hanna poured out lavishly; in the state of Iowa alone the Republicans mailed out six million pieces of campaign literature and put 6,000 workers in the field. The result was never in doubt. McKinley won by a safe margin in electoral votes, although by only a half-million popular votes. Free silver and Populism vanished in the defeat.

So far as immediate results were concerned, the great agrarian revolt of 1896 accomplished nothing. The political party that had been in power remained in power, its branches shaken by the wind of rebellion but its roots still firmly set. After McKinley's victory the Republican organization seemed more thoroughly in control than it had even in Grant's time. But the spirit of the Populists remained alive. Twenty years of agitation laid the groundwork for what was to come under Theodore Roosevelt, Woodrow Wilson, Robert La Follette, Franklin Roosevelt, and others of lesser stature who followed. Even in defeat Bryan's campaign showed the alterations that had taken place in America and the fundamental changes in the problems of democracy. Only a few months after McKinley's inauguration the United States was to engage Spain in war and emerge from it a world power, its traditional isolation ended. There would be a shift, a marked shift, from the old frontier philosophy of individualism and *laissez-faire* towards a new concept of the positive role of the state and social co-operation – a shift, as the historian Turner phrased it, 'from the ideal of individualism to the ideal of social control through regulation by law'. Modern America was about to arrive.

CHAPTER 27

PROGRESSIVISM AND REACTION
1896–1932

WAR, industrial and agricultural revolution, changes in production and transportation, new social groupings and patterns – these shaped the structure of twentieth-century America. The rapid industrialization of the national economy effected a new kind of division of labour, hastened the growth of the factory system, opened up transportation, and altered the nation's financial framework. Agriculture found itself part of a different economic scheme. The chief fact about twentieth-century America was that its developing social complexity changed the relationship of individual to individual and of section to section. American life after 1900 was interdependent, not independent. It took some time for Americans to adjust to this fact.

The most significant development in American politics from 1900 to 1920 was the Progressive movement. Surveying contemporary life, liberal thinkers were dissatisfied with what they saw. The Federal government appeared to some of them to be controlled by a privileged few who ran it for the benefit of the railroads, the banks, and the manufacturing and mining corporations. The subsequent revolt against such 'government by privilege' was the culmination of a protest long brewing, from the Grangers through the Populist agitation of the nineties. The Social Gospellers, too, contributed their share, and the ideas of social planners such as Bellamy, Lloyd, Lester Ward, George, and others, did much to undermine the foundations of the old individualistic, *laissez-faire* philosophy. The 'muckrakers', a group of crusading journalists and novelists who specialized in exposure of graft and corruption, played a part, men and women such as Ida Tarbell, Lincoln Steffens, Ray Stannard Baker, and Upton Sinclair.

The reformers of the progressive era approached con-

temporary problems with pragmatic confidence. The im-
balances and injustices of politics and society could be
solved, they believed, sensibly and practically, by returning
economic, political, and social institutions to a larger degree
of popular control. Their aim, therefore, was to formulate
new social and political doctrines for a nation whose wealth
and political power had apparently outstripped its ability to
cope with the problems these things brought. Old theories
were scrutinized and rejected, the machinery of government
inspected and repaired, traditional political and economic
patterns broken and rearranged, the better to square with
democracy. For thirty years before 1900 the underprivileged
and repressed raised voices of protest from city and farm.
All that was needed in 1900 was a set of leaders.

The first signs of progressivism came from the cities, where
urban reformers locked in conflict with local political
machines. In the states, at almost the same time, 'progressives' fought 'stalwart' conservatives for control of state
legislatures, and inevitably the same impulse of reform was
transferred to national politics. The progressive movement
advanced regardless of party lines; both Republican and
Democratic organizations were sharply divided between
'insurgents' or 'progressives' and 'conservatives' or 'stal-
warts' by 1908. The liberal wing of the Republican party
failed to capture party control, but the Democratic progressives succeeded.

Progressive programmes varied with leaders and sections.
Some stressed economic and social objectives – trust regulation, control of public utilities, tax reforms, prohibition of
child labour, public health programmes, educational reforms, conservation of natural resources. Others emphasized
the need of democratizing political machinery, proposing the
initiative and referendum, direct primary elections, secret
ballots, home rule for cities, corrupt practices acts, and
better election laws. But all held the same objective, the
advancement of the welfare of the majority of the people by
the extension of the power and purpose of the state. Both
held the same basic philosophy, in no way different from

that of other reform movements that preceded them, that the cure for the ills of democracy was more democracy.

Lord Bryce observed in 1888 that city government was 'the one conspicuous failure of the United States'. The facts bore him out. The swift growth of the city after 1870 made it especially vulnerable to machine rule, and the great bosses – Magee in Pittsburgh, Croker in New York, Lomasny in Boston, Butler in St Louis, and others – took full advantage of antiquated, unwieldy city governments to consolidate their power. Beginning in the nineties, reform groups sprang up in nearly all of the large cities. By 1905 the movement reached the proportions of a crusade, and by 1910 some of the bosses were gone and more were in temporary retreat.

City reformers, however, soon found that the city machine was in most cases merely an extension of a larger state organization. Under the American constitutional system, most important matters of a social and political character were under the jurisdiction of state legislatures, such as the terms and conditions of labour, education, suffrage, election machinery, municipal government, and corporation char-ters. The states, then, became the next battlegrounds. In the East the reform movement was largely urban-directed. In the West the progressive leaders built on the foundations left by the agrarian revolt of the eighties and nineties. Young Theodore Roosevelt, before he went to Washington, cut his teeth on the reform movement in New York City. Woodrow Wilson made his early political reputation as reform governor of New Jersey. Albert Cummins and Jona-than Dolliver of Iowa, George Norris of Nebraska, John A. Johnson of Minnesota, Edward Costigan of Colorado, William Allen White of Kansas, Hiram Johnson of Cali-fornia, and Jonathan Bourne of Oregon, all led progressive movements in the states before they became national poli-tical figures. The greatest of them all was undoubtedly Governor Robert M. La Follette of Wisconsin, a Republican who made his home state into a veritable laboratory of progressive reform, intended 'to reconstruct our institutions to meet the requirements of a new age'. His 'Wisconsin Idea' was a practical experiment in progressivism that served as a model for others on both state and national levels, and in 1933 Franklin Roosevelt's 'New Deal' found much worth copying in La Follette's thirty-year-old programme.

While progressives asked for an extension of the power of the state into new areas of responsibility, they demanded no essential changes in the traditional political system. Socialists carried collectivism much further. American Socialism in its various manifestations had a long history, dating from the utopian societies of the eighteenth and nineteenth centuries, from Social Gospellers and Bellamyites, from Christian Socialists and Georgists. Marxian socialism came with the Germans, who in 1869 formed an American section of the First International. In 1874 the International founded the Social Democratic Workingmen's Party, which a year later became the Socialist Labor Party. Socialist Labor and Populist leaders made unsuccessful overtures to each other in the nineties, but were never able to find an acceptable arrangement for co-operation. The rigidity and revolutionism of Marxism repelled many American socialists, until in 1898 they accomplished a successful revolt against Daniel De Leon, the Marxist leader, to create the Social Democratic (Socialist) Party under the direction of Eugene Debs of Indiana, Victor Berger of Wisconsin, and later Norman Thomas of New York.

Socialists and progressives were often willing to combine in support of certain measures, but their alliance was an unsteady one. Socialism, Marxian and non-Marxian, represented an offensive movement for the eventual overthrow of capitalism. Progressivism, like its predecessor Populism, represented a defensive movement offering, for specific capitalistic ills, specific remedies which occasionally might involve collectivistic control or ownership of certain facilities of production and distribution, but never its complete domination over national social and economic life.

The progressive movement was, in effect, simply an attempt to adjust an older democratic tradition, with its belief in individual freedom and equal opportunity, to the needs of an urban, industrial economy, 'a movement' (as La Follette called it) 'of a new generation towards more democracy in human relationships'. The progressive philosophy was not radical, but liberal, not revolutionary, but evolutionary. Its leaders assumed that their goals could be reached by internal adjustment, through political means, within the existing framework, and they hoped to regulate political and economic life in such a manner as to retain eighteenth- and nineteenth-century values in a twentieth-century society. Progressivism's most conspicuous result was to prepare the way for an extension under Wilson and Franklin D. Roosevelt of the responsibilities of government, local, state, and federal, into new areas of social and economic endeavour.

The results of the election of 1896 were generally viewed as a triumph of intelligent conservatism over ignorant demagoguery. 'God's in His Heaven,' said Mark Hanna when the voters' decision was known. McKinley lived up to his billing as the 'Advance Agent of Prosperity', for almost as soon as he was inaugurated the nation's business boomed – dollar wheat, rising wages, higher corporate profits. Congress passed a Gold Standard Act, putting a final quietus on Free Silver, and approved a high protective tariff. The most striking development of McKinley's first administration, however, was a tremendous increase in the consolidation of business and finance.

'A carnival of trusts is now in progress,' wrote Henry D. Lloyd, and economist John Moody in 1904 cited 318 trusts, most of them formed after 1898, as evidence that control of business and capital was rapidly concentrating in fewer and fewer hands. The Republican administration encouraged the trend, since the party had long been committed to a policy of non-interference with business. Prosecutions of combinations ran into judicial road-blocks while the Sherman Act languished.

To meet the growth of financial and industrial consolidation, labour began to concentrate its strength. The AFL, which had 278,000 members in 1898, doubled its size in 1900 and passed the million mark in 1904, but the old problem of political action still plagued union leaders. A strong minority, thinking in terms of a third party, hoped to convert either the Socialist Labor or the Socialist party into a labour instrument, in contrast to Gompers' policy of non-partisan politics. Furthermore, Gompers' concept of a loose, federated union of craft workers failed to satisfy those who still adhered to the old Knights of Labor idea of 'one big union for all'. In 1905 Debs, De Leon, 'Big Bill' Haywood, and other labour leaders organized the Industrial Workers of the World, 'one great industrial union, embracing all industries . . . founded on the class struggle'. Though never large, the IWW was vocal, aggressive, and ably led. Its violent tactics and revolutionary methods alienated public support and gave its opponents a chance to crush it during the First World War, but during its brief existence the IWW convinced the older unions of the values of militancy.

The war with Spain overshadowed all other issues during McKinley's administration. Insurrections against corrupt and inefficient Spanish rule in Cuba had been almost annual occurrences for years. Washington's policy was carefully neutral, but by the 1890's American stakes in Cuban sugar, tobacco, and iron were large enough to cause concern to investors. The revolutionists of 1895, more successful than usual, captured the Cuban capital and a fairly large amount of surrounding territory. The Spanish occupation forces, commanded by General Weyler, suffered from guerrilla depredations and took stern measures to control suspected rebels. Atrocity stories, given wide circulation by the Pulitzer and Hearst presses, excited American sympathies, and President McKinley himself protested to Madrid over Weyler's 'uncivilized and inhuman methods'.

The Madrid government, fearful of American intervention, proceeded with great care in Cuba, but two incidents in rapid succession brought Spanish-American relations to a breaking point. The Spanish minister in Washington, writing to a friend in Cuba, made uncomplimentary remarks about McKinley; the letter leaked, the minister was recalled, but the damage was done. Then on 15 February 1898 the United States battleship *Maine*, moored in Havana harbour to protect American interests, blew up with the loss of 200 lives. Blame for the explosion was never fixed, although the American press and public immediately assumed that the Spanish were responsible. 'Remember the *Maine*!' became the battle-cry of the moment. McKinley, who did not want war, vacillated while the press screamed for revenge. 'Stop the nonsense!' headlined the New York *World*. 'Stop the trifling!' Madrid, with abject apologies, indicated it would go to almost any length to avoid war, but on 19 April Congress voted to recognize Cuban independence and authorized the use of armed force to support it. After that war was inevitable.

The Spanish War, which lasted only 115 days, was a highly popular war, long enough to prove the superiority of American arms, brief enough so that the tragedy could be ignored. The public, finding it a gloriously emotional experience, made war heroes by the dozen. Bryan served as a Colonel of a Nebraska regiment, though without the publicity that followed young Theodore Roosevelt, who organized a 'Rough Riders' regiment of cowboys and society horsemen. Northern and Southern recruits trained together, erasing some of the old bitternesses, and Joe Wheeler of Confederate cavalry fame donned Federal blue to serve in Cuba.

The United States Navy was at peak strength. The Army, sadly undermanned and badly equipped, was hardly more than a token force. Campaign strategy called first for the destruction of the Spanish Navy. Admiral Dewey found the Spanish Pacific Fleet in Manila Bay in the Philippines, and on 30 April 1898 smashed it in a swift engagement that cost the American fleet only seven wounded. An expeditionary force landed soon afterwards and in co-operation with Philippine insurgents took possession of the capital, while Spanish Admiral Cervera, commanding the Atlantic Fleet, eluded the American Atlantic Squadron and slipped into Santiago, Cuba, where Admiral Sampson blockaded him.

When Cervera, somewhat against his better judgement, attempted to escape on 3 July 1898, Sampson's force sank or beached every Spanish vessel.

The Army stood at 18,000 when war was declared. Congress voted to expand it to 60,000 and to call up 125,000 volunteers. Amid great confusion some 17,000 troops under General Shafter landed in Cuba in late June to engage in sharp fighting at San Juan Hill, Kettle Hill, and El Caney. After the destruction of Cervera's fleet the Spanish defenders of Santiago surrendered and General Miles, who replaced Shafter, moved on to take Puerto Rico without incident. With its fleet gone and its armies cut off, the Spanish government asked for an armistice. At the peace negotiations in Paris the American representatives drove a hard bargain, demanding that Spain withdraw from the western hemisphere, that Cuba be recognized as an independent nation, and that the Philippines and Puerto Rico become American territories. Since the United States controlled only a very small portion of the Philippine archipelago, Spain balked at ceding her entire claim but gave in; some years later the United States belatedly gave her twenty million dollars in payment. The treaty was signed on 10 December 1898, and though it met strong opposition in Congress from anti-imperialist elements who found colonial possessions undesirable, it was ratified. The United States, having defeated a European nation in war, acquired an overseas empire in the Pacific, established control of most of the Caribbean, and became an imperial power.

The war with Spain could have been avoided. American diplomats handled their affairs with great skill, and Spain for its part went to unusual lengths to avoid hostilities. But the nation looked at its progress since Appomattox, felt a deep pride in its accomplishments, and hoped to prove itself a great international power, able to smash an arrogant, decadent European monarchy. The decisive factor in precipitating the Spanish War was neither political manœuvring nor diplomatic failure, but popular mood. 'It wasn't much of a war,' said Roosevelt, 'but it was the best we had.'

At the same time it marked a definite turning point in United States foreign policy. For the first time America deliberately extended its sovereignty beyond the North American continent. For the first time America accepted control of territories to which it had no intention of granting eventual statehood. And for the first time the United States, in establishing a colonial system, assumed full responsibility for the future welfare of an alien people.

The debates in Congress over the Spanish peace brought the argument over imperialism out into the open. Nineteenth-century Americans, enthusiastic over expansion, had long assumed it to be their 'manifest destiny' to occupy the entire continent, while agrarian slave-holders had once cast covetous glances at Central and South America. But after the Civil War a new kind of 'manifest destiny' took shape – economically, not agriculturally motivated – concerned with investments, raw materials, and markets. In 1898 the United States had reached a stage of economic development in which a search for foreign markets was inevitable. It was producing a surplus of nearly everything, had heavy financial stakes abroad, and needed a favourable balance of trade. In its attempt to make one, it found itself in direct competition with Europe. Nor was the United States alone in its economic imperialism, for China lay prostrate under European domination, and Africa was in the process of being split up among the European powers.

Stronger arguments than economic necessity supported American imperialism, the same arguments once employed to justify the Louisiana Purchase, the Monroe Doctrine, and the Mexican War. Americans believed, as they had since the days of Jefferson and Paine, that it was their mission to spread democracy, to bring American civilization to benighted people and backward areas. 'Americanizing the world', said Theodore Roosevelt, was the nation's destiny. The acquisition of colonies therefore meant that 'little brown brothers' in the Philippines and repressed Cuban colonials were to be Christianized and civilized as part of the white man's burden. Current European racist theories of

Gobineau, Cuno, and Houston Chamberlain found eager support in the United States, which was, wrote Josiah Strong, the future home of the Anglo-Saxon race, 'the principal seat of its power and the centre of its influence'. Senator Albert Beveridge of Indiana tied economic and racist imperialism neatly into one package by remarking, 'We are Anglo-Saxons, and must obey our blood and occupy new markets, and if necessary, new lands.' Social Darwinism also lent its weight to the imperialists; superior, strong peoples must absorb the weak and inferior. 'Small states', said Senator Henry Cabot Lodge, 'are of the past and have no future.' And then there was the simple argument from strategic necessity. Captain (later Admiral) A. T. Mahan pointed out that since the United States needed naval bases for its own protection, 'Whether they will or no, Americans must now begin to look outward.'

Opposed to imperialism was a long isolationist tradition and a deep American belief in the self-determination of peoples. The mission of America, some believed, was to construct in the New World a peaceful, open society, free from entangling alliances with the contentious nations of the Old. Domestic issues, not foreign, were the pressing problems, and the progressives in particular urged abstention from foreign entanglements lest the whole reform movement lose its impetus at home. Increased territory abroad merely meant increased expense without profit. It meant, said Bryan, 'heavier taxes, Asiatic emigration, and an opportunity to furnish more sons for the army'. Furthermore, acquiring a colonial empire by undemocratic means endangered democracy itself. 'This nation', wrote Bryan, 'cannot endure half republic and half colony, half free and half vassal.'

The expansionists won. Congress announced that it had no desire to annexe Cuba (annexation also meant assumption of the Cuban debt) but American troops stayed there until 1902, leaving behind them the brilliant work of Walter Reed of the Medical Corps, who freed the tropics from the scourge of yellow fever. The Cubans framed a constitution in 1901, but before they could attain self-rule Congress established Cuban bases for the United States fleet and retained the right (exercised in 1906 and 1917) to intervene in Cuban affairs when American interests seemed to be in danger. American investments in tobacco, sugar, utilities, and mines secured American control over the island economy and Cuba became largely a United States dependency. Puerto Rico, which was annexed, has had a history much like Cuba's. Its two-crop system of sugar and tobacco attached it immediately to the United States economy and it is still almost wholly dependent on American markets. The island attained a measure of home rule in 1900, and in 1917 Puerto Ricans were granted United States citizenship.

By annexing the Philippines the United States inherited the thorniest problem of all. Disappointed at not gaining independence, the Filipino insurrectionists who had plagued the Spanish for generations turned on the Americans, involving a 60,000-man expeditionary force in a brisk three-year war. In 1902 the islands were granted the status of an unorganized territory, and in 1907 they received partial self-government. The Philippines, it was hoped, might become the chief channel of United States Far Eastern trade; the hope never materialized, but Washington nevertheless assumed at heavy expense the task of sanitation, education, and economic development. In 1916 the United States announced that it would withdraw completely from the Philippines as soon as they established a stable, democratic government. In 1934 Congress granted Filipino independence, effective in 1945. The conduct of the Filipino people in World War II and the emergence of high-calibre native leadership soon afterwards proved the wisdom of the decision.

The colonial commitments of the Treaty of Paris accurately forecast the drift of American foreign policy. Since it dominated Caribbean and Latin American affairs, the United States turned towards the idea of a 'Pax Americana', based on a reaffirmation of the Monroe Doctrine. Santo Domingo, a country of perpetual revolution and heavy

American investment, became a protectorate in 1905; in 1916 United States Marines entered to put down insurrection and ran the country under military rule for eight more years. Haiti consistently refused the offer of a protectorate, but in 1915, again with the aid of the Marines, the Haitian government signed a trade treaty giving the United States control of the island's economy – the last American troops did not depart until 1934. The Virgin Islands, purchased from Denmark in 1917, served chiefly as naval bases. Governed by the Navy until 1931, they were finally transferred to the Department of the Interior. In Nicaragua the Marines put down a revolution in 1912 and remained in virtual control of Nicaraguan policies until 1933.

Colombia became an object of interest to the United States because it owned the Isthmus of Panama, the best route for an inter-oceanic canal. A French company had already tried to construct such a canal, and Congress in 1903 voted to buy its title to the canal route. The Colombian government refused to sell. In return for promises of co-operation the State Department assisted a group of Panamanian revolutionists in setting up an independent state under American protection. The new government immediately granted a lease for the canal route for an initial payment of ten million dollars – a Rooseveltian operation of great efficiency if of questionable ethics, as evidenced by an apologetic payment of twenty-five million dollars to Colombia in 1912. A Canal Zone government was established in 1904, and the Canal itself, a monumental engineering project, was completed by the United States Army.

Strong and wealthy Mexico was a different matter. Diaz, who became dictator in 1877, encouraged American investments and punctiliously co-operated with the United States government. By 1910 American interests controlled huge slices of Mexico's resources, including 80 per cent of its railroads and 70 per cent of its oil, while Diaz' regime had begun to totter. Wilson gave immediate recognition to the government of Madero, who drove out Diaz in 1911, but two years later Madero fell to Huerta, whom the United States refused to support. Wilson, who respected Madero, was determined to overthrow his tyrannical successor. American troops landed at Vera Cruz and Huerta fled, leaving the government to Carranza, whose regime Wilson was willing to recognize. The bandit chieftain Francisco Villa, however, kept up a constant war against both Mexican and American troops, finally invading New Mexico and killing several American citizens. Pershing's Army Regulars pursued Villa fruitlessly until the outbreak of hostilities in Europe, and American entry into World War I turned attention elsewhere.

There were other indications that the traditional American aversion to foreign entanglements was rapidly fading. Russian, French, and German penetration of China after its defeat by Japan in 1895 caused considerable alarm in London and Washington. In 1899 Secretary of State John Hay proposed an 'open door' policy, asking that those nations with Chinese interests allow other nations access to the China trade, and succeeded in obtaining the approval of the major European governments. Again in 1900 the United States contributed to the international force that put down the anti-foreign Boxer rebellion.

From the Spanish War to the mid-thirties the United States followed an imperialistic policy of intervention and annexation, with more and more emphasis on trade expansion and financial penetration into South and Latin American areas. Theodore Roosevelt in particular reaffirmed and extended the Monroe Doctrine, writing that the United States must shape its foreign policy 'with the view to the ultimate removal of all European powers from the colonies they hold in the Western hemisphere'. Taft followed the Rooseveltian line, while Woodrow Wilson, though less aggressive, followed it in part.

Increasing resentment against American domination of Caribbean and Latin American countries after World War I forced the United States to adopt a more temperate course. In 1928 the State Department formally repudiated Theodore Roosevelt's extremist interpretation of the Monroe Doctrine, and in 1936 it relinquished its long-held right to intervene in Latin America. Since 1930 the trend of United States foreign policy has been away from overt or undue influence on hemispheric affairs, with reliance instead on 'dollar diplomacy' to maintain American leadership.

Early twentieth-century imperialism has had its good and bad effects. It brought colonies, some of which proved to be unprofitable headaches. It created tremendous administrative problems, obvious injustices, pervasive national guilt-feelings, and increasing involvement in European politics. Most of all the period of imperialistic expansion, for better or worse, broke down the old isolationist tradition. Theodore Roosevelt, Taft, and Wilson all made strong pleas for the establishment of an international court of justice, and by 1914 the United States had negotiated arbitration treaties with most European nations except Germany and Austria. When the United States acquired the beginnings of an empire, it acquired with it certain commitments and responsibilities in global affairs, as it had reason to realize in 1917 and 1941.

Victory and prosperity made McKinley's re-election in 1900 almost a certainty. For vice-president the Republicans chose Theodore Roosevelt, Governor of New York, whose record as a reformer and military hero made him a nationally known figure. The Democrats countered with Bryan again, but good times and Mark Hanna's efficient organization defeated him easily. McKinley's assassination, barely six months after his inauguration, threw the Republican party into confusion.

Theodore Roosevelt, McKinley's successor, was only forty-three years old when an assassin's bullet elevated him to the Presidency. Young, energetic, and independent, already committed to progressive politics, he seemed to be the leader the reformers prayed for. He was an excellent administrator, a genius at political organization and public relations, and a man of devastating personal charm. His rise had been spectacular – assistant secretary of the Navy, Spanish War colonel, Governor of New York, Vice-Presi-

dent – all within the space of five years. His liberal tendencies bothered Hanna, who opposed his nomination at the
convention, and his sudden translation to the White House
worried Republican leaders. Yet on his record Roosevelt
was less a radical than an enlightened conservative; his
political programme was remedial rather than revolutionary. He was, to his credit, the first President since the
Civil War to comprehend the changes taking place in
American life, and he approached contemporary problems
with energy and intelligence. Considering himself an 'accidental President', he soon reassured the party leaders
that he intended to carry out McKinley's policies to the
letter.

Roosevelt's first term produced nothing sensational. He
raised progressives' hopes by frequent sallies against 'male-
factors of great wealth' and by his promise of a 'square
deal' for capital and labour, but he was willing to work
with the Republican bosses. His foreign policy was decidedly
imperialistic and aggressive. 'Speak softly and carry a big
stick,' he said; enforce and extend the Monroe Doctrine;
expand America's hemispheric influence and keep Europe
out.

On domestic issues Roosevelt proceeded carefully. Promising swift action against the trusts, he ordered his Attorney General to institute suit against the Northern
Securities Company, a Hill-Morgan combination, and
cracked it in 1904. At the same time he argued against
indiscriminate attacks on monopoly; there were, he said,
'good' and 'bad' trusts, and only the 'bad' deserved prosecution. His forays against big business slowed down considerably after 1902, leading La Follette to comment causti-
cally that after the smoke of Roosevelt's battles died away,
it was astonishing to find how little ground had been won.
He did, however, intervene in the violent coal strike of
1902, brought by the United Mine Workers against the
Pennsylvania operators. His programme for the conservation of national resources was a solid achievement. Progressives of both parties, though disappointed, nevertheless

supported him in 1904 in the hope that in another four years he could show real results.

Some conservative Republican leaders would have preferred to drop Roosevelt in 1904, but his popularity was too great. Hanna's death left him in virtual control of the party organization, which nominated him by acclamation at the convention. The Democrats rejected Bryan in favour of Judge Alton Parker of New York, a conservative, colourless candidate, hoping thereby to attract anti-Roosevelt Republicans. The result was an overwhelming victory for Roosevelt.

Reactions to Roosevelt's second term were mixed. He attacked trusts, bosses, and reactionaries; he advocated income and inheritance taxes, pushed conservatism programmes, speeded up the construction of the Panama Canal, and pursued an aggressive foreign policy. He broke the tobacco, beef, and fertilizer trusts, but somehow there were more trusts when he left office in 1908 than there were in 1904. At the end of his term progressive leaders criticized his record, admitting at the same time that he had faced powerful conservative opposition in Congress. Still, after seven years in the Presidency, Theodore Roosevelt left no ineradicable mark on the pattern of American political, social, or economic life. He had undoubtedly tried hard to be a liberal, but as Lincoln Steffens thought, he was 'a politician much more than he was a reformer'.

Roosevelt announced that he would not be a candidate in 1908, and though he could easily have had the nomination, he kept his word. He chose his successor William Howard Taft, a large, affable, indeterminate man with an excellent record as judge, governor of the Philippines, and Secretary of War in Roosevelt's cabinet. The Democrats returned to Bryan for the third time, but the Republicans were too strong. Taft, campaigning on the promise that he would devote himself to 'the constructive work of suggesting to Congress the means by which the Roosevelt policies shall be clinched', won an easy victory. After receiving congratulations, Roosevelt went to Africa to hunt big game.

Taft inherited a bundle of problems. The 1908 Republican platform contained a number of vague promises which it was Taft's business to carry out; a strong body of conservative Republicans in Congress were determined to prevent him from doing so. There was also in Congress a block of Republican senators and representatives from the Midwestern states (old Granger-Populist territory) equally determined to force Taft and the party itself to adopt a progressive programme. These Republican 'insurgents', led by La Follette of Wisconsin in the Senate and by Norris of Nebraska in the House, harried Taft at every turn until he found himself listening more and more to the conservative wing of his party. By 1910 the Republican organization was seriously split. In early 1911 La Follette and others founded the National Progressive Republican League, hoping to wrest control of the party from Taft, and the Republican newspapers called for Roosevelt's return. 'Teddy, Teddy, come blow your horn', a popular parody ran,

> The cow's in the meadow, the sheep's in the corn;
> The boy you left to tend the sheep
> Is under the haystack, fast asleep.

Roosevelt came back to the sound of trumpets. He was not the same Roosevelt who had left fifteen months earlier, for his African trip gave him time to think and to arrange his scattered political impulses into a more coherent philosophy. Particularly strong on him was the influence of Herbert Croly, whose book, *The Promise of American Life*, he read carefully in Africa. When he landed, Roosevelt had developed a rationale of progressivism called 'The New Nationalism', which in effect involved a stronger national government for the attainment of constructive social and economic ends. The aim of the New Nationalism was to combine 'the Hamiltonian principle of national political responsibility and efficiency with a frank democratic purpose'.

Roosevelt accepted a post as editor of *Outlook* magazine and began to publicize his programme, while jockeying for position in the presidential race of 1912 continued within the Republican party. Insurgent elements rallied behind La Follette. Conservatives, who doubted Roosevelt's reliability, backed Taft, while Roosevelt refused to commit himself but left the way open for a draft. A good many progressive Republicans, however, feeling that La Follette was too far to the left to win if nominated, quietly withdrew support from him while covertly building a Roosevelt boom. Finally, in early 1912, they jettisoned La Follette, asked Roosevelt to run, and received his acceptance.

The 1912 pre-convention campaign was a violent three-way fight. La Follette attacked both Roosevelt and Taft as 'fake progressives'; Taft denounced Roosevelt and his aides as 'neurotics' out for revenge; Roosevelt called Taft a 'traitor to the progressive cause'. At the convention the Republican National Committee, making short shrift of the Roosevelt organization, quickly nominated Taft. Roosevelt had come too far to turn back, so a call went out for a meeting in Chicago to choose a 'progressive' Republican candidate. In an atmosphere of hysterical enthusiasm reminiscent of 1896, the Chicago rump convention nominated Roosevelt. The 'Bull Moose' party (Roosevelt told a reporter, 'I feel like a bull moose') was under way.

Democrats watched the Republican civil war with interest. Bryan, three times a loser, decided not to run, and the party itself was divided between a more-or-less liberal western wing and an eastern conservative wing. The conservatives favoured Champ Clark of Missouri, while the liberals favoured Woodrow Wilson, Governor of New Jersey. Bryan threw his weight behind Wilson, a comparative newcomer to politics, and in so doing guaranteed his nomination.

An unusual campaign followed. Wilson stayed out of the bickering between Taft and Roosevelt while La Follette and dozens of Republican progressives refused to endorse either one. As a result Wilson not only kept the liberal Democrats but attracted large numbers of Republicans, winning with 345 electoral votes to Roosevelt's eighty-eight and Taft's eight. So Woodrow Wilson, some-time Johns Hopkins student, political scientist of note, president of Princeton, and reform Governor of New Jersey, became the twenty-eighth President, carrying with him to the White House the hopes of liberals and progressives everywhere.

Wilson, a Virginia-born Scotch Presbyterian scholar, was exactly what he looked like, a cold, austere professor of history. Until he was fifty-four his only experience in practical politics was one term as a governor, and he possessed neither commitment to nor strong ties with the party that elected him. What he knew of government he knew from books – from Bagehot, Gladstone, Burke, and Bryce – and not from the hurly-burly of ward politics. Until 1910 his political thinking seemed strongly conservative, though his writings showed a slow trend toward the progressive politics of La Follette and the insurgents. Like Jackson, he believed deeply in the rule of the people and in the duty of the chief executive to provide strong, positive party leadership. Educated in the tradition of British nineteenth-century liberalism, he conceived of himself as a sort of prime minister, directing his party and nation as he believed best.

Wilson's political philosophy was built about what he called 'The New Freedom'. 'There is one basic fact', he said, 'which underlies all the questions that are discussed in the political platforms of the present moment. That singular fact is that nothing is done in this country as it was done twenty years ago.' A government constructed on the theory that men live best when let alone, he believed, did not suit the economic and social organization of the twentieth century. To develop a 'new freedom', the nation must evolve a new concept of democratic individualism, with the government serving as co-ordinator and protector of the individual's rights. The things that Wilson feared most were the trust and its companions, special privilege and concentration of power. Government must remove that 'hindrance of hindrances', the stifling of competition, so that the old days of individual enterprise might come again. The New Freedom was therefore a rebirth of the old freedom, a restoration of individual competition – freedom for small business against the trust, for farmer against banker and manufacturer, for labourer against employer. The New Freedom meant 'a revival of the power of the people, the beginning of an age of thoughtful reconstruction'.

Wilson's choice of a cabinet encouraged his supporters. None of his appointees came from the inner circle of Democratic bosses, and all were considered able men. His most important appointment was that of Bryan as Secretary of State; William McAdoo ờf California became Secretary of the Treasury; Secretary of Commerce Redfield was a tariff reformer; Attorney General McReynolds was a known 'trust-buster' from Taft's administration. Wilson's inaugural address, one of the finest of presidential documents, launched his first term on a high level. 'Our duty,' he said,

'is to cleanse, to reconsider, to restore, to correct the evil without impairing the good, to purify and humanize every process of our common life without weakening or sentimentalizing it. There has been something crude and heartless and unfeeling in our haste to succeed and be great. . . . We have come now to sober second thought. The scales of heedlessness have fallen from our eyes. We have made up our minds to square every process of our national life with the standards we so proudly set up at the beginning and have always carried in our hearts.'

Thus Woodrow Wilson hoped to bring traditional democracy into tune with an urban-industrial America.

His victory, said Wilson, was not simply a change of drivers in the same wagon going down the old road. The Democratic triumph, he believed, represented an indictment of the whole course of recent politics and a mandate for a thorough reorganization and redirection of American political life. There was little in his programme that had not already been suggested by numerous progressive, liberal, and reform leaders who had preceded him. He pledged his administration to a revision of the tariff, a revision of banking and currency laws, a programme of agricultural aid, effective anti-trust laws, and constructive social legislation. Redemption of those promises meant extending Federal authority over ever-widening social and economic areas, creating the powerful government urged by the Populists and Theodore Roosevelt.

With the aid of a Democratic majority in Congress Wilson redeemed nearly all his pledges within two years. His first message to Congress, asking for a revision of the tariff, was answered by the Underwood Tariff. The ink was hardly dry on the Underwood bill when Wilson was back in Congress with the question of banking and money, the traditional Jacksonian-Granger-Populist issue. Congress responded with the Federal Reserve Act of 1913, creating a system of regional reserve banks, recognizing paper as the country's money, and providing for a contracting-expanding currency.

'I am for big business,' Wilson said, 'and I am against trusts.' The argument was not between big and small business, in his opinion, but between business and unfair monopoly. Legislate against unfair business methods, bar illicit practices, keep competition open and free – this was Wilson's principle, not Roosevelt's of allowing the trust to exist and then controlling it, nor Bryan's of splitting big businesses into little ones. In 1914 Congress approved the Federal Trade Commission Act endowing the Commission with investigative and regulative powers, outlawed 'unfair methods of competition', and supplemented the Sherman Act by establishing evidence on which anti-trust prosecutions might be based; the Clayton Anti-Trust Act, enacted the same year, reinforced and clarified the Sherman Act. Other bills, rolling through Congress, extended his programme. The seventeenth Amendment to the Constitution, ratified in 1913, established direct election of Senators, an old progressive issue. The La Follette and Adamson Acts improved working conditions and shortened hours for seamen and train-men. A child-labour bill became law in 1913.

America's involvement in the First World War ended Wilson's schedule for domestic reform, yet the record shows that during his administrations more legislation of a progressive nature was passed, and the foundations for more laid, than under any previous administration since Jackson's. In the post-war years the dominant trend of government moved far away from the principles of the 'New Freedom', until the 'New Deal' resurrected portions of its rusty programme.

The period 1900–14 saw the emergence of modern American society. One of the major factors in its development was the current revolution in transportation and communication. The period of uninhibited railroad building was past, but the application of the gasoline engine to transportation opened up an entirely new area of expansion. Duryea, Haynes, Olds, Ford, and others experimented with 'horseless carriages' at the turn of the century, and in 1909 Ford began production of his famous and durable Model T. General Motors, formed in 1908 by W. C. Durant, soon rivalled Ford. By 1914 the automobile was well within the price range of the middle income class, and a million autos were on the roads. The Wright brothers' tentative flights at Kitty Hawk dunes in 1903 were to have their effects twenty years later.

By 1900 telegraph systems spanned every section of the country. The Bell Telephone Company controlled telephonic communication almost as completely as Western Union controlled the telegraph. Marconi's wireless, perfected in 1901, became standard equipment on ships, but proved to be less useful on land. The demand for electricity created by Edison's incandescent electric lamp and by the introduction of trolley cars in the cities led to giant hydroelectric developments, while the manufacture and sale of electric equipment encouraged the rise of giant electrical supply firms such as General Electric and Westinghouse.

These new means of communication directly affected manufacturing and marketing. They broke down isolation and sectionalism, binding the nation more closely together than ever before, accelerating the trend toward urbanism, stimulating the growth of suburban settlements. The great new industrial firms created by the automobile, the electric light, the telephone (and later the aeroplane) opened up completely fresh fields of business enterprise and made new uses for a variety of raw materials – the automobile alone helped to establish a whole new empire based on gasoline and oil. As transportation and communication facilities improved, so the nation's living habits changed. The automobile created new problems of crime, education, morals, traffic, markets; the United States became a nation on wheels.

Perhaps the most obvious shift in the social pattern after 1900 was reflected in the changed status of women. The Industrial Revolution put women into factories and business; the growth of the city gave them vocational opportunities as clerks, stenographers, social workers, and teachers, all of which became almost exclusively female professions. Economic independence gave women a greater degree of domestic independence (especially after the introduction of machinery into the home) and consequent freedom from much of the drudgery of household tasks. With time for economic, social, and political activity, women used it. Women's clubs sprang up in profusion, until by 1914 the Federation of Women's Clubs counted more than a million members. By the opening of World War I women were a significant force in American social and economic affairs.

The chief woman-inspired reform of the period was the prohibition of alcoholic liquors. The nineteenth-century temperance movements faded before the Civil War, but after it the rate of liquor consumption (and of poverty and crime) increased alarmingly in the cities. In 1873 a group of Ohio women founded the Women's Christian Temperance Union to work with the churches in prohibiting the sale of liquor by law. Both Protestant and Catholic groups supported the WCTU, which obtained prohibition legislation in six states and hundreds of localities. Carrie Nation, a Kansas lady who hacked up saloons with a hatchet, was possibly the most spectacular crusader against alcohol, but the organizational skill of Frances Willard, dean of women at Northwestern University, had more effective results. The Anti-Saloon League, founded in 1893 as a logical outgrowth of the WCTU, merged the major prohibition societies into a powerful lobby that eventually succeeded in passing the eighteenth Amendment in 1920. The importance of these groups, however, lay not so much in their battle against alcohol, but more in the fact that they initiated a nation-wide network of women's organizations and developed a set of leaders with useful political experience.

Their real struggle, of course, came with the attempt to establish votes for women. The question of female suffrage harked back to the reform movements of the early nineteenth century, but by 1890 its objectives broadened to include equal pay for equal work, liberalized divorce laws, elimination of the 'double standard' of morality, and legal recognition of women's rights. The National Woman Suffrage Association followed the aggressive leadership of Susan B. Anthony; the American Woman Suffrage Association adopted the more conservative tactics of Lucy Stone. After 1890, when the rival organizations merged to present a solid front, male opposition rapidly crumbled. By 1914 eleven states had granted the vote to women, and the nineteenth or 'Susan Anthony' Amendment to the Constitution was ratified in 1920.

The trend toward liberalism traced by politics and reform marked other aspects of American life. By the turn of the century the battle between modernism and fundamentalism in religion was nearly over. Discouraged at the inroads of Social Gospellers and modernists, representatives of the fundamentalist sects met at Niagara in 1895 to adopt a body of conservative doctrine and to found new theological training schools such as the Moody Bible Institute of Chicago. Theirs was a rearguard action, however, for most Protestant churches readily accepted the socialized, modernist point of view. The Federal Council of the Churches of Christ in 1905 and the Methodist Council in 1908 both adopted creeds aimed at 'making the influence of Christ effective in *all* human relations'. Episcopal, Congregational, Baptist, and Unitarian bodies declared themselves favourably disposed to 'useful activity' on progressive, liberal lines. The greatest single change in the American religious pattern was the result of increased immigration from Southern Europe. Catholic Church membership in the United States grew from nine million in 1807 to eighteen million by 1920, chiefly concentrated in Eastern cities, where Catholics gained an economic and political position comparable to that of the Baptists and Methodists in the South. Catholicism's foreign origins and its monolithic church structure caused fear and hostility among Protestant sects, but under the leadership of Cardinal Gibbons the Catholic Church quickly became Americanized. Protestant-Catholic clashes, particularly over the relation between church and state, have since frequently developed, but rarely to serious proportions.

Social reformers, political progressives, and labour leaders in the late nineteenth and early twentieth centuries all demanded legislation embodying various reforms. Since the majority of jurists tended to favour a conservative interpretation of the law, reform legislation constantly ran into judicial road-blocks. Prevailing legal opinion considered the law an inflexible, axiomatic body of precedents, the Constitution a fixed and absolute legal standard; therefore the courts, state and federal, struck down dozens of bills, particularly on the ground that they interfered with the fourteenth Amendment. Supreme Court Justices Fields and Sutherland and others in lesser courts erased laws governing child labour, working hours, industrial safety and health regulations, workmen's compensation, minimum wages, pensions for the blind, and the like. Before reforms could succeed, the basis of legal decisions had to shift from the positivist concept that the law and the Constitution expressed eternal and unchanging truths, to a relativist concept that both must accommodate themselves to changing social needs and conditions.

In this shift both evolution and pragmatism played a major part. The leaders of the new relativist interpretation were Roscoe Pound and Oliver Wendell Holmes, Jr. Pound, who became dean of Harvard Law School in 1910, used the term 'social jurisprudence' to describe his concept of law as an ever-adapting, dynamic social institution. Dozens of young lawyers who received training under him became key figures in the New Deal reforms of the thirties. Holmes, 'the great dissenter', left an even deeper impress on American legal tradition. After a brilliant career on the Massachusetts Supreme Court he was raised to the Federal bench by Roosevelt in 1902. The law, to Holmes, settled no disputes; judges settled them by interpreting the law in terms of the majority experience, the necessities of the times, public policy and welfare, and prevalent moral and political facts. The real test of truth, he wrote, is 'the power to get itself accepted in the competition of the market'. Holmes was joined later by Louis Brandeis, a Wilson appointee to the Court, who believed even more strongly than Pound or Holmes in weighing public needs against private values in making legal decisions. More or less alone at first, Holmes, Brandeis, and the relativists gained ground. In the twenties, driven by social and economic pressures, the courts finally surrendered to the trend toward 'social jurisprudence'.

Another American institution, the press, underwent drastic modifications after the turn of the century. Though the old magazines still existed – *Harper's*, *The Century*, *The Atlantic*, *The North American Review* – the lion's share of the market went to cheaper, more sensational newcomers such as *McClure's*, *Munsey's*, *Collier's*, and *The Saturday Evening Post*, under shrewd editors like S. S. McClure, Frank Munsey, Edward Bok, and Cyrus Curtis. The development of the linotype machine, the typewriter, the high-speed press, and telegraph wire service changed the content of newspapers as well as of magazines. While the nineteenth-century newspaper had been chiefly an organ for the dissemination of news and editorial opinion, its twentieth-century descendant became less an editorial instrument than a profit-making business. Daily newspapers took on the appearance of magazines, with comic strips, sports pages, bed-time stories, advice to cooks and lovers, syndicated columns, and serialized novels.

Like other ventures of the period, the press suffered from consolidation. Chains absorbed smaller papers into empires, Hearst's, Pulitzer's, and others. 'Yellow journalism' increased circulation and profits with sensationalism, emotionalism, sex, 'sobsister' reporting, crime news. Though the accuracy and excellence of reporting might vary with the paper, the fact that news and features were usually gathered and distributed by wire-service syndicates tended to standardize content. The growth of chains and press associations closed the door on the era of personal journalism represented by Greeley, Bennett, Godkin, Bryant, and the great nineteenth-century editors.

Contemporary American painting reflected the prevailing war between traditionalists and moderns, between classical academicians and rebels. Building on the work of Winslow Homer and Thomas Eakins, a New York group founded the 'ashcan' school of native realism; the work of John Sloan, George Luks, Everett Shinn, George Bellows, and their followers caused hot arguments among critics. French impressionism influenced others. The famous 'Armory Show' of 1913 introduced Picasso, Van Gogh, Cézanne, and other 'moderns' to painters and public, leaving behind an army of imitators. In general the gulf between American and European art narrowed considerably after 1900. Architecture, sculpture, and design reacted swiftly to European trends, and Americans themselves began to develop a more mature, sophisticated, international frame of mind.

Music lagged somewhat behind art as a field of creative activity. Until the establishment of urban cultural centres, interest in musical performance and composition remained on a popular, folk level. The most vital musical force in the late nineteenth century was the Negro, whose cake-walks, fiddle songs, spirituals, and blues were the nearest to a native music that the nation possessed. Minstrel shows (based on Negro music though performed by black-faced white men) became popular in the seventies and eighties; with them the songs of Dan Emmett and Stephen Foster travelled the country. After the Civil War Confederate military band instruments fell into the hands of Negroes who began to improvise music of their own, based on religious and folk tunes of Irish, Spanish, British, and African origins. In New Orleans Negro bands played in dance halls and brothels, at funerals and weddings, evolving a singular type of two-beat and later four-beat music called 'ragtime' and 'jazz'. After 1900 jazz entered its so-called 'classical period', with the appearance of great Negro musicians like Buddy Bolden, King Oliver, Bunk Johnson, Jelly-Roll Morton, and Louis Armstrong. When the river-boats carried jazz up the Mississippi to Memphis, St Louis, Kansas City, and finally to Chicago, it shook off its local and racial origins.

Interest in serious music came with the growth of cities, increased immigration, and the perfection of Edison's phonograph. German, Scandinavian, and Bohemian groups usually organized their own orchestral and choral societies almost as soon as they arrived in America. The New York Philharmonic Society, founded in 1842, struggled hard until after the Civil War, when Theodore Thomas made it into a stable and much-improved organization. Thomas, a German immigrant, carried his musical enthusiasm to other cities, helped to found the Boston Symphony and the Chicago Symphony, serving intermittently as conductor of both. New York's Metropolitan Opera Society was established in 1883 with the assistance of several millionaires and by 1914 the 'Met', with Toscanini as conductor and Enrico Caruso as its main attraction, was almost a national institution. Both the symphony and the opera in the United States, however, depended on imported music and talent. Only a few native composers or performers, such as Edward McDowell and Emma Eames, gained any prominence.

The drama boomed after 1865, and until 1914 enjoyed probably the greatest period of prosperity and popularity in its history. It was an age of great producers – Frohman, Belasco, Hammerstein – and of polished actors – Edwin Booth, E. H. Sothern, Richard Mansfield, Maude Adams, Otis Skinner, and Maurice Barrymore. But the theatre suffered from mediocre playwriting and from the trend towards consolidation. The introduction of the 'star' system, the competition of the cinema, the concentration of theatres in a few major cities, and the tightening control of chain ownership killed off the travelling stock company and closed many smaller theatres. On a popular level melodrama remained a perennial favourite. Plays of common life with a villain, a hero, and a persecuted heroine (*Nellie the Beautiful Cloak Model*), thrillers (*Chinatown Charlie the Opium Fiend*), and old standbys (*Uncle Tom's Cabin*) drew large audiences year in and year out. Vaudeville, the American version of the British variety show, had its heyday after 1885, when Keith's in Boston and Tony Pastor's in New York started the first continuous performances. It developed great popular stars like Lillian Russell and Weber and Fields, as well as a host of actors and comedians who moved later into movies and radio. For the rougher trade it developed burlesque, with double-entendre jokes, undraped girls, and eventually the strip-tease. But vaudeville and burlesque, like the legitimate theatre, soon fell under centralized control and became big city entertainment.

Every form of entertainment after 1900 felt the impact of the motion picture, which eventually became the largest single influence on the American cultural pattern. In 1903 E. S. Porter, Edison's cameraman, by producing *The Great Train Robbery*, the first continuous-story feature, changed the motion picture from an amusing toy to large-scale entertainment. An attempted corner of the industry in 1914 was defeated by invoking the Sherman Act, and the movie business turned into a fiercely competitive struggle among several huge companies. After 1916, profiting from the wartime closing of European studios, American movie-makers seized control of the major share of the world market. Bold and imaginative directors such as David Wark Griffith and talented stars of the calibre of Chaplin sensed the possibilities of the new medium and raised the level of cinematic production. Movie stars set national fashions (good and bad) in speech, dress, action, and ideas, but in general the predominantly middle-class virtues portrayed by the movies for mass audiences tended to reinforce established cultural patterns. Since New York (later Hollywood) produced standardized products for all sections and classes, the movies exerted a strong nationalizing, standardizing influence. Since movie-making is a profit-making business, American producers have rarely troubled with experimentation in the European manner, nor have they considered the cinema primarily an art form.

Pre-Civil War foreign observers unanimously observed the American passion for sports, especially horse-racing, foot-racing, rowing, and prize-fighting. After the War base-ball began to eclipse all other pastimes in popularity. Hundreds of amateur teams were formed by veterans who learned the game in army camps, and the first professionals, the Cincinnati Red Stockings, scheduled games in 1869. In 1876 eight professional teams founded the National League, which dominated the sport until the appearance of the rival American League in the nineties. The two leagues declared peace in 1903, justifying the first 'world's series' championship play-offs. Football, adapted from rugby in the sixties, took its present form during the eighties. By 1900 it was especially popular in Eastern colleges and universities, but deaths and injuries among players mounted so high that many institutions banned it until rule changes were made in 1906 by the National Collegiate Athletic Association. Basket-ball, invented in 1891 by a Canadian, James Nai-smith, had a slow start, yet by 1930 it drew the largest attendance of any American amateur sport. Boxing was legally barred in many states and communities until it attained respectability (Theodore Roosevelt was an enthusiastic amateur) at the time of World War I. Horse-racing's connexions with gambling caused every state to pass anti-betting laws; patronage of the wealthy, legalized betting, and construction of public tracks revived interest in it after the First World War.

* * *

World War I was the most decisive event in the history of American foreign relations. Although the State Department suspected that Europe was a powder-keg, the sudden explosion of June 1914 caught both the public and the government off guard. The United States was a world power, irrevocably involved in global events, though neither its government nor people fully realized the fact and those who did were often unwilling to accept it. The outbreak of war in Europe made American isolationism the major issue of the generation.

The first American reaction to European declarations of war after August 1914, was an almost unanimous desire for neutrality. Wilson's proclamation of August stressed the need to be 'impartial in thought as well as in action'. This was Europe's war, not America's, and neither Wilson nor Bryan, his Secretary of State, wished to repeat the mistakes of 1812.

But, as in the Napoleonic era, the path of the neutral proved to be strewn with obstacles. At first the United States refused to allow American loans to the warring nations, lest financial commitments grow too large, while Wilson declared an 'open trade' policy to maintain American rights of trade with any participant. Both decisions benefited the Allies far more than Germany. England and France held large assets in the United States which they liquidated to purchase American goods; since Britain controlled the seas, few but Allied ships reached American ports. When Allied credit seemed exhausted, Wilson's government found itself in an impossible position. The United States economy, geared to wartime demands, would be seriously damaged if its export trade were cut off; on the other hand, both Wilson and Bryan recognized that foreign loans threatened American neutrality. Under pressure from industry, agriculture, and banking, Wilson gave in, until by 1917 loans to the Allies reached 2,000 million dollars while those to Germany totalled only twenty-seven millions. The American financial stake in an Allied victory was high.

Wilson's 'open trade' policy was not wholly satisfactory. Britain blockaded the Central Powers, published a list of trade restrictions, and black-listed American firms suspected of trading with Germany. In each case British proclamations followed recognized international law, but in their observance the British Navy sometimes stepped on American toes. State Department protests of minor violations of United States rights on the seas received cavalier treatment, yet American public opinion remained friendly. England's acts cost no lives; American shipping firms were compensated (sometimes over-generously) for their losses.

German violations provoked a different reaction. As Winston Churchill predicted, Germany's announcement in 1915 of a submarine blockade of England brought immediate protests from the United States. The Imperial Government of Germany, Wilson informed the Kaiser, would be held 'to a strict accountability for property endangered or lives lost'. The torpedoing of the British liner *Lusitania* on 7 May 1915, with a loss of 128 American lives, put United-States–German relations under severe strain. Wilson's note of 9 June, again demanding 'strict accountability', brought Bryan's resignation, since Bryan believed it meant war, and the sinking of the *Arabic* in August, with two American lives lost, brought the break closer. Though the German ambassador promised that his government would stop indiscriminate torpedoings, Germany in February 1916 resumed unrestricted submarine warfare. Another note from the United States elicited a vague reaffirmation of the 1915 pledge, but by this time American opinion was thoroughly aroused.

Nevertheless, a hard kernel of isolationist resistance remained in the United States. Arbitration as a means of settling international disputes was firmly ingrained in American foreign policy. The World Peace Foundation established a million dollar fund in 1910; that same year Andrew Carnegie built a 'peace palace' at The Hague and gave ten million dollars to the Carnegie Foundation for International Peace. Norman Angell's *The Great Illusion* and William James' *Moral Equivalent of War* (both published in 1910) impressed thoughtful Americans with war's futility. In Congress La Follette, Norris, Lindbergh, and other Midwesterners opposed any act that might lead to war, and in 1916 Wilson's supporters barely over-rode a bill to forbid American travel on armed ships.

Isolationist sentiment was strong, but interventionist feeling was stronger. Theodore Roosevelt, a bitter critic of Wilson's 'soft' policy, was perhaps the most bellicose of the interventionists. More thoughtful and temperate minds, however, after wrestling with the problem, came to the conclusion that 'self-complacent isolationism' was impossible in a twentieth-century world. The war, wrote Herbert Croly in *The New Republic*, was 'a challenge to the United States to justify its independence. The nation cannot be independent in the sense of being isolated' – an echo of Wilson's statement that 'We did not set this Government up in order that we might have a selfish and separate liberty.'

America's moral dilemma was best illustrated by Wilson's personal struggle. He realized that war meant the end of his programme of domestic reform, so bravely and successfully begun; as a student of history (and a member of the American Peace Society) he knew war to be a grim and inconclusive settlement of differences. He knew something of the imperialist beginnings of war and something of the ways of power politics; he disliked and distrusted armed force. Yet at the same time he rejected everything that Imperial Germany represented, and was so steeped in the Anglo-American tradition that it was manifestly impossible for him, or for others like him, to maintain absolute neutrality. Britain and France held the right cause, he believed, and in a struggle between right and wrong, he found it difficult to follow an isolationist line if it seemed to favour the wrong. The internationalist in Wilson triumphed over the isolationist, as it did in the mind of the American public at large. The war was to Wilson a holy crusade to 'make the world safe for democracy', with a vision beyond it of a peace 'planted upon the tested foundations of political liberty'.

The election of 1916 cut in half the heated debate over America's relation to the war. Though some prominent Democrats disagreed with Wilson's foreign policy, the party nominated him for a second term almost without dissent, choosing Tom Marshall of Indiana as his vice-president. The Republicans hoped to unify anti-Wilson feeling by choosing a 'safe' candidate rather than the unpredictable and strident Roosevelt. Their convention picked Charles Evans Hughes, a Supreme Court Justice more or less un-committed on the prevailing issues and a man whose dignity and probity were designed to appeal to liberal and conser-vative alike. The remnants of the 'Bull Moose' organization hoped to nominate Roosevelt and continue the revolt of 1912, but Roosevelt, who wanted to defeat Wilson even more than he wanted to be President, refused and advised his followers to vote for Hughes.

The Democrats based their campaign on the domestic achievements of the 'New Freedom' and the slogan, 'He kept us out of War', though Wilson, realizing the narrow margin by which America remained at peace, explained that involvement might come sooner than his supporters knew. Hughes conducted a conservative and dignified campaign. Roosevelt attacked Wilson violently up and down the land, warned that his re-election would be 'a damage to the moral fibre of the American people'. The Republican and 'Bull Moose' vote combined could have defeated Wilson, but a large segment of the Progressive vote swung to him. As it happened, his margin of victory was slim. Only late returns from California clinched his election, 277 electoral votes to 254.

Wilson firmly believed that the United States wanted peace, and as soon as the election was over he asked the warring powers to clarify their war aims so that a basis for ending the conflict might be found. The Allies, having suffered huge losses and a succession of defeats, resented his request but complied; Germany refused to co-operate. Nevertheless Wilson had hopes of a 'peace without victory', a hope shattered by Germany's announcement in January of 1917 of unrestricted submarine war. In the light of his previous commitments there was little Wilson could do but sever diplomatic relations, an act Congress approved at once. Speaking optimistically of 'an armed neutrality', the President and Congress created a Council of National Defence, increased the strength of the National Guard, and authorized the construction of four new battleships. In February and March German submarines sank eight American ships. On 2 April Wilson asked Congress for a declaration of war.

The President based his war message on four major points: unrestricted submarine sinkings, German sabotage in American industry, the failure of armed neutrality, and the Prussian threat to American and global security. 'It is a fearful thing,' he said, 'to lead this great and powerful people into war . . ., but the right is more precious than peace, and we shall fight for the things which we have always carried nearest our hearts.' The Senate responded with a declaration of war two days later, and on Good Friday 1917 the House concurred.

The United States entered World War I on the Allied side for a variety of reasons, but one is clear: America could not afford to do otherwise. It is true that American loans to the wartime trade with the Allies gave the nation a heavy financial interest in an Allied victory. Yet American bankers and manufacturers, however important they considered overseas loans, consistently favoured neutrality, where the profits lay, rather than war, which meant mounting taxes and government regulation of industry. It was also true that British propaganda was singularly good and German bad, British diplomacy excellent and German inept. Yet neither loans nor propaganda nor diplomacy put the United States into war. The plain fact is that the United States realized it could not afford to take the risk of allowing Germany to supplant Britain as the dominant force in Europe. England, for nearly a hundred years, had contributed to American security by maintaining control of the seas and a European balance of power. Britain and France were known quantities; Germany, a new strange power, was both unknown and unfriendly. Secretary of State Lansing observed in 1916, 'On no account must we range ourselves even indirectly on the side of Germany . . . German imperialistic ambitions threaten free institutions everywhere.' Wilson's determination that the world must be made safe for democracy stated the real reason for America's entry. So long as military autocracy existed in Europe American democracy was in danger.

The United States Army was not prepared for war. Many Americans at first believed that ships and loans constituted the most effective assistance the United States could give the Allies, but German victories and Allied losses in 1917 made it imperative that an expeditionary force be created at once. Though volunteering was good, Congress passed a Selective Service Act in May 1917 to make more efficient use of American manpower. Eventually twenty-four million men registered for the draft, of whom almost five million entered some branch of military service. Thirty-two training camps were established to receive the draftees, and as they had in 1861, raw recruits poured in from Kansas farms and Eastern cities, from Louisiana swamps and Tennessee mountains. Equipment was scarce and training elementary. Six months of drill and firing practice fitted a draftee for battle, while Officer Training Camps graduated combat leaders in ninety days. Meanwhile General Pershing, commander of the Expeditionary Force, landed in France with a small contingent of soldiers in June 1917. About 200,000 more made the Atlantic crossing before 1918, and the pace increased after March 1918.

The Navy, with several new ships nearly completed, was much better prepared than the Army. By mid-1917 eighteen destroyers were operating in the North Atlantic and within a year five American battleships joined the British fleet. The great American contribution to the sea war was its anti-submarine and convoy work. Britain in 1917 was losing one of every four merchant ships leaving its ports; the addition of American destroyers to convoy duty aided materially in lowering the rate. American minelayers also laid a major share of the North Sea minefield that bottled up the main body of the German fleet.

Pershing from the first insisted on the maintenance of a

separate American Army in France, though Foch and Haig hoped to brigade American troops with British and French units. He won his point, and in late 1917 the Americans took over a quiet sector on the Western front. Prospects for victory looked bright to the Germans and Austrians. The Italian defeat at Caporetto virtually knocked Italy out of the war, and in early 1918 the Soviets overthrew the Kerensky government in Russia, signed an armistice with the Central Powers, and released a half-million seasoned soldiers for the Western Front. Germany immediately launched a heavy offensive against the British, and later in the spring struck along the Marne. Whatever his feelings about a separate command, Pershing did not hesitate to place his troops at Foch's disposal. The First Division fought at Cantigny, the Second at Belleau Wood, and the Third at Château-Thierry.

When the Allied lines held the initiative passed to Foch, who acceded to Pershing's wish. The First and Second Armies, aided by French colonials, participated in the counter-offensive of 1918, while in September the Americans in force attacked at Saint-Mihiel salient, taking 16,000 prisoners with light losses. Later in the year Pershing's men mounted an attack in the Meuse-Argonne offensive for forty-seven consecutive days, cracking the Hindenburg Line. The 'big push' in the autumn of 1918 broke the back of German resistance. On 3 October the German government communicated with Wilson, asking an armistice, followed by a similar request from Austria-Hungary. When Wilson refused to deal independently with the Central Powers, Allied commissioners met with German representatives in early November, and on 11 November 1918 an armistice ended the war.

Direct American military contributions to the First World War were much smaller than those of Britain and France; nevertheless they were decisively timed. The American army suffered 125,000 casualties (half of them battle deaths), inconsiderable losses compared to those of the Allies, though sustained in only six months' action. But the United States had a million men in France at the end of the war, and the prospect of facing an ever-growing American army had

obvious effects on German morale. The United States' entry
into the conflict brought confidence to battle-weary nations
who had endured three years of bloody stalemate. With the
industrial might of the United States on their side, and with
the daily arrival of thousands of self-assured, fresh troops,
the Allies felt an immediate lift.

The greatest American contribution, however, was the
high-minded idealism of Woodrow Wilson. His famous
'Fourteen Points' of a just peace, embodied in his speech to
Congress in January of 1918, gave the Allied cause its most
potent ideological weapon. If the world could have 'open
covenants openly arrived at', freedom of the seas, autonomy
and liberty for peoples, redress of ancient wrongs, and a
'general association of nations for mutual guarantees of
political independence and territorial integrity' – then the
end of 'the war to end war' promised hope to victor and
vanquished alike. 'Meester Veelson's' vision, which unfortunately others may not have shared, seemed to offer a basis
for a just and enduring peace. Germany's claim that it never
received at Versailles what Wilson promised made it easier
for Adolf Hitler, a generation later, to convince the German
people that they had been tricked into an unnecessary
surrender.

The war had tremendous internal effects on the United
States. Far more so than the Spanish or Civil Wars, World
War I provoked an intense nationalism that almost completely obliterated sectional feeling. With twenty-four million men at the call of the Federal government, five million
of them under military regulations, the force of Federal
power was felt by American citizens as never before. Wartime life was strictly regimented by Federal decree, with
industry, food, fuel, housing, even news controlled by
Federal boards and bureaux. In later years during the New
Deal attack on the depression, and mobilization for World
War II, the experience of World War I provided both
pattern and personnel for similar extensions of Federal
control.

Congress at the beginning of the war gave Wilson sweeping authority, much of which he delegated to Boards or Commissions, for the most part appointed by him and responsible to him alone. The problem of total mobilization lay with the Council of National Defense, composed of cabinet officers and an advisory planning board. The War Industries Board, headed by Bernard Baruch (later an advisor to Franklin Roosevelt in World War II), was responsible for co-ordinating industrial effort, regulating production, shifting factories to a wartime basis, and planning use of raw materials. The Shipping Board took over the merchant marine and built new ships to replace submarine losses. The Railroad Administration put the rail lines under federal control, paying rent to the rail companies, while other boards took over grain elevators, warehouses, telegraph lines, and telephone services. The Department of Labor assumed responsibility for housing workers in mushrooming industrial cities. Herbert Hoover, head of the Food Administration, fixed prices, regulated production and distribution, and designated 'wheatless' and 'meatless' days to conserve foodstuffs. The Fuel Administration controlled consumption of coal and oil; the War Trade Board licensed exports so that American goods did not fall into enemy hands; the War Finance Corporation lent capital to expanding industries. The task of mobilizing public opinion fell to the Committee on Public Information, whose executive secretary, George Creel, worked tirelessly to 'sell the war' with the latest advertising methods. To finance the war Congress raised income, corporation, and excess profit taxes, imposed a variety of new taxes, and authorized the sale of government bonds. Using methods pioneered by Jay Cooke in the Civil War, the Treasury sold 21,000 million in 'Liberty Bonds' to small investors.

Labour gained a great deal from the war. Gompers' appointment to the Council of National Defense meant the recognition of organized labour as capital's equal and lifted union morale. To avoid crippling strikes and indiscriminate use of the injunction Wilson created the Nation War Labor Board to hear disputes between labour and management.

The Board handled more than a thousand cases, fixing the principle of collective bargaining firmly in the public mind. With a flood of new workers into war plants union membership jumped 37 per cent. The demands of war production created new opportunities for Negroes, who moved by thousands into Northern industrial cities. At the close of the war labour enjoyed full employment, high wages, a shorter working week, arbitration and collective bargaining, and, above all, general public respect.

The one conspicuous failure of the United States in World War I lay in the field of civil liberties. War propaganda played on its 'hate the enemy' theme so effectively that tolerance, free speech, and freedom of thought and opinion suffered. Congress, in response to demands for internal security legislation, passed the Espionage Act of 1917 and the Sedition Act of 1918, both more far-reaching in effect than any previous laws in American history. State laws against subversion and disloyalty were even more drastic. Federal authorities arrested and gaoled 1,500 persons, among them Eugene Debs, who had polled a million votes as Socialist candidate for President in 1912. The worst offenders were private patriotic groups and individuals who tracked down 'slackers', 'yellowbacks', and 'Pro-Germans' with hysterical intensity. German-Americans suffered especially; German music was banned, universities dropped courses in Goethe and revoked honorary degrees granted to German scholars – even sauerkraut became 'Liberty cabbage'. A few sensible men, such as Holmes and Brandeis, who counselled against stifling democracy during a war to preserve it, went largely unheard. Wilson's prediction that war meant 'the spirit of ruthless brutality will enter into every fiber of our national life' came true very soon.

The real test of American maturity came with the peace. The Peace Conference met in Paris on 18 January 1919, after slightly more than four years of war, thirteen million casualties, and incalculable expenditures of money and materials. The plenary sessions of the Conference mattered less than the 'Big Four' meetings which set the actual terms of settlement. Lloyd George, representing the world's largest empire and one-quarter of its population, had been elected on the slogan 'Make Germany Pay!' Clemenceau, France's 'Tiger', was a narrow, vindictive old man with little interest in anything except France's immediate future. Orlando, Italy's delegate, wanted new territory and sat out much of the conference in a huff. All four representatives were keenly aware of aroused public opinion at home, and in the end, after much bickering, Wilson was forced to make many concessions to conflicting interests and old hatreds. Not even the victors were satisfied with the Treaty of Versailles, but Wilson pinned his faith to the League of Nations Covenant it created, believing that the League might settle peaceably the disputes and wrangles bound to arise from the Treaty itself. That his dream of a peaceful and orderly world community did not materialize was not wholly his fault.

The Treaty found a rough road ahead when it was submitted to the Senate for ratification in July of 1919. The question at issue, said Wilson, 'is whether we can refuse the moral leadership that is offered us, whether we shall accept or reject the confidence of the world'. There were few serious objections to most of its terms, but many to the League of Nations idea, particularly to Article X of the League Covenant, by which members were pledged 'to respect and preserve as against external aggression the territorial integrity and existing political independence' of all other members. Some were based on partisan political considerations, some on Wilson's presumably high-handed methods in framing it without proper consultation with Congress, some on fears of entanglement in foreign wars.

In the Senate the Republicans held a majority as a consequence of the 1918 elections, while control of the Senate Committee on Foreign Relations was firmly in Republican hands. Nearly all Senate Democrats favoured the Treaty. A small group of Republicans was willing to support it with mild reservations, a larger number was willing to pass it with major changes (especially without Article X), and an 'irreconcilable' group of Republicans and a few Democrats refused to approve it in any form. There was also powerful opposition to the League outside of Congress. Theodore Roosevelt attacked it violently, and wealthy isolationists such as Frick and Mellon contributed to a huge campaign against 'The Evil Thing with a Holy Name'. Yet the League had powerful support too. The American Federation of Labor, the American Bar Association, the Federal Council of Churches, and thirty-two state legislatures endorsed it; ex-President Taft and ex-candidate Charles Evans Hughes courageously supported Wilson and the League against their own party leaders.

The key to the League's defeat lay ultimately in the hands of Senator Henry Cabot Lodge of Massachusetts, chairman of the Senate Committee on Foreign Relations. Lodge had for years favoured an association of nations, but his personal antagonism to Wilson and his adherence to party politics were stronger than his internationalist leanings. The Republicans hung amendments on the Treaty, fought Wilson on each one, and wrangled over them on the Senate floor for four months. Wilson himself set out on a nation-wide tour to carry the argument directly to the people, but weary, ill, and worn, he suffered a paralytic stroke in September 1919 and thereafter could put up only a wavering resistance. In March 1920 the Senate voted an end to the war with Germany without ratifying the Treaty, but Wilson vetoed the resolution. Not until the Republican victory of that year did the resolution pass and the war with Germany actually end.

By its refusal to accept membership in the League of Nations the United States implicitly refused to accept world leadership in the peace. Had it entered the League with its full weight, there is a bare possibility that the mistakes of Versailles might have been mitigated and World War II at least delayed, if not prevented. The rejection of the League by the most powerful nation to emerge from the war made international co-operation both difficult and hazardous, and had much to do with the League's failure to meet its challenges a decade later. Wilson's warning that if the League were defeated the United States might have to fight World War I all over again, came back to haunt America.

Though the American people never had a chance to vote directly on the League, congressional opposition to it was obviously based on a large segment of public opinion. American thinking after 1919 was prevailingly disillusioned, nationalistic, and isolationist. The nation had just completed its first great adventure in global politics and did not like it. Few lamented the League's demise during the twenties, and Wilson's lonely death in 1924 brought few twinges to the national conscience. As late as 1937 with another world war about to break, a poll showed that 70 per cent of those who had an opinion on the matter believed that the United States' entry into World War I had been an error. War propaganda backfired badly; the Allies seemed to be human after all, and the squabblings at Paris were not pretty. It became popular to claim that America had been tricked into war by slick British propaganda, by bankers and munitions makers, by clever politicking. It was all over, the nation rolled in wealth, business boomed, and the war was long ago and far away. The American people would not be easily fooled again.

Throughout the twenties revisionist historians, ably aided by politicians and the press, proved not only that World War I but also the Civil War and perhaps the American Revolution need not have happened. The terms of Versailles were carefully analysed and the manoeuvrings of 1900–14 scanned to show that Britain, France, and Russia were not blameless and that Germany possibly had a case. It was fashionable to be objective, sceptical of men and motives, rigidly neutral toward moral issues, emphatic about economic ones. Thus World War I became 'Wilson's War', brought on by an impractical college professor; his aim of 'making the world safe for democracy' was twisted into an impossible dream and his vision of a peaceful world commonwealth derided as unrealistic idealism.

Foreign relations during the twenties were chiefly concerned with problems left over from war. The Washington government lent more than 10,000 million dollars to the Allies, usually at 5 per cent interest, and as soon as hostilities ended the debtor nations clamoured for cancellation, or at best, adjustments in both interest and principal. Most of the money, it was argued, had been used to purchase war materials in the United States and never left the country; furthermore, the loans might well be considered as America's contribution to a cause for which Europe had suffered much more heavily in men and materials. American tariff barriers prevented liquidation of the debts by trade, while payment in gold would wreck European currencies.

American opinion, however, regarded a debt as a debt; Coolidge's classic remark, 'They hired the money, didn't they?' reflected the attitude of those who understood neither the intricacies of international finance nor the prostration of post-war Europe. Arguments over war debts embittered feelings on both sides, creating the myths of 'Uncle Shylock' abroad and 'dishonest ingrates' at home. The British settlement of 1923 somewhat mollified American opinion, but negotiations with France, Italy, and Belgium were long and unsatisfactory. Though Hoover announced a moratorium on war debts in 1932 a moratorium was hardly enough. In 1932 six debtor nations defaulted. In 1934 others followed, convincing many Americans that it was useless to do business with 'faithless foreigners' and reinforcing the isolationist trend of the early thirties.

Ironically, the Republican party that defeated the League made long strides toward international co-operation under Coolidge and Hoover. By calling the Washington Conference on Limitation of Armaments in 1921, Harding hoped to end the frantic naval rivalry among Britain, Japan, and the United States. Secretary of State Hughes proposed a plan of armament reduction which was adopted in revised form by most of the major powers, though Japan later renounced all such agreements in 1934. In 1927 Coolidge suggested another conference which turned out less successfully. At the same time the 1921 Conference paved the way for a four-power pact (Britain, France, Japan, and the

United States) to keep peace in the Pacific, and for a nine-power pact for control of Chinese affairs.

Plans for a World Court of International Justice under the League Covenant found the Republican leaders favourably disposed to American participation. Coolidge gave the Court his personal support, and in 1925 the House declared in favour of joining the tribunal. However, there were still those who feared a recurrence of Wilsonism, and after long debate the Senate crippled the resolution with cautious reservations. While the Senate worked over a compromise, the United States began a programme of careful co-operation with the League, sending observers and advisers to 'non-political' League conferences until by 1930 the United States had five permanent representatives in Geneva and a record of attendance at more than four hundred League meetings. Secretary of State Frank Kellogg, with Coolidge's approval, negotiated a series of arbitration treaties, culminating in the signing of the Kellogg-Briand pact in Paris in 1928. Ultimately sixty-two nations approved the agreement in principle and renounced war as an instrument of national policy. Although the American public was enormously cheered by Kellogg's achievements, less optimistic observers pointed out that the pact made no provisions for its enforcement and could hardly be construed as a broad step away from isolationism. Japan's attack on China in 1931 illustrated their point.

Herbert Hoover, a man of cosmopolitan views and international experience, approved and expanded Coolidge's foreign policy. As a Quaker and as an engineer, Hoover hated war's immorality and waste. Although he announced himself opposed to the League of Nations, he urged adherence to the World Court and after careful preparation submitted the necessary legislation for American participation to Congress. Again the 'irreconcilables', aided by the press, rallied enough isolationist sentiment to defeat it, one of the great disappointments of Hoover's life. At his suggestion Ramsay MacDonald called the London Conference of 1930 to discuss naval disarmament, and although the final agreement was only a partial victory for disarmament, it passed the Senate without hampering amendments. In 1932 Hoover electrified the World Disarmament Conference at Geneva by proposing that all existing armaments be slashed by one-third, an idea that was enthusiastically buried with oratory. Hoover's sincere, statesmanlike, somewhat visionary plan simply did not fit the temper of a world already coming apart at the seams.

American public opinion in the period 1920–32 was about equally divided between isolationist and internationalist thinking. America's entrance into the First World War emphasized Wilson's idea that 'We are participants, whether we would or not, in the life of the world', and Republican administrations of the next decade (particularly under the enlightened leadership of Hoover) went far beyond any previous policies of international co-operation. At the same time American statesmen always faced at home a strong determination to avoid foreign entanglements, keep up trade barriers, and emphasize domestic progress – just as they faced abroad the hostility of a ravaged Europe, sinking into fascism, toward a rich and expanding America. The United States, remarked Coolidge, needed no importations, 'industrial, intellectual, or political'. The sharp division of opinion forced American foreign policy into a middle path. The United States was willing to participate in internationally flavoured pacts and agreements, but unwilling to bind itself either by machinery or promises to actual involvement in European or Asian affairs. With the onslaught of World War II the United States reluctantly faced again, as it did in 1917, the problem of finding a compromise foreign policy.

Wilson hoped that the election of 1920 might decide the issue of the League of Nations for once and all, but it did not. The Republican National Convention, after some argument, adopted a platform endorsing some sort of international organization, but not Wilson's League. Since death removed Theodore Roosevelt from the scene in 1919, the race for the nomination was wide open. It was won by

Warren G. Harding, an Ohio newspaperman, with Calvin Coolidge of Massachusetts as his companion on the ticket.

Harding, an impressively handsome man of extremely limited talents, took an ambiguous stand on the League issue. Since thirty-one prominent Republicans, including Hoover, issued a statement favouring a league of nations, while Lodge and the Republican 'irreconcilables' spoke strongly against it, no one could be quite sure what a vote for Harding meant in terms of international politics. The Democrats nominated James Cox of Ohio for President, Franklin Delano Roosevelt (Wilson's able young Assistant Secretary of the Navy) for vice-president, and pledged an absolute continuance of the Wilsonian foreign and domestic programmes. The public itself, weary of debate and oratory, wanted nothing so much as what Harding called 'a return to normalcy'. Harding won by a seven million majority, and carried a Republican Congress into office with him.

A genial, kindly man who liked to play poker with his friends, Harding was a perfect tool for the party politicians. Cursed with a curious inability to judge men and issues, he was shortly at the mercy of the most cynically corrupt set of rascals to appear in politics since Reconstruction days. Within two years one cabinet member went to prison, two more barely escaped it, and various minor government officials were either convicted of graft or forced to resign. Harding himself seems to have been untouched by the scandals, but he saw enough of what was going on to shake him severely. His health broke under the strain and he died during a trip to Alaska in August 1923. Calvin Coolidge, an impeccably honest man and a good administrator, cleaned up the mess and restored respectability to the Republican party.

The Republicans meanwhile busied themselves with reversing the direction of Wilsonian policy. Congress swiftly withdrew the wartime powers it had granted the Chief Executive, dissolved the more powerful boards and commissions, and returned to the time-honoured McKinley principle of 'less government in business and more business in government'. Congress cut Federal expenditures, reduced corporation taxes, withdrew Federal controls from business, raised tariffs, subsidized new industries, and drew the teeth of the F C C, the I C C, and the Federal Reserve Act.

Coolidge phrased it succinctly – 'The business of America is business.' Big corporations grew bigger, bigger even than in McKinley's day, ending in a complex enormity that corporation executives themselves sometimes could not fathom. In 1930 fifty per cent of the nation's corporate wealth was controlled by two hundred companies; the tobacco, utilities, aluminium, chemicals, dye, communications, and steel trusts eclipsed in size and power anything on the scene in 1900. Agriculture did not fare so well, for after a sharp recession in 1921 farm prices dropped while farm production increased. The farmers organized again – the Farmers' Union, the American Farm Business Federation, the Non-Partisan League, the revitalized Grange – and sent a strong 'farm bloc' to Congress without much encouragement from the Republican majority. Labour was restive. War left the unions powerful, and since the shift to a peace-time economy brought reduced wages and longer hours, hundreds of strikes plagued industry. Courts dusted off the injunction, reaffirmed the implications of the fourteenth Amendment, and followed a uniformly conservative course.

The nationalism generated by war carried over into the peace in the form of a campaign against 'Reds', incidentally aimed at labour and liberalism. The Russian Revolution provoked a Red-hunt in which the radical, the nonconformist, and the unorthodox were relentlessly tracked down by Federal and state authorities. Attorney General Palmer headed a drive to seize 'communists' (a term he tended to interpret very broadly) and gaoled some 6,000 persons, most of whom were released for lack of evidence. At the height of the scare robbers killed a paymaster during a Massachusetts factory hold-up. Nicolo Sacco and Bartolommeo Vanzetti, both suspected anarchists, were arrested for the crime and tried in an atmosphere of anti-foreign, anti-radical rage. Though the majority of liberal opinion ranged

itself on the side of the suspects, the two were finally electro-
cuted in 1927. The wartime influx of Negroes to Northern
cities touched off race riots; with the assistance of Henry
Ford's Dearborn newspaper, anti-Semitism appeared on the
scene. The Ku Klux Klan, dormant since 1900, was quickly
revived. Nourished by anti-Negro, anti-Catholic, anti-
Jewish, and anti-foreign patriots, the Klan claimed four
million members by 1924 and held the balance of political
power in several Northern states. By 1926 the wave of
hysteria and intolerance had run its course, though a persistent small stream remained to swell into another flood
after World War II.

The overwhelming fact about the twenties, though, was
that they rolled in money. Presidential messages to Congress,
someone remarked, sounded like the chairman of the board's
report to stockholders. Except for agriculture, mining, and
textiles, the national economy reached the highest level of
profit yet recorded in American history – and the best thing
was that it would never end, for American business leaders
were convinced that 'prosperity is permanent'. The war
impoverished Europe and destroyed much of its productive
capacity; mass production and efficiency increased American production; instalment buying widened the purchasing
market; new industries, such as the automobile, radio, and
movies, made new jobs and new markets; the favourable
attitude of the Federal government spurred business confidence and encouraged new ventures. Stock market speculation attracted thousands of new investors, leading John J.
Raskob of General Motors to predict that any man who
could invest $15 a week could within twenty years have
$80,000 in cash and $400 a month income. America bulged
with money and trusted those who had it. The public
'worshipped at the knees of business', remarked George
Norris, the Nebraska insurgent, and made an oracle of
Ford. The captain of industry enjoyed public confidence as
never before. It was up to him, one commentator believed,
'to finish the work that religion, government, and war have
failed to do . . .'

Calvin Coolidge, a New Englander with a reputation for silence, was shrewd enough to keep quiet and take the credit. The Republicans nominated him again for President in 1924 and promised four more years of 'Coolidge prosperity'. The Democrats, after a rowdy convention, could not decide between William McAdoo, a Californian from Wilson's cabinet, and Alfred Smith, the popular governor of New York. Finally they compromised on John W. Davis, an able West Virginia corporation lawyer. Certain labour groups, socialists, discontented farm organizations, and Bull Moosers formed the Progressive party and ran Robert M. La Follette for President. But the time for old-fashioned political revolt was over; the American public was too confident of the future to listen to the old Wisconsin fighter. Coolidge slaughtered his opponents at the polls, beating Davis by seven million votes and La Follette by ten million. 'An air of optimism pervades the nation', wrote a leading magazine after the election, and the country settled down with 'Silent Cal' and permanent prosperity.

The temper of the twenties was ambivalent. On the one hand it was officially confident and optimistic. The nation must move forward, said John Dewey, with 'faith in the active tendencies of the day' and 'the courage of intelligence to follow whither social and economic changes direct us'. Hoover thought that the country had 'finally eradicated the causes of poverty'; Bruce Barton showed that Christianity was the best basis for a 'business civilization'; people liked Emile Coué's popular formula of 'Every day in every way I am getting better and better.'

Yet it was also a time of doubt and cynicism, the result of war, confusion, and the increased tension and complexity of the post-war world. The war to end war ended in disillusion, 'normalcy' turned into corruption, the 'noble experiment' of prohibition produced drunkenness and gangs. For the first time since the founding of the Republic responsible thinkers questioned the efficacy of the American democratic process. H. L. Mencken jeered at the 'homo boobiens' who comprised the American electorate, Sinclair Lewis pilloried business and the small town in *Babbitt* and *Main Street*, and Walter Lippmann's studies in public opinion indicated that the popular mind was irrational, gullible, easily misled. The *Army Training Manual* of 1928 listed the effects of democracy as 'mobocracy . . . demagogism, license, agitation, discontent, anarchy'. Church attendance fell off, until by 1929 more people attended movies than churches. The United States, intellectuals agreed, lacked a cultural tradition and suffered from commercialism; its moral inhibitions, provincialism, and herd-psychology stifled the creative intelligence.

One reaction was the desire to be 'emancipated'. War shattered the traditional codes of Puritan and Victorian morality by which Americans had lived, and there was nothing at the moment to replace them. Freud and Watson supplanted Darwin as a topic of conversation, reinforcing the popular preoccupation with extraversion and individualism. Old moral axioms disappeared in talk about glandular secretions, inhibitions and repressions, and stimulus-response patterns; ideas and desires once rarely mentioned became normal and healthy; moral doctrines once unanimously accepted were outmoded in terms of the new psychology. Bobbed hair, short skirts, and frank talk about sex marked the emancipated sophisticate, and there was a rise in the divorce rate as well as much discussion of 'companionate marriage'. Sports and spectacles became a national mania during the Golden Age of Jack Dempsey, Red Grange, Suzanne Lenglen, and the 'million dollar gate'; of jazz, the 'shimmy', and the 'song hit'; of 'flappers' and 'sheiks', of Rudy Vallee, Rudolph Valentino, and the movie-star 'idol of millions'.

In sport the trend toward professionalism became stronger during the twenties, and the crowds attracted by football, baseball, and basketball, made sporting events into highly lucrative ventures. The gate receipts of college football, particularly, converted the game into a business. College stadia, holding from 30,000 to 90,000 spectators, appeared in profusion and highly-paid coaches joined university staffs. Professional baseball organized an intricate interlocking system of major and minor league clubs which grossed millions of dollars yearly. The sports themselves, especially football and baseball, developed into mechanized games of extreme complexity. The modern American approach to sport is a technological one. Sports of personal prowess, with the exception of boxing, have become less popular than those emphasizing organized co-operation and a distribution of responsibility among specialists – in American terms, 'team play'. The particular player has in most games a special function to perform, at which he is often incredibly expert, while the manager or coach fits his function into the overall pattern of the game itself. American sport exhibits a chess-like rationale, requiring a tremendous knowledge of moves, countermoves, and of what players call 'the percentages' of success in any one. For this reason the coach or manager is of paramount importance in American sports; it is he who controls the play of each individual, plots strategy, and plans his 'attack' or 'defense' in semi-military fashion. Organized sport in America, as several commentators have pointed out, probably serves as a war-substitute of some importance. Possibly no other aspect of American life illustrates the American's respect for skill, efficiency, and technological organization. The American tradition in sport is a professional, not an amateur tradition. The approach is one of studied efficiency; popular heroes are in most cases professional or quasi-professional, not amateur athletes.

The temper of the twenties showed most clearly in its literature. Willa Cather's and Ellen Glasgow's sensitive novels of regional realism carried on the older tradition, and Edith Wharton continued in the path of expatriated Henry James. Robert Frost, the spiritual descendant of Whittier, Lowell, and Emerson, wrote poetry in the New England tradition; Edwin Arlington Robinson's verse reflected the influence of Tennyson and Browning; Vachel Lindsay, less a rebel than he thought, followed the course staked out by Whitman. But a whole set of 'new poets' appeared after

Harriet Monroe founded *Poetry* magazine in 1912 – Amy Lowell, Sara Teasdale, Robinson Jeffers, Marianne Moore, Edgar Lee Masters, Wallace Stevens, E. E. Cummings, Carl Sandburg, Ezra Pound – all rebels against conventionalism and romanticism. A 'lost generation' of 'sad young men' wrote cynical, hedonistic, rebellious novels and plays – Ernest Hemingway, John Dos Passos, Eugene O'Neill, Maxwell Anderson, Sherwood Anderson, Elmer Rice, William Faulkner – while F. Scott Fitzgerald's brittle, brilliant novels of the 'jazz age' caught the flavour of contemporary life perfectly.

Artists exiled themselves to Paris's 'left bank' or New York's Greenwich Village, where they could create in a friendlier, more emancipated atmosphere. Critics engaged in sharp arguments over American tradition, Van Wyck Brooks and the 'radicals' contending that American cultural life was sterile, bloodless, hag-ridden by provincialism and Puritanism. In opposition, Babbitt at Harvard and More at Princeton condemned the literature of the day and called for a 'new humanism', a return to older standards of artistic harmony and restraint. While critics argued, the artists themselves experimented endlessly with style and technique, as Joyce, Gertrude Stein, Proust, and Eliot were experimenting in Europe. Before it ended the twenties emerged as one of the most vital and stimulating periods in American literary history.

Calvin Coolidge could easily have had the Republican nomination for President in 1924, but when he announced that he 'did not choose to run' the mantle of succession fell on Herbert Hoover, his capable Secretary of Commerce. The party's platform simply re-stated the domestic and foreign policies of the preceding administrations, promising continued prosperity with not only 'a full dinner pail' but 'a full garage'. The Democrats nominated Alfred Smith of New York (known nationally as 'Al'), a New York City product, a Roman Catholic, and a 'wet' opponent of prohibition. Smith's record as governor of New York stamped him as a liberal and his Bowery accent and winning personality made him the favourite of millions, but the triple handicap of being a 'wet', a Catholic, and a New Yorker was too much. Hoover won by a huge majority in both electoral and popular vote, cracked the solid South, and carried a Republican Congress in with him.

Hoover entered the Presidency with a spotless reputation and solid public support. His wartime and post-war services as Chairman of the Belgian Relief Commission and Food Administrator had carried his name all over the world, leading the London *Nation* to call him 'the biggest man who has emerged on the Allied side'. His background, however, was chiefly in mining, business, and administration. He was unaccustomed to the give-and-take of politics, and his economic and political philosophy dated from the days of Carnegie and Sumner. He believed in strict individualism, *laissez-faire*, survival of the fittest, open opportunity, and an unhampered profit system. An intelligent conservative, he conceived himself to be the defender of older ideals of economic enterprise, modified to meet the contemporary needs of financial and industrial life. He was also inflexible, doggedly holding to preconceived ideas, with a trace of the authoritarian in him. Yet he was an honest, able man, with internationalist views, capable of being a distinguished President. People had faith in 'The Great Engineer'.

Hoover's first move was to redeem two campaign promises. First, he established the Federal Farm Board and the Agricultural Marketing Act, both designed to stabilize farm markets and prices. At his suggestion Congress next plunged into a revision of the tariff, in which Hoover wanted 'limited changes'. Congressional protectionists, however, emerged with the Smoot-Hawley tariff which raised rates nearly 7 per cent over the already high tariffs of 1922. Hoover criticized the bill, but signed it over loud protests from abroad and from more than a thousand American economists. How Hoover would have proceeded with his domestic programme will never be known, for the Big Prosperity Bubble blew up in the autumn of 1929.

Even before it broke some economists were sceptical of the boom of the twenties. Over-production, the slow rise of real wages, and falling prices were straws in the wind as early as 1926. Stock prices built up in dizzying spirals (old-timers nostalgically remember R.C.A. shares at 549) but the few analysts who preached caution were shouted down. Wall Street went into a slow decline in early October 1929, and on 24 October the panic hit. Sixteen million shares changed hands, fifty leading stocks fell forty points a day, thousands of big and little investors were wiped out, messenger boys bought well-known stocks at a dollar a share.

Nobody really believed it. Hoover thought the break would end in sixty days or so. Secretary of the Treasury Mellon looked for 1930 to be 'a normal year', but nevertheless the recession spread. Both agriculture and industry had over-expanded; international trade was out of balance; artificial price levels were maintained by monopolistic control; credit, especially in instalment buying, had been badly overdone. The United States hit the bottom of the trough in early 1932, when the National Bureau of Economic Research drew an appalling picture of the national economy. Stock prices were down 83 per cent, productive output down 40 per cent, wages down 60 per cent, dividends down 57 per cent. Fifteen to seventeen million unemployed roamed the streets, credit froze at the source, money depreciated to half its value. The carnival of the twenties was over.

The Hoover administration did a good job in fighting the depression, but what it did was far from enough. Minimizing the seriousness of the situation, Hoover urged 'business as usual' and waited for the depression to wear itself out. He raised the tariff and reduced taxes to encourage business, made Federal Reserve credit easier, and asked industry to expand production and retain wage levels. In early 1932 he established the Reconstruction Finance Corporation to loan money to industry, banks, and farmers; near the end of his administration he expanded its powers and functions in an effort to get business going again. The difficulty was that Hoover, thinking in terms of *laissez-faire* and 'rugged individualism', at no time threw the full weight of the Federal government into the battle against the depression. His programme was, in effect, a palliative designed to remedy temporary conditions until permanent prosperity reasserted itself – as he believed it must.

The depression hung like a cloud over the political conventions of 1932. Republicans faced the presidential election with something less than enthusiasm; they met, adopted a colourless programme, and nominated Hoover for another term. The Democrats met with the highest hopes in years. Their logical candidate, on the basis of his 1928 campaign record, was 'Al' Smith, but after some pre-convention horse-trading the nomination went to Franklin D. Roosevelt, Governor of New York. The platform the convention gave him was not much, but it mattered less than the man who ran on it.

Roosevelt's acceptance speech, the famous 'New Deal' speech, was a ringing promise to get something done. This was, he said, an industrial civilization, creating 'new problems for those who would remain free'. The great problem of the times was the 'new despotism' of 'industrial dictatorship', the rule of 'economic royalists'. Opportunity was stifled by monopoly; private enterprise was too private; it was privileged, not free and open. There were too many poor, too few well-to-do. 'Throughout the nation', he continued, 'men and women, forgotten in the political philosophy of the government of the last years, look to us here for a more equitable opportunity to share in the distribution of national wealth.' 'I pledge you, I pledge myself', he concluded, 'to a new deal for the American people.'

Roosevelt proved to be the best campaigner the Democratic party ever had. The New Deal, born in his Chicago acceptance speech, emerged as a sweeping, long-range political, economic, and social reorganization that, if instituted, would mark a major shift in the direction of American domestic policy. To Hoover the contest was between two widely different philosophies of government; the New Deal was 'a challenge to liberty' and its supporters 'exponents of a social philosophy different from the traditional American one'. The nation must choose, he said, between individualism and regimentation, between liberty and Federal bureaucracy. As the campaign wore on it was evident that Hoover planned a return to the happy, prosperous days of early 1929. Roosevelt planned a new, different kind of American society.

Roosevelt's lead in the balloting was never in doubt, and by midnight of election day it was certain that he had been elected by the largest vote then recorded in American history. Hoover carried only six states, while both Houses of Congress went overwhelmingly Democratic. The landslide that carried Roosevelt into office, like the landslides that swept Jackson and Jefferson into the White House, was an expression of discontent. His vote was a victory for the depression, as well as a desperate nation's vote of confidence in a man who seemed to know where he was going.

Roosevelt's inaugural address on 4 March 1933, promised 'action, and action now' in this 'dark hour of national life'. 'The only thing we have to fear,' he said, 'is fear itself'.

We do not distrust the future of essential democracy. The people of the United States have not failed. In their need they have registered a mandate that they want direct, vigorous action. They have asked me for discipline and direction under leadership. They have made me the present instrument of their wishes. In the spirit of the gift I take it.

Thus the New Deal began.

CHAPTER 28

NEW DEAL, FAIR DEAL, AND GLOBAL CONFLICT

FRANKLIN DELANO ROOSEVELT, a distant cousin of Theodore, was a wealthy, landed New Yorker descended from early Dutch settlers. His background included travel abroad, exclusive Groton School, Harvard, and Columbia Law School. In 1905 he married Eleanor Roosevelt, a sixth cousin, and in 1910, at thirty, he was elected to the New York State Senate, the first Democrat in a generation to hold a legislative seat from his rock-ribbed Republican district.

In 1912 Roosevelt supported Wilson at the national Republican convention. As a reward he was made Assistant Secretary of the Navy, where he did outstanding work in building up the service before and during World War I. A thorough believer in the 'New Freedom', young Roosevelt absorbed much of it during his Washington years, and in 1920, when he was paired with Cox on the Democratic presidential ticket, he gave Wilson a personal pledge to carry on his programme if elected. After the dismal Democratic defeat, he retired from politics to resume the practice of law.

A little more than a year later, at thirty-nine, Roosevelt was struck by poliomyelitis, paralysed from the waist down. Through a long six-year fight against illness he spent his time in correspondence, establishing a wide acquaintance with Democratic party leaders. He appeared in public but once, to nominate Al Smith at the 1924 National convention, but he was nevertheless a potent behind-the-scenes force in the party organization. In 1928 he ran successfully for the governorship of New York, and again in 1930. As governor, Roosevelt did a competent though not spectacular job. At the time of his nomination for President in 1932 he was known as a good party man with a fine radio presence, a 'safe' candidate, and a mild liberal.

When Roosevelt assumed the Presidency he possessed a

thorough knowledge of practical politics and limited administrative experience. His political philosophy was disorganized and unformed; not until the later stages of the 1932 campaign did he seem to arrange his ideas into a coherent pattern, expressed most clearly in his book, *Looking Forward*, in 1933. He possessed monumental self-confidence, great mental and physical energy, a marked capacity for growth, and (as one of his advisers said), 'a frightening receptivity to ideas'.

Roosevelt was an intuitive politician, willing to experiment, working from day to day with a 'let's see if it will work' technique. He was never a master planner, nor can one find in his New Deal any unity of programme. His greatest asset was his ability to discover, express, and translate into action the trends of popular opinion. Since Lincoln no man in public life had a more sensitive finger on the public pulse or a greater skill in seizing and exploiting the opportune moment. And 1932, of course, presented a magnificent opportunity, with the nation confused, bewildered, deep in the trough of depression.

The task of the moment in 1932 was to beat the depression, which Roosevelt promised to do with 'bold, persistent experimentation'. From March to July, during the famous 'Hundred Days' of 1933, anti-depression measures passed Congress with incredible speed. The Emergency Banking Act loosened credit and increased the amount of money issued by the Federal Reserve. The nation went off the gold standard, placed an embargo on gold and silver exports, and reduced the gold content of the dollar. The Banking Act of 1933 guaranteed the safety of bank deposits through the Federal Deposit Insurance Corporation; other agencies were established to make credit easier; and a year later the Securities Exchange Act appeared to control stock market practices.

For farm relief, Congress passed the Agricultural Adjustment Act, governing farm production, prices, and surpluses. The State Department and Congress hastened to frame trade agreements with Canada and Europe, particularly in agricultural produce. Though invalidated in 1936 by the Supreme Court, the A.A.A. reappeared in more acceptable and expanded form in 1938. For direct relief of unemployed young men Congress authorized the Civilian Conservation Corps, later adding the National Youth Administration to assist deserving students by providing part-time jobs. The Federal Emergency Relief Act of May 1933 (later superseded by the Works Progress Administration) created relief jobs directly and indirectly by making grants available to state and local governments. The Reconstruction Finance Corporation, a Hoover hold-over, continued to extend loans to private business through the Commodity Credit Corporation, while the Farm Credit Act, a corollary of the Triple-A, re-financed farm mortgages and eased farm credit.

For business and industry, Congress passed the National Industrial Recovery or 'Blue Eagle' Act in June 1933, intended to stabilize production, keep up wages, regulate hours and labour standards, and ban unfair trade and labour practices. By the time it was ruled unconstitutional in 1935, twenty million labourers worked under 500 different industrial codes. The NIRA also carried with it a gigantic relief programme, involving the Civil Works Administration, the Public Works Administration, and the Works Progress Administration, all of them designed to create jobs for nearly four million people. The Tennessee Valley Authority, born in May of 1933, was admittedly an experiment in Federally-owned public utilities, establishing a vast power empire cutting across seven states. After it in the next two decades came similar developments at Hoover Dam, Grand Coulee, Bonneville, Fort Peck, and elsewhere, as well as a Rural Electrification Act to carry electricity to isolated areas. The ratification of the twenty-first Amendment in 1933, cancelling the eighteenth (Prohibition) Amendment, had no relation to the anti-depression or reform portions of the New Deal Programme, but was rather the result of disillusionment with a 'noble experiment'.

1934 and 1935 saw fewer relief measures and more 'bold experimentation'. The Social Security Act, the most far-reaching piece of social legislation in American history, ended thirty years of agitation for old-age pensions, unemployment insurance, indigent relief, maternity and child welfare, and public health benefits, but not health insurance. The Resettlement Administration of 1935 attempted to help the farmer by withdrawing marginal land from use, lending funds for homes, and re-financing mortgages. The Wheeler-Rayburn Act of 1935 gave the Federal government increased power over interstate utilities, and a new tax bill, known as the 'soak-the-rich' tax, increased corporation and undivided profits taxes. As Roosevelt's first term drew to an end, the list of measures passed by Congress and of executive orders issued from the White House made a total of twenty-one major bills and hundreds of minor ones.

Public confidence in unions, shaken in the twenties, grew in the thirties as the quality of labour leadership improved. The Supreme Court changed its personnel and its attitude toward labour legislation, and labour took advantage of the favourable policies of the New Deal to consolidate its gains. Many of the 'pump priming' measures of 1933 and 1934 were intended to give direct assistance to the working-man. Most helpful to unions was section 7A of the N.I.R.A. code, which granted labour the right to organize and bargain collectively 'without interference, coercion, or restraint by employers'. After a brief wave of strikes in 1932, Roosevelt in 1933 created the National Labor Board to mediate disputes arising from the N.I.R.A., superseding it with the National Labor Relations Board in 1934. After the Supreme Court invalidated the N.I.R.A., Congress passed the Wagner Act to safeguard 'the practice and procedure of collective bargaining' and authorized the N.L.R.B. to administer it. By 1937 the agency had handled 5,000 disputes, arbitrated 2,000 strikes, and conducted 1,400 union elections.

The A.F.L. added a million and a half members to its rolls between 1932 and 1935. The A.F.L., however, organized on a craft-union basis, left untouched the masses of unskilled labour in the basic heavy industries. In 1936 a number of unions, led by John L. Lewis' United Mine

Workers, organized the Committee for Industrial Organization to unionize mass-production industries such as automobiles, steel, textiles, rubber, and aluminium. After repeated internal squabbles the A.F.L. formally ejected the C.I.O. unions, who changed their name to the Congress of Industrial Organizations and proceeded in their campaign against big industries. The C.I.O., using more aggressive methods, soon outstripped the A.F.L. in membership and by the late thirties had succeeded in realizing most of its immediate objectives, though both Ford and 'Little Steel' held out against it for several more years. Stormy old John L. Lewis, who was succeeded by Philip Murray in 1940, finally pulled his U.M.W. out of the C.I.O. in 1942.

By 1936 opposition to Roosevelt had coalesced within the Democratic party, some of whose leaders accused him of fostering a 'New Deal' party within its framework, of overspending, of extending bureaucracy, of dangerously increasing Federal authority. Al Smith and other prominent Democrats bolted the party to join a group of wealthy businessmen in the American Liberty League, an organization charged with fighting 'the Red New Deal with a Soviet seal', as the Chicago *Tribune* called it. The Republican convention chose Governor Alfred Landon of Kansas as its presidential candidate, and the Democrats lost no time in re-nominating Roosevelt, with John Nance Garner of Texas as his running mate. The campaign was an uninteresting one, for there was little doubt of the outcome. Roosevelt won by 523 electoral votes to eight, with a popular majority of nine million, while Congress went overwhelmingly Democratic. The vote seemed a clear endorsement of the New Deal, and Roosevelt promised four more years of the same.

He started on his second term with renewed energy. The Supreme Court had killed much of the early New Deal legislation, and lawyers seemed to be casting glances at both the Social Security and the Wagner Acts. The 'Nine Old Men' of the Court, said Roosevelt, were 'miners and sappers' of the Constitution and foes of progress. In 1937 he suggested a plan for reforming the Federal judiciary, touching off a heated argument that took up most of the year. The Court itself settled the matter by shifting its direction ('a switch in time that saved nine', someone remarked) and when several aged Justices retired Roosevelt replaced them with his own appointees.

After Congress stymied several Roosevelt-sponsored bills, the President attempted in the congressional elections of 1938 to 'purge' the Democratic party of its conservative, anti-New Deal elements, but failed. At the same time a sharp business recession in 1937 and early 1938 showed that the New Deal was not invulnerable. In late 1939 war broke out in Europe, and Roosevelt's domestic programme abruptly stopped. After September 1939 nearly all legislation introduced and debated in Congress, and all partisan political issues, were directly or indirectly influenced by World War II. The New Deal was finished.

The New Deal was not at all new. It was eclectic, borrowing from everything that had preceded it, representing the culmination of a half-century of political development. Roosevelt, taking office during a national crisis and working almost without opposition for three years, simply had an unparalleled opportunity for policy-making granted to none of his predecessors. Some of what he did was done hastily, some was frankly experimental, and much was primarily designed to rescue the American economy from the worst depression in its history. Older liberals complained that the New Deal 'Brain Trusters' paid little attention to the forms and techniques of true democracy. Conservatives claimed Roosevelt's policies were leftist; liberals criticized them as over-timid. Actually Roosevelt, in comparison to the administration that preceded him, followed a middle way. He was no doctrinaire, but ready always to try one plan, then another, or several simultaneously, sometimes veering to right or left but ending in the centre of the road.

The New Deal was by no means an attempt to change the capitalistic system of free enterprise. It was, Roosevelt said, 'a reform in order to preserve it', and to make it serve public ends more thoroughly. 'We seek', he explained, 'to guaran-

tee the survival of private enterprise by guaranteeing conditions under which it can work.' It must therefore be regulated in the public interest, to obtain stability, equilibrium,
and 'balance in our economic system'. Neither Bryan, nor
Theodore Roosevelt, nor Wilson, nor La Follette would have
disagreed.

The New Deal failed, nevertheless, to arrest the trend
toward consolidation in American economic life. The
depression accelerated the growth of monopoly by driving
weaker firms to the wall, to be absorbed by more durable
corporations. At the same time monopoly was to some extent
being replaced by oligopoly, that state of economic affairs
in which so few sellers existed in particular fields that they
dominated the market, despite theoretical competition with
each other. In 1937, after five years of the New Deal, three
firms produced 80 per cent of the nation's automobiles, three
companies made 60 per cent of the steel, and one aluminium
company controlled nearly 100 per cent of the output.
About all that Roosevelt could do was to eliminate some of
the more obvious violations of anti-trust legislation. Since
the New Deal, the trend towards monopoly and oligopoly
in American business life has continued.

The distinguishing trait of the New Deal was its broad
extension of Federal authority over American life, and the
assumption by the Federal government of large new areas
of social and economic responsibility. In effect, it created a
national state, powerful enough to define and enforce a
national interest. The New Deal thus had its roots deep in
the 1890's and the early 1900's, in the agrarian revolt, in the
Populist protest, in early Progressivism. In employing
Hamiltonian means to achieve Jeffersonian ends, the New
Deal looked more like Theodore Roosevelt's New Nationalism than Wilson's New Freedom. Roosevelt hoped, he said,
'. . . to remake national life after a fashion which, whether
the old prosperity returned or not, would yield a larger
sense of social justice and meet the demands of a new democracy.'

Only by a greater assumption of Federal authority did he

feel that this could be done. Of all the New Deal's principles, this had the most lasting influence on American politics. As the New York *Times* remarked in 1938, 'The unmistakable fact is that an increasing number of Americans, irrespective of party lines, have come to regard, as both necessary and desirable, a larger share of responsibility on the Government's part . . .' The issue itself, refusing to die, has since provided a basis for endless political debates. Did the New Deal extend and preserve the values of individualistic capitalism, as it claimed to do, or was it the entering wedge of an American collectivism, the first blueprint of a 'welfare state'?

The depression gave a distinct shock to American intellectual life. 'The climate', wrote the President of the Carnegie Foundation, 'changed from one of optimism to one of acute pessimism.' If the standards and values of the twenties no longer seemed valid in a time of social disintegration, a reexamination of the ideological foundations of modern America was in order.

First to be questioned was the cult of the practical and pragmatic, in religion, philosophy, education, and business life. Quite possibly, some thinkers concluded, a pragmatic test of ideas to live by, if it produced war and depression, was insufficient. F. S. C. Northrop, Thurman Arnold, and others attacked the 'pragmatic realism' of contemporary philosophy and found it lacking in direction. President Robert Hutchins of the University of Chicago inveighed against pragmatism and ethical relativism in education, calling for a return to the speculative spirit of the medieval university and condemning the 'service station' concept of American education. Catholic neo-scholastics, following the lead of Maritain and Gilson in France, regarded the rift between the intellectual and spiritual in contemporary society as productive of ethical insensitivity in social, political, and economic life. In Protestant theological circles a reaction set in against 'practical' religion. 'The middle-class paradise which we built', wrote Karl Barth, 'is in decay', and like the Catholic Thomists he and others censured 'socialized' religion as a confusion of secular and divine. Reinhold Niebuhr, the most influential of the Protestant theologians, reaffirmed in new terms the old Calvinist doctrine of original sin, preaching a twentieth-century return to orthodoxy.

In the churches themselves, nevertheless, the trend toward socialized religion continued. Despite the warnings of Barth, Niebuhr, and the Neo-Thomists, many clerics believed that depression demanded even greater participation by the Church in everyday life. The Federal Council of Churches' creed of 1932 went far beyond its original statement of 1908, asking for 'social planning and control of the credit and monetary systems and economic processes for the common good'. The Central Conference of Rabbis adopted a Programme of Social Justice, and Pope Pius XI urged stronger Catholic participation in reconstructing the social order. Attendance in all but the highly ritualistic churches, however, continued to decline, while a bewildering variety of new sects appeared. Jehovah's Witnesses and other fringe denominations grew in membership; the fantastic 'I AM' movement of the mid-thirties claimed a million members; Father Divine's New York 'peace heavens' filled with disciples who chanted 'Father Divine is God, is God, is God.' The Buchmanite or Oxford Group, founded by an American Lutheran in England, attracted a respectably large following among intellectuals, and Catholicism made numerous converts.

The doctrines of Karl Marx held a particular attraction during the depression years for rootless intellectuals, who searched not only for a solution to contemporary problems but for a centre of anti-fascist resistance. Marxist economic, social, historical, and aesthetic concepts were thoroughly explored by critics, writers, the 'little magazines', and *avant garde* political thinkers. The Bolshevik trials, the Hitler-Stalin pact, and the Russian invasion of Finland alienated numerous Marxist and Marxist sympathizers, convincing disenchanted artists and intellectuals of communism's unadaptibility to the American scene. Though the influence of Marxism in the United States was much less pervasive in the thirties than later investigators have assumed, interest in it contributed to a more careful reconsideration of contemporary problems in class relationships, economy, politics, and critical thought.

The rise of fascism was a matter of much deeper concern to the thinkers of the thirties. Some Americans returning from Europe voiced approval of the totalitarian methods of Hitler and Mussolini, although many were repelled by the anti-Semitic and anti-intellectual aspects of fascism. Native semi-fascist groups – the Bund, the Khaki Shirts, the Silver Shirts, the Crusaders – found encouragement in racist circles and even a few sincere thinkers expressed the belief that totalitarianism was perhaps a 'wave of the future' to which the United States must eventually adjust. Formal fascist organizations, however, attracted comparatively few members. The appeals of Huey Long of Louisiana for his 'Every Man a King' movement, and the Social Justice Crusade of Father Coughlin, a Detroit priest, aroused more enthusiasm. The slow recovery from hard times elicited a great deal of talk about the need for masculinity, discipline, and orderliness in American civilization, and evoked some popular admiration for the efficiency of totalitarian methods. Since neither Mussolini nor Hitler in the early and mid thirties seemed to pose a direct threat to American interests or security, the public in general remained largely indifferent to the spread of fascism in Europe.

To the creative artist, wrote Louis Adamic, the depression era was 'a time of transition and profound frustration . . .' The spectacle of economic collapse at home, plus communism and fascism abroad, aroused poets, novelists, dramatists, and critics to a re-examination of the native 'usable past'. The negativism and hedonism of the 'lost generation' disappeared in the depression. The novel in particular turned into a favourite vehicle of social criticism and protest in the early thirties. John Dos Passos' trilogy, *U.S.A.*, was a savage indictment of the whole drift of American society since the turn of the century. James T. Farrell drew a grimy picture of adolescent vice and frustration in Chicago; John Steinbeck, in a series of novels ending with *The Grapes of Wrath* (1939) took up the cause of migrant workers and displaced 'okies' in the Far West; Erskine Caldwell's *Tobacco Road* (1932) was a satiric handling of the Southern poor white. Proletarian novels and poems, in which aggressiveness of message often took precedence over art, appeared in profusion.

By the end of the decade, however, with the threat of fascism looming from abroad, many American artists turned their eyes homeward. Nationalism, frowned on by the writers of the twenties, became fashionable as World War II approached and Left Bank refugees fled from Europe. Expatriates, Marxists, and aesthetics, surveying the native tradition, discovered in it a set of values worth salvaging in an unstable world. One group of Southern critics and writers attacked the civilization of industrial America and urged authors to take their stand on the old aristocratic, pre-Civil War traditions of Southern life. MacLeish, Sandburg, and Benêt wrote unashamedly American poems; Dos Passos found strength and purpose in the democracy of eighteenth- and nineteenth-century America; William Faulkner launched on a long, complex study of his native South; Ernest Hemingway overcame his youthful distrust of positive ideas; Thomas Wolfe, in the manner of Whitman, found his inner life inextricably entangled with the soul of America. Among the critics, Van Wyck Brooks, mellowing with the years, began a glowing, multi-volumed reappraisal of the native literary tradition, while Vernon Louis Parrington traced the development of American ideas in aggressively Jeffersonian-Jacksonian terms. The socially-conscious novels of the early thirties faded before a new aestheticism which appeared in a resurgence of 'little magazines' and schools of 'new critics' who approached art in terms of its technical competence and the moral integrity of its ideas.

Painting, music, and architecture of later thirties and early forties were concerned chiefly with attempts to find a means of grafting European modernism on native roots. In painting Grant Wood, Thomas Hart Benton, and John Stuart Curry (all Midwesterners) led a regionalist movement away from European inspiration; New York artists, such as Ben Shahn and Stuart Davis, tended to follow international rather than regional trends. Classicism still dominated American public architecture, though the influence of the Finn Eliel Saarinen and the Frenchman Le Corbusier reinforced Frank Lloyd Wright in his lifelong battle for American modernism. In designing homes, American architects discovered (as the painters had) numerous regional styles – the Western ranch-house, the Southern plantation house, the Pennsylvania Dutch house, the Cape Cod house of New England – and tried to evolve from them architectural designs adaptable to modern tastes and needs.

Musically the United States reached maturity in the thirties. The great popularity of the radio made the public at large music-conscious, and symphony concerts, complete operas, and recitals by the best artists came into millions of homes at the turn of a dial. Music appeared more often in public school curricula, and civic orchestras provided free concerts in smaller communities. American singers and performers, capable of holding their own with European artists, began to appear on opera and concert stages. American composers like Aaron Copland, Roy Harris, Walter Piston, and Leonard Bernstein gained respect in their own right. Jazz, which lost its racial connotations in the twenties, flourished on records, radio, and in theatres. A few composers, notably Gershwin and Blitzstein, hoped to graft it with traditional music, but both classical and jazz purists protested against their efforts.

Roosevelt's terms as President coincided with a period of ruthless aggression in Europe and Asia, beginning with Japan's invasion of Manchuria in 1931 and ending with Japan's defeat in 1945. Before Roosevelt's second term was well started it was apparent that foreign affairs must take precedence over domestic. Yet the American political sys-

tem, both its parties and its institutions, were traditionally
so geared as to subordinate foreign to domestic policy.

The American reaction to European and Asian events of
1935-9 was an overwhelming desire for peace and neutrality.
The public regarded neither Hitler nor Mussolini as threats
to American security, and until the invasion of Poland and
shooting war, nothing in Europe seemed to impinge directly
on American affairs. Most Americans until 1941, the State
Department later reported, 'did not accept the thesis that
a European war could vitally affect the security of the
United States, or that an attack on the United States by any
of the Axis powers was possible'. Few Americans sympathized with German or Italian fascism, but at the same
time the majority regarded the problem of fascism as something for Germans and Italians to settle. Disillusioned with
memories of an earlier world war, fearful of entanglement in
another, protected by two oceans, Americans simply believed it best for the United States to stay away and
keep out. Congress, therefore, representing the drift of
public opinion, consistently favoured an isolationist, neutral
policy.

Roosevelt, Secretary of State Cordell Hull, and their
advisers were far ahead of the public in their thinking –
perhaps too much so. Roosevelt, after his 1935 warning that
Americans could not 'hide their heads in the sand', frequently reminded the nation of its stake in world security.
But his 'quarantine the aggressors' speech in Chicago in
1937 evoked such heated cries of 'warmonger' and 'hysterical internationalist' that he tempered his subsequent
warnings considerably. Since he had to campaign in 1936
and again in 1940, and the Democratic Congress faced re-
election in 1938, neither Roosevelt nor his party dared
proceed too fast or too far. Both Roosevelt and Hull were
internationally minded. Congress, particularly the Senate,
was not. Foreign policy thus became a tug-of-war between
the President and Congress after 1933, with Congress attempting to tie the Chief Executive's hands and Roosevelt
trying equally hard to free them.

Roosevelt and Hull hoped to discourage the fascist nations by improving machinery for collective security. As a step in this direction Roosevelt asked Congress in 1934 to pass the Reciprocal Trade Agreements Act to stimulate international trade with free countries by providing an expanding-contracting tariff. At almost the same time, as if in reply, Congress passed the Johnson Bill, forbidding loans to governments in default on previous debts, a direct slap at foreign financial entanglements. A year later Roosevelt and Hull urged greater collaboration with the League of Nations, asking American entry into the World Court. This the Senate refused. In 1933 the President requested legislation permitting embargoes on trade with aggressor nations. Congress instead moved in 1935 to establish embargoes on trade with, and prevent loans to, any belligerent nation. Roosevelt signed the Neutrality Act of 1935 with reluctance, pointing out that since it did not discriminate between aggressors and victims, it assured European dictators of American non-interference. Nor did the Act itself work well, since it applied only to actual implements of war and failed to prevent shipment of useful materials to Italy after its Ethiopian invasion. Congress nevertheless reaffirmed the Act in 1936 and 1937, and although both Roosevelt and Hull begged its reconsideration in early 1939, the Senate blocked its repeal.

The American reaction to the 'shooting war' of late 1939 was swift. Opinion was overwhelmingly sympathetic to the Allies, though most Americans hoped to avoid direct participation by serving as 'the arsenal of democracy'. With German militarism rampant in Europe, Congress revised the Neutrality Act to allow Britain and France to place huge military orders in the United States. But Under-Secretary of State Welles, after a trip abroad in January 1940, had a gloomy report to make; in both France and Britain morale was low, armaments short, preparations for war lagging. Later in the spring Germany overran Norway, Denmark, Holland, Belgium, and Luxembourg, cut across France to the Channel, nearly trapped the British and French at Dunkirk, and then turned toward Paris. Paris fell on 14 June, four days later Italy joined Germany, and the great air war on Britain began.

The fall of France was a tremendous shock to the United States. Americans suddenly realized that Japan, Germany, and Italy held control of Europe, Africa, and Asia (except for Russia) and that if Britain collapsed nothing remained between the United States and a totalitarian world. The nation faced the prospect of existing between the jaws of a nutcracker, never secure, always endangered, committed to a defensive, armed future. Answering cries for action, Roosevelt pledged swift rearmament, a bipartisan foreign policy, and immediate aid to Britain. Congress quickly appropriated funds to expand the army, navy, and air force, authorized millions in aid to the Allies, and in September 1940 passed the first peace-time conscription bill in American history. Roosevelt by executive order transferred fifty over-age destroyers to the hard-pressed British fleet in return for a string of Atlantic bases, sent rifles and surplus arms, tankers and cutters.

The presidential elections of 1940 came in the midst of pessimism and uncertainty, with Japan making threatening gestures in the Pacific, Europe nearly prostrate under the fascist heel, the Luftwaffe hammering at Britain. The single issue of the party conventions and the campaign was war. Republicans, sharply divided between isolationists and interventionists, chose Wendell Willkie, a dark horse corporation lawyer, after an extremely bitter convention-floor battle. Willkie's nomination represented an isolationist defeat, for he was in agreement with Roosevelt's foreign policy and repeatedly said so. The Democrats re-nominated Roosevelt for a precedent-shattering third term, with Henry Wallace of Iowa second on the ticket. Since both party candidates saw eye-to-eye on foreign policy, it was hard to find clear-cut issues in the campaign. Roosevelt won handily, carrying thirty-eight states, but Willkie polled more votes than any other Republican candidate up to that time.

After the 1940 election the split between isolationist and internationalist emerged more sharply than ever. Willkie, after the election, openly threw his weight to Roosevelt and Hull, who believed that American involvement in the war on the side of the Allies was inevitable, and in case of further Axis victories, desirable; Frank Knox and Henry Stimson, both Republican appointees in Roosevelt's cabinet, agreed. A number of prominent men in political and private life, determined to keep the United States out of any war, believed that the Rooseveltian policy of 'aid to the Allies short of war' would assuredly drag the nation into it. Britain and France, they were convinced, were bound to lose, and the United States must not waste materials and money on a lost cause. America could live in peace with victorious fascist nations, whose aggressive intent had been, they thought, grossly exaggerated; living in a fascist-controlled world, in Herbert Hoover's opinion, 'would not be pleasant but it could be done'. In Congress Senator Robert Taft of Ohio and Senator Burton Wheeler of Montana led the opposition to Roosevelt's and Hull's foreign policy, while outside Congress Colonel Charles A. Lindbergh and Colonel Robert McCormick (publisher of the Chicago *Tribune*) gained wide support for the isolationists.

Roosevelt, however, consistently pushed his 'aid to the Allies' plan. In 1941 he suggested that a 'lend-lease' programme, instead of the old 'cash and carry' system, be instituted in the purchase and shipment of arms abroad. This set off the most violent debate of the year. Opposed by potent isolationist forces in and out of Congress, and particularly by the powerful America First Committee, the Lend-lease plan consumed weeks of discussion before it finally passed Congress. 'Approval of this legislation,' said Senator Wheeler, 'means war, open and complete war. I therefore ask the American people before they supinely accept it, Was the last World War worthwhile?' Lend-lease also elicited Roosevelt's famous 'Four Freedoms' speech, outlining, as Wilson had with his Fourteen Points, America's aim in aiding the Allies – to insure in the post-war world freedom of speech, freedom of religion, freedom from want, and freedom from fear.

Lend-lease helped the Allies, but not enough to forestall a German invasion of Middle Europe and the Balkans or an Italian conquest of Greece and North Africa. In June 1941 the United States froze Axis assets, closed Axis consulates in the United States, and Germany launched its attack on Russia. Extension of the lend-lease programme to Russia again precipitated protest, but since it was clear to the isolationists that a Russian defeat, however desirable, would serve only to increase the Axis threat to America, Congress voted to include the Soviet Union.

From June to December 1941 the record of American foreign policy was filled with un-neutral acts. In August Roosevelt and Churchill met on shipboard to prepare and sign the Atlantic Charter, a programme for world security after 'the final destruction of Nazi tyranny', thus placing the United States in the unique position of a neutral co-signer with a belligerent to a statement whose avowed purpose was the defeat of another belligerent. American destroyers patrolling the North Atlantic were frequently fired on by German submarines, and frequently fired back. After two destroyers and several merchant ships were lost, the Senate and the House agreed to revise the Neutrality Acts to arm merchant ships and to allow them to enter combat zones. Undoubtedly, by the autumn of 1941 the United States was engaged in an undeclared war with Germany. Though there was still hopeful talk of 'aid short of war', it was merely a question of time. Japan cut the time short.

Neither the United States nor the League of Nations had effectively opposed Japanese aggression in the Pacific since 1931. The Japanese Army seized Manchuria in the early thirties, and swept through China toward the East Indies while the United States and Europe were occupied with their own problems. Though Hoover denounced Japanese conquests, he also pointed out that so long as the Japanese committed acts which 'do not imperil the freedom of the American people', the United States would refrain from decisive action. Nor was Congress willing to apply pressure on Japan. Even after Japan's announcement of the 'New

Order' in Asia (which the United States officially refused to recognize) American opinion was still overwhelmingly neutral.

German and Italian successes impressed Japan's military leaders, and in September 1940 the three powers signed a military pact obviously aimed at the United States. Both Roosevelt and Hull, well aware of American unpreparedness, for the next eighteen months followed a careful course designed to gain time. By spring of 1941 Japan's Foreign Minister Matsuoka, convinced of imminent Axis victory in Europe, set his nation in motion for war. Prince Konoye, the leader of the peace party, was replaced by the bellicose Tojo, and on 25 November a Japanese naval task force, well briefed and well prepared, sailed for Pearl Harbor, Hawaii, the base of the United States Pacific Fleet. On 6 December Roosevelt sent a personal appeal for peace to Emperor Hirohito, a message intercepted and suppressed by the Japanese Army. On 7 December the Japanese surprise attack hit Pearl Harbor, almost completely shattering the base. Simultaneously an attack on the Philippines neutralized General MacArthur's air force, and three days later the British lost two battleships off Malaya. Japan, the master of the Pacific, could land its armies practically at will wherever it chose. The United States declared war on Japan on 8 December. Germany and Italy, fulfilling their bargain with Japan, declared war on the United States on 11 December.

Pearl Harbor resolved in an hour the dilemma the American people had faced since 1939. The nation suddenly realized that it could not have peace and an Axis defeat at the same time. Since 1939 the United States had been a limited belligerent, true, but the Rooseveltian policy of partial participation did not of itself lead to final involvement in the war. The United States, as in 1917, was neither forced nor manœuvred into war; it entered the war because it could not stay out. If America, from 1939 to 1941, had appeased the dictators, refused to lend its moral weight and its industrial might to the Allies, abandoned the European democracies and the Philippines, Pearl Harbor need not have happened. But the alternative – existence as an armed island, between the Rising Sun and the Swastika – was one the nation could not choose.

The strategy agreed upon by the Allies was based on two decisions: first, to defeat Germany while containing Japan; and second, to co-ordinate and unify all Allied economic, political, military, and diplomatic policies. In the opening phases of the war the United States, a late entry, was committed to a defensive strategy, its power in the Pacific damaged, its huge industrial potential only partially mobilized. Before it could shift to the offensive the nation had to organize and equip itself as swiftly as possible for a war in which its opponents already possessed the initiative.

The pattern of mobilization followed fairly closely that of World War I. The Office of War Mobilization, headed by James F. Byrnes, held the responsibility of working with the Army and Navy Departments to insure co-ordinated effort. The War Production Board, established in 1942 as the successor to the National Defense Advisory Commission, supervised the task of converting industry to a war-time basis, while the Defense Plant Corporation, a subsidiary of the R.F.C., planned and built government-owned war plants. By 1943 60 per cent of American industry had been completely converted to war production, with a capacity at least equal to the combined total of the Axis powers. The Office of Civilian Defense trained air-raid wardens, auxiliary firemen and police, plane spotters, and emergency medical personnel. The Office of War Information handled news at home and propaganda abroad.

The wartime agencies that had most far-reaching effects on the daily life of the average American, however, were those directed by the Office of Economic Stabilization. The War Manpower Commission, which controlled both Selective Service and industrial employment, touched the destinies of nearly every American family. The Office of Price Administration established rent ceilings, rationed food, fixed prices, and battled with black markets, sometimes against strenuous opposition. The Office of Defense Transportation supervised nearly all public transportation; railroads, unlike the practice of World War I, remained in private hands subject to O.D.T. control. The War Labor Board, created to arbitrate in strikes and grievances, kept labour-management friction at a minimum; the most serious strikes were those of the United Mine Workers in 1943 and 1945. To finance the cost of the war, which was about four times that of World War I, Congress increased excise and income taxes sufficiently to cover 46 per cent of expenditures. The balance was raised by the sale of interest-bearing bonds to private investors, also a useful anti-inflation device for absorbing excess spending power.

In 1941 the United States, as General Arnold expressed it, held two advantages – the distance of oceans and precious time contributed by British and French resistance. Japan held virtually complete control of the Pacific, with China cut off from aid, India menaced, the Philippines, Singapore, and the strategic Pacific islands in Japanese hands. The problem of prosecuting even a defensive Pacific war was primarily one of supply, with 2,000 miles of sea between American industry and the fighting front. Under-manned British, Australian, New Zealand, Dutch, and American forces fought savagely to hold their lines, and in the Solomons campaigns of 1942 they checked the Japanese advance for the first time.

The Battle of the Coral Sea and the Battle of Midway broke Japan's naval superiority in the Pacific. In late 1942 and early 1943 United States Marine and naval forces began an offensive on Guadalcanal, turned back a Japanese counter-attack in New Guinea, and after six months of hard fighting consolidated strong positions in the islands. Australian, New Zealand, and American forces then began an island-hopping movement, sealing off or by-passing Japanese-held bases while their planes hammered at Japanese supply lines. By the end of 1943 the Allies, holding both sea and air supremacy, had evolved a long-range strategy – land forces under MacArthur were to advance along the New

Guinea coast and eventually into the Philippines, while naval forces under Admiral Nimitz moved along the island chains toward Japan, establishing bomber bases for attacks on Japanese-held territory and on Japan itself.

Following these plans, landing forces began penetration of the Marshalls and the Mariannas, taking Saipan, Guam, and neutralizing the huge base at Truk while MacArthur's forces pushed into New Guinea. By the autumn of 1944 Allied planes were over the Philippines. In October assault boats landed at Leyte, and the United States Fleet, by defeating the Imperial Navy at the Battle of Leyte Gulf, virtually drove the Japanese from Philippine waters. American troops landed on the Philippine island of Luzon in late 1944 and in February 1945 took Manila. The fall of Iwo Jima the same month provided a new base for air strikes at Japan, and by spring the Allies had control of the air over Formosa and the China coast. Other landings at Okinawa placed Allied planes within 300 miles of the Japanese homeland. Throughout 1944 Chinese, British, Indian, Australian, and American troops fought in Burma, hoping to open a supply line into China. British troops took Rangoon and Mandalay in 1945, and the Burma Road, hacked out of the jungle, opened a China route, though the war ended before the Chinese could be sufficiently trained and equipped to play an offensive part in the conflict.

Experimental atomic fission was achieved by European scientists before the War. British and American physicists began serious work in nuclear fission in 1939, while the fascist governments of Germany and Italy drove out several key scientists (among them Albert Einstein, Lise Meitner, and Enrico Fermi) who carried into exile valuable information and priceless research skills. Roosevelt in 1939 appointed an advisory committee on uranium, and in 1940 placed the committee under the jurisdiction of the National Defense Research Council, In the autumn of 1941 it was suggested that the United States, Britain, and Canada pool resources. This was done, and when the project reached the production stage it was placed under the control of the

United States Army and charged with the manufacture of an atomic weapon. After the expenditure of some 2,000 million dollars, the first atomic bomb was exploded at Alamagordo, New Mexico, on 16 July 1945.

A division of opinion existed from the first over the use of atomic weapons in warfare. The German surrender of May 1945 left Japan the sole enemy, and proponents of the bomb pointed out that a successful invasion of the Japanese homeland might cost between one and two million lives. On the other hand, many condemned a mass slaughter of civilians as the sort of barbarism the United Nations fought against, claiming that Japan, already under heavy air attack, was virtually at the point of surrender. A possible quick ending of the war, however, weighed heavily in the considerations of President Truman and his advisers, and the decision to use the bomb, concurred in by Churchill, was unanimous.

On 6 August 1945 a single Air Force B-29 dropped an atomic bomb on Hiroshima, leaving 128,000 dead, missing, and injured. Three days later another dropped on Nagasaki, one day after Russia, completing its Yalta pledge, declared war on Japan. On 10 August Japan asked for peace, and the next day the American Secretary of State, acting on behalf of the Allies, submitted surrender terms. Japan surrendered on 14 August, signing the final peace on 2 September.

Adolf Hitler, in December 1941, believed that the entrance of the United States into the war came too late to save Britain and France from defeat. The United States, however, was better organized for war than in 1917, its productive capacity expanded by lend-lease, its Navy at wartime strength, one and a half million men in training under the conscription laws of 1940 and 1941. By June 1942 there were sufficient ground troops in Europe to justify formation of an American command under General Eisenhower, while American planes in increasing numbers operated with the Royal Air Force from England. In 1942 and early 1943 the British were able to clear North Africa, and in June an Anglo-American force invaded Sicily. The great invasion of Italy, beginning in September 1943, led to the capture of

Rome in early 1944, after which an Allied army of various elements began the slow, bloody advance up the Italian boot.

After the German attacks of 1941 and 1942 dashed themselves to pieces on stubborn Russian resistance, Roosevelt, Churchill, and Stalin met at Cairo and Teheran to plan a general offensive. In July of 1943 the Russians began a two-month advance, while air strikes from Britain seriously damaged German war production. As part of the combined offensive strategy, Allied forces invaded France on 6 June 1944, landing in Normandy and securing the port of Cherbourg. German lines of defence and communication in France crumbled swiftly, and by August the German army was fighting desperately along the Seine. That same month the American Seventh Army landed in Southern France and began a swift slash up the Rhone Valley. With the fall of Paris a few days later, all invading Allied forces joined facing the German frontier, ready to begin a series of co-ordinated drives.

By early 1945 Hitler's armies were hopelessly caught between the Russians, advancing towards Berlin from the north-east, and the British, French, and Americans, from the south-west. By March the Russians were within thirty miles of Berlin, the Allies crossing the Rhine. German troops in Italy and Austria surrendered, and on 2 May Berlin fell. Five days later the German army made its unconditional surrender.

The impact of World War II on American foreign relations was much greater than that of World War I. In the Second World War the United States from the first committed itself more completely to international collaboration than ever before in its history. During the war and after it, the nation faced point-blank (as it had in 1920) the problem of world-wide collective security, and there is no evidence to show that either the government or the public shirked a decision. Throughout the war the American government worked closely with the Allies and with the heads of anti-Axis states, compiling an unprecedented record of international co-operation at Casablanca, Quebec, Moscow, Cairo, Teheran, Bretton Woods, Dumbarton Oaks, Yalta, and Potsdam. The Senate, traditionally an isolationist stronghold, in 1943 pledged the United States to join 'an international authority with power to prevent aggression and to preserve the peace of the world'. In April 1945, a few days after Roosevelt's death, the United Nations met in San Francisco to complete its organization with full American support, and in July the Senate ratified the U.N. Charter by a vote of 89 to 2, marking the end of a long isolationist road. 'Let us not hesitate', said Truman in words both Wilson and Roosevelt would have approved, 'to join hands with the peace-loving nations of the earth . . .'

Almost as soon as the Peace of Potsdam was signed, however, some of the first flush of internationalist enthusiasm died away. The chief difficulty was Russia, a nation the United States had steadily avoided since 1919. The wartime alliance of America and the Soviet Union was uneasy, and Roosevelt bent every effort during the war to win the confidence of Russian leaders. At Yalta in 1945 he agreed to a great-power veto in the U.N. Security Council, Russian annexation of East Poland, Polish annexations of German territory, and Russian dominance in Yugoslavia and Manchuria. In addition, Yalta established the controversial partition of Germany into four military zones, and the four-power control of Berlin. Roosevelt contended that he could not have prevented these concessions, and it is true that he did receive in return a Russian pledge to enter the war against Japan and promises of post-war co-operation.

Russia's post-war policies were hardly designed to inspire confidence in her one-time allies. Friendly relations between the U.S. and the U.S.S.R. swiftly deteriorated, beginning with Russian violations of the Yalta agreements concerning Poland and Romania. The rush of Russian communism into the power vacuum left by the collapse of Germany and Japan, and the rise of communist influence in France and Italy, excited apprehension in American diplomatic circles.

At the Potsdam peace talks of 1946 Truman and Secretary of State Byrnes concluded that it was hopeless to expect further Russian concessions and that Russia intended to prolong post-war chaos as long as possible. With British and French support, the United States announced a 'get tough' attitude toward Russia. The Truman Doctrine of 1947 committed the United States to a policy of containment of Russian expansion, and to a policy of alliance with the remaining democratic and anti-communist nations, including some strange bedfellows such as Franco's Spain, Tito's Yugoslavia, and Perón's Argentina.

Under the terms of the Truman Doctrine the United States poured money into Greece and Turkey, while the 'Marshall Plan', or European Recovery Programme, budgeted 5,000 million dollars a year to anti-communist nations. In addition, in 1949 the United States signed the North Atlantic Pact, an eleven-nation alliance aimed directly at Russia; 'armed attack against one or more' of the member countries was to be 'considered an attack against them all'. The Russian counter-move to the Truman Doctrine was the establishment of the new Cominform at Warsaw in 1947, and of an Economic Mutual Assistance pact involving Russia and her satellite neighbours. Meanwhile, arguments over the interpretations of the Potsdam agreements caused increasing friction between Russia and the Allies in Germany. In protest against announced plans to set up a West German state, the Soviet ordered a blockade of Berlin in June 1948, and released it only after Britain, France, and the United States supplied the city by air for nearly a year. Nevertheless, the West German state came into existence in 1949, with Russia immediately countering by creating the German Democratic Republic in its own zone of control.

The United States and Russia met again head-on in the Far East. At Yalta Stalin agreed to enter the war against Japan within three months of a German surrender, a promise kept to the day. Japan, however, was on the brink of defeat, and the United States refused to allow either

Russia or China, whose contributions to the Pacific war were negligible, to share in more than an advisory capacity in the post-war control of Japan. After some discussion General Douglas MacArthur was designated as Supreme Allied Commander of the Far East, supported by a four-power council of representatives from the United States, Russia, Great Britain, and China. The United States, however, clearly dominated the council.

Until the end of 1946 MacArthur pursued a policy of liberal reform in Japan, whose new government was modelled closely on Britain's. By 1947, however, growing tension between the United States and Russia emphasized Japan's usefulness to the United States as an economic and military outpost against Soviet expansion. The Japanese government swung perceptibly to the right, the reform policies disappeared, and Japan began rearming under the terms of the peace treaty drawn up in 1951.

When the Japanese surrendered in August 1945, the Chinese Nationalist forces of Chiang Kai-shek and the Chinese Communist armies began a race for possession of the coastal areas and Manchuria. The United States did everything in its power to help Chiang, while the Communists received aid from Russia. After intensified fighting between Nationalist and Communist armies, President Truman in 1945 sent General George Marshall to China to attempt mediation. Marshall succeeded in arranging a brief truce, but in thirteen months of negotiation got nowhere in adjusting differences between the warring groups. On his return he advocated withdrawal of support to Chiang, a recommendation Congress refused to follow. Though the United States subsequently sent between two and four thousand million dollars' worth of aid to China, the Nationalist government steadily lost support and territory.

In 1949 and 1950 the Communists, sweeping through the coastal cities, drove Chiang's armies to Hainan and finally to Formosa, where they most certainly would have been trapped had it not been for American intervention. The Washington government, following the Truman Doctrine, declared Formosa vital to American Far Eastern defence and ordered the United States Navy to protect it from Communist invasion. The outbreak of war in Korea and the subsequent entry of Chinese Communists into it transferred the Chinese problem elsewhere.

World War II's experiences served to increase American interest in Central and South America. After 1941 the 'good neighbour' policy became something more than an expression of good will; hemispheric solidarity, American diplomats recognized, was a matter of political and military necessity. Widespread pro-Naziism, in Brazil and Argentina, both with large German populations, led the State Department to make a sincere though belated courtship of South America, including the announcement that the United States was ready to lend seventy million a month to needy Latin American nations. The Act of Chapultepec, signed shortly before the San Francisco U.N. Conference, reaffirmed but modified the Monroe Doctrine. Instead of viewing hemispheric protection as the unilateral responsibility of the United States, it defined an attack on any American nation as an attack on all, and pledged all to joint responsibility for the common defence.

The Chapultepec agreement, however, did not settle all hemispheric differences. American tariff barriers against South American grain and meat were long-standing causes of friction, especially with Argentina, whose dictator-president, Colonal Juan Perón, was a consistent, clear, and open antagonist of 'Yankee imperialism'. Post-war economic adjustments with Argentina lessened tension appreciably. Though recognizing distinctly the totalitarian nature of Perón's regime, the State Department carefully worked out compromises that modified, at least, some of its anti-American bias.

Meanwhile, Soviet-American conflict in the United Nations continued. The U.S.S.R., with a minority of U.N. support, used its veto freely to block action, even on minor matters; the United States, with majority support, sometimes forced decisions on questions the Russians were sure to veto. The Soviet representatives, however, were far more guilty of disrupting U.N. efforts to keep peace and encourage unity, often creating ill-feeling and disharmony in areas where none need exist. The titanic struggle for dominance in its councils has hampered U.N. efforts severely since 1946, and will continue to do so so long as the United States and the Soviet Union collide in foreign policy.

The effect of World War II on internal affairs in the United States has been extremely far-reaching. Even more than in World War I mobilization extended the power of the Federal government over every segment of American society, with the result that the historic issue of states' rights versus federalism became the most hotly-discussed political question of the post-war years. Public opinion, as expressed in every election since 1944, has been divided on the issue. The American people, if their voting records provide any indication, want freedom of choice and open economic competition without undue federal interference; at the same time they want federal protection against inflation, price drops, unemployment, depression, social and economic dislocation. In effect, post-war America is moving toward a modified capitalism, with insurance against capitalism's risks as well as opportunity to enjoy its benefits. The current political problem is to find a reasonable balance between extremes of federalism and decentralization.

Socially the war marked a great forward step for racial and nationality minority groups, with the Negro making the greatest stride of all. A major population shift, beginning in 1919, placed 20 per cent of the American Negro population in the cities of the North and West by 1940. Serious racial tensions developed, and minor race riots occurred during the war years, culminating in a particularly violent outbreak in Detroit in 1943. Yet despite white-Negro friction, the Negro made distinct social and economic progress under wartime conditions. Industry, faced with an unprecedented demand for labour, opened doors previously shut to black men and women; the C.I.O. and the A.F.L., which had long before adopted bi-racial policies, brought Negro workers by thousands into the labour unions. Beginning in 1932 the Negro voter shifted his allegiance to the Democratic party and under the New Deal programme gained a great deal of political power. Since 1930 the number of Negro voters has increased from 200,000 to 1,100,000. In a number of cities their vote is a decisive factor, and Negroes hold many elective offices as well as other positions of civic responsibility in North and South.

Roosevelt in 1941 forbade racial or religious discrimination in employment and appointed a Fair Employment Practices Commission to enforce his order, a practice copied in several Northern states. The Supreme Court during the forties upheld the right of Negroes to sit on juries, vote in primary elections, and to receive equal educational facilities. Truman's civil rights programme, recommended to Congress in 1948, failed against strong Southern opposition, but Southern states themselves recognized their responsibility to the Negro and began to modify old 'jim crow' laws and customs. 'White supremacy' in America is by no means dead, but on the racial issue the South is no longer so solid as it was before World War II.

The American record toward minority groups in the Second World War was an improvement over that of World War I, except for the treatment of Japanese nationals and Japanese-Americans. Feeling against the Japanese after Pearl Harbor was intense and unselective, and Nisei, or American-born Japanese, of whom the West Coast had many, bore the brunt of war-time intolerance. As a measure of military security 100,000 men, women, and children of Japanese descent were evacuated from the Pacific Coast states to relocation camps in the interior, sometimes under conditions of extreme hardship. Long-smouldering racial hatred, stemming from economic rivalry between Japanese and white agricultural and business interests in the West, led to talk of permanently expelling Japanese from the area. After the war, however, most Japanese returned to their homes and businesses without appreciable difficulty.

The most striking consequence of the war on public

opinion was a tremendous surge of anti-communist, anti-Russian feeling, intensified by the breakdown of Soviet-American relations in 1946 and by the outbreak of the Korean war. The existence of a tightly-controlled, Soviet-directed Communist party in the United States, at a time when the United States and Russia were engaged in conflict over world leadership, posed a national dilemma. The United States was firmly committed to anti-totalitarianism, and revered its tradition of free thought and free expression. How far should restrictions on Communist or quasi-Communist activity go? How far might the accepted principle of 'free trade in ideas' be safely followed? The problem of establishing internal security while protecting civil liberty had troubled the nation before – in the days of the Alien and Sedition Acts, in the abolitionist controversy, in the Civil War, in World War I – but the 'red scares' of 1919 and 1920 seemed destined to be repeated in virulent form, aided by a favourable press.

The Smith Act of 1940 made it a crime to advocate the forcible overthrow of any United States government, to disseminate such doctrines in printed form, or to belong to any organization that advocated such action. The Federal Bureau of Investigation, an agency of the Justice Department, was granted broader powers to deal with espionage and subversion in 1945. Politicians found anti-Communism an attractive vote-getting device, and members of Congress and of state legislatures, beginning in 1947, asked for 'loyalty oaths' among civil service employees, teachers, and government officials. Congressional and legislative committees probed labour unions, government agencies, schools, universities, the movies, and publishing houses for evidences of Communist infiltration, sometimes harrying suspects without proper regard for process of law or traditional civil rights.

The facts behind the 'red scare' were foreboding enough – Russian successes in eastern Europe and China, the Berlin blockade, Russian obstructionism in the U.N., discovery of Communist espionage in atomic research in Canada and

England, the conviction of Alger Hiss, a respected State Department official, for perjury. Yet the facts were never sufficient to account for the hysteria that struck the public during the period 1947 to 1952, nor for the toleration by the public and the press of frequent abuses of civil rights in the search for subversives. The culmination of anti-Red political activities came after 1950 with the work of Senator Joseph McCarthy, who made widespread charges (usually under senatorial immunity from suit) against private citizens and government officials. In the midst of the furore Justice Jackson of the Supreme Court ruled in 1950 that the Communist Party was a conspiracy rather than a political party, and a mounting number of legal decisions agreed. Local and state laws outlawing the Communist Party appeared in many states, some upheld, some disallowed by the higher courts. In 1950 Congress passed the controversial Internal Security (McCarran) Act over Truman's veto, making it unlawful to conspire to establish a totalitarian dictatorship such as a communist state.

The presidential elections of 1944 came as the tide of war turned in the Allies' favour. Roosevelt, ill and worn, was reluctant to run for a fourth term, but since there seemed to be no one to replace him he quickly accepted the Democratic nomination. Henry Wallace of Iowa, vice-president since 1940, impressed the party leaders as too unstable for another term, and at the convention the choice for second place fell to Senator Harry Truman of Missouri. The Republican National Committee eliminated Taft and Willkie (he was not even invited to speak at the convention) in favour of Thomas Dewey, whose record as a 'gang-busting' district attorney and as governor of New York made his name known the nation over.

The campaign was a lively one. Roosevelt made only a few public appearances, but Dewey launched an aggressive attack against the New Deal as a quarrelsome, inefficient bureaucracy of 'tired old men', promising instead a youthful, energetic administration. The momentum of war and New Deal reform carried Roosevelt through. His electoral majority, though large, did not accurately reflect his smaller popular majority of three and a half million. Much of his strength lay in the urban vote and in the support given to him by the unions through the C.I.O. Political Action Committee, founded in 1944. A few months after his inauguration Roosevelt was dead, the New Deal and the prosecution of the war in Truman's hands.

Harry Truman, a product of Missouri machine politics, was a politician from the ground up, stubbornly loyal to his party, his friends, and his benefactors. Sent to the Senate by powerful Kansas City bosses, he had a comparatively undistinguished record before he was placed on the national ticket as the only eligible Midwestern Democrat. A humble, sincere man, apprehensive at the responsibilities suddenly thrust upon him, he pledged an unflagging devotion to Roosevelt's principles and to the continuance of the New Deal.

Truman's path was a hard one. He inherited a dragging war, a sudden peace, and a recalcitrant Congress. Politically he stood somewhat to the right of Roosevelt, and after a series of wrangles New Deal appointees left his administration in droves, Wallace, Byrnes, Ickes, and others. The end of the war brought popular demands to make peace quickly, drop price and wage controls, 'bring the boys home', and return life to normal as swiftly as possible. The spread of post-war inflation surged upward, and a plague of strikes and work stoppages struck industry. Truman's uncertain approach to post-war problems seemed to stamp him as an ineffective successor to the self-confident Roosevelt.

The Republicans in Congress took advantage of Truman's inexperience, mangling most of his proposals beyond recognition and blocking others. Congressional leadership on domestic issues fell to Senator Robert Taft of Ohio, Republican foreign policy to Senator Arthur Vandenberg of Michigan. Taft, a President's son already known as 'Mr Republican', was a deeply isolationist conservative opposed to almost anything smacking of the New Deal. Vandenberg, an isolationist turned internationalist, was a broader and more flexible man whose foreign policy resembled Roosevelt's and Truman's. The resurgence of the Republican party began in the congressional elections of 1946, which returned a Republican majority to Washington for the first time since 1928.

The struggle between Truman and Congress after 1946 occupied the remainder of Truman's term. Following Vandenberg's advice, Congress accepted the Truman Doctrine and the Marshall Plan, but Old Guard Republicans, skilfully led by Taft, won most of the rounds on domestic issues. A wave of strikes in 1946 and 1947, with John L. Lewis' United Mine Workers leading the way, convinced a good many Congressmen that uncontrolled labour was as dangerous to economic stability as uncontrolled management. The Taft-Hartley Act of 1947 therefore established curbs on union powers, banned the closed shop, authorized injunctions in jurisdictional strikes, required union financial statements, demanded non-Communist affidavits of union officials, and outlawed certain types of strikes. Unions attacked it vehemently (although admitting the validity of some of its provisions), Truman vetoed it, and Congress passed it over his veto. Both the C.I.O.-P.A.C. and the A.F.L.-P.A.C. entered the 1948 elections with the act as their major target.

Taft was the organization's choice for nomination at the Republican convention of 1948, but Dewey, despite his loss in 1944, remained the popular idol. Dewey won the nomination, and started a slashing, confident campaign. New Dealers in the Democratic party would have preferred to jettison Truman (there was talk of drafting General Dwight Eisenhower, then president of Columbia University) but no one could agree on a substitute. An unenthusiastic convention nominated Truman, while the Northern wing of the party rammed home a sweepingly liberal platform, including a strong civil rights plank that immediately alienated the race-conscious South. Dissident Southern Democrats formed a States' Rights (Dixiecrat) party and nominated Governor J. Strom Thurmond of South Carolina.

The Progressive Party, a Communist-liberal coalition, ran Henry Wallace on a platform reaffirming the New Deal and advocating co-operation with Russia.

Republicans, viewing the split in the Democratic party and basking in the favour of an almost uniformly anti-Truman press, approached election day with supreme self-confidence. All public opinion polls gave Dewey a decided edge, and even Democrats privately admitted that Truman had no chance. But Truman refused to give up. His battles with Congress had forced him to liberalize his political thinking, sharpen up his political techniques, and evolve a positive programme of his own. He called Congress into special session, offered his programme, and when the Republican majority defeated it he took to the road on a 'whistle-stop' tour of the nation. Flaying the 'do-nothing' Congress in hamlets and cities, evoking admiring cries of 'Give 'em hell, Harry!' Truman turned into a forceful, rough-and-tumble political leader of real appeal. The election, a shattering upset, surprised everyone but Truman. Thurmond took four states, Wallace none, Dewey sixteen, and Truman the rest, though his margin of victory was less than two million votes out of forty-nine million cast.

Truman's Fair Deal programme, the centre of controversy during his second term, was born in his speech to Congress in January 1949. By a 'fair deal,' he said, he meant the realization of 'the promise of equal rights and equal opportunities which the founders of our Republic proclaimed'. His programme had a familiar ring, since it comprised most of the unfinished business of his first term plus national health legislation – a civil rights bill, repeal of the Taft-Hartley Act, public housing, farm subsidies, price and wage controls, more T.V.A.-type power projects. The Fair Deal involved a greater extension of Federal authority and responsibility than even Roosevelt had asked, leading to Republican cries of 'socialist', 'welfare state', or as Hoover called it, 'a disguise for the totalitarian state'. After 1949 this accusation became one of the most effective Republican political weapons.

Truman's victory was no landslide, and the Democrats, lacking a genuine mandate from the voters, fell on the defensive. The Republicans, denied a term of office to which they felt entitled, fell into the role of an irreconcilable opposition. Nor did Truman control Congress. Anti-Truman Democrats, chiefly from the South, frequently joined Republicans to block Fair Deal legislation, and after the 1950 elections reduced the Democratic majority to the vanishing point Truman was virtually helpless. Most of the Fair Deal went down the drain, although he did succeed in passing through Congress a boost in the minimum wage law, some public housing, and extended coverage under the Social Security Act. In his foreign policy, until 1950, Truman fared somewhat better. Congress expanded the European Recovery Programme, ratified the North Atlantic Treaty, and gave the President power to revise tariffs under the Reciprocal Trade Agreements Act.

Determined to avoid Wilson's error, Roosevelt in 1940 had proclaimed a bipartisan foreign policy, consulted with Republican leaders on major decisions, and placed prominent Republicans in his cabinet. So long as Vandenberg remained in charge of Republican foreign policy this worked well, but after the Michigan Senator's illness removed him from an active role in Senate affairs (he died in 1951) bipartisanship broke down. After 1950 Congressional Republicans made increasingly bitter denunciations of Truman and his Secretary of State, Dean Acheson, and showed a marked reluctance to continue in the Vandenberg tradition. By 1951 the attack on Truman and Acheson involved five major criticisms: alleged softness toward Russia, blundering in China and in the U.N., failure to force European unity against Russia, waste in foreign aid, and Communist (or semi-Communist) infiltration of government agencies. After the beginning of the Korean conflict the Truman-Acheson foreign policy became the most important single political issue.

Well before the close of World War II the Soviet Union, China, Great Britain, and the United States agreed to

Korean independence after Japan's defeat. By an agreement presumably made at Yalta, the thirty-eighth Korean parallel became the dividing line of responsibility, Russia to control the north, the United States and other nations the south. In South Korea, after internal flare-ups between Korean conservatives and radicals, the United States created the Republic of Korea and held elections in 1946, with the result that Syngman Rhee and the rightist elements gained control of the government. Both the United States and Russia discussed a merger of the two zones, but since each wanted the merger under a government friendly to itself, no decision could be reached. An open election, the United States believed, would create a pro-American government; Russia evidently agreed, and hoping that the removal of foreign forces might assist a successful Communist coup, suggested withdrawal of all troops from both zones. Both sides began training and arming Koreans in preparation for the eventual withdrawal, the U.S.S.R. arming North Koreans better and faster. Russia recalled its forces in early 1948, the United States following six months after.

On 24 June 1950 North Korean army units crossed the thirty-eighth parallel in a drive toward the Korean capital of Seoul, announcing that they came to liberate South Korea from the rule of Rhee and unify all Korea. While the South Korean army rapidly dissolved, the United States at Secretary Acheson's behest introduced into the United Nations Security Council a resolution calling on the North Koreans to withdraw. Meanwhile President Truman ordered General MacArthur, the Supreme Allied Commander in Tokyo, to send air and sea forces into Korea, with ground troops to follow, an action, said Truman, 'taken as a matter of basic moral principle'. With Russia and its veto absent, the Security Council approved a resolution that all U.N. members furnish military aid to the South Korean Republic, asking unity of command under American auspices and designating MacArthur as Commander-in-Chief of the U.N. forces. Congress, supporting the Council, extended the draft, increased taxes, and speeded up armament production.

The R.O.K. army, however, lost ground rapidly to the well-trained North Koreans, until the combined South Korean and U.N. troops held only a small area about Pusan. MacArthur mounted an offensive in the summer of 1950 that drove the North Koreans back across the thirty-eighth parallel and by November had them pinned against the Manchurian border. In that month Chinese Communist troops from Manchuria appeared in North Korean lines. On 24 November MacArthur ordered American units to attack Chinese positions. The counter-attack that followed drove the outnumbered U.N. armies back to the thirty-eighth parallel, where their lines held.

The entrance of Communist China into the Korean conflict on a 'volunteer' basis created a distinct difference of opinion between MacArthur and Truman over the conduct of the war. Truman, convinced that Russia and not China was the real antagonist, favoured treating Korea as a holding action, committing only a portion of American strength to checking the Chinese while building up anti-Russia strength in European and other Far Eastern danger spots. Under no circumstances, he and his advisers believed, should the Korean action be allowed to develop into a full-scale war against China, leaving Russia free to continue its advance across Europe and the Middle East.

MacArthur, seeing sweeping victories denied him, voiced his disapproval of the plan determined by his superiors. He made an unauthorized truce offer to China, with the implied threat of extending the war to the Chinese mainland, and disregarded Department of Defense orders forbidding public statements of policy by Army officers. In April 1951 he wrote a letter to Representative Joseph Martin, House Republican leader and a bitter foe of the Truman administration. Martin immediately published the letter, which expressed strong criticism of the Korean strategy, and on 11 April 1951, President Truman, with the unanimous consent of his military and civilian advisers, removed MacArthur as U.N. Commander and replaced him with General Matthew Ridgway.

MacArthur's dismissal created a bewildering uproar. The frustrations of cold war and Korean stalemate led many to see merit in MacArthur's simple, forceful approach, and numerous groups opposed to Truman and Acheson sprang to the General's defence. MacArthur staged a triumphal return to Washington, where Congressional committees conducted a curious, inconclusive investigation of State and Defense Department policies. MacArthur himself, after a dramatic exit speech to Congress, retired to private business and interest in him rapidly waned. Not long after his removal Russia's U.N. representative, Jacob Malik, proposed peace talks in Korea. Both North and South Koreans agreed, but after months of conferences nothing was accomplished.

As a result of the Korean war and *l'affaire MacArthur* the United States adopted a long-range militarization programme and a much more aggressive attitude toward Russian expansion. Congress speeded up economic aid to Europe, and the State Department worked energetically to consolidate European alliances and to unify American and European resources. The decisive action taken by the United States in Korea committed it irrevocably to intervention in global politics, for better or for worse. In the race for world authority between communism and democracy, America accepted full responsibility for free-world leadership.

At the close of World War II the American people, as they had after World War I, wished nothing more than to live at peace in an isolated hemisphere, untouched by European or Asiatic disturbance. America had everything any American could wish – wealth, personal and political liberty, high living standards, unexploited resources, a free and stable government – and nothing held more appeal to the average American than simply the preservation of the *status quo*. But it was clear that the isolationism of the twenties and thirties was both unworkable and undesirable in the post-war world. The Second World War released tremendous forces in the war-ravaged countries of Europe

and Asia, where the *status quo* meant unreasoning nationalism, poverty, distress, oppression, and revolution. Of all the
nations to emerge from World War II, only the United
States and Russia were in a position to exert immediate,
forceful leadership, and Russia, by reason of its totalitarian
structure and imperialistic commitments, was in the better
position to act. That the United States accepted world
leadership against the new totalitarian threat, a leadership
forced on it by inexorable events, is proof of its attainment of
national maturity. No administration, during this or any
foreseeable future generation, is likely to relinquish it
willingly.

Throughout Truman's second term his relations with
Congress steadily deteriorated. Their losses in 1944 and
1948, Republicans reasoned, stemmed from 'me-tooism',
that is, promises to do what Roosevelt and Truman had
done, but to do it better. After 1948 the party leaders
adopted a frankly conservative, anti-New Deal, anti-Fair
Deal line, concentrating their attack on the 'creeping
socialism' and 'blundering foreign policy' of both Roosevelt and Truman. Some liberal Republicans did not like
the tactics; some conservative Democrats did. Strange
coalitions therefore appeared in Congress, Southern Democrats occasionally joining Northern Republicans to thwart
Truman, liberal Democrats and Republicans rushing to his
assistance.

Harry Truman was a rugged and stubborn fighter, but
he did not possess Roosevelt's flair for the dramatic, and
what Roosevelt would have made a crusade became in
Truman's hands simply a political squabble. After 1950
rebellious anti-Truman Democrats and Republicans in
Congress treated the President with little more than contempt; for the first time in 160 years Congress tried to force
the resignation of a cabinet member (Acheson) and very
nearly succeeded. Enthusiastically aided by the press,
Republicans and their minority Democratic allies launched
an offensive against the President unmatched for rancour

since the days of Andrew Johnson. By the time of the 1952 presidential conventions, Harry Truman, like Johnson, was thoroughly discredited in the eyes of the public.

Senator Taft, twice frustrated, quickly declared himself a candidate for the Republican nomination and began a vigorous pre-convention campaign in early 1952. A great deal of sentiment, however, developed in favour of General Dwight Eisenhower, then commanding the North Atlantic Treaty Organization forces in Europe, who made no political statements and refused for some time to reveal his party affiliations. Eisenhower supporters among Republicans entered his name in several state primary elections, and after noting that he did well, the General in June 1952 resigned from the Army, declared himself a Republican, and returned to give his first frankly political speech at Abilene, Kansas. Taft's long service in the Senate and his years of experience made him the favourite of the conservative party leaders, but Eisenhower's military reputation and his wide popularity gave him greater public support. At the Chicago convention in July a violent struggle between Taft and Eisenhower delegates ended in an Eisenhower victory.

Truman had announced in March 1952 that he would not seek re-election, thereby leaving the field open to numerous hopefuls, among them Senator Estes Kefauver of Tennessee, Senator Richard Russell of Georgia, Averell Harriman of New York, and Vice-President Alben Barkley of Kentucky. Kefauver, nationally known for his televised investigations of crime and racketeering, went to the convention a solid favourite. However, a last-minute mobilization of liberals swung the convention to Adlai Stevenson, the Democratic governor of Illinois, a virtual unknown who had given his state an enlightened and progressive administration. Stevenson, after some hesitation, accepted the nomination, pledging a continuance of New Deal and Fair Deal policies.

The 1952 campaign was extremely bitter, centring about five major issues: high taxes; the so-called Fair Deal 'welfare state'; waste and corruption in Federal agencies;

alleged infiltration of pro-Communists into government posts; and especially the Truman-Acheson foreign policy with regard to Korea, Russia, and European aid. Significantly, both candidates agreed on an internationalist foreign policy, though minor isolationist groups appeared in both parties.

Republican promises to end the Korean stalemate, reduce taxes, and pursue a strong anti-Russian course proved to be decisive factors in the election. Eisenhower won a sweeping victory, with 449 electoral votes to Stevenson's eighty-nine and a popular majority of seven million. Undoubtedly Eisenhower's personal popularity provided the Republicans with their biggest advantage, since he ran far ahead of the rest of the Republican ticket; the Republicans on 5 November held a majority of but one in the Senate and three in the House. For the first time in twenty years the Republican party controlled the executive and legislative branches of the American government, and for the first time since Hoover the Republican party had both the responsibility and the power to direct national policy.

Dwight Eisenhower entered the White House with tremendous popular support and little political experience. Virtually insulated from partisan politics during forty years of Army service, he had been far removed from the bitter battles between New Deal, Fair Deal, and Old Guard. His Cabinet appointments indicated the alignment of power centres within his administration; many came directly from business, chiefly from large corporations, and as one member of his cabinet frankly stated, 'We're here in the saddle as an Administration representing business and industry.' Yet the appointment of Martin Durkin, a Democratic labour leader, to the post of Secretary of Labor came as a surprise and led the labour unions to hope for favourable concessions.

Eisenhower's chief interest in the early days of his office centred on foreign affairs – the stalemated Korean war, the organization of the European Defence Community, the final phases of the North Atlantic Treaty Organization, the continuation of foreign economic aid, and the development of a world trade policy. John Foster Dulles, the new Secretary of State, was an internationally-minded and experienced diplomat. The death of Premier Stalin and an apparent shift in Russian and Chinese policy enabled Dulles and the U.N. to negotiate a truce in Korea, on approximately the same grounds as those recommended earlier by Truman and Acheson. Indecisive as it was, the Korean agreement still provided a temporary solution to the tangled Asian problem and redeemed a Republican campaign pledge. For the first time since 1950 the State Department believed it had an opportunity to seize the initiative in Russo-American relations, and while continuing to deal cautiously with the new Malenkov regime, Dulles expressed hope of a better settlement. Eisenhower's hope of stimulating 'profitable and fair world trade', however, ran into stiff opposition from high-tariff Republicans. The fate of E.D.C., N.A.T.O., and foreign aid remained shrouded in uncertainty, and it seemed clear that the Administration's foreign policy was due to encounter rough going from the isolationist, nationalist wing of the Republican party.

The Republicans moved slowly during their first year in office, feeling their way after twenty years as a minority party. Despite Eisenhower's popular victory, the party he represented was hardly unified, and from the beginning many Republicans showed signs of restlessness on matters of foreign and domestic policy. Some Republicans thought that the President was too slow in breaking away from the foreign policy of the Democrats, particularly in relations with the Allies; others thought him tardy in reversing the Democratic trend to the 'welfare state'. Party factions asserted themselves even before Eisenhower's inauguration. For a time Senator Taft held the factions in line, but his death in mid-1953 left the party without an experienced leader.

In domestic affairs the Republican record during its first year was indecisive. Labour, a substantial segment of which had supported Eisenhower in expectation of obtaining revisions in the Taft-Hartley law, split with his administration within a few months. Durkin resigned, claiming violations of specific promises to amend the act, and the C.I.O. and A.F.L. both expressed annoyance at lack of action from the White House. Midwestern farmers and Western cattlemen, confronted by a serious drought and declining prices, displayed familiar signs of agrarian restlessness. Meanwhile attacks on the civil service system, suspension of the public housing and community development programmes, proposals to dispose of Federally-owned industrial and power projects to private business, and the transfer of offshore oil reserves from Federal to state ownership created fears that twenty years of social and economic progress might swiftly be cancelled. Others, after two decades of protest against an expanding Federal authority, welcomed a reversal of the trend begun by Franklin Roosevelt and continued by Truman. Many major issues – farm policy, trade, Taft-Hartley amendments – were passed over for 1954.

The focus of the Eisenhower administration for its first year was often on investigation rather than legislation. Three Congressional committees concentrated their inquiries on communism in the United States, seeking out subversion in unions, schools, churches, and the press. Overshadowing all other investigators was Senator McCarthy, who did not hesitate to challenge the Eisenhower administration itself. Many Americans were disturbed over the implications of the widespread loyalty investigations, believing that the methods employed seriously endangered American liberties. Abroad the word 'McCarthyism' gained currency as a symbol of incipient American fascism, colouring American foreign relations. Although President Eisenhower was reputed to be antagonistic to improperly conducted investigations, his Attorney General levelled charges at ex-President Truman and others of his administration.

President Eisenhower during his first year placed no definite legislative programme before Congress. His own domestic and foreign programme could be inferred, however, from press conferences and occasional speeches. First, he seemed interested in removing much of the influence of the Federal government from domestic affairs. His attitude toward this, the major political issue of the past quarter century, represented a 'middle-of-the-road' policy of retaining the concept of long-range Federal planning while keeping Federal authority over social and economic life at a minimum. Second, as an avowed internationalist, he was concerned with pursuing a somewhat stronger foreign policy than that of his predecessor, while at the same time hoping to avoid entrapment by its critics. Here he faced, as Acheson and Truman before him, the powerful nationalist bloc within the Republican party which had by its constant attacks imprisoned the State Department in a ring of criticism, robbing it of flexibility, morale, and reputation. Third, Eisenhower hoped to re-establish the identity of Congress by making it the ally and not the enemy of the Chief Executive. Apparently he had no intention of being a 'strong' executive, in the tradition of Jackson, Lincoln, Wilson, or the two Roosevelts, whose battles with Congress are legendary. Since the tendency has nearly always been for Congress to seize leadership unless the executive branch swiftly forestalls it, the results of Eisenhower's determination to 'get along with Congress' remained to be seen.

Since contemporary American society is a mass society, the question it has faced since the turn of the twentieth century is, Can individual integrity and individual values be preserved in a standardized civilization? The contemporary thrust toward orthodoxy in the United States is of course neither new nor distinctively American. It has characterized modern life since the completion of the industrial revolution, though the United States has perhaps found it more difficult to resist than older societies. The conformist trend has produced in American society a deep sense of insecurity, the effect of a widening dichotomy between a traditional belief in the validity of the individual and an equally strong traditional belief in the judgement of the crowd. There is as a result an inner conflict in American life, manifested in the major areas of social and intellectual endeavour, a struggle to maintain individuality in a mass-dominated, insecure world that the nineteen-fifties neither understands nor trusts.

The pressure to conform induced by a mass society is nowhere better illustrated than in the history of American publishing since 1930. The depression drove smaller independent newspapers, journals, and publishers either out of business or into more financially stable chains, with the result that the control of publishing, particularly of newspapers, gravitated into fewer and fewer hands. As advertising revenues and circulation profits became more important than ever to a newspaper's existence, publishers became more sensitive to outside pressures; the press that survived the depression was for the most part cautious and orthodox. There were and are, however, notable exceptions. Since 1932 coverage of foreign affairs has tended to be nationalistic and coverage of domestic affairs conservative, sometimes reflecting special interests rather than public attitudes. *Time* magazine, founded in 1923 by Henry Luce, began a new style of summarized news presented in distinctively styled prose, and elicited a host of imitators. Luce's *Life*, begun in 1936, made the picture magazine popular; combined with *Time* it gave Luce Publications a strong influence in journalism, inclined toward nationalism and conservatism. *Readers Digest*, founded in 1922 by DeWitt Wallace, presented 'digests' of the 'best' articles of the week. It too attracted dozens of imitators, including digests of summaries and summaries of digests, most of them as orthodox as their prototype. The popularity of comic books, 'confession' magazines, and cheap novels testifies to the continuing strength of the subliterary tradition that has existed since the days of the dime shocker and the penny dreadful.

The close of the First World War saw the appearance of great new communication media – movies, radio, and later television – appealing to audiences in the millions. Entertainment became a transcontinental business, dominated by a few corporations and a relatively small number of executives, to whom box-office receipts and advertising fees were more important than originality, initiative, or art. The movies established the pattern for the entertainment industry in the twenties, followed with minor variations by radio and television, and it was assumed by all that their function was to provide the nation with vicarious pleasure, escape, or reassurance. Hollywood developed into a fantastic never-never land, a stylized version of the romantic dreams of the frustrated and repressed, its films following well-tried formulas and usually avoiding controversial issues. While sociologists have expressed fears that the unreal world thus presented daily to millions might make it difficult for the average American to adjust to reality, little has been offered to prove that their fears are justified.

The importance of Hollywood within the framework of American culture is often exaggerated, but nevertheless it remains the arch-interpreter of Americanism to the rest of the world. In the cinema, the literary, the unliterary, and the illiterate throughout the world now sit in on the work of Americans; since Americans are working in a medium in which they are unquestionably powerful and generally competent, it is not altogether surprising that Europeans, Africans, and Asians are inclined to take as typical of America this one art in which American achievement is supreme. Yet the picture of American life exported by Hollywood is neither true nor whole, presenting instead an America that never was, or was only in part. Unfortunately, the rise to influence of Hollywood has come at a time when Americans must take over from Europe some of Europe's century-old duties. They have, in the moving-picture industry, a vehicle by which they can convey to the world their own purposes and their own faith. Instead the movies have often revealed to the world only that America which is the heir to Europe's decay; they have not shown the other America, the heir of Europe's strength, which in the New World has taken on a vigour all her own. It is doubly unfortunate that by its persistent proclamation of the delights of orthodoxy, Hollywood had made more difficult than ever the task of the rebel, at a time when the world at large needs to revive the habit of asking questions, testing anew the aims of modern life, and reassessing contemporary standards.

The most evident trend of American life since World War II has been the widespread emphasis on reliability, predictability, and conformity. There is still in modern America a widespread subconscious suspicion of the thinker and the theorist, perhaps an extension of the old frontier distrust of the specialist. The expressed aim of many educational authorities is the teaching of 'adjustment to life', the necessity of social approval, and the ready acceptance of mass values by the individual. Recent thinkers have proudly proclaimed themselves 'new conservatives', dedicated to a cautious evaluation of the new and unorthodox, while the fifties have been filled with the warnings of intellectuals exorcising the liberalism of the thirties and forties. The discrediting of the American tradition of dissent seems to be another signal of insecurity, under-confidence, and of the trend toward a conformist, outer-directed civilization.

Nevertheless there still exist in present-day America powerful counterbalances to standardization. The United States is a big country, so populous that the acts and ideas of a minority may give a false impression that they constitute a sweeping movement, particularly to European eyes. Zootsuiters in New York, gangs in Chicago, divorces in Reno, or Klans in the South represent nothing more than fractional divergences from the main stream of American life. It is also a tremendously diverse country, a tangled skein of sections, localities, and groups to which the citizen holds powerful allegiances. There is no such thing as 'a typical American', for dissimilarities of background, geography, politics, race, environment, religion, and economic status prevent his existence. The customary European question, 'What do Americans think about this or that?' is unanswerable. Americans think in terms in multiple allegiances and not infrequently as individuals – much to the despair of politicians, advertisers, publishers, business men, and labourleaders. They also possess a healthy scepticism and a stubborn independence. The radio commercial may go unheard and the advertising slogan unread, the political exhortation may pass easily in at one ear and out of the other, the charlatan may disappear at the turn of a radio or television dial. No matter what evidence may be cited as proof of American crowd-mindedness, it is significant to note that the single most popular form of recreation in the United States is Walton's lonely sport of fishing.

The sum of America and Americans has been traditionally difficult for Europeans and Asians to grasp, even for those more perceptive observers who detect the words but not the tune of American life. The key to an understanding of the United States lies in the fact that it is an experiment in the making, never made. It is a society of change and movement, operating fluidly within a framework of compromises. The core of the American experiment is that principle expressed in a long tradition of slogans (which Americans love) beginning with the Declaration of Independence itself and its phrase 'the pursuit of happiness', which is still the basis of its society. Conceived in the eighteenth century as an individual search, the pursuit has come to be understood in the twentieth century in larger social terms. The quest may sometimes have been diverted into blind alleys or perverted into meaningless activity, but again it has been charted and channelled toward better ends. The United States today, as in the eighteenth century, firmly believes in its mission to give the world something greater than Coca-cola, gum, gangster novels, and slang. The only way that Europe and Asia can understand America is to accept it on these, its own terms.

BIBLIOGRAPHY

IT would be impertinent and impossible to attempt to discover or select from among the many general histories of the United States. Suffice it to say that S. Morrison and H. S. Commager, *The Growth of the American Republic* (1930, 2 vols.) and A. Nevins and H. S. Commager, *A Short History of the United States* (1943) together with J. T. Adams' brilliant and provocative *The Epic of America* (1932) are good general histories. J. D. Hicks, *A Short History of American Democracy* (1949) gives a point of view which is rather different from these because of the author's Middle-Western outlook.

There are many series covering the whole field of American history. A. Schlesinger and D. R. Fox (Eds.) *The History of American Life* (1927–44, 12 vols.) is a good series, each volume written by an authority. H. Commager and R. Morris (Eds.) 'The New American Series' is still in progress and is planned to extend to some forty volumes. 'The Rivers of America Series' is a multi-volumed regional history with much social, political, military, and economic information; all the books are written with an eye on the general reader.

C. and M. Beard, *The Rise of American Civilization* (1927, 2 vols.) remains one of the most important and interesting studies. V. L. Parrington, *Main Currents in American Thought* (1927–30, 3 vols.), though written with a Jeffersonian-Jacksonian bias, is nevertheless one of the most stimulating discussions of intellectual and political history, and M. Curti, *The Growth of American Thought* (1943) is essential background reading.

S. F. Bemis, *A Diplomatic History of the United States* (1937, 6th edition 1949) and T. A. Bailey, *A Diplomatic History of the American People* (4th edition 1950) are two standard works. W. Binkley, *American Political Parties: Their Natural History* (1943) is a lively and readable account of politics for the general reader, and R. Hofstadter, *The American Political Tradition and the Men Who Made It* (1948) contains excellent essays on men and events in American politics from Washington to Roosevelt. C. B. Swisher, *American Constitutional Development* (1943) is sound, but no bibliography of American Constitutional development is complete without James Bryce, *The American Commonwealth* (1893), still a classic treatment. A recent addition to the essential list is D. W. Brogan, *An Introduction to American Politics* (1954).

The standard history of education is E. P. Cubberley, *Education in the United States* (rev. ed. 1934), while more detail can be found in P. Monroe, *Founding of the American Public School System: A History of Education in the United States from the Early Settlements to the Close of the Civil War Period* (1940).

A. P. Stokes, *Church and State in the United States* (1950, 3 vols.) is a solid study; W. W. Sweet, *The Story of Religion in America* (rev. ed. 1939) is specially written for the layman, and W. L. Sperry, *Religion in America* (1946) is specially written for the British layman. D. W. Wecter, *The Saga of American Society: A Record of Social Aspiration* (1937) is an entertaining book on manners, fashions, and social aspirations. H. Wish, *Society and Thought in Early America* (1950) and *Society and Thought in Modern America* (1953) are penetrating and comprehensive treatments of intellectual history from colonial times to the present day.

H. V. Faulkner, *Economic History of the United States* (6th edition, 1949) is probably the best one-volume treatment. J. Dorfman, *Economic Mind in American Civilization* (1946, 3 vols.) is more learned but still fascinating, and V. S. Clark, *History of Manufactures in the United States* (1916–28) though now somewhat outmoded is still of some importance. C. Wittke, *We Who Built America: The Saga of the Immigrant* (1939) and O. Handlin, *The Uprooted* (1953) are both excellent studies of immigration and immigrants. S. Dunbar, *A History of Travel in America* (1915, 4 vols.) is old but has not been superseded. J. Schafer, *The Social History of American Agriculture* (1934), R. Burlingame, *March of the Iron Men* (1938), and *Engines of Democracy* (1940), and H. Faulkner and M. Starr, *Labor in America* (rev. ed. 1949) are all interesting studies of particular aspects of economic history.

The two books by Burlingame, which are studies of economic technology and its impact upon society, are particularly well written for the average reader.

R. Spiller and others (Eds.), *The Literary History of the United States* (1949, 4 vols.), is an exhaustive study by a group of scholars, particularly valuable for its excellent biographies. Supplementary to this is C. Van Doren, *The American Novel, 1789–1939* (1940), A. M. Quinn, *A History of American Drama* (1936, 2 vols.), and A. Kazin, *On Native Grounds* (1942), a most readable survey of literary history. H. Lehmann-Haupt, L. C. Wroth, and R. G. Silver, *The Book in America: A History of the Magazine: The Selling and Collecting of Books in the United States* (1951), J. D. Hart, *The Popular Book: A History of America's Literary Tastes* (1950), treat literature from a rather different angle. Reference should also be made to F. L. Mott, *American Journalism: A History of Newspapers in the United States Through Two Hundred and Sixty Years, 1690–1950* (1950) and *A History of the American Magazine, 1641–1850* (1939). V. Loggins, *The Negro Author* (1931) is a most useful book in a neglected field, though it needs to be brought up to date.

H. W. Schneider, *A History of American Philosophy* (1946) is the best survey.

On American music, J. T. Howard, *Our American Music: Three Hundred Years of It* (1931, 3rd edition 1946) is interesting but less effective than it might be. C. Larkin, *Art and Life in America* (1949) is a brilliant illustrated history of painting, sculpture, and architecture, and John Walker writes a provocative introduction and some excellent notes to the panorama of two hundred years of American painting in *Paintings from America* (1951). For the lighter side of American life, see F. R. Dulles, *America Learns to Play* (1940).

F. J. Turner, *The Frontier in American History* (1920), is important both to the state of American history and to the state of American historiography. It has had many fruits, among them R. A. Billington and J. B. Hedges, *Westward Expansion: A History of the American Frontier* (1949), and R. Lillard, *The Great Forest* (1948) are worth reading.

Each of the minority groups has had its histories. For good general reading see J. H. Franklin, *From Slavery to Freedom: A History of American Negroes* (1947) and, a fine piece of journalism, R. Otley, *Black Odyssey* (1949). D'Arcy Mc-Nickle, *They Came Here First: The Epic of the American Indian*, is lively. The standard reference book on the Indians is still F. W. Hodge, *Handbook of American Indians* (1907–10, 2 vols.).

For printed documents see H. S. Commager (Ed.), *Documents of American History* (1934), and for maps, J. T. Adams and R. V. Coleman, *Atlas of American History* (1943).

The best account of the period immediately following the War of 1812 is G. Daingerfield, *The Era of Good Feelings* (1952), while W. Cresson, *James Monroe* (1946), is the most satisfactory biography of the author of the Monroe doctrine. C. Fish, *The Rise of the Common Man 1830–50* (1935), and F. J. Turner, *The United States 1830–50* (1935) are excellent briefer treatments. A. M. Schlesinger, jr., *The Age of Jackson* (1945), is a superb account of the Jacksonian era, and Marquis James, *Andrew Jackson* (vol. I, 1933; vol. II, 1937) is the authoritative life. For the numerous reform movements of the period, the reader should consult A. Tyler, *Freedom's Ferment* (1944); R. Billington, *The Protestant Crusade* (1938), and relevant chapters of C. Madison, *Critics and Crusaders* (1947). A Ekirch, *The Idea of Progress in America 1815–1860* (1951 ed.) outlines the philosophical and ideological backgrounds of reform. F. O. Matthiessen, *American Renaissance* (1941), and Van W. Brooks, *The World of Washington Irving* (1944) and *The Flowering of New England* (1936) are admirable studies of literary men and movements of the pre-Civil War years. Good biographies of literary figures include R. Rusk, *The Life of Emerson* (1949); J. Grossman, *James Fenimore Cooper* (1950); H. Canby, *Thoreau* (1939); L. Howard, *Herman Melville* (1951); M. Van Doren, *Hawthorne* (1949); R. Stewart, *Hawthorne* (1948); and H. Allen's histrionic but lively *Israfel: The Life of Poe* (1934). A satisfactory general treatment of the Mexican troubles is J. Rippy, *The United States and Mexico* (rev. ed. 1931).

Among studies of the decade preceding the Civil War,

Bibliography

A. Craven, *The Coming of the Civil War* (1950) and R. Nichols, *The Disruption of Democracy* (1948) are outstanding. W. Dodd, *The Cotton Kingdom* (1919), U. B. Phillips, *Life and Labor in the Old South* (1929), and F. Gaines, *The Southern Plantation* (1925) are still useful studies. C. Eaton, *A History of the Old South* (1949), and F. Simkins, *The South Old and New* (1947), are both excellent and recent; however, a ten-volume *History of the South*, ed. W. Stephenson and E. Coulter, is in preparation. For an understanding of Southern civilization and temperament, no reader should neglect W. J. Cash's minor classic, *The Mind of the South* (1941). The political battles of the pre-war era are treated by H. Simms, *A Decade of Sectional Controversy 1851–1861* (1941), and in greater detail by A. Nevins, *Ordeal of the Union* (2 vols., 1947). The best study of the great Southern leader is C. Wiltse, *John C. Calhoun* (vol. I, 1949; vol. II, 1954). W. S. Jenkins, *Proslavery Thought in the Old South* (1935), is a good exposition of the Southern position on slavery; A. Lloyd, *The Slavery Controversy 1831–60* (1939), is also informative. R. Nye's study of Garrison and the abolitionists will appear in 1955. The most satisfactory history of the American Negro is J. H. Franklin, *From Slavery to Freedom* (1947); however, Booker Washington's *Up From Slavery* (1901) and R. Holt's *George Washington Carver* (1947) give excellent pictures of two Negro leaders. For the literary trends of the period, see V. Brooks, *New England: Indian Summer* (1940).

Adequate one-volume military histories of the Civil War include F. Pratt, *Ordeal by Fire* (1950), and G. Milton, *Conflict* (1936), but for real insight into the war the reader would do well to consult *The Photographic History of the Civil War* (8 vols., 1911), with the magnificent Brady photographs. For men and events of wartime politics, see A. Nevins, *The Emergence of Lincoln* (2 vols., 1950); E. Coulter, *The Confederate States of America 1861–65* (1950); and B. Hendrick, *Statesmen of the Lost Cause* (1943), and *Lincoln's War Cabinet* (1946). Among biographies of military leaders, D. S. Freeman's *R. E. Lee* (4 vols., 1945), Freeman's *Lee's Lieutenants* (3 vols., 1942–4), and L. Lewis, *Sherman: Fighting*

Prophet (1932) are outstanding. Lewis' four-volume biography of Grant was cut short by his death after *Captain Sam
Grant* (1950); a good understanding of Grant can be gained
from his own *Memoirs* (2 vols., 1885–6). Biographies of
Lincoln are numerous. A good introduction to Lincoln,
however, is P. Angle, *The Lincoln Reader* (1947), while
B. Thomas, *Abraham Lincoln* (1952), is a superb one-volume
biography. C. Sandburg, *Abraham Lincoln: The Prairie Years*
(2 vols., 1926), and *Abraham Lincoln: The War Years* (4 vols.,
1939), is a brilliantly written longer study. *The Collected
Works of Abraham Lincoln*, ed. by R. Basler, appeared in
8 volumes in 1953.

A competent one-volume study of Reconstruction is P. H.
Buck, *The Road to Reunion* (1937); E. Coulter, *The South
During Reconstruction* (1947), is recent and scholarly, and
W. Hesseltine, *U. S. Grant Politician* (1935), is a good con-
sideration of Radical politics. However, no reader should
miss Henry Adams' *Education* (1907), a classic account of an
intelligent man's search for values in a confused era. A.
Nevins, *The Emergence of Modern America* (1927), and A.
Schlesinger, *The Rise of the City* (1933), trace social and
economic changes in the period. For the opening of the
West, see H. Hubbart, *The Older Middle West* (1936); R.
Riegel, *America Moves West* (rev. ed., 1947); R. Billington,
Westward Expansion (1949); H. N. Smith's provocative study
of the West as fact and myth, *Virgin Land* (1950); O.
Winther's worthwhile *The Great Northwest* (1946); and par-
ticularly W. P. Webb, *The Great Plains* (1931). Mark
Twain's *Roughing It* (1873) is still an enjoyable account of
gold-mining days; S. White, *The Fortyniners* (1920) treats the
California rush, and G. Willison, *Here They Dug the Gold*
(1946), is a lively study of Colorado's. J. Dobie, *The Longhorns* (1941), is a readable history of the cattleman's West.
Biographies of the literary figures of the period include A.
Paine's *Mark Twain* (1912) and J. Ferguson's more satisfactory *Mark Twain: Man and Legend* (1943); N. Arvin, *Whitman*
(1938); and H. Canby, *Walt Whitman: An American* (1943).

J. Hicks, *The Populist Revolt* (1931), and the relevant chapters of R. B. Nye, *Midwestern Progressive Politics* (1951), are good sources of information concerning the political upheavals of the eighties and nineties. There is no adequate modern study of Bryan, but his book, *The First Battle* (1896), provides an insight into the man's mind. H. Commager's *The American Mind* (1950) contains some penetrating essays on intellectual trends at the turn of the century, while O. Cargill, *Intellectual America* (1941), is particularly useful for its treatment of American-European cultural relations in the period. L. Mumford, *The Brown Decades* (1931), surveys the arts in America from 1865 to 1900, and S. Warren, *American Free-thought 1860–1914* (1943), is a good treatment of radical theology. The social history of the nineties is handled well by L. Morris, *Postscript to Yesterday* (1947); T. Beer's *The Mauve Decade* (1926), though mannered, is good reading. The rise of 'big business' is treated in B. Hendrick, *The Age of Big Business* (1919), T. Cochran and W. Miller, *The Age of Enterprise* (1942), and H. Faulkner, *The Decline of Laissez-Faire 1897–1917* (1951), while Faulkner's *The Quest for Social Justice* (1931) is an excellent survey of trends in social and economic reform. B. Hendrick, *Andrew Carnegie* (1932), and A. Nevins, *Rockefeller: A Study in Power* (2 vols., 1940, revised 1953), are good biographies, though Carnegie's own writings, still easily available, give an even better view of the industrialist psychology.

The latter chapters of Nye, cited above, survey the conflict between conservatism and liberalism in the early years of the twentieth century. L. Filler, *Crusaders for Liberalism* (1939), is an excellent treatment of the muck-rakers and other reformers, and the sweep of reform from 1865 through 1952 is brilliantly done by E. Goldman, *Rendezvous with Destiny* (1952). La Follette's *Autobiography* (1913) and Wilson's *The New Freedom* (1913) are essential to an understanding of the politics of the pre-World-War-I years. E. Morrison has edited *The Letters of Theodore Roosevelt* (8 vols., 1954), while J. Blum's *The Republican Roosevelt* (1954) is an astute study of T.R. as politician. B. and F. La Follette, *La Follette* (2 vols., 1953), and R. Ginger, *The Bending Cross: A Bio-*

graphy of Eugene Debs (1949), are outstanding. For the administrations of Wilson, Josephus Daniels, *The Wilson Era* (2 vols., 1946), is a valuable source of information. R. S. Baker's *Woodrow Wilson : His Life and Letters* (8 vols., 1927–39) is a standard reference work; A. Link's *Woodrow Wilson: The Road to the White House* (1947) is the first volume of a definitive life.

A useful running account of events from 1900 to 1925 may be found in M. Sullivan, *Our Times* (6 vols., 1926–35). Of the numerous books on American participation in World War I, P. Slosson, *The Great Crusade and After* (1930), and C. J. H. Hayes, *Brief History of the Great War* (1928), are competent; B. Crowell and R. Wilson, *How America Went to War* (6 vols., 1921), is exhaustive, while H. Barnes, *Genesis of the World War* (rev. ed., 1929), is a revisionist's view. D. Birdsall, *Versailles Twenty Years After* (1941), and T. Bailey, *Woodrow Wilson and the Lost Peace* (1944), take contrasting positions; A. Nevins, *The United States in a Chaotic World* (1950), is a good survey of American foreign relations from 1920 to 1950.

H. Faulkner, *From Versailles to the New Deal* (1951), is an excellent brief account of trends during the twenties, while B. Mitchell, *Depression Decade* (1947), L. Gurko, *Angry Decade* (1947), and D. Wecter, *The Age of the Great Depression* (1948), deal with the thirties. F. Allen's *Only Yesterday* (1933), Allen's *Since Yesterday* (1940), and L. Morris, *Not So Long Ago* (1949), are all charmingly written social histories of life between World Wars. D. Brogan, *The Era of Franklin D. Roosevelt* (1950) is the best British study of the New Deal era, while B. Rauch, *The History of the New Deal* (1944), is perhaps the best American account; however, Roosevelt's own *Looking Forward* (1933) is a valuable primary source. Of F. Friedel's projected six-volume biography of Roosevelt, two volumes appeared in 1952 and 1954; until its completion, R. Sherwood's *Roosevelt and Hopkins* (1948) remains a useful source. S. Rosenman has edited *The Public Papers and Addresses of Franklin D. Roosevelt* (13 vols., 1948–50), but B. Zevin, ed., *Nothing to Fear* (1946), is an easily available one-volume collection of Roosevelt's major speeches. J. Ickes, ed., *The Secret Diaries of Harold Ickes* (3 vols., 1955), provides a fascinating though highly personalized picture of New Deal inner politics, and W. White, *The Taft Story* (1954), is a competent study of one of the New Deal's bitter opponents. The best biography of the famous twentieth-century industrialist is A. Nevins and F. Hill, *Ford* (1954), though Walter Chrysler's *Life of an American Workman* (1950) is an interesting autobiographical account of another manufacturer.

A. Nevins, *The New Deal and World Affairs* (1950), B. Rauch, *Roosevelt from Munich to Pearl Harbor* (1950), and H. Feis, *The Road to Pearl Harbor* (1950), are useful surveys of Rooseveltian foreign policy. E. Reischauer, *The United States and Japan* (1950), is an excellent study of Far Eastern relations. Among primary sources for the period Cordell Hull's *Memoirs* (1948), W. Millis' edition of *The Forrestal Diaries* (1951), Sumner Welles, *The Time for Decision* (1944), and the United States State Department, *Peace and War: United States Foreign Policy 1931–1941* (1942), are important. Of the United States Army's official 99-volume *History of World War II*, six have appeared at this writing; S. Morrison's semi-official *History of Naval Operations in World War II* is planned for 13 volumes, of which the first appeared in 1947, while W. Craven and A. Cate, *The Army Air Forces in World War II* (1948–   ), is also an unfinished multi-volumed history. A useful short history of American participation, however, is F. Pratt, *War for the World* (1950). D. Eisenhower, *Crusade in Europe* (1948), and O. Bradley, *A Soldier's Story* (1951), are accounts by important participants. Problems of post-war foreign policy are treated by the Brookings Institution, *Major Problems of United States Foreign Policy* (1950), and T. A. Bailey, *America Faces Russia* (1950). Penetrating discussions of the controversy over loyalty and security are A. Barth, *The Loyalty of Free Men* (1951), Elmer Davis, *But We Were Born Free* (1954), and H. Commager, *Freedom, Loyalty, and Dissent* (1954).

For discussion of the development of mass entertainment media in recent times, see L. Jacobs, *The Rise of the American*

Film (1939); L. White, *The American Radio* (1947); and G. Seldes, *The Great Audience* (1950). There are few satisfactory studies of recent American poetry, one being H. Gregory and M. Zaturenska, *A History of Modern American Poetry 1900–1940* (1944). J. Beach, *American Fiction 1920–1940* (1941); M. Geismar, *Writers in Crisis* (1942); and M. Cowley, ed., *After the Genteel Tradition* (1936), are good introductions to the major American novelists of the twentieth century. For studies of individual novelists, poets, critics, and others, consult the *Library of American Biography* series (40 volumes) and *American Men of Letters* series (22 volumes), both in preparation, and the introductions to the *Portable* series of anthologies, especially M. Cowley's *Portable Faulkner* (1946) and *Portable Hemingway* (1944).

INDEX

Index

723

Index

Hayes, Rutherford B., 560, 561, 562, 589, 591

Health problems, 143, 575

Hemingway, Ernest, 584

Henricopolis University, plans for, 31

Henry VII, 10, 11

Henry, VIII, 11, 12

Henry, John, 298, 299

Henry, Patrick, 136, 157, 158, 187, 193, 194, 197, 235, 253, 256

Henry the Navigator, 2

Henson, Josiah, 434

Hill, A. P., 502, 504, 505

Hillsborough, Lord, 168, 169

Hiroshima, 684

Hitler, Adolf, 643, 684

Holland, 1, 8; alliance with France, 118; alliance with United States, 224, 225; at war with England, 98, 225; overseas expansion, 95 ff.; prosperity, 96; religious toleration, 97; trade, 95 ff.; United New Netherland Company, 42. *See also* Netherlands.

Hollywood, 708

Holmes, Oliver Wendell, 581

Holmes, Oliver Wendell Jr, 630, 631

Holy Alliance, 342

Hood, John B. 478, 489, 505, 512 525, 526, 527, 530

Hooker, Joe, 491, 492, 501 ff., 513, 514

Hoover, Herbert, 644, 649, 650, 651, 655, 658 ff., 678, 679, 696

Howe, Gen., 218, 219, 226, 233,

Howe (Lord George Augustus), 183

Hudson, Henry, 96

Hudson river, 42, 96

Hudson's Bay, 115; Charter, 115; Company, 116

Huguenots, in South Carolina, 9, 13, 128

Hull, Gen., 301, 302, 303

Hume, David, 233, 234

Huron, Lake, 114

Ideology, development, in colonies, 160, 240

Illinois, 336, 337, 345, 346, 422, 433; Anti-Nebraska Convention (1856), 451

Immigration to U.S.A., 329, 389, 390, 539, 540, 572, 575, 630; exclusion Bill, 595

Imperialism, American, 112, 594, 613, 614 ff., 689

Independence, Declaration of, 150, 196, 209, 210, 214, 216, 217, 240, 272, 410, 414, 475. *See also* Revolution, American.

India, 2, 12, 14, 121, 123, 125, 127

Indian College scheme, Virginia, 30 ff.

Indian Boundary Line, 134; Frontier Wars, 133, 134; Reservations, 133, 134. *See also* American Indians.

Indiana, 296, 337, 346, 348, 358; helps fugitive slaves, 433; joins Union, 345, 422

Indians, of Asia, 14

Industrialism, 131, 344, 347, 356, 357, 366, 374, 387 ff., 450, 463, 492-3, 494, 536 ff., 545, 562 ff., 589, 627, 628, 654, 665, 690, 694; effect of inventions, 386 ff. *See also* Tariffs.

Industry, captains of, 564-5, 568, 654

Inflation. *See* Currency.

Ingersoll, R. G., 579. *See* Religion.

Inventions, effect on industry, 386, 545 627, 631, 633

Iowa, 422, 427, 437, 539

Ireland, and English settlement, 20; and John Wilkes, 176

Iroquois, 116, 118

Irving, Washington, 330, 331, 332, 393

Isolationism, 327, 605, 615, 619, 627, 636, 637, 638, 647, 648, 651, 675, 677, 678, 679, 686, 700

Jackson, Andrew, 158, 207, 212, 242, 300, 309, 326, 339, 342, 349, 359, 362, 363, 364, 366, 367, 368, 369-94, 419, 422, 423, 440, 444, 467

Jackson, Thomas Jonathan ('Stonewall'), 478, 479, 484, 488, 489, 490, 491, 501, 502, 503

James I, 20, 23, 24, 30, 36

James II, 83, 88, 90, 98, 116

James Bay, 116

James, Henry, 584, 585, 586

James, William, 585, 586

James river, 23, 59, 236

Jamestown, settlement, 19, 22-37, 38, 41, 114

Japan, 96, 436, 595, 596, 674, 677, 679, ff., 687, 688, 691

Jay, John, 223, 224, 238, 255

Jazz, 633, 674. *See also* Music.

Jefferson, Thomas, 144, 148, 152, 153, 157, 196, 197, 206, 207, 208, 210, 211 ff., 235, 242, 243, 244, 246, 247, 248, 251, 258, 259, 261, 262, 264, 268, 270, 271, 272, 280 ff., 292, 293, 294, 295, 326, 327, 347, 349, 359, 360, 362, 372, 373, 403, 414, 440, 575

Jenkinson, Anthony, 13

Jesuits, expulsion from New World, 112

Johnson, Andrew, 509, 551, 552, 553, 554

Johnston, Gen. Albert Sidney, 478, 484, 486, 487

Johnston, Joe, 478, 482, 483, 484, 488, 497, 499, 514, 515, 525, 526, 531, 533

Jones, John Paul, 204

Journalism, journalists, in America, 134, 135, 631, 632. *See also* Newspapers

Index

Judicial force, 282, 283, 344. See also Judiciary; Law; Marshall; Supreme Court.

Judiciary, 245, 252, 630, 667–8. See also Supreme Court.

Kansas, 437 ff., 539; legislature, 438, 439, 448; settlers, 438–9

Kellogg-Briand Pact, 650

Kentucky, 246, 261, 292, 337, 345, 346, 360

Key, Francis Scott, 307, 308, 326, 389

King George's War, 119, 120

'Knownothing' party, 441, 442, 455–6

Korean war, 689, 692, 697 ff., 704

Ku Klux Klan, 559, 560, 562, 654

Labour, 543, 544, 570, 595, 602, 626, 653, 704, 705; apprentices, 27, 28, 30; in Britain, 75; in the United States, 386 ff., 434; indentured, 27, 28, 29, 75; in Virginia, 27, 28, 29, 76; organization of, 388 ff., 440–1, 493, 570 ff., 599, 610 ff., 644, 665 ff., 690, 691, 695, 703; problems (post-Civil War), 535, 539. See also Slavery.

Lafayette, Marquis de, 204, 205, 206, 218, 228, 235, 260

La Follette, Robert M., 608 ff., 620–3, 637, 655

Land, jobbing, 134; laws, 347, 492; settlement, 172, 193, 197, 347, 356, 357, 545 ff., 555

Laurens, Henry, 225, 238

Law, lawyers, 155, 156, 157, 158, 173, 245, 282, 283, 344, 569, 630, 631, 667

League of Nations, 646, 647, 648, 650, 676

Lee, Arthur, 177, 223, 225

Lee, Charles, 203, 228, 231, 273

Lee, R. H., 136, 159, 187, 216, 235, 327

Lee, Gen. Robert E., 38, 200, 212, 213, 454, 466 ff., 473, 478, 479, 483, 488, 489, 490, 491, 501, 502 ff., 525, 530 ff.

Lee, William, 224, 225

Legislation, colonial, control of, 131, 167

Legislative force, 282. See also Law; Marshall; Judiciary; Supreme Court.

L'Enfant, Pierre, 264, 265

Levingstone, William, 146

Lewis and Clark expedition, 288, 289, 290, 347, 421

Lewis, John L., 666, 667, 695

Lewis, Meriwether, 288, 289, 290, 347

Lexington, Massachusetts, 190, 194, 197

Liberty, Sons of, American group, 176, 180, 181, 187, 195

Libraries, public, 140, 147, 403, 577

Lincoln, Abraham, 200, 212, 250, 346, 349, 351, 373, 382, 407, 449–80, 481 ff., 541, 549; Amnesty Proclamation (1863), 549, 550; assassination, 532–3; at Gettysburg, 507; 'copperheads',

treatment of, 508; Emancipation Proclamation (1862), 508, 521, 522

Literacy, in modern America, 330, 378, 576

Literary activities, literature, 47, 48, 71, 73, 103 ff., 145, 147, 148, 150, 213, 214, 268, 269, 275, 276, 277; French, 149, 208, 209; in modern America, 331, 332, 392, 393, 496, 581 ff., 637, 656, 657–8, 672–3. See also Culture.

Livingston, Robert, 287, 288

Lloyd George, David, 646

Locke, John, 75, 85, 109, 148, 160, 161, 271

Locofoco movement, 388, 389

Lodge, Henry Cabot, 615, 647

London, Virginia Company of, 22, 23, 27, 28, 29, 30, 35, 36, 37, 41, 43, 58

Long Island, 237

Longfellow, Henry Wadsworth, 330, 332, 392, 581

Longstreet, 478, 489, 491, 501, 503, 505, 506, 512, 513

Lords of Trade, 63, 84, 88, 89, 91, 92. See also Trade.

Louisbourg, 119, 120, 121, 123

Louisiana, 8, 116, 119, 335, 345, 346, 360; ceded to Spain, 126; French refugees, 127; negotiations with France, 284, 286; Purchase, 287, 288, 289, 310, 344, 361, 362; secession from Union, 458

Lowell, James Russell, 334, 392, 406, 424, 525, 581

Loyalists, 198, 199, 231, 238, 246

Lutheranism, 95

Lyceum system of education, 577

MacArthur, Gen., 688, 698, 699, 700

Madison, James, 207, 243, 247, 248, 249, 250, 251, 253, 255, 256, 257, 258, 259, 261, 292, 295, 296, 298, 299, 300, 303, 306, 307, 325, 339, 412, 462

Magellan, Ferdinand, 5, 14

Mail order houses, founded, 598

Maine, 48, 63, 80, 88, 361; and the Virginia Coy of Plymouth, 23, 42; French domination, 55; joins Union, 345

Manchuria, 688

Manhattan Island, 42, 96

Marconi, 627

Marines, United States, 617, 682

Marlborough, Duke of, 113, 120

Marshall, Gen. George, 688

Marshall, John, Chief Justice, 242, 257, 268, 282, 283, 335, 343, 344, 370, 371

Marshall Plan, 687, 695

Marxism, 671, 672

Mary I, 13, 59

Maryland, 58–62, 88, 193, 195, 246, 307, 366; agricultural wealth, 40, 67; capital, 62, 69; education, 73; estates, 61; labour in, 76; origins, 24, 60; planters,

727

Index

Negroes, 28, 29, 143, 252, 309, 414, 415, 445, 446, 465, 528, 535 ff., 550 ff., 561, 562, 569, 572, 599, 645, 654, 690, 691. *See also* Abolitionists; Anti-slavery movement; Slave trade.

Nelson, Thomas, 235

Netherlands, and United States, 224; expansion in North America, 41, 42; trade with England, 10, 11. *See also* Holland.

Neutrality Act (1935), 676

Nevada, 544, 546

New Amsterdam, 56, 78, 97, 98

New Deal policy, 661, 662, 663 ff., 693 ff.

New England, 79, 80, 118, 304, 310, 329, 335; architecture, 102, 103; boundary, 60; aristocracy, 40; colonies as separate entities, 43; commerce, 40, 67, 347, 348; Confederation, 129; Council, 43; culture, 100 ff.; currency restriction, 133; economic reasons for immigration, 43; escape route for slaves, 433; foundations of, 38–57; importance to American way of life, 38; industrialism, 339, 360; literature, 47, 48, 71, 103 ff.; migration, 336; preachers, 49, 50; religious reasons for immigration, 39, 42, 43, 44, 45; Salem Witch Trials, 50–2; Territory and Dominion, 88; trade, 56, 63, 67, 130, 134, 191; university, 33. *See* Pilgrim Fathers; Plymouth; Puritans; Revolution, American.

New England Restraining Act, of British Parliament, 193

New English Canaan, the (Morton), 48, 49

New France, 94, 115, 118

New Hampshire, 56, 63, 80, 88, 129, 191, 245, 254, 301, 366, 374; origin, 55; Rockingham memorial, 301; Royal charter, 55

New Haven, 54, 102, 106. *See also* Connecticut.

New Jersey, 78, 79, 80, 81, 82, 109, 129, 154, 166, 193, 195, 228, 245, 329; Plan 252

New Mexico, 114, 115, 420, 424, 425, 544

'New Netherlands', 42, 78, 93–9

New Orleans, 126, 286, 287, 300, 308, 358, 537, 538; battle of, 308, 309, 310, 326; French settlers at, 115, 121

New Plymouth, 55

New Somerset, 55

New Sweden, 95

New York, 78, 79, 98, 99, 102, 118, 128, 131, 140, 145, 147, 154, 159, 163, 167, 168, 177, 178, 185, 195, 197, 217, 218, 219, 228, 235, 236, 237, 255, 278, 301, 329, 346, 359, 366, 390

New York Harbour, 96, 99

Newfoundland, 15, 18, 59, 60, 118, 130

Newport, Capt. Christopher, 23

Newspapers, 154, 155, 177, 275, 510, 631, 632, 707. *See* Journalists; Publishing.

Niagara, Fort, 133

Nicaragua, and U.S.A., 617

North Atlantic Treaty Organization, 697, 703

North Carolina, 69, 128, 129, 158, 174, 197, 254; cotton trade, 67; currency troubles, 131, 132. *See also* Cotton; South Carolina; Trade.

North Dakota, 544

North, Lord, 170, 171, 173, 179, 180, 191, 235, 237

Northampton county, Virginia, 136

Northampton, Mass., 108

North-east Passage, 12, 14

'Northern Virginia', 41

North-west Passage, 14, 116, 289

Nova Scotia, 118, 127

Nuclear fission, work in, 683, 684

Oglethorpe, Gen. James, 113, 119

O'Hara, Gen., Yorktown surrender, 237

Ohio, 118, 121, 123, 291, 292, 336, 337, 345, 346, 348, 358, 422, 433, 440

Ojeda, 3

Oklahoma, 544

Oligopoly, 669

Onete, 114

Ontario, Lake, 123

Orchestras, 633. *See also* Music.

Oregon, 289, 347, 421, 423, 424, 427

Origins of American colonies, 24

Otis, James, 129, 135, 136, 159, 161, 163

Ottawa river, 114

Ottawas, 121, 133

Owen, Robert Dale, 401

Oxford, University of, influence on Colonial education, 33, 73; of Pennsylvania, 150; of various states, 402, 575; Presidents, 576

Pacific Fur Company, 347

Paine, Thomas, 148, 151, 206, 213, 214, 215, 216, 271, 335

Painters, painting, 277, 278, 291, 587, 632, 658, 674

Pakenham, Sir Edward, 308, 309, 326

Palmer, Edward, 33

Palmerston, Lord, 417, 428, 520, 521

Panama Canal, 428, 617, 621

Pan-American Congress (Pan-American Union), 596

Paris, American commissioners in, 220, 221

Paris, Treaty of, 126, 127, 417, 616

Parliaments, and colonial policies, 137, 161 ff.

Index